PEOPLE OF VIRTUE

NORDIC INSTITUTE OF ASIAN STUDIES
NIAS Studies in Asian Topics

16 Leadership on Java *Hans Antlöv and Sven Cederroth (eds)*
17 Vietnam in a Changing World *Irene Nørlund, Carolyn Gates and Vu Cao Dam (eds)*
18 Asian Perceptions of Nature *Ole Bruun and Arne Kalland (eds)*
19 Imperial Policy and Southeast Asian Nationalism *Hans Antlöv and Stein Tønnesson (eds)*
20 The Village Concept in the Transformation of Rural Southeast Asia *Mason C Hoadley and Christer Gunnarsson (eds)*
21 Identity in Asian Literature *Lisbeth Littrup (ed.)*
22 Mongolia in Transition *Ole Bruun and Ole Odgaard (eds)*
23 Asian Forms of the Nation *Stein Tønnesson and Hans Antlöv (eds)*
24 The Eternal Storyteller *Vibeke Børdahl (ed.)*
25 Japanese Influences and Presences in Asia *Marie Söderberg and Ian Reader (eds)*
26 Muslim Diversity *Leif Manger (ed.)*
27 Women and Households in Indonesia *Juliette Koning, Marleen Nolten, Janet Rodenburg and Ratna Saptari (eds)*
28 The House in Southeast Asia *Stephen Sparkes and Signe Howell (eds)*
29 Rethinking Development in East Asia *Pietro P. Masina (ed.)*
30 Coming of Age in South and Southeast Asia *Lenore Manderson and Pranee Liamputtong (eds)*
31 Imperial Japan and National Identities in Asia, 1895–1945 *Li Narangoa and Robert Cribb (eds)*
32 Contesting Visions of the Lao Past *Christopher Goscha and Søren Ivarsson (eds)*
33 Reaching for the Dream *Melanie Beresford and Tran Ngoc Angie (eds)*
34 Mongols from Country to City *Ole Bruun and Li Naragoa (eds)*
35 Four Masters of Chinese Storytelling *Vibeke Børdahl, Fei Li and Huang Ying (eds)*
36 The Power of Ideas *Claudia Derichs and Thomas Heberer (eds)*
37 Beyond the Green Myth *Peter Sercombe and Bernard Sellato (eds)*
38 Kinship and Food in South-East Asia *Monica Janowski and Fiona Kerlogue (eds)*
39 Exploring Ethnic Diversity in Burma *Mikael Gravers (ed.)*
40 Politics, Culture and Self: East Asian and North European Attitudes *Geir Helgesen and Søren Risbjerg Thomsen (eds)*
41 Beyond Chinatown *Mette Thunø (ed.)*
42 Breeds of Empire: The 'Invention' of the Horse in Southeast Asia and Southern Africa 1500–1950 *Greg Bankoff and Sandra Swart*
43 People of Virtue: Reconfiguring Religion, Power and Morality in Cambodia Today *Alexandra Kent and David Chandler (eds)*
44. Lifestyle and Entertainment in Yangzhou   *Lucie Elivova and Vibeke Børdahl (eds)*

People of Virtue

Reconfiguring Religion, Power and Morality in Cambodia Today

Edited by

ALEXANDRA KENT AND DAVID CHANDLER

People of Virtue: Reconfiguring Religion, Power
and Morality in Cambodia Today

Edited by Alexandra Kent and David Chandler

Nordic Institute of Asian Studies
Studies in Asian Topics, no. 43

First published in 2008 by NIAS Publishing
Nordic Institute of Asian Studies (NIAS)
Leifsgade 33, 2300 Copenhagen S, Denmark
E-mail: books@nias.ku.dk
Online: http://www.niaspress.dk/

© NIAS – Nordic Institute of Asian Studies 2008

While copyright in the volume as a whole is vested in the Nordic Institute of Asian Studies, copyright in the individual chapters belongs to their authors. No chapter may be reproduced in whole or in part without the express permission of the publisher.

British Library Cataloguing in Publication Data

People of virtue : reconfiguring religion, power and moral
   order in Cambodia today. - (NIAS studies in Asian topics ;
   no. 43)
   1. Theravada Buddhism - Cambodia 2. Cambodia - Religion -
   21st century 3. Cambodia - Social conditions - 21st century
   4. Cambodia - Moral conditions
   I. Kent, Alexandra II. Chandler, David P.
   294.3'91'09596

ISBN 978-87-7694-036-2 (Hbk)
ISBN 978-87-7694-037-9 (Pbk)

The publication of this volume was assisted by a generous grant awarded by the Bank of Sweden Tercentenary Foundation, Stockholm.

Typesetting by NIAS Press
Produced by SRM Production Services and printed in Malaysia

Contents

Acknowledgements • ix
Contributors • xi

SECTION 1 – HISTORICAL CHANGE

1. Alexandra Kent and David Chandler: *Introduction* • 1
2. Alain Forest: *Buddhism and Reform: Imposed reforms and popular aspirations. Some historical notes to aid reflection* • 16
3. Anne Hansen: *Modernism and Morality in the Colonial Era* • 35
4. Alex L. Hinton: *Truth, Representation and the Politics of Memory after Genocide* • 62

SECTION 2 – DESIRED IDEALS

5. John Marston: *Wat Preah Thammalanka and the Legend of Lok Ta Nen* • 85
6. Alexandra Kent: *The Recovery of the King* • 109
7. Erik Davis: *Between Forests and Families: a remembered past life* • 128

SECTION 3 – REMAKING MORAL WORLDS

8. Judy Ledgerwood: *Buddhist Practice in Rural Kandal Province, 1960 and 2003. An essay in honor of May M. Ebihara* • 147
9. Kobayashi Satoru: *Reconstructing Buddhist Temple Buildings: an analysis of village Buddhism after the era of turmoil* • 169
10. Eve Zucker: *The Absence of Elders: Chaos and moral order in the aftermath of the Khmer Rouge* • 195
11. Penny Edwards: *The Moral Geology of the Present: Structuring morality, menace and merit* • 213

SECTION 4 – QUESTIONS OF CHANGING CULTURE

12. Heng Sreang: *The Scope and Limitations of Political Participation by Buddhist Monks* • 241

13. Ven Sovanratana: *Buddhist Education Today: progress and challenges* • 257

14. Christine Nissen: *Buddhism and Corruption* • 272

15. Vandra Harris: *Development Workers as Agents of Cultural Change* • 293

16. Heng Monychenda: *In Search of the Dhammika Ruler* • 310

Index • 319

FIGURES

0.1. Map of Cambodia • xvii

3.1. Preah Dhammacariyeavangs Et • 36

3.2. Um Sur • 37

4.1. Tuol Sleng buildings • 71

4.2. Photograph of executed prisoner, Tuol Sleng • 72

4.3. Skull map of Cambodia, Tuol Sleng • 73

5.1. Temple gate of Wat Preah Thammalanka • 87

5.2. Shrine of the Wat Preah Thammlanka vihara • 89

5.3. Principle Buddha image of Wat Preah Thammalanka vihara • 90

5.4. Painting of Lok Ta Nen • 92

5.5. Ven. Sar Lang, current abbot of Wat Preah Thammalanka • 101

6.1. *Don Chi* with matted hair • 113

6.2. Statue of Preah Ko and Preah Keo • 116

6.3. *Naga* tunnel • 118

6.4. Empty sockets of missing statue's feet • 119

6.5. Prasat Sosar • 121

6.6. Buddha statue with bamboo 'forest' • 122

7.1. Miss Yaan as a girl Kheum • 129

7.2. Miss Yaan as a woman • 141

9.1. Preah Vihear, Wat San Kor • 177

9.2. Preah Vihear, Wat Prasat • 178

9.3. Preah Vihear, Wat Preah Krasang • 178

9.4. Preah Vihear, Wat Krasang Mean Rutthi • 178
9.5. Chenh vossa, Wat San Kor • 179
9.6. Chenh vossa, Wat Prasat • 180
9.7. Chenh vossa, Wat Preah Krasang • 180
9.8. Chenh vossa, Wat Krasang Mean Rutthi • 180
10.1. Phnom Yong Kmauch • 201
10.2. Large Phnom Yong Kmauch • 201
14.1. Poster showing how 'Corruption Breeds Poverty' • 274
14.2. Cycle of trust and corruption • 278
14.3. Poster showing the moral burden of corruption • 279
14.4. Khmer New Year ceremony, monks receive donations from the laity and offering blessing in return • 281
14.5. A monk chanting at Khmer New Year ceremony with donations in front of him • 286
14.6. An old man and patron from a rural village watching over his household from his hammock • 288
16.1. The relationship between religion, the nation and the king • 311

TABLES

9.1. Penetration of manufactured products into households of two villages • 174
9.2. Variation of building materials of house roofs • 174
9.3. Basic data of four *wat*s in San Kor • 176
9.4. Recent changes at Wat Prasat • 182
9.5. Statistics for men of Veal village who were monks or novices • 183
14.1. Integrity rating showing that state institutions rank very negatively compared to private and Buddhist institutions • 277
14.2. Vocabulary, from extortion to gifts out of kindness • 291–292

Acknowledgements

The conference from which this book originally springs, 'Reconfiguring Religion, Power and Moral Order in Cambodia', held in Varberg, Sweden 26–29 October 2005, was generously sponsored by the Bank of Sweden Tercentenary Foundation, the Swedish School of Advanced Asia Pacific Studies, the Nordic Institute of Asian Studies, the International Institute of Asian Studies and the Centre for Asian Studies at Lund University. We wish to express our thanks to all these sponsors for making this important event possible. Special thanks are owed to the Bank of Sweden Tercentenary Foundation for also supporting this publication.

We also wish to express our appreciation of the contributions to the conference and to this volume. Although not all of those in attendance at the conference appear in this book, their presentations and insights have nevertheless influenced the final outcome. We thank Ashley Thompson, Joakim Öjendal, Jan Ovesen, Ing-Britt Trankell, Maurice Eisenbruch, Ian Harris, Chhom Kunthea, Elisabeth Moltke, Malin Hasselskog, Mona Lilja, Kristina Jönsson, Karel van Oosten, Sandro Campana Wadman and Trudy Jacobsen. Both the conference and the production of the volume were marked by consistent enthusiasm and positive input in ways other than purely textual.

Comments and guidance provided by the anonymous referee were greatly appreciated. Warmest thanks are due to the staff of NIAS Press for their exceptional support, patience and professionalism.

The Nordic Institute of Asian Studies in Copenhagen provided a stimulating institutional environment and practical support throughout this project. Alexandra Kent thanks her family, Jonas, Claudia and Raoul for providing such a lively and positive home environment, which has been every bit as important in the production of this volume.

Contributors

Chandler, David

David Chandler is Emeritus Professor of History at Monash University, Melbourne, Australia, where he taught between 1972 and 1997. He has also held teaching positions at the University of Paris, The University of Wisconsin, Cornell University and the University of Michigan. He has written seven books about Cambodia, including *A History of Cambodia* (first published in 1983, 4th edition, 2007), *The Tragedy of Cambodian History: Politics War and Revolution since 1945* (1991), *Voices from S-21: Terror and History in Pol Pot's Secret Prison* (1999) and *Facing the Cambodian Past: Selected Essays 1972–1994* (1995). <dpchandler@mac.com>

Davis, Erik

Erik Davis teaches in the Department of Religious Studies at Macalester College in the United States. He is currently completing his doctoral dissertation at the University of Chicago on the topic of funerary rituals and the role of death in Khmer culture. He conducted fieldwork for nearly three years, concentrating on funerary and memorial rituals in contemporary Cambodia. While in Cambodia, he was involved with the Buddhist Institute, where he helped lead a folklore research and publication project, and with the Center for Khmer Studies. He holds a masters degree from the University of Washington in Seattle. <erik.w.davis@gmail.com>

Edwards, Penny

Penny Edwards is Assistant Professor of Southeast Asian Studies at the University of California, Berkeley. She specialises in the modern cultural and political history of Cambodia and Burma, with a focus on textual, material and visual narratives of national, religious, gender and racial identity. Her most recent publication is *Cambodge: The Cultivation of a Nation, 1860-1945* (Hawai'i University Press, 2007). She has authored a number of academic articles and is joint editor of *Pigments of the Imagination: Rethinking Mixed Race* (a special issue of the Journal of Intercultural Studies, February 2007), *Beyond China: Migrating Identities* (Centre for the Study of Chinese Southern Diaspora, Research School of Pacific and Asian Studies, Australian National University, Canberra, 2002) and *Lost in the Whitewash: Aboriginal-Asian Encounters in Australia, 1901 to 2001* (Humanities Research Centre, Australian National University, Canberra 2003). She also serves on the board of directors of the Center for Khmer Studies in Cambodia, which is a member institution of the Council of American Overseas Research Centres. <pennyedwards@berkeley.edu>

Forest, Alain

Alain Forest is Professor of History of the Indochinese Peninsula at the University of Paris 7/Denis-Diderot. He is the author of *Le Cambodge et la colonisation française: Histoire d'une colonisation sans heurts (1897-1920)*, Paris, L'Harmattan (1980); *Le culte des génies protecteurs au Cambodge: Analyse et traduction d'un corpus de textes sur les neak ta*, Paris, L'Harmattan (1992); *Les missionnaires français au Tonkin et au Siam (XVII/e/-XVIII/e /siècles): Analyse comparée d'un relatif succès et d'un total échec*, (Livre 1: Histoires du Siam, Livre 2: Histoires du Tonkin, Livre 3: Organiser une Église, convertir les Infidèles), Paris, L'Harmattan (1998). He is the editor of several volumes, including a series on Asian religions and society in four volumes. He is currently working on a manuscript dealing with the history of religion in Cambodia and an edited volume devoted to contemporary Cambodia. His research interests include the study of contacts between the societies of Southeast Asia and the Occident as well as the study of religious phenomena. <alain.forest@sabouraud.net>

Hansen, Anne

Anne Hansen is Associate Professor in the Department of History at the University of Wisconsin Milwaukee, where she also directs the Comparative Study of Religion Programme. Since receiving her PhD in the Study of Religion at Harvard University in 1999, she has pursued work on the history and development of Theravada Buddhism in Southeast Asia and particularly on Buddhist ethical thought and literature in colonial Cambodia. Her most recent publication is her book *How to Behave: Buddhism and Modernity in Colonial Cambodia*, Honolulu, University of Hawai'i Press (2007). Her current and future projects include research on prophetic histories in nineteenth and twentieth centuries in Cambodia (with Judy Ledgerwood) and a book on Southeast Asian Theravadin narrative literature and art. <awhansen@uwm.edu>

Harris, Vandra

Vandra Harris completed her doctoral degree at the Centre for Development Studies, Flinders University, South Australia in 2005. Her doctoral research concerned development practitioner attitudes to culture, power and participation in Cambodia and the Philippines. She then spent 6 months at the Nordic Institute of Asian Studies conducting post-doctoral research on the partnership policies of the Swedish and Danish development agencies. She is currently tutoring in politics and development studies at Flinders University. <vandra.harris@flinders.edu.au>

Heng Monychenda

After living under the Khmer Rouge regime for nearly 4 years Heng Monychenda fled to the Cambodian/Thai border in 1980 and became a Buddhist monk, disrobing in 1997. From 1985 to 1992 he directed the Khmer Buddhist Research Center at Site 2 refugee camp, exploring the relationship between Buddhism and Khmer society and how Buddhism might help prevent further tragedy in Cambodia. In 1990 Monychenda founded the non-governmental organization Buddhism for Development (BFD) to promote socially-engaged Buddhism in Cambodia. He returned to Cambodia in 1993 and established BFD in Battambang province. Today BFD has eight branches throughout the country. Monychenda received his Masters Degree in Public Administration from John F. Kennedy School of Government, Harvard University in 1998. He has written numerous books on engaged Buddhism in Khmer and is widely known in Cambodia as the main figure behind socially-engaged Buddhism in the country. <bfdkhmer@bfdkhmer.org>

Heng Sreang

Heng Sreang is currently a lecturer teaching philosophy at the Royal University of Phnom Penh (RUPP) and at Pannasastra University of Cambodia (PUC). He was awarded a Bachelor of Arts degree in philosophy by the Royal University of Phnom Penh in 1999 and was sponsored by the Catholic NGO New Humanity to study at the Ateneo de Manila University in the Philippines, where he received a Master of Arts in philosophy in 2004. In 2005 he followed the training programme offered by the Centre for Khmer Studies, Phnom Penh, entitled 'Capacity Building in Cambodian Higher Education Programme'. This programme focused on Contemporary Southeast Asia and included periods of fieldwork in Vietnam and Thailand. <hengsreang@yahoo.com>

Hinton, Alex

Alex Hinton is Associate Professor of Anthropology and Global Affairs at Rutgers University. He is the author of *Why Did They Kill? Cambodia in the Shadow of Genocide* (University of California Press, 2005) and three edited collections, *Annihilating Difference: The Anthropology of Genocide* (University of California Press, 2002), *Genocide: an Anthropological Reader* (Blackwell, 2002), and *Biocultural Approaches to the Emotions* (Cambridge University Press, 1999). <ahinton@adromeda.rutgers.edu>

Kent, Alexandra

Alexandra Kent is an Associate Professor of Social Anthropology based at the Nordic Institute of Asian Studies, Copenhagen. She completed a doctoral study of a Hindu revitalization movement in Malaysia at Goteborg University, Sweden in 2000. Since 2003 she has been working on the revival of Buddhism in Cambodia, exploring its role in the regeneration of community and moral order. Her publications include a monograph entitled *Divinity and Diversity: A Hindu Revitalization Movement in Malaysia* (NIAS Press, 2005) and articles on religious revival in Malaysia and in Cambodia. <alix.kent@swipnet.se>

Kobayashi Satoru

Kobayashi Satoru earned a Masters Degree in Human and Environment Studies at Kyoto University in 1996. He began research in Cambodia in 1998, and this has included extensive fieldwork in a rural setting from 2000 to 2002. He is currently a research fellow of the Japanese Society for the Promotion of Science. His work has appeared in *Southeast Asian Studies* (Center for Southeast Asian Studies, Kyoto University, Japan). <kobasa@cseas.kyoto-u.ac.jp>

Khy Sovanratana

The Venerable Khy Sovanratana is a Rajagana Fourth Class with the ecclesiastical title 'Preah Tepsattha' in the national Sangha Council of Cambodia. Khy Sovanratana is a Personal Advisor to the Buddhist Supreme Patriarch of Cambodia. He is currently a Lecturer and Vice-Rector of Preah Sihanouk Raja Buddhist University and a visiting lecturer in psychology at Pannasatra University of Cambodia, Phnom Penh. Having won a scholarship in 1995 to further his studies, he graduated with a Bachelors Degree in Buddhist Philosophy from the University of Kelaniya, Sri Lanka, in 2000. In 2002, he obtained his Masters Degree in Buddhist Philosophy from the University of Kelaniya, Sri Lanka. In 2005, after one-year training, he received a teaching qualification majoring in Education Science and English from the National Institute of Education, Ministry of Education, Youth and Sports, Phnom Penh. Besides his extensive academic responsibilities, he has attended conferences and symposiums in Hong Kong, Russia, France, Switzerland, Sweden, United States and Japan. <sovanratana@yahoo.com>

Ledgerwood, Judy

Professor Ledgerwood is a cultural anthropologist whose research interests include gender, refugee and diaspora communities and the transnational movements of people and ideas. Her current research is focused on Cambodian Buddhism and ideas of cultural identity. Her dissertation was on changing Khmer conceptions of gender in Khmer refugee communities in the United States. After she completed her degree, she taught and conducted research in Cambodia for three and a half years. She taught as a visiting professor at Cornell University and the Royal University of Fine Arts in Phnom Penh. From 1993 to 1996, she was a research fellow at the East-West Center in Honolulu and has taught Anthropology and Southeast Asian Studies at Northern Illinois University since 1996, where she is currently Chair of the Department of Anthropology. <T20JLL1@wpo.cso.niu.edu>

Marston, John

John Marston's interest in Cambodia dates to the 1980s, when he worked in refugee camps in Thailand and the Philippines. He completed his PhD in Anthropology at University of Washington in 1997. Since then he has taught at the Center for Asian and African Studies at El Colegio de México.

He is the co-editor of *History, Buddhism, and New Religious Movements in Cambodia*, published by University of Hawai'i Press. <jmars@colmex.mx>

Nissen, Christine

Christine Nissen holds a Masters Degree in Ethnography and Social Anthropology from the University of Aarhus, Denmark. Her Masters dissertation analyses local understanding and perceptions of corruption in relation to social and moral order and Buddhism in Cambodia. She conducted fieldwork in rural Cambodia and worked for the Cambodian branch of Transparency International, Center for Social Development in Phnom Penh for two and a half years. She was co-initiator of the 'Languages of Corruption' network, an attempt to strengthen and expand analytical and practical explorations of local understandings of corruption. Her publications include: *Living under the Rule of Corruption: An Analysis of Everyday Forms of Corrupt Practices in Cambodia*, Center for Social Development, Cambodia, 2005 (www.csdcambodia.org); *Corruption and Cambodian Households: Household Survey on Perceptions, Attitudes and Impact of Everyday Forms of Corrupt Practices in Cambodia*, Center for Social Development, 2005, 'Country Report on Cambodia' in *Global Corruption Report 2005*, Transparency International, 2005. <Christine@joker-nissen.dk>

Zucker, Eve

Eve Zucker received her PhD in Social Anthropology from the London School of Economics in the United Kingdom in June 2007. Since 1994 she has lived and worked in Cambodia on three occasions for a total of just over three years. One year was spent living in rural southwestern Cambodia, where she conducted her doctoral research concerning the remaking of moral order in the aftermath of violence. Prior to this Eve Zucker had worked as a research intern for the Cambodia Genocide Programme at Yale University, participated in various Cambodian higher-education projects within Cambodia and actively involved herself with the Khmer community of Southern California. She holds a Masters Degree in anthropology from the University of Wisconsin at Madison, and a Bachelors degree in philosophy from the University of California, San Diego. Her PhD thesis is entitled *Memory and Re-making Moral Order in the Aftermath of Violence in a Highland Khmer Village in Cambodia*. <emzucker@yahoo.com>

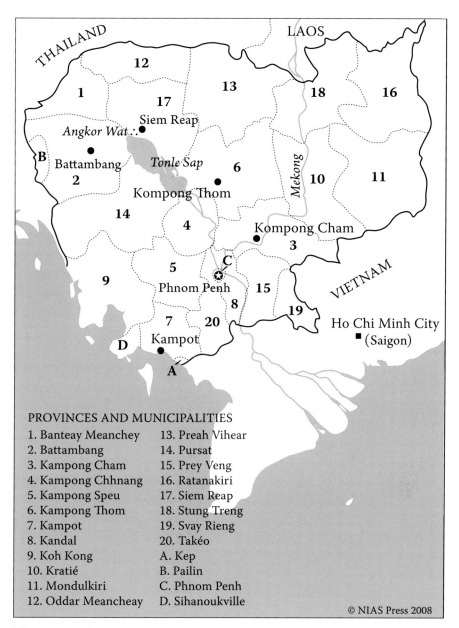

Map 0.1. Cambodia

SECTION I
Historical Change

CHAPTER 1

Introduction

Alexandra Kent and David Chandler

The signing of the Paris Peace Accords in 1991 ushered in a new era for Cambodia after decades of devastating violence and conflict. The last 15 years have witnessed the dawning of important research on Cambodian culture, religion and morality, though researchers involved in this are still relatively few, and are spread across the globe. Until recently, very little had been written in English on Cambodian religion and no overall introduction was available. Two recent publications in this field have, however, begun to alter this situation: Marston and Guthrie's (2004) edition *History, Buddhism, and New Religious Movements in Cambodia* and Harris' (2005) *Cambodian Buddhism: History and Practice*.

This book aims to make a contribution to this burgeoning field of study. It arose from a conference held in Varberg, Sweden in October 2005 entitled 'Reconfiguring Religion, Power and Moral Order in Cambodia', organized by Alexandra Kent. The conference included 21[1] presentations that discussed the dynamic way in which religion, power and moral order in Cambodia interplay, both shaping and being shaped by historical events.

On the surface, the book may seem to be narrowly focused – exploring well-defined themes in a single country – but the chapters address major questions that are of interest to a global, English-speaking audience. These include such topics as how community may be repaired after violent conflict, how religion and politics are interwoven and how moral order and historical change impact upon one another.

Religion and morality are everywhere concerned with power. Throughout Southeast Asia religion has always been suffused with concerns about power: individual potency, protection and strength, the powers of nature. The Southeast Asian cosmos is still understood by many Southeast Asians, including many Khmer, as energized by an animating or divine radiance, which is in continual flux and is both indispensable and potentially dangerous. The repair of popular religion after destruction and violence may therefore provide a means for dangerous power to be domesticated in the service of the community. It may also help the recovery of local cosmology, social integration and political order. The regeneration of the ritual life of a community may also offer a way for people to formulate and relate to their collective stories through a symbolism that recalls a shared cultural origin. However, the particular ways in which representatives of religion and of morality may become involved in hegemonic political and secular affairs, both past and present, may call into question these individuals' credibility and moral authority. It is therefore important to explore the processes by which a community like Cambodia is attempting to recover moral order after violent conflict both in relation to indigenous values and experience, and as embedded in social relations and history.

Most of the chapters in this book are grounded studies that examine the contemporary interlacing of power with morality in lived situations. They address one another in harmonies, yet also speak in chorus of Cambodia's troubles today and her pursuit of order in large part through reference to her past.

RELIGION, POWER AND MORAL ORDER IN THE CAMBODIAN PAST

Many scholars have conceived of power in classical Southeast Asia as unevenly distributed, concentrated in and emanating from potent centres, particularly kings, who manifested it in their ability to control the physical and social world over which they held dominion. Cambodia's Angkorean era, classically defined as falling between 802 A.D. and 1431 A.D. (although the overriding significance of both dates has been called into question) offers a substantial corpus of inscriptions and archaeological evidence from which we know that power at this time, like kings, ancestors and the more demanding Hindu gods, was both necessary and dangerous. In the Empire's strongest moments – under Jayavarman V, Suryavarman I and II and Jayavarman VII – religion, power and the moral order seem to have been fused in the institution of kingship, and echoes of this conceptualization persist in the popular mind to this day, as Kent's chapter in this volume demonstrates. The monarch was credited with access to divinity, which meant that he could channel its power into the world and thus ensure prosperity and regeneration. The official moral order, however, came 'down' from those with power, legitimized and ritualized by the religious paraphernalia at the 'top' of the Hinduized state. No institutional means of curbing royal power existed (Mabbett and Chandler 1995: 69). Kings were praised as beings *above* society, as embodiments of virtue (Chandler 1998 [1983]: 46). If the king behaved appropriately, as in China and classical Vietnam, it was thought that he could influence worldly conditions, such as the weather and crops.

The inscriptions tell us very little about the world of ordinary people. Whereas political power was supposedly coextensive with the potency of the encompassing centre, unofficial religious practices were more ambiguous and more down to earth. Evidence of this underlying religious world can be found in aerial photographs showing thousands of small temples, almost all dismantled now, which were once scattered over the Angkorean landscape. Some of these must have served not only as homes for seemingly Indian gods but also as ancestral temples, honouring the forebears of the people who had had them built.

Obedience may be forced, or taken for granted, but reverence is harder to command, and we may assume that the decentralized religious realm of ancestral spirits and local deities was not amenable to control by the state. Ordinary people would have had local deities of their own to appease and family networks to nourish and maintain and these may have contained a subversive element not visible in the official line recorded in the inscriptions, which say little about everyday struggles for status or power even among the elite, and nothing about everyday social life. However, although there clearly was vibrant religious activity at the local level, there is nothing to suggest that this kind of alternate authority did much to undermine the centre's monopoly on power, except in periods of dynastic weakness or disarray. A strong king, surrounded by a talented and energetic entourage, was master of all he surveyed.

State power around Angkor weakened in the so-called Middle Period, and kings and their entourages shifted southward to the vicinity of Phnom Penh during the fifteenth century. Various ecological factors appear to have contributed to degeneration of the Angkorean irrigation and water transport system. Thai invasions of the Angkor region also played a part. During the thirteenth century, a major cultural change occurred as Theravada Buddhism was brought to rural communities, presumably by missionizing mendicant monks. The religion reproduced itself locally through the ordination of village youths who had strong local loyalties and became rich fields of merit. By the fourteenth century, if not before, a decentralized monastic system thus established itself kingdom-wide, making centralized power now subject to moderation by legitimate, alternate authorities among the commoners.

Theravada Buddhism took root not only in villages but also in the royal court and indeed undocumented royal and elite conversions may well have inspired thousands of other Cambodians to follow suit. By the mid-sixteenth century, the Cambodian monarch had become the protector and patron of the Buddhist faith rather than the embodiment of a Hindu deity, or as identified with the Buddha, like Jayavarman VII. Official religion still legitimized the power of the meritorious centre but it also offered a new means of morally checking it. With the weakening of the prestige of legendary warrior kings and the Hindu cults associated with them, and of royal power *vis à vis* Siam and more generally in territorial and military terms, the public idealization of martial prowess faded, and a somewhat quietist moral order took root in Cambodia that fitted the philosophical framework of Theravada Buddhism; these were not people who were commanded, or willing to build Angkor Wat.

The decline of Angkor as an exemplary center, then, coincided with a shift in religious practices in the upper reaches of society from those associated with Hindu gods, temples and priests to those linked to a relatively open monastic order, written and recited codes of conduct (the *chbab*, often written by monks) and the notion of individuals earning merit, living peacefully in society, cultivating virtue and moderation. Merit making and meritorious behaviour became the *sine qua non* of civilization, with civilized space exemplified by the *wat* with its *sima* and tutelary spirits – the *neak ta* – protecting it from the amoral and dangerous wilderness outside. Each individual was now free to negotiate their particular relationship to the moral order and to achieve 'un pouvoir personnel' within 'un socialisme particulier' (Thierry 2003: 121). As the population shrank and kingly power became diffuse, kings lost the capacity to mobilize powerful armies; local power bases and patronage networks developed instead.

Without a strong, militarized state Cambodia was poorly equipped to resist the encroachment of Siam and Vietnam. The royal family was sometimes split by divergent loyalties, to the one or the other neighbour state. The 1830s and 1840s were especially destructive decades in Cambodia. Siamese armies invaded the kingdom several times and Cambodia sometimes fell under the slightly disdainful protection of Vietnam. Buddhism in these years also fell into disarray. By the mid-1800s a multitude of independent *sangha*s or congregations of monks coexisted and reports from the period describe an unruly monkhood that was obedient to no central authority (Harris 2005). King Norodom (r. 1864–1904) strove to reimpose royal control over Cambodia, but rebellions broke out under dynastic pretenders, regional overlords and millenarians giving voice, ideologically, to the deep moral crisis of the time and the longing for the restoration of idealized conceptions of order (Hansen 2004; see also Hansen in this volume). A self-image was born of the Khmer, after centuries of greatness, becoming in their decline the innocent victims of predatory neighbours and therefore meriting protection from a friendlier outside power. Cambodia was by now virtually a failed state. It was at this point that the French offered Norodom their open-ended and ambiguous protection.

The protectorate (1863–1953) brought a major shift in the constellation of religion, power and moral order, as Forest describes in this volume. While providing security to the kingdom, the French undermined the power both of the monarchy and of the *sangha*. In 1866, the French created a new, modern capital city for Norodom at Phnom Penh and after the 1880s, the king lost the authority to punish, pay or promote his subjects.

In the first decades of the twentieth century, the French also imposed a series of administrative regulatory systems upon the *sangha* and in 1943, regulations for a wholesale reorganization of the *sangha* were drawn up. The previous, somewhat confused and informal system was now replaced by modern, bureaucratic routines and an ecclesiastical structure that mirrored the government's organization of civil society into provinces, districts and sub-districts (see Harris 2005). The French also began modernizing Cambodia's education system by using monks as teachers of modern curricula in the *wats*.

The French usurpation of Cambodia's moral and political centre was not, however, accepted without protest. In the early decades of the colonial era, rebellions inspired by millenarian religious leaders known as *neak mean bon* (meritorious people) continued to erupt, presenting alternate discourses on order and identity (Hansen 2004). Later on, protests in 1916, 1925 and the so-called Umbrella War of 1942 (a peaceful protest march performed by a thousand umbrella bearing monks in protest against the arrest of one of their number)[2] are examples of how resistance was enacted both by secular and religious actors (Edwards 2004). From the 1900s onwards, French intervention into 'an area of society long deemed sacred and outside the orbit of worldly political power, namely the Cambodian

Buddhist *sangha*' (ibid.: 63) became increasingly heavy-handed. Efforts were directed to suppressing Buddhist instigators of resistance as well as to clamping Thai influence over modernization of the *sangha*. In an effort to achieve the latter, the Buddhist Institute was founded in 1930, with an associated Commission des Moeurs et Coutumes du Cambodge. Ironically, the institute soon took on a role as moral custodian of national culture and some of its members began to think in terms of anti-colonial, Buddhist nationalism. The French responded by sentencing one of the main proponents to death in 1942,[3] thus inciting further resentment among both the laity and the *sangha*. The country then edged towards independence on 'a breaking wave of Buddhist activism and martyrdom that had its seeds in the late nineteenth century' (Harris 2005: 228).

As the colonial hold on Indochina weakened, Cambodia's monarch, Norodom Sihanouk, who had been crowned by the French in 1941, began polishing his Buddhist credentials. In 1947 he entered the monkhood for three months and he soon became a sponsor of the religion. When the colonial authorities left in 1953, Sihanouk abdicated the throne, and as a 'private citizen' presented himself as the 'father' of his people, over whom he radiated protective power and compassion. He also tolerated no opposition, but his conduct sometimes drew discreet criticism from high ranking members of the *sangha*, whose moral standards Sihanouk did not feel obliged to follow either as a politician or in his personal behaviour. By employing Buddhism as part of his catchy ideology of 'Buddhist socialism', he claimed moral legitimacy as patron and protector of religion.

For all its capriciousness, Sihanouk's rule during the 1950s and 1960s was a relatively harmonious time, in which a strong centre and flourishing *sangha* satisfied most people's moral expectations. The image of Cambodians as blameless victims of outside powers persisted, with Sihanouk's encouragement, but Cambodians also saw themselves as a people innately blessed by destiny and protected by Sihanouk, the Buddha, local monks and the spirits of the land. A cultural refrain of this time was that the invincibility of the Khmers was ensured by their adherence to Buddhist virtue.

This time of innocence came to an abrupt end, however, when the Vietnam War spilled over into Cambodia. General Lon Nol, allegedly with American support, usurped Sihanouk's position at the centre via a coup in 1970. Lon Nol saw himself as a predestined Buddhist chief of state who should lead his people in a religious crusade against communism. Using

Buddhism as a mantle and justification, he embarked on a xenophobic assault on Vietnamese 'unbelievers' (*thmil*), a logic that foreshadowed the racialist campaigns of the Khmer Rouge against Vietnam. Lon Nol's Khmer Republic was, however, soon crushed under the weight of the Vietnam War, America's violent intervention, the energy of his opponents, and its own incompetence. As things deteriorated, the centre proved to be utterly impotent as provider of protective 'shade' for the periphery. A moral vacuum resulted, waiting to be filled.

17 April 1975, when the Khmer Rouge marched into Phnom Penh and seized power, took nearly everyone by surprise. The Party was rushed into power under wartime conditions, immediately after its unexpected victory. In January 1976 a new constitution was promulgated and the name of the country now became Democratic Kampuchea (DK). With extraordinary circularity, we may detect in the Khmer Rouge rhetoric echoes of the Angkorean mindset, though now in the new, but partially concealed guise of Marxism-Leninism and according to a pattern of bizarre structural inversions, as depicted in Hinton's chapter in this volume. Buddhism and all other religions were formally abolished by the Khmer Rouge leaders. Public statements now dealt with grandeur, with 'enemies' and success, while the regime became increasingly intent upon an open-ended struggle to defeat enemies both internal and external.

The Party leaders were convinced that they could overturn Cambodia's time-honoured, hierarchical power relations, and that they could rapidly produce a society without exploiters, exploited, rich or poor. However, it seems clear that insofar as underdogs took power under the DK they tended to act in the same overbearing manner that their superiors had employed for many years. Hierarchical order was simply inverted – broken glass floated, to quote a Cambodian proverb; the young, the 'wild', the uneducated and the poor were empowered to impose order upon the old, the 'civilized', the educated and the rich.

Under DK, power again emanated from the centre. The concealed leaders of the Party, or *Angkar* (the 'Organization'), envisioned themselves as the new, moral substitute for the *sangha*. Alternate, pre-revolutionary sources of domestic or community-based power – the *sangha*, older family members, and local spirits – were discredited. The moral order was now rendered as the imposed, historically inevitable egalitarianism of the impoverished population, supposedly liberated from the shackles of the past and from a wide range of dominations. *Angkar* forcibly removed what it saw as the sources of oppression – markets, money, venal officials and private property. The moral order of DK was inseparable from the actions of an omnipotent Party, keyed to what it called the wheel of history (*kong pravatasas*), which acted like a juggernaut and could change direction without warning. A grim saying of the period ran: 'The wheel of history turns ceaselessly. Don't put your hand or foot into it or they will certainly be cut off' (Chandler 2002: 16).

Ironically, the DK's egalitarian rhetoric meant that politics once again came from 'above' the population, and moral order was imposed upon the people by force, ostensibly for their own good.

In January 1979, the Vietnamese invaded and established a subservient Cambodian regime in Phnom Penh within days. The Vietnamese sought to impose a non-Khmer form of socialism on Cambodia's exhausted population, and to prevent the Khmer Rouge from regaining power. They reopened markets, reintroduced money, rebuilt roads, hospitals and schools and stood by as hundreds of thousands of Cambodian returned home or fled the country.

Like previous Cambodian regimes, the People's Republic of Kampuchea (PRK) sought to reconfigure power, religion and the moral order in Cambodia to suit its geopolitical needs. Unable to bolster their legitimacy through the monarchy since Sihanouk had placed himself in opposition to them, the Vietnamese turned instead to the *sangha*, and encouraged a partial revival; the restoration of *wat*s and the selective ordination of monks were permitted, though monks were regarded as state employees, they were issued with identity cards and were forbidden to practise alms rounds. Nevertheless, as families reassembled and as the violence of life under DK effectively disappeared, many politically harmless aspects of pre-revolutionary religious life, such as wedding and funeral ceremonies and seasonal rituals, reappeared throughout the country.

Of particular significance in this orchestrated revival was the reordination in September 1979 of seven selected former monks under the direction of a contingent of Vietnamese and Khmer Krom monks (see Keyes 1994). The youngest of these monks, Ven. Tep Vong, who was then 47 years old, was later appointed head of a unified Cambodian *sangha*.[4] Shortly after this, Tep Vong was named Vice-President of the Khmer National Assembly and Vice-President of the Central Committee of the Khmer United Front for the Salvation of Cambodia – worldly roles rarely if ever given to members of the *sangha* in other countries. The power of the *sangha* to act as an autonomous moral critic of centralized political power was thus more or less paralysed. The institution of the *sangha* now operated beneath and within the realm of central power.

THE CHANGING POWER OF RELIGION TODAY

The Vietnamese never achieved the legitimacy they sought among Cambodians, and when the end of the Cold War meant that Soviet support dried up, Vietnam began to pull back, withdrawing completely from Cambodia by 1989. The Paris Peace Accords were signed in 1991, and after a UN-administered period and a national election in which over 90 per cent of registered voters went to the polls, politics fell into the hands of Prime Minister Hun Sen and his Cambodian People's Party (CPP). This was the renamed Kampuchean People's Revolutionary Party, which had ruled Cambodia during the Vietnamese period. A new era of internationalization was ushered in. The international community began buttressing the Cambodian economy with foreign aid and support for democratization and decentralization, shifting the competition for power, perhaps, from war to elections (Roberts 2001: 32).

In late 1991, Sihanouk returned to the country from years of comfortable exile in China and North Korea. In 1993 he became king again, and resumed his role as supreme patron of the *sangha*, reinvesting supreme patriarchs for the two previously existing monastic orders: Ven. Tep Vong for the larger, influential *Mahanikay* and Ven. Bour Kry for the far smaller *Thommayut* Order. This means that Tep Vong, a politicized monastic figure, was positioned at the pinnacle of the Cambodia monkhood. In the 1990s, ordinations opened up to men of all ages, and monks with better monastic credentials began returning from periods of exile overseas. The swelling ranks of a new generation of impatient young monks mean that the religious legitimacy of today's newly appointed ecclesiastical hierarchy is questioned by many, as Heng Sreang discusses in this volume.

Along with the dramatic changes in Cambodia's political economy during the 1990s (see Hughes 2003), democratization propelled elements of the *sangha* more deeply into party political processes. The universal adult suffrage ensured by the 1993 constitution meant that monks were included in the electorate for the first time. In Thailand, by contrast, monks (and even female ascetics, *mae chi*) to this day forgo the right to vote upon ordination, thus ritually demonstrating that the ordained state is beyond the reach of politics. Politicization and fragmentation has bedeviled the *sangha* in Cambodia throughout its existence. Today, these problems have taken on a new guise as the *sangha*'s politicized leadership and absorption into the electorate have deeply entangled monks in the tensions of the emerging party political system. This has occurred largely at the expense of their moral autonomy. Wary of monks' moral credentials, popularity and possible support for the opposition, the CPP government often tries to woo them with hefty donations that are delivered with a dose of surveillance and menace (Hughes 2006), or to control their political activities by force[5] (see e.g. Frommer 2003). Groupings of monks can be roughly identified as allied to particular political parties (Harris 2001). No matter how they are intended, religious statements are now often interpreted as politically edged. For instance, just prior to the 2003 elections supreme patriarch Ven. Tep Vong argued that it was inappropriate for monks to use their vote. Regardless of the religious justification for this statement, it was widely understood by Cambodian skeptics as an expression of Tep Vong's support for the CPP and as his attempt to prevent monks from demonstrating and encouraging support for the opposition. Even monastic activities that might appear to be apolitical – such as the development of a well-supported Vipassana meditation movement by the monk Ven. Sam Buntheoun, who was shot to death in 2003 by an unidentified assassin – may be labeled by others as promoting particular political agendas (McDermid and Sokha 2005).

Young monks can be particularly vulnerable to the elite's rough-shod political efforts at co-optation, control and coercion. Many are from poor backgrounds, and need accommodation, food and education. Leadership in many temples is also weak and sometimes corrupt (Guthrie 2000) and the government's readiness to resort to violence to contain the monkhood makes many monks afraid to act as the moral moderators of power that most people still consider monks should be. Many Cambodians feel that a tamed *sangha* will be of no use to anyone and that monks can only maintain the trust of the people if they remain independent of government and free to express opinions on ethical issues such as corruption (Kalab 1994: 70).

Cambodian villagers have long been suspicious of city people but, as Michael Vickery noted in 1962, many out-of-the-way villages at that time had evolved nearly autonomous, autarkic lifestyles that were of little interest to central power-holders (see Vickery 1999 [1984]: 1–4). Today, however, democratization, the liberal market system and improved communications mean that the 'centre' is reaching out into 'the periphery' in new ways and that the periphery is aware of the centre in ways that were not possible in the 1960s. The new economic conditions have rendered farmers vulnerable to the profiteering of the powerful, the poor are often forced off their lands and their access to resources, such as fish and forests, is rapidly diminishing as these are taken over by speculators. Part of this penetration of the periphery takes the form of intervention in temple affairs by powerful members of today's elite (Kent 2007). Patronage of temples by the powerful is nothing new in Cambodia but it is now taking place under new political and economic conditions and in the context of a *sangha* that has yet to recover both morally and intellectually after the years of repression. As the powerful now seek approval and sustenance within a consumer-driven global arena, they forge new, rigidified relations of dominance and dependence among the Cambodian masses. The weakened state of today's *sangha* and the loss or demoralization of elders who would once have been the upholders of local morality (see Zucker in this volume) mean that cultural resources for mobilizing local solidarity and putting a moral brake on the powerful are hard to find.

Despite this bleak scenario, religion is still regarded by a great many Cambodians as their only hope. Both mainstream and non-mainstream foci of religious power are cropping up in Cambodia. Some attract substantial resources, often from overseas Khmer. These foci can tell us much of Cambodian desires for order and the structures that may either aid or hinder its reconfiguration. Some development initiatives, recognizing this, have attempted to selectively appropriate 'tradition' in the sculpting of new forms of cultural order.

Young men now entering the monkhood are brought into contact with the *dhamma*'s (truth, teaching, eternal order) timeless message concerning salvation and righteous leadership. The *dhamma* may provide a framework through which these young men can formulate moral critique of contemporary society. Such critique may be acutely relevant for a disenchanted generation of poor young men witnessing today's power abuses. The religious world of the Khmers, though constrained, retains its potency and only time will tell how today's young monks may influence the flux of power in the coming years.

OUTLINE OF THIS BOOK

The chapters in this volume have been arranged under four headings: Historical Change, Desired Ideals, Remaking Moral Worlds and the Practicalities of Changing Culture.

The first section contains a broad historical introduction followed by three chapters, which tie religious change to historical processes in Cambodia's past. Alain Forest's historical overview of Buddhist reform in Cambodia describes some of the complexity of Cambodian religion and explores the implications of reform for notions of purity, autonomy and control of religion. Anne Hansen examines the modernization of Cambodian Buddhism through the latter part of the nineteenth and the early part of the twentieth centuries. Echoing some of the themes introduced by Forest, Hansen examines the new Buddhist moral values among the blossoming Buddhist intelligentsia of the colonial period, particularly those of rationalism, authenticity and purification. Alex Hinton explores the politics of memories of the Khmer Rouge – how memories of the period have been utilized in Cambodia to represent her traumatic past to herself and to shape her future.

The second section uses recently gathered ethnographic data to examine some of the ideals that Cambodians relate to from their past in their hopes of building their future. Using the legend of a pre-Pol Pot monk renowned for magical powers, John Marston explores how legend may fulfil people's 'imaginary need' to find continuity with the past and political and spiritual direction for the future. Similarly, Alexandra Kent's chapter uses two vignettes, one of a lay woman and one of a lay-nun (*don chi*), to capture one way in which Cambodians imagine reconfigured order and civilization through reference to symbols buried in her past. Erik Davis' chapter introduces us to the dream-like reality of one woman's memory of her previous lives. In this realm of memory, Davis identifies the power of desire as it subverts and informs conventional ideas of social and moral order.

The third section is also based on recent ethnography and events, which are analysed in relation to the issue of social repair in Cambodia after the rupture with the past. All four chapters share the theme of Cambodian concerns about moral decline. The first two discuss this decline in relation to monks, the third is concerned with the loss of moral elders and the fourth examines the government's strategies to redefine morality. Judy Ledgerwood's chapter takes data from Kandal province, Kobayashi Satoru's from Kompong Thom province, Eve Zucker's from Kompong Speu province and Penny Edwards' from Phnom Penh. Ledgerwood shows that merit making remains at the core of village Buddhism despite the fact that most of the young today grew up without experience of Buddhist practice. Kobayashi Satoru describes how religious tradition and modernity are themselves being re-/constructed through the process of temple reconstruction. The temple, he asserts, is an arena for the intersection – as well as compromise and protest – of different people's social spaces. Zucker turns her attention to the impact upon a community of the loss through death or demoralization of its lay bearers of social and moral order – the elders. The final chapter in this section, Penny Edwards' contribution on the moral geology of the present, examines the government's laissez-faire approach to personal and mob violence, particularly directed towards perceived suspects, and its increasingly active engagement in the policing of female corporeal, sexual and conjugal morality as a means of advancing a particular scheme of social ethics.

The final section deals with day-to-day practicalities and questions involved in restructuring culture and moral order today. Heng Sreang builds upon his field research concerning monks' involvement in politics today, involvement that requires cautious navigation of the political landscape. Ven. Khy Sovanratana's contribution provides an account of the history of Buddhist education in Cambodia and its reconstruction today and draws attention to positive developments, in terms of rapidly increasing numbers both of institutions and monk students, and also to some major challenges: the government's prioritizing of secular education and consequent shortage of resources flows to Buddhist education. Christine Nissen explores Buddhism's role in discourses of corruption. While the politicization of Buddhism is seen as a kind of moral pollution of sacred space, the Buddhist logic of merit and karma also play directly into the moral economy of corruption. The chapter by Vandra Harris examines the roles and attitudes of development workers who endeavour to change Cambodian culture in selective ways – at once critiquing and celebrating aspects of both Cambodian tradition and Western cultural features. The final chapter, by Heng Monychenda, ends the book with a Cambodian vision of the future. Writing from the perspective of active engagement in the application of Buddhist ideas to contemporary development, he describes the significance of the notion of the Dhammika leader, and goes on to suggest that if each person was to emulate this idea, politics could be re-enchanted and 'Dhammocracy' developed.

It is hoped that this collection will encourage further scholarship and debate among people interested not only in the future of Cambodia, but also among scholars of other post-conflict settings and those examining the intersections in Cambodia and elsewhere between ideas and practices that affect power, religion and moral order.

REFERENCES

Chandler, D. 1998 [1983]. *A History of Cambodia*. Chiang Mai: Silkworm Books.

—— 2002. 'S-21, the Wheel of History, and the Pathology of Terror in Democratic Kampuchea' in Ledgerwood, J. (ed.) *Cambodia Emerges from the Past: Eight Essays*. DeKalb: Northern Illinois University.

Edwards, P. 2004. 'Making a Religion of the Nation and its Language: the French Protectorate (1863–1954) and the Dhammakāy' in Marston, J. and Guthrie, E. (eds.) *History, Buddhism, and New Religious Movements in Cambodia*. Honolulu: University of Hawai'i Press.

Frommer, J. 2003. 'Wat Threatens pro-SRP Monks' *Phnom Penh Post*. Phnom Penh.

Guthrie, E. 2000. 'Buddhist Temples and Cambodian Politics' in Vijghen, J. (ed.) *People and the 1998 National Elections in Cambodia*. Phnom Penh: Experts for Community Research

Hansen, A. 2004. 'Khmer Identity and Theravada Buddhism' in Marston, J. and Guthrie, E. (eds.) *History, Buddhism and New Religious Movements in Cambodia*. Honolulu: University of Hawai'i Press.

Harris, I. 2001. 'Sangha Groupings in Cambodia'. *Buddhist Studies Review* 18: 73–105.

—— 2005. *Cambodian Buddhism: History and Practice*. Honolulu: University of Hawai'i Press.

Hughes, C. 2003. *The Political Economy of Cambodia's Transition 1991-2001*. London: RoutledgeCurzon.

—— 2006. 'The Politics of Gifts: Tradition and Regimentation in Contemporary Cambodia'. *Journal of Southeast Asian Studies* 37: 469–489.

Kalab, M. 1994. 'Cambodian Buddhist Monasteries in Paris: Continuing Tradition and Changing Patterns' in Ebihara, M., Mortland, C. and Ledgerwood, J. (eds.) *Cambodian Culture since 1975: homeland and exile*. London: Cornell University Press.

Kent, A. 2007. 'Purchasing Power and Pagodas: the sīma monastic boundary and consumer politics in Cambodia'. *Journal of Southeast Asian Studies* 38: 335–354.

Keyes, C.F. 1994. 'Communist Revolution and the Buddhist Past in Cambodia' in Keyes, C.F., Kendall, L. and Hardacre, H. (eds.) *Asian Visions of Authority: Religion and the Modern States of East and Southeast Asia*. Honolulu: University of Hawaii Press.

Mabbett, I. and Chandler, D. 1995. *The Khmers*. Oxford: Blackwell.

Introduction

Marston, J. and Guthrie, E. 2004. 'History, Buddhism, and New Religious Movements in Cambodia'. Honolulu: University of Hawai'i Press.

McDermid, C. and Sokha, C. 2005. 'Chronicle of a Death Foretold' *Phnom Penh Post*. Phnom Penh.

Thierry, S. 2003. *Les Khmers*. Paris: Editions Kailash.

Vickery, M. 1999 [1984]. *Cambodia 1975–1982*. Chiang Mai: Silkworm Books.

NOTES

1. Professor Judy Ledgerwood was unable to attend. Her contribution was read by Dr Anne Hansen.
2. Hem Chieu who taught at the École Superieure de Pali, Phnom Penh, was vehemently opposed to French attempts to romanize the Khmer script. He was arrested on 17 July 1942 for his participation in opposition activities. He died the following year in prison, aged 46.
3. The execution was, however, not carried out.
4. The *Thommayut* Order, a far smaller, royally sponsored division of the *sangha*, introduced into Cambodia from Thailand under King Norodom, was thus effectively merged with the larger, traditional *Mahanikay* Order.
5. The most notable example of this is the violent crackdown on protesting monks in 1998, discussed in Heng Sreang's chapter in this volume.

CHAPTER 2

Buddhism and Reform: Imposed reforms and popular aspirations
Some historical notes to aid reflection*

Alain Forest

Very little is known about the religious history of Cambodia between the thirteenth and twentieth centuries. The best one can do, in fact, is to elaborate on hypotheses about the changes that took place in the fourteenth and fifteenth centuries, when Cambodia shifted from religious heterogeneity, with brahmanical cults honouring Siva ('the king of the gods, the god of the king' *devaraja*) and Vishnu coexisting with diverse forms of Theravada and Mahayana Buddhism, to the uncontested superiority of a form of Theravada Buddhism stemming from a reform that took place in Ceylon in the second half of the twelfth century.[1] The main thrust of this reform was in relation to the *sangha*, and in this sense the reform was comparable to the Cistercian reform in the West. They are both extremely simple and they are both still in force.

The precepts that a Buddhist monk must honour are stipulated very precisely. There are 227 of them. The text that enumerates these precepts forms the *patimokkha*, a text that is recited by the monks every fifteen days, without the presence of the faithful. The monks must also confess any breaches of the precepts they may have committed. The recitation and the scrupulous respect for the *patimokkha* clearly distinguish the monastic community – the 'virtuosi' to use a phrase of Max Weber's – from the community of the faithful.

---

* *Translated from the French by David Chandler*

In return, the precepts insure that the monk is always in a state of sanctity, as required by the faithful. It falls to the faithful to protect the religion because they must act in such a way that the monks can devote themselves without interference to meditation, to gaining knowledge of texts – which were specified and reviewed in the course of the reforms – and to respecting rules, so that the religion is perpetuated. The faithful are also responsible for providing food and lodging for the monks and for protecting them from possible aggressors. All of this behaviour constitutes the 'gift' – the meritorious act *par excellence* – that bears good fruit, shaping the future *kamma* of the donor and potentiating favourable rebirths. In this sense, the monk resembles a 'rice field of merit'. It is understood (and here we encounter the imperative for sanctity again) – that the fructification of the gifts depends on the sanctity of the monk receiving them. A good rice field will produce good grain, but a faithful layperson will not draw any merit from a bad field.

THE SINGHALESE REFORMS

Establishing the sanctity of the monks so that progress could be made in the cycle of rebirths in the direction of Deliverance is one of the bases of the Singhalese reforms. The king played an essential role in the process as the first of the faithful and the first protector of religion. It fell to him to see that the corpus of scriptures was copied and kept in its entirety. It was also his responsibility to make sure that the monastic discipline was respected and, since the monks were forbidden to use violence, to defrock bad monks if necessary. In order to make sure that he carried out his responsibilities well, the king would take care to choose a *sanghareach* (literally 'a king of the *sangha*') – usually an eminently respectable monk – who would guide and advise the king (see also Heng Monychenda's chapter in this volume).

This essential complementarity between sovereign and *sangha* explains why Theravada Buddhism, despite the universality of its message, was in practice built upon local *sangha*s and around kings and princes (or other authorities in recent times) and is the most powerful vector for the constitution around these kings of 'national' societies.

The position assigned to the king by the Singhalese reforms was probably one of the reasons for the enthusiasm with which reformed Theravada was received in Pagan among the Mons in what are now Burma and Thailand, and among the Thai princes who were then gaining power over societies in the upper Menam and middle Mekong. After creating new kingdoms in this region, the princes extended their reach southwards, to the detriment of the Angkorean Empire and its allies, up until the kingdom of Ayutthaya was established in the 1350s.[2] Evidence suggests that these Thai princes found in reformed Theravada a powerful means of making the societies over which they gained control cohere around their own person.

THERAVADA BUDDHISM IN CAMBODIA

This form of Theravada Buddhism arrived quite late in Cambodia. The available evidence suggests that the process of conversion took a relatively long time, and may have gone on over almost two centuries, from 1215 to 1400.[3] Although major religious transformation had begun in the twelfth and thirteenth centuries with Jayavarman VII and his family's adoption of Mahayana Buddhism, it would be too much to assume a straightforward cause-and-effect relationship or an immediate continuity between this and the massive conversion to Theravada at least a century later. We know that the Buddhism that Jayavarman VII professed was strongly rejected by the court at Angkor, but scholars have perhaps failed to consider that the rise of Theravada may in fact have sprung from this break with Mahayana. In this regard, it is interesting to note the bas-reliefs of the second enclosure of the Bayon, which was essentially devoted to the rehabilitation of Brahmanism. These emphasize the personage of the ascetic[4] who seems now, in the mid-thirteenth century, to have become the valorized person *par excellence.* Reverence towards this kind of figure may analogously have contributed to valorization of the 'virtuoso' monk of Theravada.

Cambodian monks who adhered to the new reform certainly did not remain inactive. Monks circulated between different monasteries and religious exchanges were stimulated by the dynamism of monastic communities in neighbouring countries (Lanna, Sukhotai and later Siam and Lan Xang). It has been suggested that one of Jayavarman VII's sons was in Ceylon soon after King Parakkamabhu's reform and he would then have been one of the small group who later disseminated reformed Buddhism. If this was so, the presence of a son of Jayavarman VII at the origins of the reform would support a kind of anteriority of Cambodian Theravada and it would also suggest an active role for Cambodian monks in the conversion of the peninsula. Such involvement by Cambodian monks is better attested much later, in the mid-fifteenth century, when eight Cambodian monks joined with 25 others from Chiang Mai in a trip to Ceylon to study and be re-ordained, before returning to Chiang Mai to take up residence there.[5] It is also more than likely that Cambodian monks were present at the Buddhist Council assembled in Chiang Mai by King Tilok in 1477.

Powerful popular aspirations doubtless contributed to the success of the new monachism in Cambodia.[6] Notably, with the exception of a short period during the troubled reign of Jayavarman VII in the thirteenth century, when people were particularly concerned about the future, laypeople had been largely excluded from interrogations about the afterlife, the search for a happy rebirth and the cult of dead forebears in the royal cults at Angkor. The reformed monachism, however, could offer everyone, regardless of social status, consolation and the possibility and above all the means of Deliverance. In contrast to the status of the Brahman, the status of the Buddhist monk (*bhikkhu*) was from then on open to everyone. The central sanctuary of the Angkorean temples, which was only accessible to a few privileged officiants, was replaced by the Buddhist reliquary (stupa or *chedei*) and the basilica (temple, or *vihear*), which was a large assembly hall open to all the faithful.

Finally, the sources[7] suggest that royal adherence and protection provided a decisive impetus for the implantation of the new religion. Successive defeats by the Siamese together with enormous demographic losses suffered by the Angkorean empire[8] prompted the last Angkorean kings to adopt the religious system that seemed to have provided so much power to the Thai princes. Moreover, in the economic and demographic turmoil that accompanied the abandonment of Angkor and the shifting of the capital to the South, numerous monasteries were founded and maintained within or around the successive new capitals (Sithor, Phnom Penh, Longvek). Evidence suggests that this – drawing on the model practised at Angkor *vis à vis* the Brahmans – was the preferred way of drawing and keeping the population close to these new establishments.

Cambodian Buddhism is thus a relatively 'young' phenomenon, whose consolidation depended on the interaction of three distinct forces: the conviction and aspiration of influential monks who ensured real 'sanctity', faith in the Buddha and deep attachment to the monks by the faithful, and attention and protection from the sovereign. This consolidation took place against a background of powerful syncretism and considerable formalism as far as the crucial elements of Buddhist monachism were concerned. At the same time, successful integration gave rise to reinterpretations of local and brahmanical beliefs.

A SYNCRETIC RELIGIOUS MILIEU

The rigour of Cambodian Buddhism is partly due to the fact that it did not develop in isolation but with the comings and goings of and study visits by monks to monasteries in neighbouring countries. We have already noted the trips made to Ceylon by some Cambodian monks with monks from Chiang Mai to strengthen their engagement, as well as the presence of Cambodian monks at the Council in Chiang Mai in 1477.[9] This kind of movement continued right up until the twentieth century. The importance of Siam – Ayutthaya and later Bangkok – as the source of dissemination, teaching practice and the perfecting of Buddhism, indeed for everything of concern to Cambodian monastic authority from the early seventeenth century until the early twentieth century, is well known. Also, we should not overlook the simultaneous importance of exchanges between Cambodian and Laotian monks via present day northeastern Thailand (Isan). This region was at that time one of passage, meeting and cohabitation of Lao and Cambodian people and it was also renowned for its forest monks, who were devoted to very demanding ascetic and meditation practices.[10] These ongoing exchanges enabled mutual control and emulation in the exactitude of meditative, ascetic and esoteric practices – which in fact seemed to be relatively normalized and 'controlled'. The precepts of the *patimokkha*, conditions for ordination, the practice of meditating and of seeking alms, conformity to ritual times (fasting after midday, claustration in a monastery during the *vossa* or rainy season), the rejection of personal interpretations of the Scriptures and the oral knowledge of these were respected and perpetuated identically in the region. This helped enforce the monachal integrity and 'sanctity' that formed the basis of Theravada Buddhism.

Complementarily, the new Buddhism sank roots into society by integrating traditional beliefs while also reinterpreting them. There is no contradiction, for instance, between the Buddhist and the rural conceptions of time. Buddhism also admits the existence of multifarious divinities: diverse malevolent beings (phantoms, ghouls, etc.) and beneficent ones (various protective genies) that inhabit the universe. According to the Buddhist message, all of these beings and divinities are more or less happy existences that are subject to the sad cycle of death and rebirth. All of them are thus concerned with the Buddhist promise of Deliverance. Some of these beings accept and uphold this message – protecting good Buddhists as they do so – while others (such as the Christian and Muslim God, often assimilated with Mara in old Siam) reject the message and must be guarded against.[11]

Thus Indra, the king of the divinities, recovered the pre-eminence he had enjoyed at the time of the Buddha's preaching, and became the leader of those divinities who supported the Master. He is almost always represented riding on his three-headed white elephant[12] on the eastern fronton of Buddhist temples above the principal entrance. Vishnu was celebrated mainly as his *avatar* Rama. In a reinterpretation of the *Ramayana* (*Reamker* in Cambodia), Rama became the image and the exemplar of a Buddhist 'king of men'.[13] As for Siva, his fate is most interesting. His name (Preah Eysor) lives on in legends and stories and he has remained one of the divinities that specifically protects kings (along with Indra, Vishnu, Ganesa, etc.). In addition, he became the Great Hermit, an example of asceticism, and the possessor of a wide range of magical powers. Nowadays he is often represented in paintings near Buddhist monasteries, dressed in white. His mount, the bull Nandin, has been transformed into Preah Ko (the sacred cow) and has also become the symbol of Gautama Buddha, whose zodiacal sign is the bull and whose Cambodian name, Kodom, begins with the syllable Ko. More generally, Angkorean times and the memory of brahmanical dominance slipped into the domain of myth but were recalled as a time of the privileged alliance between men and *nagas*, the serpent-divinities and masters of the soil and wealth who lived beneath the earth.

The theme of the protective *naga* – easily Buddhicized since Buddhist teachings and iconography represent the *naga* as the protector of the Buddha[14] – provoked such widespread popular enthusiasm that the *naga* became virtually a totem animal,[15] whose image and magical abilities remain apparent everywhere. Agricultural tools such as the sickle, the plough and the ox-cart, and architectural motifs such as the roofs and balustrades of Buddhist temples include representations of the *naga*. Moreover, the animal is associated with the protective genies (that defend territories against external enemies and punish people who fail to respect them). Gradually these protective genies became 'existences' responsible for protecting those who respect the Buddhist religion and punishing others such that statues of the *neak ta* are regularly installed inside monastic enclosures. Some have even been discovered and solemnly introduced by the abbots of monasteries.

In the course of this evolution, the actual 'function' of the monk changed very little. Devoted to meditation and sanctity, and in this way seen as the catalyst of great merits benefiting the faithful, the monk also became an efficacious dispenser of blessings[16] and, inevitably, the possible dispenser of immediate benefits. Certain monks were appreciated for their gifts as healers or bone-setters, and they acquired reputations in the process.

A reading of different Cambodian sources leads one to think that the great moment of synthesis occurred in the sixteenth century.[17] A new era seems to have opened at the beginning of the century, with the coming to power of a man of the people, Kan, and then with the reconquest of the throne by a prince from the traditional royal family, Ang Chan. The sixteenth century can be described as a century of readjustment. At last a city (the complex of Longvek/Udong) became the uncontested capital of the 'king of kings'. Monastic foundations and the sovereigns' largesse toward them flourished once again. Moreover, Cambodia's powerful neighbour, Siam, found itself confronted with the rise to power of the Burman kingdom of Ava. This indeed enabled the Cambodian kings to push back the Siamese menace and to religiously reinvest the site of their ancient capital, Angkor. Several Angkorean sites still bear witness to the Buddhist fervour of these kings and, perhaps, to their attempt to make Angkor a sort of magically protected space, sheltered from future Siamese attacks. Certain temples of the 'Great City', such as Angkor Wat, were transformed into Buddhist reliquaries or, as in the case of the Baphuon, into a gigantic reclining Buddha (in the position of entering *nibbana*). Moreover, the combination of the reclining Buddha and the reliquary inside Buddhist temples that seems characteristic of the epoch testifies to the emphasis placed at this time on Deliverance, or *nibbana*, symbolically represented for viewing or for the meditation of monks and the Buddhist faithful.

The same period, particularly during the reign of Ang Chan, is associated with the development of a harmonious syncretism: in oral literature Ang Chan is in fact often identified with statues and other evidence of the Angkorean era and the erection of these in the form of protective genies.[18]

THE WEAKENING OF CAMBODIA'S POWER

The capture and destruction of Longvek in 1594 by King Naresuan of Ayutthaya were cataclysmic, with Naresuan emptying the Cambodian capital of its riches and objects endowed with magico-religious power (sacred texts, statues) that were assembled there (see also Kent's chapter in this volume).[19]

From then on, the vital centre of Cambodian Buddhism shifted to Ayutthaya and after 1767 to Bangkok. Monks destined to become the most respected Venerables of the Cambodian *sangha* came to the monasteries of these two capitals, as did the *achar*s and learned men who were to maintain the intellectual life of the kingdom, including the performance of rites and other expressions of religious life. From a religious point of view, the new Cambodian capital of Udong was little more than an extension of its Siamese counterparts.

After the fall of Longvek and the chaos that then reigned in the land of the Khmer – including the trauma of a king converting to Islam (Reamthipodey, r. 1642–1660) – other developments in Cambodian Buddhism between the end of the seventeenth and the mid-nineteenth centuries can be sketched in.[20]

Firstly, Cambodian Buddhism became from then on saturated with millenarian beliefs in the coming dissolution of Gautama's Buddhism and the arrival of the future Buddha (Maitreya) and the return of glorious times. Most Cambodians saw the sacking of Longvek as the capture by Siam of the magico-religious power of Cambodian kings. It is indeed true that Khmer writing was considered at Ayutthaya to be sacred, in the same way as Pali. The Cambodians then began waiting for the reappearance of Lord Preah Ko (Sacred Cow), who had disappeared with his brother Preah Keo (Sacred Jewel) during the fall of Longvek.[21] In the same way the cult of Maitreya grew.[22] Nowadays Maitreya statues can often be seen on the altars of temples, often at the base of a platform where statues of the Buddha are placed. Maitreya is represented with the trappings of a king in glory, dressed as a warrior prince with a jewel (*keo*) in the middle of its forehead. These sometimes form the focus of discoveries of highly popular 'persons of merit' (*neak mean bon*). It is thought that these people have come to establish a perfect kingdom and they often become the core around which popular rural movements of discontent crystallize.[23]

A second trait is the tendency towards esotericism, with the elaboration of texts, rituals and types of meditation that give access to a more accomplished rebirth, in the 'religious' sense of the term, which is to say a rebirth that leads more rapidly to sanctity and Deliverance.[24]

Somewhat different, though in a similar spirit, is a tendency towards more extreme asceticism, which is expressed in the movement known as 'forest monks'. Even if these men were attached to a monastery – or more likely to a master – they usually devoted themselves to solitary meditation in the forest or on a hill. They were highly respected, even feared, and could be extremely stubborn about protecting their monastic ideal. This created tensions in the monastic order. Finally, during this unstable time, the faithful, notably the *achar*s, came to play a decisive role in safeguarding, perpetuating and dynamizing Cambodian Buddhism.

As we have seen, representations concerning the retribution of acts (*kamma*) and obtaining merits constituted the foundations of popular Buddhism. The faithful were convinced that giving to monks and monasteries constituted the meritorious act *par excellence,* and was thus the best means of obtaining a good rebirth and good *kamma* for the future. At the same time, they made sure that the sanctity of the monk who received their gifts was irreproachable so that these gifts could bear 'good fruit'. Finally, the 'gift' became part of the strategies used by individuals or families for acquiring prestige. In giving to the pagoda, a faithful Buddhist displayed his integration into society and the size of his gift expressed his social status while also 'capitalizing' on merits for ensuring a good future.

DISRUPTION AND UNITY

These powerful representations stimulated real dynamism at the popular level. Providing for a monk became a veritable need for individuals and for society. The faithful of all categories therefore became occupied with welcoming, feeding and clothing monks, with erecting monasteries for them complete with a temple and a sala, and with meticulously maintaining these buildings.[25] At the same time, laypeople kept a close eye on the sanctity of their monks – without which their meritorious efforts would be in vain. The symbiosis between the population and the monastery was even more pronounced, of course, because most men would have spent time in the monastery either as a child 'servant' of a monk, or as a novice or monk themselves for at least a period of their lives. Some of them, the *achar*s, even acquired special competence in the monastery in knowledge of the Scriptures, prayers and rituals.

It is no exaggeration to say that Khmer Buddhism has survived because of popular consent and popular initiatives (and the strong interdependence between the faithful and the monks), and because of royal protection. Buddhism was the only real enduring, unifying factor in this divided and desolate country. It also drew strength from the harmonious synthesis that developed between Buddhism and the rites and practices for obtaining happiness, health and prosperity in the immediate future: the cult and invocation of protective genies, diverse entities and divinities, various agrarian rites, and the 'magical' techniques certain monks were thought to have mastered. No contradiction was observed between techniques for preserving short term happiness, accumulating merit for obtaining a better rebirth or a better life in the middle term, or Deliverance in the long term. Thus all ceremonies, whatever they may have been (for example, the annual honouring of protective genies) were soon matched with more specifically Buddhist ceremonies that involved making offerings to monks, 'feasts to make merit'. At the same time, beneficent entities, such as protective genies, managed to become Buddhicized guarantors that preserved both Buddhist and traditional social ethics.

We should add, however, that certain conceptions of Theravada Buddhism had, conversely, to come to terms with more traditional beliefs. Beliefs concerning death are a case in point. Although Theravada postulated that actions, meritorious or not, only had their positive or negative repercussions for the person who performed them, since *kamma* was strictly individual, it had to compromise on this point and allow for the idea of ' transfer of merits'. That is to say that the faithful could 'transfer merits' to deceased relatives so that these people could escape a bad rebirth.[26] Similarly, despite its insistence on cremation for ensuring a good rebirth, Theravada had to accept the idea that the souls of the dead return annually, during the feast of the dead, to be nourished and comforted by the living before being sent back to the places where they normally reside.

These are the general characteristics of traditional Cambodian Buddhism[27] – characteristics that are found in more or less the same form in neighbouring Siamese and Lao societies. Indeed, the first movements that sought to adapt Buddhism to the modern world came from Siam (see Hansen's chapter in this volume) supported in the 1830s by Mongkut (the future Rama IV) who, after being kept from the throne on the death of Rama II in 1824, retired to monastic life.

THE BIRTH OF THE THOMMAYUT ORDER

Mongkut's was an extremely active retreat. He understood that his country needed to modernize in order to contain Western powers.[28] Countering the claims of Anglo-Saxon Protestant missionaries that conversion to Protestantism was a prerequisite for modernization, Mongkut argued vehemently that Buddhism was quite compatible with science and that Siamese modernization would come about through people's deepening knowledge of Buddhism and its compatibility with progress. In this way Mongkut took command of an elitist religious reform. Knowing that the old order of monks who were loyal to the 'Great School' (Khmer, *Mahanikay*) would be reluctant to take part in reforms, he established a new school known as the 'Renewed Dhamma' (Khmer, *Thommayut*), which welcomed an elite group of princes and nobles and was not only more open to western innovations but was also better equipped to confront them intellectually.

Having made a great impact upon Siam, the reforms soon made their way to Cambodia, where disorder was peaking in the shadow of Vietnam's attempts to absorb the country (1835–1848). A fragile peace was established in 1848 with the arrival of King Ang Duong (r. 1848–1869). Under close Siamese supervision, this king worked hard to re-establish a semblance of administration and law. After his death, King Norodom (r. 1860–1904) called for a French protectorate in 1863 and this distanced Cambodia from Siam. Paradoxically, and at great cost to the French, King Norodom conceived of the protectorate essentially as a system of aid in favour of himself and he felt free to disregard any reform that seemed to run counter to his personal interests.

Thus the *Thommayut* order seemed to remain marginal to Cambodia, and the future Venerables of the *Mahanikay* order – and, for that matter, of the *Thommayut* – continued to go for training to Bangkok, until the French were able to put a stop to this.

Many indications suggest that the French protectors looked with distrust on relations between the Cambodian and Siamese *sangha*s, the latter being considered to exercise influence over the Bangkok court. For this reason, the protectorate authorities were particularly mistrustful of *Thommayut* monks, whom they considered to be quarrelsome – perhaps because they were better equipped to defend their interests on account of their privileged backgrounds. The French were disturbed by the relations that the monks established with the monastic elite in Bangkok. Much later, King Chulalongkorn's (Rama V) proclamation in 1902 established identical rules for all the monasteries of Siam, tightening control over them and circumscribing their movements and this inspired the Protectors to take action of their own. The French choice in 1904 of a new sovereign, Sisowath (r. 1904–1927), who had cooperated with them, allowed the French to advance some important initiatives.

The first set of religious reforms inspired by the French broke the links between Siamese and Cambodian Buddhism. This was definitive and was widely accepted since doing so sounded a note of national pride. The reform overlooked the need to endow Cambodia with institutions that were independent of those in Bangkok and this situation led, in 1909, to the creation of two schools of Pali in Phnom Penh and at Angkor, schools that were replaced in 1914 by the creation of a Superior Pali School in Phnom Penh, and a movement that led to the creation of the Buddhist Institute in 1930.

The 1914–1918 war and a few incidents involving monks returning from Bangkok and being accused of pro-German propagandism or of supporting Norodom's son, Prince Yukanthor[29] (and this was a pure pretext) furnished the authorities with a pretext to enforce the control and supervision of monks and to restrict their movements (1916).[30] From then on, candidates for ordination needed to have a certificate of good conduct issued by their village chief; after their ordination, monks needed to procure a certificate of ordination and be prepared to present it to the authorities. Village chiefs had to be notified about the movement of monks on their arrival and departure by *achar*s, who were responsible for all omissions and false declarations. Authorizations to visit Bangkok were only given to monks who had completed their studies and had obtained a diploma from the Pali School in Phnom Penh.[31]

A second aspect of the reforms dispossessed laypeople of their autonomy in the religious domain. For example the construction of new monasteries was regulated because it was thought that Cambodians spent too much on their monasteries. The French also tried to curb the expression by laypeople of ideas and opinions about religion. It was argued that these expressions exacerbated the conflicts between monks, between monasteries and between the two orders, *Mahanikay* and *Thommayut*. Finally, a pyramidal, hierarchical structure was set in place. This regulated more strictly the relationships between monasteries at the national level, and awarded pre-eminence at the provincial level to a superior monk who was nominated by the governor of the province and approved by the Minister of the Interior and Religion. At the same time, special tribunals were established to deal with the disputes that arose on religious matters.

Moreover, these disputes were not infrequent because, paradoxically, the agreement reached between the throne and its protectors helped to restructure and reinforce the higher social classes (princely families, and old or new families of high royal functionaries). This led to a greater affinity among these groups for the *Thommayut* order. French sources testify to numerous conflicts between the two orders and these were often settled by the King. The disagreements were commonly motivated by the fact that certain monks were pushing their formerly *Mahanikay* monasteries toward the *Thommayut*, despite opposition from the faithful. It should be noted that from this time on monasteries were more subject to the judgement of superior authorities than to the judgement of laypeople.

A third aspect of the reforms can be traced neither to legislation nor to the will of the colonial power. It came rather from a 'spirit of reform' that permeated all kinds of religious representations and discourse. This affected not only the French authorities and savants but also, more generally, the great majority of Westerners as well as the Siamese elites who were sensitive to Protestant propaganda, and it also reached some of the Cambodian elite. It soon became common to denounce and to write lessons for Buddhists about the perversion of 'true' Buddhism (essentially an Orientalist reinvention and reinterpretation of the Scriptures). This perversion included magical practices and supernatural beliefs into which Cambodians, to make things worse, were used to pouring their meagre riches.

The introduction of the dichotomy between true religion and superstitions, in the guise of reformist renewal, was liable to explode the solid traditional synthesis by which Theravada Buddhism was rendered not as a pure and simple intellectual construction but as the basis of the composite of systems of relationships constituting social space. If this idea of reform was not instantly traumatic, in the long term it certainly engendered a profound malaise.

The break between Siamese and Cambodian Buddhism, the blocking of laypeople's religious initiative and the deepening divide between religion and superstition had some important secondary effects.

1. The break with Bangkok opened Cambodian Buddhism to the influence of Cambodian elites in French Cochinchina (Kampuchea Krom), elites that had access to a better system of education in Cochinchina. An emblematic person from this group is Son Ngoc Thanh, one of the first assistant directors of the Buddhist Institute and an eminent figure in Cambodian nationalism. The considerable influence of the Kampuchea Krom elites was expressed in an intensification of the theme of safeguarding the purity of religion and, by extension, the purity of the Khmer 'race'. These elites were peculiarly sensitive to the need to preserve the purity of customs and religion in the face of the demographic dynamism and superiority complex of the Vietnamese, but also in their hope for the return of the Cambodian provinces of

Cochinchina to Cambodia.³² They were consequently among the first to begin blaming the Protectorate, whose authorities were interfering with Buddhist affairs and were suspected of trying to subvert religion and thus pave the way for the demise of the Khmer nation.³³

2. However, serious disagreement began to emerge within Cambodian society itself on the question of the purity of the 'true' religion, and two viewpoints stood in opposition. The majority of Cambodians, both laypeople but particularly monks, held (and continue to hold) that purity rests upon the preservation of traditional customs and interpretations of Buddhism. An entirely different position, adopted by certain Westerners and an increasing number of Cambodian elites, held that Cambodian Buddhism, like mediaeval Christianity, needed to be stripped of the superstitions that were perverting it. These maintained that monks should engage in the intellectual study of original texts in order to restore the authenticity of the Buddhist religion.

The first notes of discord to appear were in the ambiguous responses within all milieux, including the *Thommayut,* to the work of the reformist monks Chuon Nath (1883–1969) and Huoth Tath (1891–1975), who made the reinterpretation of texts the core of their programme, thereby hoping to overcome the differences between the *Mahanikay* and *Thommayut.*³⁴

This conflict between conservatives and reformers was temporarily arrested in the 1930s by the birth of nationalist sentiment. The issue of Buddhist reform seemed to recede from public debate, dissolving after the 1940s in the tide of hope about building a new, harmonious, post-colonial society, and eclipsed by slogans and theories of 'Buddhist socialism' during Sihanouk's Sangkum Reastr Niyum movement (People's Socialist Community, 1955–1970) and, finally, by the complete effacement of Buddhism between 1975 and 1979.

However, the root of the conflict persisted and resurfaced regularly in various guises. There was dispute over Romanization of the Khmer alphabet in the 1940s and later over any form of simplification of the Khmer writing system or modernization of the language. In the 1960s, for instance, Chuon Nath and intellectuals such as Keng Vannsak proposed that Khmer was too dependent upon Pali and Sanskrit roots to allow for the creation of new terms.

The cleavages related to Buddhist reform were and remain particularly complex. The spirit of reform has undeniably won and many Cambodians have internalized the disastrous dichotomization of 'true' Buddhism and 'superstitions', in a manner leading them to believe that they have little to say in religious matters. However, the tension between reform and preservation has never been resolved and it has, with few exceptions, become indelibly imprinted on the heart of every Cambodian. This has meant that the debate has become internalized, with confusion giving way to demagogic slogans, esotericism and escapes into millenarianism, which continues to flourish today.

At the end of the last century, initiative and decision-making in religious matters passed between central power and monachal power while the dynamism and aspirations of ordinary laypeople – notably their reconciliation of the Buddhist message with the pursuit of immediate boons – were progressively invalidated.

This evolution again makes the relationship between power and the *sangha* crucial. Currently, the recognition of Buddhism as an official religion and the revival of constitutional monarchy may appear to renew the perennial relation between faith and what was established by the Ceylonese reforms. But to what extent can the bases of that relation – a central power that protects the religion and also oversees the authenticity of the scriptures and maintains monastic discipline – be reintroduced?

The issue of reform begs other questions concerning:

- the possible religious foundations of Khmer Rouge totalitarianism: the relation between preservation of religious purity and the obsession with purity that characterized the Khmer Rouge 'sect';
- the accelerated individualization of religion following the Khmer Rouge cataclysm, an individualization that is now taking three directions: 1) stress on the individual nature of the Buddhist search for Deliverance (and meditation) 2) a chaotic search for religious alternatives such as various gurus or reinvented Brahmanism and 3) conversion to Christianity;
- the orientation of Buddhist practices toward a cult of the dead, which continues even today to be a foundation for the attachment of the society to Buddhism;
- the relationship between religion and politics (see Heng Sreang's chapter in this volume) and, more generally, Buddhism's role in contemporary society (not simply as a kind of NGO) and in opening Cambodian society up to the rest of the world rather than enclosing it in a mystical universe. Following a recent statement by Benedict Anderson, one might also question the capacity of overseas Cambodians to participate fruitfully

in these reflections when they tend to see Cambodia as a repository of traditions and beliefs from the past.

But these issues must not eclipse the fundamental question of the reform and its implications for the relationship between power and the *sangha*, and which in turn affects individual and collective initiatives. Is it viable to reconsider and revive the foundations and dynamism of the Ceylonese Buddhist reform in Cambodia today?

REFERENCES

Bizot, F. (1976) *Le figuier à cinq branches. Recherche sur le bouddhisme khmer.* Paris: PEFEO.

Chandler, D. (2007) *A History of Cambodia.* 4th edition, Boulder: Westview Press.

Dolias, J. (2001) *La Perception de l'Océan par les Cambodgiens*, Doctoral dissertation, l'Institut National des Langues et Civilisations Orientales (INALCO).

Edwards, P. (2007) *Cambodge: The Cultivation of a Nation (1860-1945).* Honolulu: University of Hawai'i Press.

Forest, A. (1979) *Le Cambodge et la colonisation française. Histoire d'une colonisation sans heurts (1897–1920).* Paris: L'Harmattan.

—— (2001) 'Jésus vu par les bouddhistes' in Gerard Cholvy (ed.) *Figures de Jésus-Christ dans l'hjistoire.* Montpellier: Centre Regionale d'histoire des Mentalités (Univerisité de Montpellier), pp. 101–109.

Khin Sok (1988) *Chroniques royales du Cambodge (De Baña Yât à la prise de Lanvaek).* Paris: PEFEO.

Khing Hoc Dy (1993) 'Le conte historique de Brah go brah kaev', *Cahiers de l'Asie du Sud-Est,* INALCO, No. 29–30 (a homage to Solange Thierry).

—— (1998) 'Les romans classicus Khmers et les jataka extra-canoniques' Paper presented at the colloquium 'Religious Diffusion and Cultural Exchanges on the Indochinese Peninsula'. University of Hamburg.

Leclère, A. (1899) *Le bouddhisme au Cambodge* Paris: E. Leroux.

Mak Phoeun (1984) *Chroniques royales du Cambodge (Des origines légendaires jusqu'à Paramarâjâ Ier)*, Paris: PEFEO.

—— (1998) 'Quelques aspects des croyances religieuses liées aux guerres entre le Cambodge et le Siam (XVè-XIXè siècles)'. Paper delivered at the colloquium 'Religious Diffusion and Cultural Exchanges on the Indochinese Peninsula'. University of Hamburg.

Saveros Pou (1977) *Ramakerti (XVIè-XVIIè siècles) et Etudes sur le Ramakerti.* Paris: PEFEO.

Tiyavanich, K. (2003) *The Buddha in the Jungle.* Chiang Mai: Silkworm Books.

Thompson, A. (2004) 'The future of Cambodia's Past: a Messianic Middle-Period Cambodian Royal Cult' in John Marston & Elizabeth Guthrie (eds), *History, Buddhism and New Religious Movements in Cambodia*, Honolulu: University of Hawai'i Press.

Wade, G. (1998) 'The spread of Theravada tradition in the T'ai polities of Yunnan 14th–18th centuries.' Paper presented at the colloquium 'Religious Diffusion and Cultural Exchanges on the Indochinese Peninsula'. University of Hamburg.

Wyatt, D. (2002) *Siam in Mind* (the chapter on Nakhon Phanom). Chiang Mai: Silkworm Books.

NOTES

1 The reform took place at the initiative of King Parakkamahabu I (r. 1153–1186), who wanted to end the divisions between the ministries on the island, decisions that had political implications.

2 The creation of the kingdom of Lan Xang (Luang Prabang and Vientiane) took place in the same period.

3 The use of Pali in a monastery foundation stele in 1308 indicates that Theravada had already become established at Angkor.

4 At the north entry, there is a representation of Siva transforming himself into a flaming lingam, a symbol of the purifying power of asceticism.

5 See Geoff Wade (1998) 'The spread of Theravada tradition in the T'ai polities of Yunnan 14th–18th centuries.' Paper presented at the colloquium 'Religious Diffusion and Cultural Exchanges on the Indochinese Peninsula'. University of Hamburg.

6 The twelfth and thirteenth centuries marked the beginning of a generalized adhesion on the part of Southeast Asian peoples to messages of Deliverance: Islam in the island world, Theravada Buddhism on the continent, not to mention the subsequent conversions to Christianity in islands untouched by Islam and in the present-day Philippines.

7 Primarily the royal chronicles, cf. Mak Phoeun (1984) *Chroniques royales du Cambodge (Des origines légendaires jusqu'à Paramarâjâ Ier)*, Paris, PEFEO.

8 Insofar as most of the population passed under Siamese control, or were destabilized by the conflicts.

9 We should take note of the influences exerted by the Chiang Mai monasteries on the religious and literary production of the entire peninsula. For example, a number of apocryphal, but edifying stories of the previous lives (*jataka*) of the Buddha seem to have been elaborated in Chiang Mai before spreading into the kingdoms of the peninsula, a movement that encouraged similar activities in several kingdoms to create new *jataka*s, also apocryphal but revered alongside those of the Scriptures. This is what happened for example in post-Angkorean Cambodia where new *jataka*s, approved by Chiang Mai were received and from which new ones were created on the same model. See Khing Hoc Dy (1998) 'Les romans classicus Khmers et les jataka extra-canoniques' Paper presented at the colloquium 'Religious Diffusion and Cultural Exchanges on the Indochinese Peninsula'. University of Hamburg.

10   See David Wyatt (2002) *Siam in Mind* (the chapter on Nakhon Phanom). Chiang Mai: Silkworm Books, and Kamala Tiyavanich (2003) *The Buddha in the Jungle.* Chiang Mai: Silkworm Books.

11   See Alain Forest (2001) 'Jésus vu par les bouddhistes' in Gerard Cholvy (ed.) *Figures de Jésus-Christ dans l'hjistoire.* Montpellier: Centre Regionale d'histoire des Mentalités (Univerisité de Montpellier) pp. 101–109.

12   Symbol of rainfall and fecundity.

13   See Saveros Pou (1977) *Ramakerti (XVIè–XVIIè siècles) et Etudes sur le Ramakerti.* Paris: PEFEO.

14   This theme was often a feature of Angkorean statuary in the era of Jayavarman VII.

15   Replacing the crocodile, it seems. See Jacques Dolias (2001) 'La Perception de l'Océan par les Cambodgiens', Doctoral dissertation, l'Institut National des Langues et Civilisations Orientales (INALCO).

16   Collections of formulaic blessings exist, and every ceremony at which monks are present ends with blessings, accompanied by the aspersion of lustral water by the most senior monk.

17   See Khin Sok (1988) *Chroniques royales du Cambodge (De Baña Yât à la prise de Lanvaek).* Paris : PEFEO.

18   See Alain Forest (1992) *Le culte des génies protecteurs au Cambodge*, Paris: L'Harmattan.

19   See Mak Phoeun (1998) 'Quelques aspects des croyances religieuses liées aux guerres entre le Cambodge et le Siam (Xvè–XIXè siècles)'. Paper delivered at the colloquium 'Diffusions religieuses et échanges culturels en Péninsule indochinoise'. University of Hamburg.

20   Jaques Dolias (2001) 'La Perception de l'Océan par les Cambodgiens'. Doctoral dissertation, l'Institut National des Langues et Civilisations Orientales (INALCO).

21   Khing Hoc Dy (1993) 'Le conte historique de Brah go brah kaev', *Cahiers de l'Asie du Sud-Est,* INALCO, No. 29–30 (a homage to Solange Thierry).

22   See Ashley Thompson (2004) 'The future of Cambodia's Past: a Messianic Middle-Period Cambodian Royal Cult.' In John Marston & Elizabeth Guthrie (eds) *History, Buddhism and New Religious Movements in Cambodia*, Honolulu: University of Hawai'i Press.

23   The Buddha himself was considered to be a 'person of merit'.

24   See François Bizot (1976) *Le figuier à cinq branches. Recherche sur le bouddhisme khmer.* Paris: PEFEO. It noted that the cycle of deaths and rebirths is extremely long according to Theravada doctrine. Gautama Buddha himself had 550 rebirths (*jataka*s) before arriving at the human existence from which he attained Buddhahood and later *nibbana*.

25   As we know, the local organization of Theravada Buddhism is not based on territory, making it different from the parish in Catholic countries. The establishment and care of monasteries and monks are the expressions of families and clienteles, groups (sometimes neighbours, but not always) or of individuals aspiring to obtain an exceptional amount of merit and, simultaneously, to strengthen their prestige in the eyes of their compatriots. Moreover, although it may be natural for humble peasants to

frequent the nearest monastery, they are not necessarily tied to the monastery because of its proximity or for territorial reasons but because of privileged personal ties. Such and such a family or clientele go to a monastery set by tradition – or because the boys and men of these groups, when they become *bhikkhu*s, traditionally wear the robe in this 'family monastery'. A monastery or a monk well known for their sanctity (or for the pleasing voices of the monks reciting the Scriptures) also attracts the faithful, to the extent that the gifts and benefits given to these monasteries and monks are known to produce excellent merits.

26 Or so that families and friends could find each other in the after-life.
27 Adhémard Leclère's *Le bouddhisme au Cambodge* (1899), Paris: E. Leroux gives a good presentation.
28 The British, who had recently annexed the regions of the Arakan and Tenasserim at the expense of the Burmese, began putting pressure on the Siamese regarding the suzerainty of the sultanates in peninsular Malaya (Kedah).
29 On Prince Yukanthor, see David Chandler (2007) *A History of Cambodia.* 4th edition, Boulder: Westview Press, p. 180, drawing on Alain Forest (1980) *Le Cambodge et la Colonisation Francaise*, Paris: L'Harmattan: pp. 59–78.
30 Evidence suggests that it was also a question of preventing suspected criminals from taking refuge from the authorities in the monastery by ordaining.
31 See Alain Forest (1979) *Le Cambodge et la colonisation française. Histoire d'une colonisation sans heurts (1897–1920).* Paris: L'Harmattan.
32 The theme of preserving religious purity is also a powerful Buddhist doctrinal theme – it is always necessary to know the difference between what is Buddhist and what is non-Buddhist, but since the Buddhist faithful are by nature foolish they are hardly capable of making this kind of distinction and are therefore easily mistaken. This justifies the need to identify and distinguish anything that may introduce a confusion of spirits, and to struggle continuously for the preservation of religious purity.
33 Note that the Cambodian term for nation – *jati* – is the term for caste in Sanskrit and is often translated as 'race'.
34 In this regard see Penny Edwards (2007) *Cambodge: The Cultivation of a Nation (1860–1945).* Honolulu: University of Hawai'i Press. The advance of these reformist monks was then supported by Suzanne Karpélès. We know that from 1980, Buddhism was once again permitted with the nomination of a new *Sanghareach* (Venerable Tep Vong). However, another example of reformist effort was the fact that only the *Mahanikay* order was authorized and until 1983–1984 only the elderly had the right to ordain (at least theoretically, though this restriction was not widely respected). The *Thommayut*, which was considered to belong to the exploitative upper classes remained prohibited until the Paris Peace Accords and the return of Sihanouk to Phnom Penh in 1991.

CHAPTER 3

Modernism and Morality in Colonial Cambodia

Anne Hansen

In his well-known essay on modernity, 'The Painter of Modern Life,' published in *Figaro* in 1863 (the same year that Cambodia became a French protectorate), Charles Baudelaire proposed that 'every age had its own gait, glance and gesture'. Baudelaire advised going to 'some vast portrait-gallery, such as the one at Versailles' to 'verify this proposition'.[1] The 'gait, glance and gesture' of early modernism in colonial Cambodia – part of a religious reform movement that galvanized Khmer Buddhists in the early decades of the twentieth century – is perhaps better verified in the surge of photographs of monks that first began to circulate in this period, attached to the newly introduced literary forms of print hagiographies or commemorative funeral biographies. Among these photos, none better inscribes the full ethos of modernist sensibilities than a portrait of Preah Uttamamuni Um-Sur from the late1930s (see p. 37).[2]

The photo appeared in a funeral volume dedicated to Um-Sur after his premature death in 1939, as well as in the Buddhist periodical *Kambujasuriya*.[3] It shows a frail man holding a thick Buddhist commentarial text (one he had only recently translated and published in book form), his eyes focused intently on what he is reading, the image of a man who is accustomed to concentrating on and comprehending the *Dhamma-vinaya*. Even a decade earlier, when photographs first began to appear in Buddhist publications, it would have been unthinkable for a portrait of a learned monk in Cambodia to contain a depiction of a printed script rather than of a palm leaf manuscript. The first monk portrait that appeared in *Kambujasuriya* in 1927, a photograph of the recently deceased Abbot Preah Dhammacariyeavangs Et of Wat Damnak in Siem Reap, showed him seated

Figure 3.1. Preah Dhammacariyeavangs Et on a chair and holding a palm leaf manuscript, though not in a reading position.[4]

The logo of the Royal Library itself in the 1920s and 1930s – an institution that promoted the printing of Buddhist texts – depicted a seated royal figure holding only traditional Buddhist manuscripts, one made from palm leaf and the other an accordion-pleated manuscript made from mulberry bark paper. A pioneer of new methods of Pali learning, translation and the co-author of the controversial first printed scriptural translation in Cambodia in 1918, Um-Sur, at the time of his death, was considered to be the most erudite Pali scholar of his generation.

Figure 3.2. Preah Uttamamuni Um-Sur

In the photo, Um-Sur's qualities as an exemplary Buddhist ascetic are made evident from the way that the photo constructs his relationship with the camera and viewer, suggesting that his study of the *dhamma* is not at all disturbed by the obvious presence of the camera. The viewer is left with the impression that even in the self-reflexivity of this quintessentially modern moment, posed in front of the camera, Um-Sur is not simply pretending to read; he has become genuinely absorbed in the *dhamma*. Observing this stance from some distance beyond the camera, the viewer senses that here is a prominent man of his age – but also one who is somehow, simultaneously outside it, reflective of something indescribable that transcends historical categorization.[5]

This essay argues for the emergence of 'new' Buddhist moral values in the context of Buddhist intellectual developments in colonial Cambodia, values that were clustered around modernist ideas of rationalism, purification and 'authenticity'. With authenticity I refer to new notions of textual and canonical authority and a preoccupation with the legitimacy and accuracy of Buddhist practices with respect to their historical origins. Buddhist intellectuals of this period were giving new emphasis to the historical life of the Buddha, Siddhartha Gautama, and to the centrality of his teachings as conveyed in the *Dhamma-vinaya* as universal ideas that could give meaning to modern Buddhist life. These ideas, evident in the bookish portrait of the *dhamma* scholar and translator Um-Sur, were attached to a small but influential Buddhist modernist movement that developed in Phnom Penh in the 1910s and 1920s, centred among students in the monastic lineage of Preah Mahavimaladhamm Thong, a prominent Pali scholar at Wat Unnalom.[6] Coinciding with the heightened interest in the historical biography of the Buddha, the rise of a popular new print genre of monastic funeral biographies suggested how these Buddhist values – the kind of qualities authenticated by the historical life of the Buddha – could be transplanted into the lives of contemporary individuals. The funeral biographies of two key figures in the modernist 'movement', Venerables Um-Sur and Mahavimaladhamm Thong, demonstrate how these interlinking moral concepts worked to shape modern intellectual understandings of how persons should live and act in their contemporary world.[7]

BACKGROUND TO KHMER BUDDHIST MODERNISM

In the first decades of the twentieth century some Buddhist intellectuals in Phnom Penh had begun thinking in new ways about temporality and history. Their interpretations of Buddhist doctrine represented in part their effort to accommodate new scientific, religious, commercial, technological, and political viewpoints and ideas circulating in this period within their Buddhist worldviews. One outgrowth of this reinterpretation was their greater attention to delineating the social ethical values important for ordinary individuals in their everyday lives.

Since modernist scholars (and most other literati in Cambodia during this period) had been trained to think primarily through the lens of Buddhist texts and ideas, it is not surprising that Buddhist ethical reflection was the medium through which they sought to understand and express changes in their society. By giving attention to their ethical values, of course, it does not mean that we are seeing all the ways in which Cambodian Buddhists of the period actually lived and acted in the world – even with reference to the group of intellectuals discussed here. But examining ethical values does give us insight into how these particular moral actors made sense of the world, how they gave it order and meaning, and the guiding principles by which they tried to structure their lives and relationships. An examination of their ethical thought is also valuable in an institutional historical sense since these Buddhist intellectuals were among the architects of the modern Buddhist institutions that dominated *sangha* education in Cambodia throughout much of the rest of the twentieth century.

The deaths in 1927 and 1939 of two of the most important thinkers in the modernist movement, Preah Mahavimaladhamm Thong and Preah Uttamamuni Um-Sur, each gave rise to a series of biographical essays – published in Buddhist periodicals and commemorative funeral volumes – that offered reflections on the ethical values associated with modernism. Both men were understood by their compatriots to have embodied these values. Their deaths, as represented in the biographies, are surrounded by the trappings of modern life: the Royal Library and the Sala Pali (Pali high school), two important new modern Buddhist institutions; new printed vernacular translations of Pali texts; modern medicine; international pilgrims arriving on steamships; even funeral discourses chanted over microphones. Yet simultaneously, they evoke the scenes and emotions at the death of the Buddha, thus causing their biographies to reference his. As a modern and historically-oriented genre of printed monastic biography arose in Cambodia, it helped to reinforce a new ethical emphasis on rationalism and purification as modes for leading an 'authentic' Buddhist life, one based on the example of the moral perfection achieved by the historical Buddha.

Buddhist modernism in Cambodia drew on and reflected a combination of local, regional and global forces and ideas, reviewed in Forest's essay in this volume. Khmer monks' emphases on purification and rationalism as means for achieving 'authentic' understanding of the Buddhist scriptures, for example, had roots in mid-nineteenth century purification efforts intended to revitalize Buddhism within Cambodia. They also derived from the influence of the religious reformism adopted by Mongkut (later Rama IV) of Siam and his sons Chulalongkorn (Rama V) and Prince-Patriarch Vajirañana, whose Buddhist modernization program has been described as 'scripturalism', the privileging of canonical texts as the definition of religious authority.[8] Buddhist modernism also resonated with broader trends in Southeast Asia that crossed religious boundaries. Region-wide, religious modernists including Muslims in Malaya and the Dutch East Indies as well as Buddhist reformers in Siam and Cambodia were calling for reforms that emphasized new methods of scriptural translation and interpretation. They opposed older methods of learning that featured rote memorization and urged religious people to accurately understand each word of scripture and to ensure that rituals were authentically performed, according to scriptural injunctions.[9]

Buddhist and Islamic religious modernism in Southeast Asia was shaped in part by the regional and global political, economic and cultural factors that we typically associate with the onset of colonial modernity in Southeast Asia: the demarcation of national boundaries, participation in a world-wide market economy, the new (and relatively late) availability of print technologies and modern literary genres in the region, engagement with discourses of Western science, rationalism and secularism. King Mongkut of Siam's attention to Western astronomy and geography, for instance, exemplifies this kind of interaction.[10] But religious modernism was also generated by interactions between Southeast Asians and other non-Western and pan-Asian people, alliances and movements such as exchange with Buddhist missionaries and scholars in South Asia, Muslim pilgrimage to Mecca, the study of Chinese renderings of Western philosophy, and travel by religious teachers and students across different parts of Southeast Asia itself.[11]

For Cambodians of this period, the most profound external religious influences came from Bangkok. Wars and violence during the late eighteenth and early nineteenth centuries had disrupted Buddhist education to such an extent that Khmer monks and novices who sought higher learning and textual resources turned to Bangkok as their intellectual center. After 1848, when King Ang Duong took the throne in Cambodia, the interactions between Thai and Khmer Buddhists intensified even further due to Ang Duong's close ties with the Siamese throne and his reliance on Khmer monks trained in Bangkok to revitalize Buddhism in his kingdom. David Chandler has described how Ang Duong began his reign by observing the Southeast Asian tradition of consolidating political power through religious purification or revitalization.[12] In this Theravadin sense (as Alain Forest's essay in this volume explicates in greater depth) purification entailed renewing Buddhism by supporting monks, collecting Buddhist texts, building and repairing monasteries, and gathering together learned teachers and literati. As a result, some of the most prominent figures in the Khmer *sangha* in the nineteenth and early twentieth centuries were trained in Bangkok, and other monks traveled there for shorter periods to study advanced Pali or to copy and collect texts.

When they returned to Cambodia, Khmer monks carried back not only the scriptures and commentaries missing from Cambodian monasteries, but also the reformist sense of mission current in Bangkok after the 1830s: to achieve purification with respect to Buddhist scriptures, monastic practices and self-conduct.[13] Stanley Tambiah has described Thai reformism during this period as 'scripturalism', referring to Mongkut's 'concern with finding the true canon, of understanding the truth correctly and discarding false beliefs and magical practices'.[14] The religious revisions initiated by Mongkut and further extended during the reign of his son Chulalongkorn aimed at bringing Thai ritual, monastic and pedagogical practices in line with new corrected recensions of Buddhist scriptures.

The biographies of Khmer monks returning from Bangkok often describe them as having experienced an 'awakening' or 'illumination' with respect to the *Dhamma-vinaya* (the Buddha's teaching). Following the outlines of Mongkut's reforms, they were particularly interested in the *Vinaya*, the part of the Buddhist canon that clarified the rules for Buddhist monastic life, including issues of how monks should wear their robes, ritual requirements for conferring monastic ordination, and other matters that pertained to assuring the 'authentic' practice and transmission of Buddhist teachings.[15] These reformist ideas resonated with the existing religious preoccupations in Cambodia of purifying religion by rebuilding the material, literary, ritual, and educational culture of Buddhism. At the same time, some aspects of the reigning Khmer Buddhist worldview of late nineteenth-century Cambodia had begun to crumble. Older associations between merit, virtue, social standing, and political power seemed less coherent in the colonial context, as mounting French control weakened the traditional roles of the monarch and court ministers. The result was a disjuncture between Buddhist theories and literary expressions of the world and lived experience.[16] The reformist ideas that monks were bringing back to Cambodia helped to address the disjuncture and ultimately to produce a modernist faction among the younger generation of Khmer monks. These young monks were being trained in new translation methods and with a new focus on questions of authentic monastic practice as articulated in the *Vinaya*.

PURIFICATION AND MODERNISM

Before examining several Khmer Buddhist modernist writings from the late 1920s and 1930s, it is perhaps helpful to briefly consider the outlines of different international expressions of 'modernism' during this period.

This comparison makes it evident that Southeast Asian intellectuals in Cambodia, Siam and elsewhere in the region were engaged with some of the same questions that preoccupied modernists in Europe and America during roughly the same period. Both the translocal dimensions of Khmer modernism and its distinctive local hues become more apparent on this larger comparative canvas.

While the many different disciplinary and cultural applications of our current scholarly uses of language about 'the modern' are not easy to summarize succinctly, as I have suggested elsewhere, making reference to certain generalizations about modern movements can help us think about the Khmer context within a larger comparative frame.[17] 'Modernity' has been widely associated with hallmarks such as changing modes of production and exchange; changing conceptions of temporality and of the physical representation of the world; mechanization and bureaucratization; rationalism, disenchantment or demystification; the demarcation of the secular; historicist views about progress and civilizational development. 'Modernist' movements, groups and expressions are often understood as responses to these experiences. 'Modernism', as it has sometimes been defined with reference to Euro-American art and literature, is understood to both express and critique aspects of modernity and to exhibit reflexivity about being caught up in shifts of history.

Art historians and critics point to a variety of expressions of modernism in Euro-American art that resist easy categorization, yet there is some general agreement about the broad absorptions of modernists. Art historians widely cite Charles Baudelaire's 1863 essay, cited earlier, for its perception of 'modernity' as 'the ephemeral, the fugitive, the contingent, the half of art whose other half is the eternal and the immutable'.[18] Sandro Bocola suggests that as the relevance of an underlying divine nature in the world gave way for Euro-American artists in the nineteenth century, it was gradually replaced – in their modernist art – by a perception of the underlying 'predictable functioning of reality and the mutual interdependence of anonymous anorganic, organic, psychic and intellectual forces' and a unity conceived of through scientific perception.[19] Emerging currents of modernist thought in art and literature served as a source for addressing the paradox that Baudelaire had perceived.[20] Other modernists viewed their work as a practice of 'purification', that 'purified art of much that was not art'.[21]

Similarly, in the late nineteenth and early twentieth centuries in Cambodia, Buddhist thought acted as a cultural medium for simultaneously critiquing and reflecting on modern experience.²² Euro-American modernist artistic efforts to work out the perception of a changed understanding of underlying reality through radical reinterpretations of artistic styles and forms accompanied a 'turn to the universal' in art. This seems to me to resemble Khmer Buddhist modernists' attention to the particularities of local and individual ritual and conduct as a means for apprehending the universal truth contained in the *dhamma*.²³ Modernist Buddhist writers such as Chuon Nath rejected older Buddhist literary conventions and practices of textual production, but their innovations and reforms were tinged with a critical appraisal of how far modern values and behaviour had veered from the path of universal truth. 'Nowadays', Chuon Nath wrote in the 1927 volume of *Kambujasuriya* commemorating Preah Mahavimaladhamm Thong's death, 'we should be striving hard to behave according to what is right and wrong ... But we have become indifferent. We do not strive ... at all, and those of us who are ordained spend our time sowing discord with each other'.²⁴

Chuon Nath and his compatriots were intent on transforming Buddhist interpretation in Cambodia by rediscovering the authentic words and practices of Buddhism in the historical time of the Buddha. They wanted to ensure that the *dhamma*'s true meaning was fully apparent. Their methods for editing, translating and disseminating scripture involved minute attention to the mechanics of language through grammatical translations compiled into new, more readily accessible literary forms such as printed pamphlets and serialized periodicals. Yet even as they self-consciously turned away from older approaches to Buddhist learning and expression, they did not intend to appear avant-garde. Rather, their new approaches to texts reflected their changed perceptions of grammatical accuracy and their recognition of the potential reach of print media. They wanted to use these new technologies of textual production in order to 'purify' texts and bring them in line with what they understood to be the historically authentic teachings of the Buddha.

Their writings also exhibited new apprehensions of the individual as situated in history as well as in an inter-dependent collective or communal life. The Khmer writer and Pali scholar Okña Suttantabreyjea Ind's *Katelok* (c. 1921) incorporated commentary on contemporary and historical figures and situations. His greatest concern was with the state of current morality. 'What is *dhamma* in these times?' he wrote. ²⁵ His ethical treatise considered how one should behave 'right now',²⁶ contrasting the 'old' with the 'new',[27] and examining the 'modern morality that has arisen'.[28] It was necessary 'in these present times', he wrote, for 'persons who are trying to be good and pure [to recognize] what is worldly and what is *dhammic* [behaviour]'.[29] This approach to moral conduct in terms of time, delineating the present moment from *'chas'* or *'boran'*, past or ancient times, or *'mun'*, all previous time before right now, along with the distinction he draws between what is 'worldly' (or secular) and *dhammic* (or religious) seems to me to express a similar self-consciousness about temporality to the one evident in the Euro-American artistic movements described above.[30] Other modernist authors similarly conveyed historicity through various means: by employing chronology to order a discussion of the life and contributions of a particular monk, or by including a preface that specifically addressed the needs and questions of contemporary readers.[31] The historicity in their ethical writings was attached to a strong sense of communality, which stressed that the actions of one person affected those of others. Purification necessitated collective effort by all adherents of the religion, *'neak tâm sasânâ'*, the four-fold religious community or *'bârisâl'* consisting of the assembly of all four groups of monastic and lay Buddhists, male and female: *bhikkhu-bhikkhuni-obasâk-obaseka*.[32]

Like the modernism in different artistic contexts, Buddhist modernism was not a monolithic intellectual development – although it did reflect the broad values I have sketched out. Different interpreters emphasized different ideas and worked on translating different authoritative scriptural texts according to their own interests. Huot Tath's memoir recounts that the self-designation 'new' or 'modern' originated with a small group of students and Pali scholars at Wat Unnalom who, beginning around 1914, began to refer to themselves as proponents of *'thorm-thmi'*, 'new' or 'modern' *dhamma*. This 'modern *dhamma*' moniker was picked up by the group's opponents as well, and was also used (sometimes rendered as 'modernist') in French administrative records after the mid-1910s.[33] By designating their interpretation of the *dhamma* as 'new', the young monks were self-consciously challenging the traditionalism of the *'thorm-chas'*, the 'old' or 'traditional *dhamma*' group. This latter faction was critical of the new methods of Pali learning and scripturalist attitudes advocated by the younger monks, preferring instead to maintain the older traditions of knowledge and textual dissemination associated with manuscript culture. These were the very practices that the young modernists had begun to see as contributing to an inauthentic or degenerate understanding of Buddhism.[34]

RATIONALIZING THE BUDDHA, AUTHENTICATING THE DHAMMA

The shift in emphasis toward a more collective and inclusive understanding of moral purification as the basis for everyday behaviour required a new, more rationalized interpretation of the Buddha as a human exemplar rather than as the mythic character represented in *Jataka* narratives.[35] In the canonical *Mahaparinibbana Sutta*, the Buddha is ill and recognizes that he has reached the end of his life. When his devoted assistant Ananda begins to weep, the Buddha reminds him of the nature of reality: everything that is born or arises must die. The Buddha continues by giving Ananda instructions for the time after his death:

> And the Lord said to Ananda, 'Ananda, it may be that you will think: "The Teacher's instruction has ceased, now we have no teacher!" It should not be seen like this, Ananda, for what I have taught and explained to you as Dhamma and discipline [*Vinaya*] will, at my passing, be your teacher.'[36]

For Khmer modernists, the Buddha most appropriate to their rationalization project was not simply the de-mythologized historical Buddha but also the Buddha as identified with and through his teachings in the *Dhamma-vinaya*, as described in the *sutta* passage above. They argued that since genuine purification could be achieved through studying the *Dhamma-vinaya*, it was essential that practitioners have access to the authentic teachings of the Buddha. In present-day Cambodia, they feared, too many of the existing texts had been corrupted over time through scribal errors and lack of correct understanding of Pali to allow Buddhists to gain insight.[37] Following from Mongkut's reforms in Siam, the early generations of Khmer monks who had been trained in Bangkok and later, their own students in Khmer monasteries, were especially focused on careful study and articulation of moral conduct based on codes of conduct outlined in the *Vinaya*, the compendium of prescriptions for monastic behaviour contained in the *Dhamma-vinaya*.

The introduction of new educational methods including grammar, translation and other pedagogical concerns were seen as crucial for the modernists because they illuminated *Vinaya* and other scriptural knowledge. In the older manuscript culture, aspects of Buddhist doctrine and *Buddhavacana*, the 'words of the Buddha', were less important than its overarching vision that human perfection was indeed possible: represented by the epic figure of the Bodhisattva moving from rebirth to rebirth over vast spans of time. Modernist monks wanted to demythologize this cosmic vision of perfection and bring it in line with human history. The historical Buddha had achieved moral purification and although he was long dead, his insights were still present in the *Dhamma*.

The modernist emphasis on purification also raised questions about authenticity. Through clear understanding of the authentic *Dhamma-vinaya*, Buddhists could purify their conduct and bring it in line with the Buddha's *dhamma*; purifying one's own individual conduct simultaneously purified and strenthened the religious community as a whole. 'Whether performed by a householder ... or a *bhikkhu*', Lvi-Em emphasized in a 1930 sermon, this form of purification represented the 'highest kind of homage or worship to the Buddha'.[38] Like Thai Prince-Patriarch Vajirañana's observations that the *Dhamma-vinaya* itself advocated rationalism, Preah Dhammalikhit Lvi-Em suggested in his sermon that 'the true and authentic Buddhist *Dhamma-Vinay*' could be understood through the means elucidated in the *Dhamma-vinaya* itself, in short, by 'making an effort to ponder, think, analyze and reflect on teachings in Pali and to let them penetrate one's heart and mind deeply'.[39] Although it required discipline, ordinary people could attain moral purification through effort and study. Yet this route to purification demanded a certain level of discernment about the sources of *Dhamma-vinaya* knowledge. How could the ordinary Khmer Buddhist recognize the difference between authentic and inauthentic doctrine when the *sangha* was itself at odds over this very issue?

Writing as a layperson and government official, Kim-Hak (who published the first modern Khmer novel in 1939) took up this theme in a 1931 essay addressed to the lay readership of *Kambujasuriya*:

> Devout persons everywhere! It is lamentable that in these times, the doctrine of our Great Teacher is not as resplendent as it could be. For Buddhism to be gloriously resplendent requires a return to Buddhist purity, practicing the Dhamma and *Vinaya* correctly in accordance with the words of the Buddha (*Buddha-vacana*) as we have been instructed in the last words of the Buddha, spoken by the Blessed One to Ananda in the city of Kusinara.[40]

The 'last words of the Buddha' to which Kim-Hak refers, are those cited previously from the *Mahaparinibbana Sutta* in which the Buddha instructs Ananda that after his death, the '*dhamma* and *vinaya*' should be regarded as the teacher, synonymous with the Buddha himself. In his 'articles for improving Buddhism', Kim-Hak points to a dilemma for Khmer Buddhists: 'Buddhists have a belief that it is a boastful exaggeration to claim that anyone can study the *Dhamma-vinaya* correctly on his or her own.' This was problematic in Cambodia, for not only was 'the number of Khmer intellectuals too small', but within this small group of intelligentsia there was also a troubling 'absence of agreement ... about how to interpret and disseminate the *dhamma* and *vinaya*'. The contemporary acrimony within the *sangha* about scriptural interpretation, Kim-Hak stressed, was an impediment to 'realizing the greater improvement of the *sāsanā*'.[41] Kim-Hak called on all his devout readers to aid in improving Buddhism by lending support to the Sala Pali, a place dedicated to 'increase the number of learned scholars capable of rectifying the [current condition] of Buddhism'.[42] Individual lay persons could work to improve Khmer Buddhism by studying the *Vinaya-pitaka*, which was now easy to obtain, thanks to the diligent efforts of the Royal Library to 'disseminate *Dhamma-vinaya* across our kingdom for the benefit of all moral persons'.[43]

While Kim-Hak's rallying 'Methods for Improving the Condition of Buddhism in the Kingdom of Cambodia' likely reached only the small, highly educated readership of *Kambujasuriya*, modernists intended others of their printed texts to have an impact on Khmer Buddhist practice writ large. One of the most successful examples of this effort to make moral purification accessible to an array of laypeople as well as *bhikkhu*s was Chuon Nath's small book, *Gihivinayasangkhep* [A Condensed *Vinaya* for Laypeople].[44] Translated, compiled and edited by Chuon Nath 'from the Pali version of ... *Mangaladipani-atthakatha*, *Mangala-sutta* and other texts', the text was written as a reference on Buddhist comportment for traders 'so they can take this book with them easily, even during their frequent journeys'.[45] It contained lists of right and wrong behaviour as well as instructions for conducting the religious rituals most commonly practised by laypeople. The manual detailed, for example, how to seek forgiveness by speaking clearly 'toward the direction of the face of the Preah Buddha image ..., toward the stupa, the *cediya* that holds relics of the Buddha..., toward the face of an individual who is a *bhikkhu*.'[46] Having made obeisance in this manner, the petitioner 'must demonstrate with clearly-annunciated speech ... that he or she has taken refuge as an *obasâk-obaseka* [lay adherent] in the religion of the Lord Buddha, and must profess commitment to continual observance of the precepts'.[47]

EMBODYING THE BUDDHA AND *DHAMMA*

How were these values to be translated into peoples' lives? We can evaluate at least the ideal translation of a life lived as a rational modern Buddhist through biographies that were produced in the wake of the deaths of two central figures in this movement, Preah Maha Vimaladhamm Thong and Preah Uttamamuni Um-Sur. Thong's unexpected death in 1927 posed a huge crisis for modernists. Still under attack by older traditionalists in the *sangha*, Thong's colleagues and students who were pushing for reforms in Buddhist education and ritual practices had leaned heavily on his reputation as a brilliant scholar and revered *sangha* leader for credibility. This was made evident, for instance, in a poignantly timid passage in *Samaneravinaya*, the controversial 1918 text translated and edited by Huot Tath, Chuon Nath and Um-Sur that had stirred up passionate disagreement within the *sangha* over the question of whether or not Buddhist scriptures could be printed. The three young compilers of the work were censored by Supreme Patriarch Preah Dhammalikhit Sanghanayok Uk before the work was finally published in 1918 against the wishes of *sangha* traditionalists. It was composed, Huot Tath wrote, repeatedly invoking Thong's name,

> at the invitation of the Venerable Preah Mahavimaladhamm Thong, Director of the Sala Pali of Phnom Penh, who requested that the *Samaneravinaya* be compiled, edited and made ready for printing. [The work] was carried out according to his [Thong's] wishes in order to benefit all students. It was he who invited Venerables Nath, Um-Sur and myself to be the compilers of this work, and it was brought to completion in accordance with his request.[48]

Thong was a dedicated *Vinaya* scholar and translator whose vision for revitalizing Buddhism in Cambodia included his proposal to the Résident Supérieur (who soundly rejected it) that the Administration send *Vinaya* teachers 'out into the pagodas of the provincial seats in the interior to teach the *Vinaya*' in order to help aid the development of the populace:

> The Preah *Vinaya* defends against doing wrong and ordains the doing of good. Until recently, due to a lack of adequate instruction, monks and novices have not competently learned the Buddhist regulations. They ignored these regulations because they have had too much freedom. They performed wrong actions, according to their inclinations, and this caused disorder in the religion and in the Kingdom. In consequence, it would be appropriate to remedy this problem by augmenting the education in the religious regulations that are the fundamental principles of the religion

dictated by the Buddha. If this is accomplished, the task undertaken by the Protectorate to protect the Kingdom and the religion will not be in vain.⁴⁹

Entrusted by the colonial administration with an appointment to a key position as the first director of the Sala Pali, Thong was also esteemed by French scholars of Buddhism and Indology at the École Française d'Extrême-Orient. George Coedès admired Thong for his 'science and his competence', describing him as a 'handsome and intelligent figure of a *bhikkhu* whom I am honored to count among my teachers'.⁵⁰ Louis Finot wrote after Thong's death that here was a man whose 'liberal and enlightened thought was manifested in the establishment of a program that permitted the first glimmers of European science to penetrate the Cambodian clergy'.⁵¹

The commemorative biographies written by Thong's students after his death in August 1927 sounded several prominent themes. First, Thong would long be remembered for his brilliance, as the 'foremost' teacher and scholar of his age.⁵² Second, he should be honored and remembered by faithful adherence to and correct study and translation of the *Dhamma-vinaya*. Third, Thong's death itself illuminated the meaning of *Dhamma-vinaya*; his death, like his life, was devoted to revealing the authentic meaning of *dhamma*. Taken as a whole, the commemorative biographies construct connections between Thong, the Buddha, and the *Dhamma-vinaya* to give continued urgency to the mission of the modernist project of translating and disseminating the *Dhamma-vinaya.*

The realization that even Thong could become sick was a shock to his students. His body (recalling that of the Buddha's) radiated health. 'Preah Mahavimaladhamm Thong was a person who was rarely sick. He was strong and able-bodied, with such a healthy constitution that diseases rolled off his body. It was utterly surprising to all of us who knew him that this time, he happened to become afflicted with an illness.'⁵³ When his students finally came to terms with the gravity of the situation, they gathered together to help stem the progress of the disease by reciting protective *paritta* – drawn from Pali *sutta* – in his honor. Chuon Nath relates that he and other monks made 'resolutions of truth' (*saccakiriya*), 'following a tradition observed by wise ones since antiquity. By making such a resolution, one is asking that [Thong] be healed and recover'.⁵⁴ Chanted in Pali for Thong's benefit and translated into Khmer by Chuon Nath for the wider readership of the biography, the efficaciousness of the *paritta* comes from the power of the *Buddha-vacana*, words that had been spoken by the Buddha. Chuon Nath explains:

This [Pali passage] translates as follows:

> There was a king who had a very serious illness. He had heard of a certain *Bojjhanga-paritta* while staying with the elder teacher Mahacunda-thera. By the time the *paritta* was completely recited to him, he was healed. This *paritta* was endowed with the power of the seven factors of wisdom. When it was chanted, just at that time, by the power of this *paritta* that we are now chanting, the king ... had recovered from his illness. It no longer troubled him, he glowed with health.
>
> So let it be for the Venerable who is our elder teacher. Let him live to an old age ... By our words of truth that have been recited, let our danger be dissipated. By our resolutions of truth, let peace and well-being flourish from this time forward.[55]

Through their ritual efforts, Thong's students had done everything they possibly could to halt the deterioration of his health. Indeed, chanted collectively and individually by Thong's assembled students for Thong, assembled *sangha* dignitaries, other *bhikkhu*s and novices, and a throng of laypeople, the *paritta* seemed briefly to be effective.[56] Listening appreciatively to the recitations of texts compiled and edited by his students,[57] Chuon Nath reports that Thong received them with *anumodana*, the joyful acceptance of a gift that transforms it into merit, 'saying *"sadhu"* with a loud roar like that of a person who had no illness'.[58] But the much greater task – even for adept students of Buddhism – was coming to terms with the inevitability of death and impermanence. Within days, Thong's condition had worsened again. Neither chanting nor truth resolutions nor any form of medicine had effect. Thong was unable to keep down any food. Yet in spite of the severity of his illness, his final hours, as they are recounted in Chuon Nath's and Um-Sur's accounts of the event, are devoted to illuminating his students and preparing them to carry on with their work translating and propagating the *Dhamma-vinaya* in Cambodia after his death.

These descriptions of Thong's deathbed closely follow the death scene of the Buddha, who issued numerous instructions concerning the future of the *sangha* during the last watch of the night. Thong thanks his students graciously for all they have tried to do to help him, but informs them that nothing can stop the course of his illness. 'Taking care of Buddhism', Thong instructs his students, 'is what gives help to me ... Illness and death are ordinary for beings – there are not any who can escape it.'[59] While he knew this already, Um-Sur reflects, he did not really understand it clearly until Thong summoned him to his deathbed and gently chided him, 'my dear Venerable, stop worrying so much about me. Illness and death are part and parcel of the rounds of *samsara*'. These words echo the *Mahaparinibbana Sutta*, when Ananda has gone off by himself to lean against a door frame and lament. Cognizant of this, the Buddha calls for him,

> Enough, Ananda, do not weep and wail! Have I not already told you that all things that are pleasant and delightful are changeable, subject to separation and becoming other? So how could it be, Ananda – since whatever is born, become, compounded is subject to decay – how could it be that it should not pass away?[60]

In the *sutta*, the Buddha continues by praising Ananda in front of the other monks for his ability to recite the *dhamma* in ways that gratify and please the four-fold religious community. If a *bhikkhu* or layperson sees Ananda, the Buddha relays, 'they are pleased at the sight of him, and when Ananda talks *dhamma* to them they are pleased'.[61] Like Ananda, Um-Sur writes that after hearing his teacher's brief discourse on *samsara*, he began to feel relieved and even 'began to comprehend death ... a little bit'.[62] His biography of Thong follows this episode by turning attention from his own emotional state back to the elucidation of the *dhamma*, interwoven with the narration of the hours leading up to Thong's passing.

Again like the Buddha, Thong offers a final discourse from his deathbed, urging his students to turn their efforts toward 'restoring Buddhism to its illustrious splendor'. The task of 'halting illness and making death disappear is small indeed', he tells them,

> whereas the work that is larger and weightier and requires all able-bodied beings to work together is the work of Buddhism. Those who want to be helpful to the *sasana* [religion] are the individuals who are helpful to themselves, helpful to their teachers, parents, husbands and wives, friends and all those in the different directions.[63]

Inter-identifying the authority of the Buddha, the *Dhamma-vinaya* and their teacher Preah Mahavimaladhamm Thong, Chuon Nath's and Um-Sur's commemorative biographies shift attention away from the more elusive protective and healing power of the *Buddha-vacana* to its much larger social ethical impact. While *paritta*s offer some comfort, the *dhamma*'s greater power is its ability to benefit and purify whole networks of people 'in the different directions' by teaching them how to 'be helpful' to themselves and others and 'work together'. While the biographies make clear that this potential for collective transformation had yet to be realized in Cambodia of 1927, they memorialize Thong as the great scholar and teacher who clarified the urgent need for correct, authentic interpretation of the *Dhamma-vinaya* as a means of protecting and developing the whole 'Kingdom and the religion'.[64]

LIVING AND DYING AS A MODERN BUDDHIST

In 1939, Um-Sur died just as the '-ism' of modernism had ceased to hold meaning; no longer a reactionary or innovative approach to the *dhamma*, scholars from the modern *dhamma* group including Um-Sur, Chuon Nath, Huot Tath, and Lvi-Em had by this time moved into prominent *sangha* leadership positions and their views on *Dhamma-vinaya* interpretation were becoming widely accepted in educated circles. A decade after the death of Thong, the commemorative reflections on the death of Um-Sur demonstrate the extent to which modernist views of moral purification had become absorbed into a vision of Buddhism as essential to national development.

Um-Sur is depicted in one commemorative biography, written by Lokachary Chap-Bin Suvannajoto, as a man whose exemplary moral conduct benefited not only himself but his fellow monks, laypeople and the nation at large. During his lifetime, he was highly regarded and often referred to by his peers as the man who most closely resembled the ideal of the moral person, one who had achieved the remarkably high level of purification highlighted in his photographic portrait from the late 1930s.

'Since he was first ordained', Chap-Bin noted, 'Venerable tried to make his behavior bring about beneficial results for himself, for other people, and for the Buddhist teachings as well. His diligence led to the greater improvement of Cambodia, as a result of his knowledge of correct conduct according to the *Dhamma-vinaya*.' His 'diligent efforts' (*pyayam*) consisted in 'effort' in studying, practice, acting in accordance with the true meaning of the *Dhamma-vinaya*; compiling and editing *Dhamma-vinaya* texts and commentaries about the most profound teachings, such as the truth of non-self and the truth of *nibbana*; and his ability to clearly understand, teach and translate this 'subtle *dhamma*, which only a very few people can truly recognize, and which only a very few people can explicate so it is comprehensible to others'.[65]

The biography used his manner of death to illustrate how purity – manifested through his ability to concentrate on and comprehend the *Dhamma-vinaya* without distraction, even in the face of death and confusion – permeated his behavior. Before his incapacitation as he approached death, he was working desperately to finish a commentarial translation. But 'at the point at which he was nearly finished, in easy reach of the conclusion', he was overcome with consumption and 'thus prevented from achieving his desire. Racked by illness, he was no longer able to hold a pen or pencil'. Despite the most up-to-date medical care, his condition 'steadily worsened'. Yet,

> [d]uring this period of time in which his illness intensified so severely, his disposition was one of love and tranquility. He did not prohibit *bhikkhu*s, novices and lay followers from staying in his proximity. As a result, he was surrounded constantly by noise and confusion.
>
> His behavior in this instance reveals why people had such great reverence for him. [During this period of time] people around him were jostling each other to inquire after him, and many remained nearby, weeping loudly and inconsolably. They caused so much agitation that it would seem to be impossible for anyone to concentrate on the meaning of the dharma.
>
> Yet His Excellency Preah Uttamamuni Um-Sur possessed such great *satisampajañña* [mindfulness and attention] that he could remain concentrated, as he had for so long, on the meaning of the dharma.
>
> The time of his death was 2:30 on Friday in the fifth day of the second waxing moon [reign year] of BE 2482 ... He was fifty-nine years old when he passed away in a quiet and well-disciplined[66] manner in the presence of ... four *bhikkhus* [who were chanting]. His death accurately reflected and gave expression to the disposition of tranquility and quietness that characterized his being in all respects.[67]

His death scene, as Charles Hallisey has noted in response to this translation, resembles the Buddha's in that it triggers a wide-spread response called *samvega* in Pali texts – a religious emotion involving a productive yet inarticulable recognition of the reality of suffering and death, one that moves the moral person further along the Path toward purification.[68] In the *Mahaparinibbana Sutta*, the Buddha too, allows a throng of lamenting townspeople to pay their final respects to him. When he reaches his final moment, Ananda testifies to the *samvega* that the Buddha's *parinibbana* has inspired in those who are far enough advanced on the Path to be moved to a deepened insight into the nature of reality:

> Terrible was the quaking, men's hair stood on end,
> When the all-accomplished Buddha passed away.[69]

A short time later, when the laypeople are informed of the Buddha's *parinibbana*, they react more noisily:

> [T]he Mallas ... were struck with anguish and sorrow, their minds were overcome with grief so that they were all tearing their hair.[70]

Then, like the laypeople around Um-Sur, they turn to the work of preparing the funeral canopies, garlands and other preparations for a magnificent funeral. As kings from various cities learn the news of the Buddha's death, they ask that relics of his body be sent out from Kusinara for memorializing, and so the remains of the Buddha's bones are divided, memorialized and worshiped in far-flung places.

In Um-Sur's biography, we are told:

> The voices of the multitudes who came to view his body echoed and resounded with cries of: 'Oh! Our Cambodia has lost its greatest *Abhidhamma* scholar and chief advocate of peace and morality, who led both Buddhism and our nation to prosper! It is impossible to extol him highly enough! Say what you will, mere words are inadequate!'[71]

The effects of Um-Sur's death continued throughout the months until his cremation. The biography suggests that even his remains – like the Buddha's – are able to effect spiritual transformation in others. It recounts that as religious and political luminaries passed by his corpse to pay their respects,

> Preah Uttamamuni's appearance in death was of such as marvelous nature that it led a great number of clerical and lay dignitaries, foreign as well as local, to be inclined toward purity and freedom from blemish through the influence of his attainments [*guna-sampatti*].[72]

If Um-Sur in 1939 had come to represent the highest attainment of purity that the modern world could produce, it was a rationalized vision of purity. His purity had been obtained through effort in studying and comprehending the authentic Buddhist teachings disentangled from older corrupted interpretations through modern methods of grammatical study, translation and textual dissemination. It was this kind of knowledge, in Lvi-Em's words, that would move modern Cambodia forward, from darkness into light, 'as a torch for all beings in the world'.[73]

I am not suggesting that the values put forward by the modernist group including Thong and Um-Sur were philosophically or ethically alien or completely 'new' to Theravada Buddhism, of course. But as different Buddhists in different local historical contexts have interpreted and reinterpreted the Buddhist canon, they identified and valorized certain combinations of ideas and images as authentic and relevant. As is the case with Angarika Dharmapala in Sri Lanka, Mongkut and Vajirañana in Siam, and later monks and scholars such as Buddhadasa and U Nu, Khmer monks contributed to the construction and dissemination of a new 'rationalist' Theravada interpretation, which in turn has reconfigured what the tradition is and means in the world today, including the dissemination of the historicized moral exemplar of 'our' Buddha, Siddhartha Gautama.[74]

The significance of Khmer Buddhist modernism is both local and translocal. Besides helping us understand more about the history and development of modern Buddhism in Cambodia during the twentieth century, it makes clear that some Khmer were connected to the same pan-Asian and global currents of thought that were prompting modernist responses elsewhere in the world. Khmer Buddhist modernism enables us to see parts of the creative process by which, at least at the turn of the nineteenth century, new expressions about the experience of being in history and of taking part in a rapidly changing global political economy were being constructed among different groups of local intellectuals, literati and artists. The creative processes and the creative media used by religious modernists in Cambodia – intellectuals who had been trained largely in monasteries – were necessarily different than in other parts of the world. I have argued elsewhere that contemporary post-colonial scholars are perhaps not used to understanding scriptural translation as a creative process or Buddhist ethics as a medium for working out modern ways of being.[75] But if we can move past these scholarly assumptions about modernism and morality, the first three decades of the twentieth century appear as fertile a period for the outpouring of modern ideas and forms among this group of intellectuals in colonial Cambodia as among other groups in Siam, Ceylon, Japan, and France.

AUTHOR'S NOTE

This chapter owes much to conversations with Richard Jaffe, Charles Hallisey and Eduardo Douglas.

ABBREVIATIONS

D	*Dighanikaya*
NAC	National Archives of Cambodia, Phnom Penh
RSC	Fonds Résident Supérieur du Cambodge

SOURCES

Baudelaire, Charles (1964) 'The painter of modern life.' In Jonathan Mayne (trans. and ed.), *The Painter of Modern Life and Other Essays*. London: Phaidon Press, pp. 1–40.

Bechert, Heinz (1970) 'Theravada Buddhist sangha: some general observations on historical and political factors in its development.' *The Journal of Asian Studies* 29 (4), pp. 761–778.

Bibliothèque Royale du Cambodge (1930) *Buny Samputthi Putthsasânabantity* [Inauguaration of the Buddhist Institute]. Phnom Penh: Bibliothèque Royale du Cambodge.

Bocola, Sandro (2001) *Art of Modernism, 1870–2000*. New York: Taschen.

Bradley, Mark (2004) 'Becoming *van minh*: civilizational discourse and visions of the self in twentieth-century Vietnam.' *Journal of World History* 15 (1), pp. 65–83.

Chap-Pin (a.w. Cap-Pin) Suvannajoto, Lokachary (1940) *Uttamamunittherabavatti* [Biography of Um-Sur]. In: *Avasanakichcha Rabas' Preah Uttamamuni Um-Sur Dhammavinayarikkhito* [Posthumous Work of Preah Uttamamuni Um-Sur], 2nd ed. Phnom Penh: Buddhist Institute.

Chandler, David (1996) 'Going through the motions: ritual aspects of the reign of King Duang of Cambodia (1848–1860).' In *Facing the Cambodian Past: Selected Essays 1971–1994*. Chiang Mai: Silkworm Books, pp. 100–118.

Chuon Nath, Preah Krou Samasattha (1927) 'Sechteybrakas gunabadikar Preah Mahavimaladhamm Thong, Changvan Sala Pali chan khpos' [Declaration of Gratitude toward Preah Mahavimaladhamm Thong, Director of the École Supérieure de Pali], *Kambujasuriya* vol. 2, pp. 56–71.

Chuon Nath, Preah Sasânasophana and Preah Uttamamuni Um-Sur (1926) *Trayapanama Sangkhepa: Gihivinaya Sangkhepa* [Abridgement of the Three Homages]. Phnom Penh: A. Portail.

—— (1935) *Trayapanama Sangkhepa: Gihivinaya Sangkhepa* [Abridgement of the /Vinaya /for Laypeople]. Phnom Penh: Royal Library.

Coedès, George (1902) 'Liste des manuscrits khmèrs de l'École Française d'Extrême Orient.' *Bulletin de l'École française d'Extrême-Orient* II (1902), pp. 398–405.

Edwards, Penny (1999) 'Cambodge: the cultivation of a nation, 1860–1945,' PhD Thesis, Monash University.

Finot, Louis (1927) 'Maha Vimaladhamma.' *Bulletin de l'École française d'Extrême-Orient* vol. 27, pp. 523.

Ginsburg, Henry (1989) *Thai Manuscript Painting*. Honolulu: University of Hawai'i Press.

Gombrich, Richard and Gananath Obeyeskere (1988) *Buddhism Transformed: Religious Change in Sri Lanka*. Princeton, New Jersey: Princeton University Press.

Goodrich, Lloyd (1963) *The Armory show. Pioneers of modern art in America: the decade of the Armory show, 1910–1920*. New York: Praeger, for the Whitney Museum of American Art.

Groslier, Georges (1921) *Recherches sur les Cambodgiens*. Paris: Augustin Challamel.

Hansen, Anne Ruth (1994) 'Khmer identity and Theravada Buddhism.' In John Marston and Elizabeth Guthrie (eds), *History, Buddhism, and New Religious Movements in Cambodia*. Honolulu: University of Hawai'i Press, pp. 40–62.

—— (2007) *How to Behave: Buddhism and Modernity in Colonial Cambodia 1860–1930*. Honolulu: University of Hawai'i Press.

Harris, Ian (2005) *Cambodian Buddhism: History and Practice*. Honolulu: University of Hawai'i Press.

Harvey, David (1990) *The Condition of Postmodernity*. Cambridge: Blackwell Publishers.

Huot Tath, Preah Krou Samghavijja (1927) *Singalovadasutta (Dighanikaya* 31). Phnom Penh: Publications of the Ecole Supérieure de Pali, Bibliotheèque Royale du Cambodge.

—— (1993) *Samtech Preah Mahasumethathipati Kalyanamitta ropos khñom* [My *Kalyanamitta*]. Phnom Penh: Buddhist Institute.

Huot Tath, Preah Krou Samghavijja, Preah Krou Samasattha Chuon Nath and Preah Krou Vimalapañña Um-Sur (1928) [1918] *Samaneravinaya*, 2nd ed. Phnom Penh: Bibliothèque Royale du Cambodge.

Ind, Okña Suttantabreyjea (1971) [1921] *Katelok* [Ways of the World], vols 1–10. Phnom Penh: Buddhist Institute.

Jaffe, Richard (2004) 'Seeking Sakyamuni: travel and the reconstruction of Japanese Buddhism,' *Journal of Japanese Studies*, 30 (1), pp. 65–96.

Jory, Patrick (2002) 'Thai and Western Buddhist scholarship in the age of colonialism: King Chulalongkorn Redefines the Jatakas,' *Journal of Asian Studies* 61 (3), pp. 891–918.

Kamala Tiyavanich (1997) *Forest Recollections: Wandering Monks in Twentieth-century Thailand*. Honolulu: University of Hawai'i Press.

Karl, Rebecca (2002) *Staging the World*. Durham: N.C. and London: Duke University Press.

Kim-Hak (1931) '*Vithi toptaeng Preah Putthsasâna aoy chamroen tpoeng nov knung nokor Kampucha* [Methods for Improving the Condition of Buddhism in the Kingdom of Cambodia], *Kambujasuriya*, vol. 11, pp. 49–56.

Kurzman, Charles (ed.) (2002) *Modernist Islam, 1840–1940*. New York: Oxford University Press.

Ledgerwood, Judy (ed.) (2002) *Cambodia Emerges from the Past: Eight Essays*. DeKalb, IL: Southeast Asia Publications, Center for Southeast Asian Studies.

Lopez, Jr., Donald S. (ed.) (2002) *A Modern Buddhist Bible: Essential readings from East and West*. Boston: Beacon Press.

Lvi-Em, Preah Ñanabavaraviccha (1930) 'Sasâna-hetukatha.' In *Buny Samputthi Putthsasânabantity* [Inauguration of Buddhist Institute]. Phnom Penh: Bibliothèque Royale du Cambodge, pp. 3–74.

Marr, David G. (1971) *Vietnamese Anticolonialism, 1885–1925*. Berkeley: University of California Press.

Marston, John and Elizabeth Guthrie (eds) (2004) *History, Buddhism, and New Religious Movements in Cambodia.* Honolulu: University of Hawai'i Press.

McHale, Shawn (2004) *Print and Power: Confucianism, Communism, and Buddhism in the Making of Modern Vietnam.* Honolulu: University of Hawai'i Press.

Moura, Jean (1883) *Le Royaume du Cambodge,* vols. 1–2. Paris: Libraire de la Société Asiatique de l'École des Langues Orientales Vivantes.

Noer, Deliar (1973) *The Modernist Muslim Movement in Indonesia, 1900–1942.* Kuala Lumpur and London: Oxford University Press.

Reynolds, Craig J. (1972) 'The Buddhist monkhood in nineteenth-century Thailand.' Doctoral dissertation, Cornell University.

—— (1976) 'Buddhist cosmography in Thai history, with special reference to nineteenth-century culture change," *Journal of Asian Studies,* 35 (2), pp. 203–220.

Riddell, Peter G. (2001) *Islam and the Malay-Indonesian World.* Honolulu: University of Hawai'i Press.

Tai Hue-Tam Ho (1983) *Millenarianism and Peasant Politics in Vietnam.* Cambridge: Harvard University Press.

—— (1992) *Radicalism and the Origins of the Vietnamese Revolution.* Cambridge: Harvard University Press.

Tambiah, Stanley J. (1976) *World Conqueror and World Renouncer.* Cambridge: Cambridge University Press.

Thongchai Winichakul (1994) *Siam Mapped.* Honolulu: University of Hawai'i Press.

Um-Sur [a.w. Quom-Saur, Oum-Sou], Preah Krou Vimalappañña (1927) 'Sechktipa(r)nna Maranakicch robos Preah Mahavimaladhamm Thong, Changhvan Sala Pali chas khpuas' [Reflections on the Last Acts of Preah Mahavimaladhamm Thong, Director of the École Supérieure de Pali], *Kambujasuriya* vol. 2, pp. 19–37.

—— Preah Uttamamuni. (1940) *Avâsanakiccha robos Preah Uttamamuni Um-Sur Dhammavinayavikkhito* [The Last Acts of Preah Uttamamuni Um-Sur Dhammavinayvikkhito]. Phnom Penh: Buddhist Institute.

Vajirañanavarorasa, Somdetch Phra Maha Samana Chao Krom Phraya (1979) Craig J. Reynolds (trans. and ed.) *Autobiography: the Life of Prince-Patriarch Vajirañanavarorasa of Siam, 1860–1921.* Athens, OH: Ohio University Press.

Von der Mehden, Fred R. (1993) *Two Worlds of Islam: Interaction between Southeast Asia and the Middle East.* Gainesville: University of Florida Press.

Walshe, Maurice, translator (1987) *Thus Have I Heard: the Long Discourses of the Buddha.* London: Wisdom Books.

NOTES

1   Baudelaire 1964: 14.

2   I am following a modified version of the Huffman Franco–Khmer transcription system, developed by Franklin E. Huffman in 1983 and excerpted in the forward to

Ledgerwood 2002. For Khmer names and other words (such as *wat*) that have other common transcriptions in English, I follow these spelling conventions. Pali words and titles are reproduced without diacritical marks, reflecting the preference of the press.

3 *Kambujasuriya* 1939 (10–12): 1; Um-Sur 1940: *th*.
4 *Kambujasuriya* 1927 (12): 111.
5 Thanks to Michael Nau, Justin McDaniel and other members of the audience at UC Riverside who helped me read this photo during a May 2006 visit.
6 A fuller discussion of Buddhist modernism during this period can be found in Harris 2005: 105–130 and Hansen 2007.
7 Hansen 2007: 129, 149, 179.
8 Tambiah 1976: 211–212; Reynolds 1972 and 1976.
9 Vajirañanavarorasa 1979: 30; Kurzman 2002: 355 and 362.
10 Thongchai 1994: 37–61
11 Tambiah 1976: 212; Jaffe 2004: 65–96; Noer 1973: 296–299;Von der Mehden 1993: 2–15; Riddell 2001: 207–230; Marr 1971: 77–248; Tai 1992: 20–31; Bradley 2004: 67–71; Karl 2002: 164–176; McHale 2004, 144, 150, 156–163. On the influence of modern Buddhist trends in Sri Lanka during the late nineteenth and early twentieth centuries, see Bechert 1970, 775–778; Gombrich and Obeyesekere 1988, 202–240; Lopez 2002; Jaffe 2004.
12 Chandler 1996: 104–107.
13 Tambiah 1976: 211–212, 401, 405–406.
14 Tambiah 1976: 211.
15 Hansen 2007: 84–96.
16 Hansen 2004: 43–51 and 2007: 44–76.
17 Hansen 2007: 10.
18 Baudelaire 1964: 13; Harrison 1996: 189.
19 Boccola 2001: 7, 32.
20 Harvey 1990: 23.
21 Goodrich 1963: 40, 68.
22 Harvey 1990: 10–28.
23 Bocola 2001: 35; Elderfield 2004: 69, 85.
24 Chuon Nath is relaying a speech by Thong here. Chuon Nath 1927: 65.
25 Ind [1921] 1971, vol. 1: 8.
26 Ibid., vol. 1: 1, 8; vol. 4: 2, 5; vol. 5: 14.
27 Most notably in passages in vol. 1: 1 and vol. 10: 73–4, the introduction and conclusion to the text, when he refers to his reasons for composing the text.
28 Ind [1921] 1971, vol. 1: 1.
29 Ibid., vol. 1: 8.
30 Baudelaire 1964; Harvey 2000: 10–38.
31 See for example, an early example of a funeral biography (of Abbot Preah Dhammacariyeavangs Et of Wat Damnak in Siem Reap, referred to earlier in this

essay) in *Kambujasuriya* 1927 (12): 112–118; Huot Tath's prefaces for his contemporary readers in Huot Tath et al. [1918] 1928 or Huot Tath 1927.

32 For example, Ind [1921] 1971, vol. 1: 2–3 and Lvi-Em 1930.

33 Huot Tath 1993: 11–15; '*Chivabravattisangkhep nei obaseka So-Suon*' [Biography of Laywoman So-Suon], Son-Siv, 1960, NAC 16 b.27, 3; Gouverneur General, 'etat d'esprit des bonzes Mahanikays du Cambodge,' 1916, NAC RSC F. 94 b.908 10172; Minister of the Interior K. Chea, 28 June 1937, NAC RSC F.942 b.2791 23609 and Minister of the Interior K. Chea, 2 July 1937, NAC RSC F. 942 b.2791 23609. Huot Tath states that Chuon Nath later suggested that this moniker was misleading in that it gave the impression that there could be more than one *dhamma* (1993: 13). The *Thorm-thmi* faction apparently came to be known later as the 'Thammakay', but the Khmer and French sources I surveyed from the 1920s and early 1930s as well as later monk funeral biographies make no mention of this name. Penny Edwards references 'Thammakay' in a 1932–1933 French-authored report on temple schools by the Résident of Kompong Thom and in later *Nagaravatta* articles from 1937–1938 (Edwards 1999: 331–332, 338–339).

34 Huot Tath 1993: 11-13; '*Chivabravattisankhep nei obaseka So-Suon*' [Biography of Lay Woman So-Suon], 1960, NAC 27, 3; Minister of the Interior K. Chea, 'Rapport d'ensemble sur la religion Bouddhique au Cambodge,' 28 June 1937 and 'Deliberation of the permanent Commission of the Council of Ministers,' 2 July 1937, NAC RSC F.942 b.2791 23609.

35 Kamala 1997: 3–9, 32–46; Jory 2002.

36 D ii.154; these and the following translations of the sutta are from Walshe 1987: 269–270.

37 Preah Mahavimaladhamm Thong, Directeur de l'École du Pali to Ministre de la Guerre et de l'Instruction Publique, 18 February 1919, NAC RSC R.57 b.1428 16473.

38 K., *patipatti-puja*' or 'offering good conduct.' Lvi-Em 1930: 66.

39 Lvi-Em 1930: 67.

40 Kim-Hak 1931: 49.

41 Ibid.: 50.

42 Ibid.: 50–51.

43 Ibid.: 49, 51.

44 Chuon Nath 1935: 35. It appears to have been composed during the early 1920s and was first issued in a print version in 1926 with both Chuon Nath and Um-Sur listed as authors (Chuon Nath and Um-Sur, 1926).

45 Chuon Nath and Um-Sur 1935, *k*.

46 Chuon Nath 1935, 37.

47 Ibid., *n* (*xv*).

48 Huot Tath et al [1918] 1928 : 1–2.

49 Preah Mahavimaladhamm Thong, Directeur de l'École du Pali to Ministre de la Guerre et de l'Instruction Publique, 18 February 1919, NAC RSC R.57 b.1428 16473.

50 Coedès 1938: 317.

51 Finot 1927: 523.

52 The entire 1927 (2) *Kambujasuriya* was devoted to commemorative biographies and recollections of Thong. For example, see Um-Sur 1927: 25.
53 Um-Sur 1927: 19.
54 Chuon Nath 1927: 55.
55 Ibid.: 59.
56 Ibid.: 60.
57 Um-Sur gives the names of thirteen students in Thong's monastic lineage who offered *paritta* but says there were more present as well (1927: 23).
58 Chuon Nath 1927: 60.
59 Um-Sur 1927: 26.
60 D ii.144; Walshe 1987: 265.
61 D ii.145; Walshe 1987: 265–266.
62 Um-Sur 1927: 30.
63 He says 'sections,' but I take this as a reference to the 8 cardinal directions described in the *Sigalovadasutta*. Um-Sur 1927 : 26–27.
64 Preah Mahavimaladhamm Thong, Directeur de l'École du Pali to Ministre de la Guerre et de l'Instruction Publique, 18 February 1919, NAC RSC R.57 b.1428 16473.
65 Chap-Bin 1940, *kh-r*.
66 K., *riab-ray*.
67 Ibid., *r-v*.
68 'Contours of the Moral Person' Conference, Amherst MA, August 2005.
69 D ii.157; Walshe 1987: 272.
70 D ii.159; Walshe 1987: 272.
71 Chap-Bin 1940: *v*.
72 Chap-Bin 1940: *v-h*.
73 Lvi-Em 1930: 58.
74 Jaffe 2004.
75 Hansen 2007: 12.

CHAPTER 4

Truth, Representation and the Politics of Memory after Genocide

Alex Hinton

When Cambodians talk about Democratic Kampuchea (DK), the genocidal period of Khmer Rouge rule in Cambodia when up to 2 million of Cambodia's 8 million inhabitants perished from April 1975 to January 1979, they recall many paths of ruin, the memories breaking light into this time of shadows, when memory itself became a crime.

Chlat, a low-ranking provincial government official who was a student prior to DK, recalled one such path, the death of his brother Sruon. Sharp and pensive, Chlat was one of those people who might have gone far if the trajectory of his life had not been broken by the Khmer Rouge revolution. His smile echoed his life, struggling to blossom and always taut, trying to recoil. We spoke many times about his life, including the period when memory itself was a crime.

For, in their radical experiment in social engineering, the Khmer Rouge launched an assault on the past, seeking to obliterate everything that smacked of capitalism, 'privatism', and class oppression (Chandler 1999; Hinton 2005; Kiernan 1996). This attack ranged far and wide. Broadly, the Khmer Rouge targeted Buddhism, the family, village structure, economic activity, and public education – key socio-cultural institutions through which memory was ritually, formally, and informally transmitted. More specifically, they assaulted social memory by burning books and destroying libraries, banning popular music, movies, media, and styles, destroying temples, truncating communication, terminating traditional holidays and ritual events, separating family members, homogenizing clothing, and eliminating private property, including photos, memorabilia, and other mementos.

This onslaught on the past was dramatically expressed in the first significant act that the Khmer Rouge took upon attaining power: rusticating the entire urban population. Ordered to evacuate their homes with little notice, hundreds of thousands of people clogged the arteries leading out of Phnom Penh and the other provincial capitals. As they shuffled toward an unknown beginning, past the pagodas, schools, cinemas, restaurants, parks, streets, and homes that landscaped their past, the urbanites discarded a trail of memories: wads of now worthless bank notes blowing in the wind, luxury sedans that had run out of fuel, food that had rotted in the blazing heat, books too heavy to carry, and, most tragically, the bodies of the old and the infirm unable to survive the journey. And still they would bear the stain of their capitalist past.

In the new revolutionary society, each person had to be reworked, like hot iron, in the flames of the revolution. The Khmer Rouge called this 'tempering' people, literally 'to harden by pounding' (*luat dam*). One urban evacuee explained that 'the dreaded phrase was *lut-dom*. *Lut* is the part of metal processing in which a rod of metal is placed in a fire until it is red-hot and pliable.' *Dom* means the hammering – when the hot metal is put on the anvil and pounded into shape, any shape desired. *Lut-dom* described the way people were expected to be molded by Angkar ('the Organization') into the pure Communists of the future (Criddle and Mam 1987:101; see also Locard 2004: 299).

Memory was to be reshaped during this process until it aligned with the Party line, which colored the past in revolutionary red. Borrowing a Maoist metaphor that resonated with Buddhist conceptions of the wheel of life and two wheels of *dhamma*, the Khmer Rouge spoke of 'the Wheel of History' (*kang bravattesas*; see Locard 2004: 211) that, powered by natural laws that had been discerned by the 'science' of Marxist–Leninism, had and continued to move Cambodia inexorably toward communism, crushing everything in its path. This vision of the past was clearly laid out in a landmark speech given by Pol Pot on 29 September 1977 to celebrate the seventeenth anniversary of the founding of the Communist Party of Kampuchea (CPK). Not only did the speech announce publicly for the first time the very existence of the CPK and Pol Pot's leadership of it, but it also laid out the history of revolutionary struggle in Cambodia, which had faltered in 'slave', 'feudal', and 'feudo-capitalist' stages because of the lack of a proper 'political line' (Pol Pot 1977). This line only began to be ascertained, Pol Pot proclaimed, at the CPK's First Party Congress, held

28–30 September 1960 by 21 revolutionaries who locked themselves into a secret room in the rail yard of Phnom Penh.

Having discerned through 'scientific analysis' the key contradictions in Cambodian society (between 'the Kampuchean nation and imperialism, especially US imperialism' and between classes, especially 'the capitalists and the landlords'; see Pol Pot 1977: 25–26), the Party was able to light the flames of revolution that, 'like dry straw in the rice fields' during the hot season 'needs only a small spark to set it on fire' (Pol Pot 1977: 38). From that point on, Pol Pot stated, the fire spread throughout the country, enabling the revolutionary movement to defeat not just the Khmer Republic, but the United States as well. Just as the Party line had enabled the Khmer Rouge to win victory, so too would it lead Cambodia toward communist utopia faster than ever before.

Achieving this goal required the creation of a country filled with a new sort of revolutionary being who, after being 'tempered' by hard peasant labor, criticism and self-criticism sessions, political meetings, and constant indoctrination, would develop a progressive political consciousness that accorded with the Party line and history. Those showing signs of being unable to rid themselves of vestiges of the 'corrupt' past – for example, as evinced by dwelling too much on one's former life, complaining about the difficult conditions of life, failing to display appropriate enthusiasm for the revolution, making mistakes in one's duties, or missing work – were sometimes said to have 'memory sickness' (*comngii satiaramma*) (see Criddle and Mam 1987: 99). If the sickness was chronic or did not heal rapidly, it was 'cured' by execution. Indeed, execution served as the most direct and thorough means of obliterating counter-revolutionary memories of the past.

⇒ ⇐

Chlat smoked as he told me the stories of how his family trekked out of Phnom Penh in the blazing sun, at times moving only a meter in two hours, how the Khmer Rouge requisitioned his watch, diploma, and clothes, how his brother-in-law, a former military officer, was identified and led away, never to return, and how his grandfather died and was buried on the side of the road in a grave marked only by incense. The first time, he offered me a cigarette, which I declined. He smiled tightly and told me how he had begun smoking during DK when he was assigned to transport human excrement from the latrines so that it could be used for fertilizer. He explained, 'The smell was overwhelming and the cigarettes cut the stench. After I stopped working there, I continued to smoke because of hunger. I was never full but when I smoked my hunger would diminish.' Another time he told me that he smoked because his head was so busy. If he ruminated on some difficult matter like DK, smoking would ease his heart. As Chlat recalled these events, he would take a drag of his cigarette, embers briefly aglow like his memories, then ash.

We usually met in the evening at the home of a mutual friend, after Chlat had finished work at the provincial government office. The electricity would often fail and we would sit around a table dimly illuminated by a single candle and the lit end of his cigarette, which traced his profile and cast shadows against the walls. It was on one of these nights that he first told me of how his brother's path turned toward the Pagoda at the Hill of Men in 1977, in the midst of a major purge. Chlat's family had returned to his parents' birth village, where people knew the family's suspect urban background and that his older brother Sruon had worked in the import–export business there. Speaking in a low monotone, punctuated by long pauses and sudden taps of his cigarette against the ashtray, Chlat recalled how Sruon was taken to the Pagoda, which had been transformed into an extermination center:

> First we heard that trucks had been coming to take people from neighboring cooperatives to a 'new village'. Rumors spread that the people were taken to be killed. The trucks arrived at my village without warning. No one had been informed. People began to be taken away at noon. You could see that it was primarily 1975 people, particularly those who were lazy or unable to work hard, who were ordered to go to the new village . . . When [my elder brother] Sruon's name wasn't called out – he had been sick and unable to work much lately, so we were worried – he couldn't believe his good fortune. He kept telling me and my father, 'I'm really lucky. I must have done good deeds in the past to escape death, because those people are not going to a new place, they're going to be killed and discarded.'
>
> Sruon's name still hadn't been called by 8:00 that evening. He had just finished saying, 'I'm out of danger. I'm not going to die', when Sieng, the village head, tapped on our door and told Sruon, 'Gather your things. The trucks are going to take you to a new village.' Sruon stopped speaking and slowly sat down on the bed, terrified, thinking about what he suspected was going to happen to his family. Finally, he said, 'So, my name is on the list too'. Someone, I suspect it might have been a distant relative of mine who spied for the Khmer Rouge, must have gotten them to replace his name with that of my brother at the last moment. Sruon instructed his wife and children to get ready to go. He told me, 'Take care of father and our siblings. As for me, don't believe that they are taking me to a new place. There isn't

one. They are taking us to be killed.' Everything was still; no one spoke. All you could hear was the patter of the rain.

The people whose names were called were ordered to gather at a nearby pagoda. Sruon picked up his youngest child, protecting him from the rain and mud, and took his family there. It was getting late, so the Khmer Rouge ordered everyone to sleep in the pagoda that night. Guards prevented the people from leaving the premises. Children were crying from hunger because they weren't given food. The next day, at first light, the Khmer Rouge loaded everyone on the trucks and drove off. My brother and his entire family were executed at the Pagoda at the Hill of Men . . . A few days later, clothes were distributed to people in our village. They were the garments of the people who had been loaded into the trucks. I saw them give out my brother's clothes.

Chlat's memory of his brother's death is chilling, more so when one considers that, throughout Cambodia, millions of people endured similar moments of death, suffering, and terror during DK. Such memories, and the powerful emotions they evoke, have proven to be a powerful dynamic in Cambodia, as different groups have rewritten the DK past to meet the needs of the present, asserting their legitimacy and moral authority in the process.

This chapter explores several dimensions of this politics of memory, particularly that of the People's Republic of Kampuchea (PRK), the Vietnamese-backed successor of DK, which tied its legitimacy so closely to a set of discursive narratives about this violent past. In addition, we can discern another broad shift in the politics of memory in Cambodia around the time of the 1993 UN-backed elections in Cambodia. At this time, non-governmental organizations proliferated in Cambodia and discourses of reconciliation, human rights, and justice were localized, often in Buddhist terms, in another reworking of the memory of the genocidal past. New shifts can again be discerned with the July 2006 start of a UN-backed trial of former Khmer Rouge leaders. After discussing the PRK's apparatus of truth, knowledge, power, and memory, I turn to a consideration of Buddhism, which has operated both in conjunction and disjunction with the state-level narratives, as have other local-level and international discourses.

LEGITIMACY AND LIBERATION

In January 1979, when a Vietnamese-backed army invaded Cambodia, routing the Khmer Rouge, the sands of memory shifted once again. Cambodia's roads began to swell with people, some returning to lost lives and homes, others seeking new ones, still others heading toward the border and unknown places. It was a time of remembrance, as friends and family long separated came together and shared their stories of where they had been, what they had endured, and who had been lost. Then they began to rebuild their lives.

Many, like Chlat, had nothing and had to confront the immediate problem of how to survive and make a living. Eventually Chlat found a job as a teacher. At Banyan, the village located near the Pagoda at the Hill of Men in Kompong Cham that had remained empty during DK, former residents trickled back home. Amidst their greetings, they found horrific reminders of the recent past: dozens of mass graves, village wells filled with corpses, and the reek of death when the winds blew from the direction of the pagoda. They returned to what they knew best, farming the land, though now their rice fields adjoined killing fields and their plows churned the bones and clothes of the dead.

In Phnom Penh, two Vietnamese photographers who had accompanied the invading army were drawn by a stench to the grounds of Tuol Sleng (Chandler 1999: 1f.). What they found inside echoed the gruesome scenes Banyan villagers had discovered: recently executed men whose throats had been cut, some still chained to iron beds and lying in pools of blood, shackles, whips and other instruments of torture, and the prison cells of the condemned. Within days, search crews discovered an enormous cache of documentation, ranging from photographs to confessions.

In the midst of this upheaval, the newly established People's Republic of Kampuchea (PRK) faced numerous problems, ranging from an economy and infrastructure in shambles to potential famine (Gottesman 2003). Almost immediately, however, the new regime was beset by problems of legitimacy. The PRK government, headed by Heng Samrin, was closely linked to Vietnam, which had supplied roughly 150,000 troops for the invasion and wielded obvious influence over the government.

While initially welcoming Vietnam's help in overthrowing the Khmer Rouge, many Cambodians remained deeply suspicious of a country frequently viewed as a historical enemy that they believed had long secretly desired to 'swallow' Cambodian land. Many also viewed the new regime with suspicion both because, like DK, it was socialist and because a number of PRK officials – including Heng Samrin and his Foreign Minister, Hun Sen, who would be Prime Minister by 1985 – were themselves former Khmer

Rouge who had fled DK during purges of their factions. These suspicions were heightened by PRK propaganda, which at times eerily echoed that of the regime's socialist predecessor (Gottesman 2003: 60). Finally, the PRK government was to be increasingly threatened by new resistance groups and a resurgent Khmer Rouge army, which after arriving in tatters on the Thai border, was propped back up by foreign powers more concerned with Cold War politics than genocidal criminality.

Memory mixed with politics as the PRK regime set out to establish a narrative of the recent past that would buttress their legitimacy both domestically and abroad (Gottesman 2003; Ledgerwood 1997). Genocide stood at the center of this story. The new political narrative centered around the theme of a magnificent revolution subverted by a small group of evil doers, led by the 'Pol Pot', 'Pol Pot–Ieng Sary', or 'Pol Pot–Ieng Sary–Khieu Samphan clique' (Ledgerwood 1997: 82). Inspired by a deviant Maoist strain of socialism, the narrative went, this clique had misled or coerced lower-ranking cadre (including, by implication, PRK leaders who were former Khmer Rouge) into unwittingly participating in a misdirected campaign of genocide. As a result, most former Khmer Rouge cadres, including, by implication, PRK officials, were not ultimately responsible for the events that had transpired during DK.

Socialist discourses remained central to this narrative, as the PRK regime could still speak of how the revolutionary movement had 'won the glorious victory of 17 April 1975, totally liberating our country' from 'the yoke of colonialism, imperialism, and feudalism' (Gottesman 2003: 7–8).[1] In a speech given just prior to the invasion, Heng Samrin described how 'the reactionary Pol Pot–Ieng Sary gang' had begun taking Cambodia down the wrong path almost immediately upon liberation through such policies as the evacuation of the cities, forced collectivization, the abolition of money, and attack on family and village life. These acts foreshadowed 'massacres, more atrocious, more barbarous, than those committed in the Middle Ages or perpetrated by the Hitlerite fascists'. The PRK regime, in turn, staked its claim to legitimacy as the true bearers of the revolutionary mantle and, crucially, as the ones who, with the help of their Vietnamese 'brothers', had liberated the people from this hell on earth. In the PRK narrative, the regime remained the people's protector, a 'back' (*khnang*) upon which they could rely to ensure that the horrors of the DK past were not repeated. With a growing Khmer Rouge insurgency on the border, this role was of enormous importance to the populace.

While every government defines itself in terms of an imagined past and future, new regimes, particularly ones like the PRK that ascend to power with questionable legitimacy, devote enormous effort toward asserting such visions. Their mechanisms for the production of truth are varied, ranging from the codification of law to educational instruction to the creation of memorials. By bringing a number of seemingly heterogeneous institutions together, a government is able to create a functionally over-determined 'apparatus' to further its strategic goals, such as the popular interpellation of discursive narratives that enhance the regime's legitimacy and control (Foucault 1980; Said 1979).

We can see just such a process at work during the PRK, as the government used multiple institutions, discursive structures, and symbols to assert its legitimacy. One key nexus was education. On the one hand, education served as a reminder of the brutality of the DK regime, since they had largely abandoned formal instruction and turned many schools into prisons or storage areas (Ayres 2000). While there was some primary education during DK (ibid.), the Khmer Rouge believed that the former education system corrupted the minds of the young and that the best education was political indoctrination and learning through 'struggle' on the economic 'front lines'. Thus, drawing on Maoist discourses, the Khmer Rouge proclaimed: 'The spade is your pen, the rice field your paper' and 'If you want to pass your Baccaulareate exams, you must build dams and canals' (Locard 2004: 96–7).

TEACHING ABOUT THE GENOCIDAL PAST

The devastation of the past was also marked physically, both in the deteriorated condition of the schools and materials (signifying the deterioration of Cambodia under the Khmer Rouge) and, in many cases, walls marred by bullet holes (denoting the violence of the past and danger of the present). On the other hand, education represented one of the great achievements of the PRK regime, which rapidly rebuilt the school system. In a 24 September 1979 speech commemorating the reopening of schools for the 1979–1980 year, Heng Samrin invoked these themes, stressing how under the 'barbaric genocidal regime of the Pol Pot–Ieng Sary clique' the country's 'infrastructure in the domain of education and of teaching [has been] completely shattered', with the educated, including students and teachers, singled out for slaughter (cited in Ayres 2000: 126).

These sorts of discourses were explicitly incorporated into teaching materials. Thus, by 1983, a fourth-grade writing book included a poem entitled, 'The Suffering of the Kampuchean People in the Pol Pot–Ieng Sary Period', which was adorned with a graphic showing a couple being executed while a child watched in horror as a man was being hanged in the background (Ministry of Education 1983). Likewise, a first-grade moral education (*selathoa*) book included lessons on how 'The [new] Revolution has given Happiness to the People' (with a graphic showing happy citizens cheering soldiers) and 'The Pol Pot–Ieng Sary clique's Criminal Plan to Destroy [our] Race' (with a graphic that showed people being executed at a mass grave by cadre with studded clubs and bloody hoes) (Ministry of Education 1984). Essays were followed by questions for class discussion. The latter essay asked:

1. What types of criminal acts did the Pol Pot–Ieng Sary clique inflict upon the Cambodian people who were ethnic Khmer like you?
2. These despicable ones (*vea*) killed Khmer in what sorts of ways?
3. What sort of intention did these despicable ones (*vea*) have that led them to kill your fellow members of the Khmer race?

The entry provided unsparing answers to the six and seven year olds, describing 'the most savage acts of killing', such as when 'these despicable ones' dug 'enormous, deep ditches' into which they dumped their victims 'dead or alive' after striking them with hoes, axes and clubs. Women and children, the text notes, were not spared: 'Their intention was to kill and destroy Kampucheans so that they would be extinguished' (Ministry of Education 1984: 29). Such texts emphasize the difference of the 'Pol Pot–Ieng Sary clique', marking them as not Khmer, a dangerous enemy plotting the annihilation of the Cambodian race, and, by implication, as a deviant communist sect.

Reading through such school texts, we find most of the discursive narratives – which were supplemented by related photos and posters – central to the PRK's regime of truth: repeated descriptions of the 'savage' and 'criminal acts' committed by the Pol Pot–Ieng Sary clique and of the enormous suffering of the people, assertions of the 'clique's' lack of Khmerness and deviant socialism, proclamations of the everlasting friendship between Kampuchea and Vietnam, glorification of the 'great liberation' on 7 January 1979, panegyrics to the rapid progress the PRK was achieving, and tributes to the PRK army and militias that protected the people from a return of the DK past. One fourth-grade writing text that I came across, published in 1988, focused on all of these themes and more (in fact, the majority of the articles touched upon these issues), including two consecutive articles on Tuol Sleng, one ('Torture at Tuol Sleng') with a graphic of a dead prisoner shackled to an iron above a pool of blood and instruments of torture (Ministry of Education 1988: 21).

MEMORIALIZING THE GENOCIDAL PAST

Here we find one of a number of cross-linkages to other parts of the PRK apparatus of truth and memory. In contrast to the verbal focus (albeit with powerful graphics) of the school texts, PRK memorials like Tuol Sleng and Choeung Ek place emphasis on nonverbal symbolism (Ledgerwood 1997; Boreth Ly 2003).

Opened on 13 July 1980, the Tuol Sleng Museum of Genocidal Crimes is constructed to create a sense of authenticity, as if one is getting a glimpse of the prison moments after it had ceased operation (Ledgerwood 1997; Williams 2004). This sense is most immediately and forcefully connoted by the first of four buildings a visitor encounters, where one enters the seemingly still intact interrogation rooms where the last prisoners were

Figure 4.1. Tuol Sleng buildings

Figure 4.2. Photograph of executed prisoner, Tuol Sleng

hastily killed, bloodstains faintly visible on some floors. Not leaving anything to the imagination, each room includes an enlarged photograph of the executed prisoner taken just after the Khmer Rouge had abandoned the prison. The second building contains wall after wall of mugshots, taken when prisoners arrived at Tuol Sleng. The faces in the pictures show all sorts of expressions, but all are haunting, as the visitor, who has already seen building one, knows in graphic detail what their fate was.

In the third building, the visitor finds classrooms divided into small brick cells in which the prisoners were shackled next to a small ammunition canister into which they relieved themselves. A list of Khmer Rouge prison rules – the only written text of note in the building – states that a prisoner had to ask permission before doing so. The last building is somewhat more reminiscent of a 'traditional' museum, featuring glass cases with Khmer Rouge artifacts, ranging from devices of torture to busts of Pol Pot that were being built on the premises. This building has more written text than the other buildings, but is still visually dominated by the artifacts and pictures of Khmer Rouge atrocities painted by Vann Nath, a former prisoner. Until recently, though, perhaps the most impressive exhibit was located in the last room, a 12-square-meter map of Cambodia made out

Truth, representation and the politics of memory after genocide

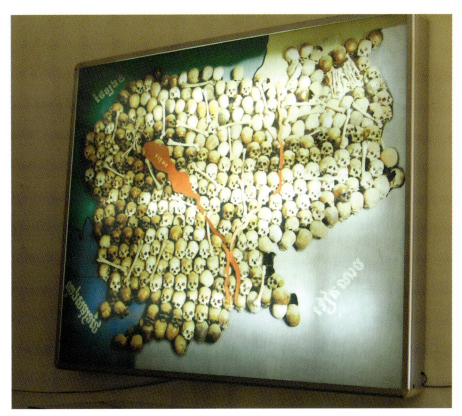

Figure 4.3. Skull map of Cambodia, Tuol Sleng

of 300 skulls, taken from provinces throughout Cambodia (Ledgerwood 1997), with waterways painted blood red.

Such skulls have become iconic of DK, serving as the focus of memorials at the 'Genocidal Center at Choeung Ek', which opened in 1980, and local memorials throughout Cambodia – including one at the site of the killing field of the Pagoda at the Hill of Men – that were constructed following a 1983 PRK directive (Hughes 2003). The skulls condense an array of referents linked to the PRK discourses of legitimacy, ranging from the death, destruction, and brutality of DK to the danger of a return of the 'Pol Pot-Ieng Sary clique'. The photos at Tuol Sleng serve a similar purpose, as Cambodians know the fate of the people portrayed and can project themselves back into the DK past when they, too, suffered greatly and faced death on a daily basis. Tuol Sleng and the memorials are also evidence, proof of the 'criminal acts' that Pol Pot's group committed.

Along these lines, (lack of) vision is a prominent metaphor in these memorials, particularly the blindfolded skull, with all of its powerful significations (see Boreth Ly 2003). Most immediately, it associates DK with a loss of memory and sensory perception. Many survivors recall DK as a time when people retreated into themselves, speaking when necessary but living in silence much of the time. Many people whispered to each other, 'Plant a kapok tree' (*dam daem kor*) a phrase that had a secondary connotation of muteness and thus also meant 'Remain mute'. Along these lines, the lack of sight is also linked to incapacitation, as people lost their freedom and agency on a daily basis. More ominously, DK was linked to incapacitation through death, both literally – the blindfolded skulls are those of dead people – and more figuratively through narratives of the disappeared and how the Khmer Rouge sometimes consumed their victim's livers, a potent act in a society where liver is linked to vitality (Hinton 2005). And then, of course, the DK regime is linked to social death and the erasure of memory.

While the victims lost their sight, the Khmer Rouge claimed to be 'all-seeing'. The DK regime was in many ways panoptic, as a network of spies kept track of what one said and did. In political tracts, the regime was described as 'all-seeing' and 'clairvoyant'. On the local level, people whispered: 'Angkar has the eyes of a pineapple.' In such ways, the theme of vision cut across PRK propaganda, suggesting the terror, incapacitation, and ignorance associated with DK.

Such sites and images interface with other dimensions of the PRK apparatus of truth and memory: holidays such as the 7 January commemoration of the 'liberation', the 20 May 'Day to Remain Tied in Hatred', PRK subsidy of publications and films about DK, the 1979 trial of Pol Pot and Ieng Sary in abstentia, PRK laws on the Khmer Rouge, and so forth.

DISSONANT NARRATIVES

Despite the power of these redundant PRK narratives and institutions, such apparatuses are never monolithic. Instead, they are always challenged from outside and within because of the mismatch between the regime's more homogeneous discourse of truth and the more heterogeneous beliefs and understandings of the populace. All the propaganda in the world about the 'Friendship of Kampuchea and Vietnam', for example, could never assuage Chlat's animosity toward the Vietnamese, a sentiment shared by some Cambodians who feel that the Vietnamese look down upon Cambodians and have sought, both in the past and in the present, to seize Cambodian territory. 'I hate them', he would tell me again and again, 'I don't have words to tell you how much I hate them.' And then he would launch into a diatribe about the malicious and scheming nature of the Vietnamese. Vietnam also figured prominently for Cambodians living abroad, many of whom, while sharing the PRK's horror of DK, viewed the PRK as a front for Vietnamese control and believed Cambodia must be 'liberated' from the PRK and the Vietnamese arch-enemy with which it was allied. This sort of narrative was also central to the rhetoric of the resurgent Khmer Rouge, who attempted to rebuild their movement by lambasting the PRK's ties to Vietnam, which, it claimed, was perpetrating genocide against Cambodians and had fabricated the 'evidence' at places like Tuol Sleng and Choeung Ek. Sadly, this anti-Vietnam stance played into the hands of China, Thailand, the United States and other Western powers that viewed Cambodia as a key proxy site in the global Cold War struggle. These countries not only supported the Khmer Rouge, but effectively allowed DK officials to maintain control of Cambodia's seat at the UN while ignoring the PRK's pleas for an international trial of former Khmer Rouge leaders (Amer 1990; Fawthrop and Jarvis 2004).

The Khmer Rouge, in turn, used this new-found legitimacy to make claims of its own about the past. Former Khmer Rouge leaders could be found making speeches to international audiences in which they not only denied that they had committed mass atrocities but argued that it was in fact the Vietnamese who were 'genocidal' ravagers (Ieng Thirith 1979:15). As for the PRK evidence, the Khmer Rouge dismissed it as a fabrication. A December 1994 radio broadcast stated:

> Concerning those skeletons at Tuol Sleng, they are purely and simply part of the psychological war waged by Vietnam in its aggression against Cambodia. The communist Vietnamese collected skulls and bones from graveyards all over North and South Vietnam, brought them by truck to Cambodia, and displayed them in an exhibition at Tuol Sleng as part of a psychological propaganda campaign to legalize their aggression against and occupation of Cambodia (16 December 1994).

The close link between the PRK and the Vietnamese proved to be a potent propaganda tool for the Khmer Rouge to gain recruits. It found echoes among the members of the post-DK diaspora, as Cambodians abroad asserted their identity and authenticity by inveighing against the Vietnamese presence in Cambodia.

With the signing of the 1991 Paris Peace Accords, the morphing of the PRK into the State of Cambodia, still led by Hun Sen's CPP faction, and the eventual UN election in 1993, the CPP apparatus was severely undermined by the discursive narratives of other Cambodian factions and Khmer abroad. Opposition parties lambasted the CPP for its ties to Vietnam; the CPP, in turn, continued to assert its legitimacy in terms of liberating and continuing to protect the populace from a return of the Khmer Rouge (particularly after the Khmer Rouge dropped out of the political process). These struggles sometimes took place over the symbolic sites associated with DK. For instance, there was debate over whether or not to cremate the remains at Choeung Ek (with the CPP asserting that this evidence should be preserved and King Sihanouk, contrarily, promoting 'reconciliation' and asserting that the souls of the dead should be allowed to rest), and over the map of skulls at Tuol Sleng (which was removed in 2003). New discourses of reconciliation emerged in conjunction with the peace process, leading to some major discursive shifts. After 1993, for example, most mention of the DK period disappeared from school texts. At the same time, human rights discourses, which had been incorporated into the language of the Paris Peace Accords and new constitution and were actively promoted by UNTAC, proliferated, often mediated through Buddhist understandings (Ledgerwood and Un 2003).

BUDDHIST UNDERSTANDINGS

Buddhism has played an interesting role throughout this process. When it was resurrected, with restrictions, by the PRK, Cambodians throughout the country began rebuilding temples and reconstituting their ritual life. The PRK saw Buddhism as an institution through which party ideals could be disseminated and its destruction under the Khmer Rouge served as another useful symbol of the abuses of DK. However, Buddhism also provided a set of understandings about the events that had occurred through notions of karma, merit, and action. It also provided a way of coping with the past through meditation and concepts of forgiveness and letting go of anger.

Thus, when speaking of the villager who was responsible for sending Sruon to his death, Chlat drew upon state-level, Buddhist, and non-state-level discourses:

> I continue to think of revenge. But this thought of revenge, it doesn't know how to stop. And we should not have this thought or the matter will grow and keep going on and on for a long time. We should be a person who thinks and acts in accordance with *dhamma*. [A person who seeks revenge] only creates misery for our society. It is a germ in society. But I continue to think

of revenge ... The people who killed my brother, who put down his name to get into the truck, are all alive, living in my village. To this day, I still really want revenge. I keep observing them. But, I don't know what to do ... The government forbids it.

To understand Chlat's remarks, and thus to begin to understand his response to the violence of the past, one must also unpack other local idioms that structure his response – in particular, the ontological resonances that give them power and force (Hinton 2005).

Buddhist understandings are often central to such responses. Thus, Cambodians sometimes say that Khmer Rouge perpetrators will 'suffer from their *kamma*'. Many invoke a Buddhist saying: 'Do good, receive good. Do bad, receive bad.' Buddhist doctrine provides an explicit ontology that explains how violence originates in ignorance and desire. If the consequences of violence are manifest in overt signs, such actions also have long-term consequences. On the one hand, violence may lead others to seek vengeance against you. On the other hand, harming others is considered a Buddhist sin resulting in a loss of merit and, most likely, diminished status in the next life.

Moreover, becoming bound in such cycles of violence and anger upsets the equilibrium that is so crucial to well-being for Cambodians, both in terms of social relations and bodily health, the two being highly interrelated in Cambodian ethnopsychology. Emotions such as anger constitute a potential disruption of this balance, signaling a disturbance in the social fabric in which a person is embedded and producing 'felt' somatic manifestations, such as pain (*chheu*), discomfort (*min sruol khluon*), dizziness (*vil*), or heat (*kdav*), symptoms that Cambodians constantly scan (D. Hinton 2001a, 2001b). The 'choking heat' of anger, then, metaphorically references the felt 'pressure' of an animating, yet potentially disruptive psychosocial process that strongly 'moves a person's heart' to act (Khmer Dictionary 1967). Chlat's invocation of heat and anger, then, indexes a culturally meaningful state of imbalance associated with the past, one that is not just an 'inner disturbance', but is a signifier of social suffering with its political and moral implications (Kleinman, Das, and Lock 1997).

Besides providing an etiology of violence and its consequences, Buddhism offers a remedy for this toxic state of being – the middle path. On the local level, Cambodians are enjoined to follow five moral precepts (*sel pram*), the first of which is the injunction not to kill. Monks preach that one must learn to control and extinguish one's anger, which arises from ignorance and desire and leads to violence and suffering. In Buddhism, the mindful way of dealing with anger is to recognize its source and to let it disappear, since anger, like everything else in the world, is impermanent. Those who continue to act in ignorance will suffer from the consequences of their actions, with their deeds following like a shadow, as one suffers through the countless cycles of birth and rebirth.

If Buddhism provides a sort of ontological justice for victims, it also suggests that their suffering is a cosmic consequence of their own (or the Cambodian collective's) bad actions in the past (see Haing Ngor 1987: 157, 312). Some viewed what was going on as the fulfillment of Buddhist millenarian prophesies, such as the well-known Buddhist predictions (*Put Tumneay*). Many of these foretold a time when demons or members of the lowest rungs of Khmer society would take over and invert the social order, leading to an assault on Buddhism and wide-spread famine and death (see Ledgerwood 1990; Smith 1989). In fact, a popular DK metaphor for the need to remain silent, 'plant a kapok tree', seems to have been taken from just such a prophesy, as Pin Yathay explains:

> Puth was a nineteenth-century sage who prophesied that the country would undergo a total reversal of traditional values, that the houses and the streets would be emptied, that the illiterate would condemn the educated, that infidels – *thmils* – would hold absolute power and persecute the priests. But people would be saved if they planted a kapok tree – *kor*, in Cambodian. Kor also means 'mute'. The usual interpretation of this enigmatic message was that only the deaf-mutes would be saved during this period of calamity. Remain deaf and mute. Therein, I now realized, lay the means of survival. Pretend to be deaf and dumb! Say nothing, hear nothing, understand nothing! (Pin Yathay 1996: 63)

On a cosmological level, such prophesies played upon Khmer understandings of purity and contamination, which are in part structured in terms of the opposition between the Buddha and demons, dhamma and adhamma, order and disorder, coherence and fragmentation (Hinton 2002; see also Kapferer 1988).

To fully understand the politics of memory in Cambodia, then, we must look not just at the larger state-level discursive structures, but at their points of articulation with and divergence from more local-level discourses and counter-discourses. In many instances, there is convergence. But, there are also important points of divergence, such as more local-level Buddhist discourses during the PRK.

This reemergence was signified dramatically by Maha Ghosananda's Peace Marches in the early 1990s, which symbolically asserted the revival of the *sangha* and *dhamma* (for example, by planting trees and through the composition of the march itself), the importance of cleansing Cambodia and oneself of anger (for example, by sprinkling holy water on the crowds), and the need to make peace symbolized by the path of the march, which connected different parts of the country, including past and present war zones (see Skidmore 1997).

More recently, these Buddhist discourses have come into tension with the global human rights discourses that are associated with another mode of remembering the past: holding a tribunal. While Buddhism promotes mindful understanding of the past, which is one Buddhist argument for holding the tribunal, it also asserts the importance of letting go of the past and freeing oneself of anger and attachment. Depending on how they are invoked, these notions may clash with assertions that the trial will enable Cambodians to attain 'justice', to finally be able to 'heal themselves', and to impose the 'rule of law'. Such discourses are linked to Western juridical models, Christian notions of forgiveness, and assumptions about the universality of psychodynamic process.

THE POLITICS OF MEMORY IN THE PRESENT

This story is being written today as Cambodia continues to struggle with the complexities of the past as a tribunal gets underway. Is this the appropriate way, at this point in Cambodian history, to deal with the past? Should the tribunal be supplemented by modalities of justice and remembering, such as a truth commission or Buddhist rituals? Or, should people just let go of their anger, forget about the past, and move on?

As I think about such questions, I wonder how people like Chlat might reply. I wish I could ask him. The last time I saw Chlat, in the summer of 2003, he was emaciated and had been sick for some time. He explained with a thin smile that he had a parasite that was resistant to medication, emphasizing the point by clenching an open hand to demonstrate how the parasite closed up whenever he took medicine. We talked for a while about his past before having dinner with a mutual friend and his son. About a year later, I received a message from that friend saying that Chlat was in the hospital on the brink of death. He had been diagnosed with AIDS – the disease that was perhaps the most devastating legacy of Cambodia's reengagement with the Western world. Chlat died a few days later.

I think that Chlat would have wanted a tribunal, though I have no doubt that he would have been critical of the corruption of the Cambodian judiciary, the hypocrisy of the international community, and failure of the process to reach people like the cadre who sent his brother to his death at the Pagoda at the Hill of Men. I picture the answers he might have given in that darkness, face silhouetted by billows of smoke and the embers of his cigarette aglow like his memories, then ash.

AUTHOR'S NOTE

I would like to thank Alexandra Kent for inviting me to contribute to this volume and for her skilful editing. I am also grateful to Leena Höskuldsson for the typesetting, and to Nicole Cooley for her comments and suggestions.

This essay is dedicated to Chlat.

REFERENCES

Amer, Ramses (1990) 'The United Nations and Kampuchea: The Issue of Representation and its Implications.' *Bulletin of Concerned Asian Scholars* 22 (3):1990.

Ayres, David M. (2000) *Anatomy of a Crisis: Education, Development, and the State in Cambodia, 1953–1998.* Honolulu: University of Hawai'i Press.

Boreth Ly (2003) 'Devastated Vision(s): The Khmer Rouge Regime in Cambodia.' *Art Journal.* Spring: pp. 66–81.

Chandler, David P. (1999) *Voices from S-21: Terror and History in Pol Pot's Secret Prison.* Berkeley: University of California Press.

Criddle, Joan D. and Teeda Butt Mam (1987) *To Destroy You Is No Loss: The Odyssey of a Cambodian Family.* New York: Anchor.

Fawthrop, Tom and Helen Jarvis (2004) *Getting Away with Genocide: Cambodia's Long Struggle Against the Khmer Rouge.* London: Pluto.

Foucault, Michel (1979) *Discipline & Punish: The Birth of the Prison.* (Alan Sheridan, trans.) New York: Vintage.

Gottesman, Evan (2003) *Cambodia after the Khmer Rouge: Inside the Politics of Nation Building.* New Haven: Yale University Press.

Haing Ngor (1987) *A Cambodian Odyssey.* New York: Warner Books.

Hinton, Alexander Laban (2005) *Why Did They Kill? Cambodia in the Shadow of Genocide.* Berkeley: University of California Press.

Hinton, Devon, Khin Um, and Phalnaraith Ba (2001a) '"Kyol Goeu" ("Wind Overload") Part I: A Cultural Syndrome of Orthosstatic Panic among Khmer Refugees.' *Transcultural Psychiatry.* 38(4): 403–432.

—— (2001b) '"*Kyol Goeu*" ("Wind Overload") Part II: Prevalence, Characteristics, and Mechanisms of Kyol Goeu and Near-Kyol Goeu Episodes in Khmer Patients Attending a Psychiatric Clinic.' *Transcultural Psychiatry*. 38 (4): 433–60.

Hughes, Rachel (2003) 'The Abject Artefacts of Memory: Photographs from Cambodia's Genocide.' *Media, Culture & Society*. 25: 23–44.

—— (2005) 'Memory and Sovereignty in Post-1979 Cambodia: Choeung Ek and Local Cambodian Memorials.' In Susan E. Cook, ed. *Genocide in Cambodia and Rwanda: New Perspectives*. pp. 269–292. New Brunswick, NJ: Transaction.

Khmer Dictionary (1967) *Vochânanukrâm Khmaer*. Phnom Penh: Buddhist Institute.

Kiernan, Ben (1996) *The Pol Pot Regime: Race, Power, and Genocide in Cambodia under the Khmer Rouge, 1975–79*. New Haven: Yale University Press.

Kleinman, Arthur, Veena Das, and Margaret Lock, eds (1997) *Social Suffering*. Berkeley: University of California Press.

Ledgerwood, Judy (1997) 'The Cambodian Tuol Sleng Museum of Genocidal Crimes: National Narrative.' *Museum Anthropology* 21 (1): 82–98.

Ledgerwood, Judy and Kheang Un (2003) 'Global Concepts and Local Meaning: Human Rights and Buddhism in Cambodia.' *Journal of Human Rights* 2(4): 531–549.

Locard, Henri (2004) *Pol Pot's Little Red Book: The Sayings of Angkar*. Chiang Mai: Silkworm.

Ministry of Education (1983) *Writing: Fourth Grade*. Phnom Penh: Ministry of Education.

—— (1984) *Moral Education: First Grade*. Phnom Penh: Ministry of Education.

—— (1988) *Writing: Fourth Grade*. Phnom Penh: Ministry of Education.

Pin Yathay (1987) *Stay Alive, My Son*. New York: Touchstone.

Pol Pot (1977) *Long Live the 17th Anniversary of the Communist Party of Kampuchea. Speech by Pol Pot, Secretary of the Central Committee of the Kampuchea Communist Party, Delivered on September 29, 1977*. Phnom Penh: Ministry of Foreign Affairs.

Said, Edward W. (1994) *Orientalism*. New York: Vintage.

Skidmore, Monique (1997) 'In the Shadow of the Bodhi Tree: Dhammayietra and the Reawakening of Community in Cambodia.' *Crossroads* 10 (1): 1–32.

Williams, Paul (2004) 'Witnessing Genocide: Vigilance and Remembrance at Tuol Sleng and Choeung Ek.' *Holocaust and Genocide Studies* 18(2): 234–54.

NOTE

1   The following quotations from Heng Samrin's speech are cited in Gottesman (2003: 7–8).

SECTION II

Desired Ideals

CHAPTER 5

Wat Preah Thammalanka and the Legend of Lok Ta Nen

John Marston

While legend is so often packaged as having a timeless quality, and as functioning with its own iconic logic outside of historical reality, it may be more interesting to explore these stories as polysemic partial truths fulfilling different imaginary needs in different layers of society – and doing so in ways that evolve over time. This chapter is about a pre-Pol Pot Cambodian monk called Lok Ta Nen, said to have supernatural powers, the object of popular legend in the rural areas of what is now Batheay District, in Kompong Cham. The word *nen* specifically means 'novice' and the word *ta* is an informal word for grandfather, so 'Lok Ta Nen' literally means Ven. Grandpa Novice, a phrase with an oxymoronic quality. This monk was also the object of a cult in the 1950s and 1960s for elite Cambodians from Phnom Penh, mostly military or members of the royal family. The renewed sponsorship of the *wat* where he was resident indicates a continuing interest in him – one colored by the current realities of Cambodian spiritual practice.

The story of Lok Ta Nen is also the story of Wat Preah Thammalanka, where he was resident, usually pronounced simply as Wat Bathom. I came to the subject of Lok Ta Nen in my attempt to understand what villagers described as the 'Brahmanic' orientation of this *wat*. In this case, 'Brahmanism' primarily refers to the use of *vetamon*, literally 'Vedic formulas', but which for our purposes might be translated as 'magic'.

While there clearly was a historical Lok Ta Nen, much of what I am going to recount here could be described as 'yarn' – bearing in mind that a yarn may be believed or half-believed. While it is never irrelevant to ask what is and is not literally true, we have to recognize that in a case like this, what is not true may be more interesting than what is, and more revealing about culture, as it resonates with fiction and myth more generally. The wild stories about Lok Ta Nen thus have an interest in and of themselves. They also have interest for what they suggest about a divide between Phnom Penh and the countryside in the 1950s and 1960s and at the present time. Part of this has to do with questions of sponsorship – how the flow of money and merit relates to a conception of the larger spiritual landscape – and we can compare the pre-war landscape with what is currently taking place at Wat Bathom in order to raise questions about the general directions that Cambodian Buddhism is taking. More broadly, they suggest something about conceptions of spiritual power among rural people and urban elites and how these may interact with each other. Although it is hard to document, all this, I believe, has come to be informed by questions of prophecy or, to put it differently, by the articulation of larger national myths with local folk traditions. There is a difference between the way Lok Ta Nen is perceived locally and the way he is perceived by urban sponsors, but the particular fusion of these different perceptions makes for interesting possibilities.

Please note that up until now I have found no written documents concerning Wat Preah Thammalanka, so my presentation is based on my visits to the *wat* and on interviews with people in Batheay district and Phnom Penh who have some knowledge of the stories. The exercise of recounting the legend of Lok Ta Nen is to some extent one collating the stories told to me by a number of people into a single narrative, and I acknowledge risks of this. Where there are striking contradictions between versions, I point these out. Although my analysis does not attempt to follow Lévi-Straussian theory, I do recognize the structural oppositions that appear when the different versions of the myth are compared. These are of interest in and of themselves, and it may be more relevant to explore this pattern than to declare one version more authentic than the other. Thus we have one informant saying that Lok Ta Nen drank alcohol when he was a monk and another saying that he only drank in periods of his life when he was not a monk. Here I think it is not so important to verify the truth as to point out that in either version Lok Ta Nen is situated at the crux of a contradiction: that he somehow embodied both the spiritual power associated with the monkhood, which implies a respect for disciplinary rules, and a kind of earthy power that was open to transgressing rules.

One should also recognize that different versions of the Lok Ta Nen story have differing degrees of coherence. For many villagers it is fragments of stories that stay in their mind, and one must keep in mind this fragmented quality at the most grassroots level; Lok Ta Nen is a few astounding details. For one local man his memories of Lok Ta Nen were an occasion to debunk the general myth. For monks with some claim to play a role similar to Lok Ta Nen, including the current abbot of Wat Bathom, the narrative has more totality – but is colored by their agendas as spiritual practitioners themselves and their desire to authenticate themselves. What is harder to grasp is the narrative as perceived by the urban elites who have shown interest in the *wat* – and here we are largely forced to infer the contours of a narrative based on the patterns of their sponsorship and the reports of their actions by rural observers.

WAT PREAH THAMMALANKA

Before describing Lok Ta Nen, I should say something about the spiritual power of the site of Wat Preah Thammalanka. The principle market town of Batheay district is P'aw. To the west of P'aw, a road extends into the countryside, past a series of villages and the *wat*s associated with them. Eventually a fork in the road curves to the left and heads past a row of

Figure 5.1. Temple gate of Wat Preah Thammalanka (courtesy of Elizabeth Guthrie)

spiritually powerful hills to parts of Kompong Chhnang province east of the Tonle Sap river, in Chul Kiri district, the region in which, according to most oral accounts, Lok Ta Nen lived before he came to Batheay.

However, Wat Preah Thammalanka is much closer to P'aw and is one of three or four *wats* along the road that are within hiking distance of another spiritually powerful hill, Phnom Choeung Prey (literally 'the hill at the foot of the forest'). On it can be found the remains of an Angkorean *prasat* which in subsequent epochs was shaped to resemble a stupa.[1] The hill and at least one other *wat*, in addition to Wat Preah Thammalanka, are popular sites for female ascetics. During the colonial period Wat Thammalanka was in Choeung Prey district, whose name indicated the central importance of the hill. It is only recently that the district has been divided in two, so that the hill and the villages associated with it are, for administrative purposes, separated.

When I asked villagers further down the road if there was a local spirit (*neak ta*) who had authority over other *neak ta* of the area (a pattern of hierarchical ranking that Forest [1992: 97] has observed), they told me that it was *neak ta khleang meung*[2] at Phnom Choeung Prey. This turned out to be, not on top of the hill, but on a slightly elevated spot in the otherwise flat forested area between Wat Thammalanka and the nearby Wat Choeung Prey, also known for *don chi* and *don ta* meditation.[3]

As a spiritually powerful site, Phnom Choeung Prey competes with one of the hills on the road to Kompong Chhnang, Phnom Taprong, on which there are pre-Angkorean ruins. Villagers there say that the *wat* at the foot of the hill, Wat Taprong, is the first *wat* in the region and one from which all others are generated by lines of ordination.[4] It also has a reputation as a spiritually powerful site, although it is not associated with female asceticism. Its most famous monk, Lok Pho Diep, is one of my sources for stories about Lok Ta Nen. (He himself, famous for his capacity to perform blessings with water, *sraoch toeuk*, is probably the closest thing to a Lok Ta Nen in the area at the present time.) He told me that Lok Ta Nen regularly paid obeisance at Phnom Taprong at well as at Phnom Choeung Prey.

SITE OF POWER

Perhaps the most important thing to emphasize about the site of Wat Preah Thammalanka is that it is perceived to be in a wooded area, about half a kilometer from the main road and some five kilometers to the national highway on another, parallel road, closer to Phnom Choeung Prey, which goes directly from the *wat* through undeveloped terrain without passing

Figure 5.2. Shrine of the Wat Preah Thammalanka vihara (courtesy of Elizabeth Guthrie)

any village. The *wat*, near the end of a shallow lake, is perceived locally as remote and has never had a community of villagers supporting it, which is to say that it does not have a solid *chomnoh choeung wat*. It has always relied on sponsorship from outside. Its remoteness would have been even more marked in the 1950s and 1960s.

Figure 5.3. Principle Buddha image of Wat Preah Thammalanka vihara (courtesy of Elizabeth Guthrie)

The reputation of the site as having spiritual power is strongly associated with the presence for as long as anyone can remember of a surprisingly well-preserved ancient statue of a royal figure in a meditating position, whose head is overarched by a multi-headed *naga*.[5] The current abbot, Ven. Sar Lang, and other people associated with the *wat*, construe it as a Maitreya image, which in Cambodia is typically depicted in royal dress. However, the crowned figure, with a naked torso up to a wide collar adornment, does not resemble Maitreya as he is usually depicted in Cambodia. Also, to my knowledge, the Maitreya is not depicted as sheltered by a multi-headed *naga*. The combination of crowned figure and an overarching *naga* is rare. In the bright gold that the statue is now painted it is hard to imagine it as an Angkorean period sculpture. However, if the antiquity insisted on by local people can be established, the concatenation of features might suggest a Mahayana image from the period of Jayavarman VII.[6]

For the purposes of this chapter, the most important point is that the residents of the *wat* consistently describe it as a Maitreya figure. On the stepped pedestal (*palang*) in the front of the *preah vihear* (consecrated shrine hall), it is surrounded by four smaller Buddha images, creating a small square, a configuration which, as Thompson has pointed out (2004), is often used to depict the Maitreya in relation to the four previous Buddhas of our era. According to the current abbot, this configuration was chosen by Lok Ta Nen.

For years the statue was situated under a tree. Tradition holds that since ancient times no one has been able to build on this site, the statue being so powerful that whoever attempted to do so would experience accidents and be unable to finish. It was only Lok Ta Nen who had sufficient spiritual power to build. When preparations were being made to build, he declaimed, 'If I am permitted to build here, may it rain', and, just as he began lighting incense for the ritual petition, it began to rain. What he built was a temporary shelter (*salom*) over the statue. Prior to the war there was never a *preah vihear* on the site.

LOCAL LEGEND

This is first and foremost a local story. Most people I asked in Phnom Penh, including persons well versed in Cambodian religion and folk customs, had never heard of Lok Ta Nen. But among those who have lived in the area near Wat Thammalanka and know the story, it is told with great relish. It is harder to say what these stories meant to urban elites who made a cult out

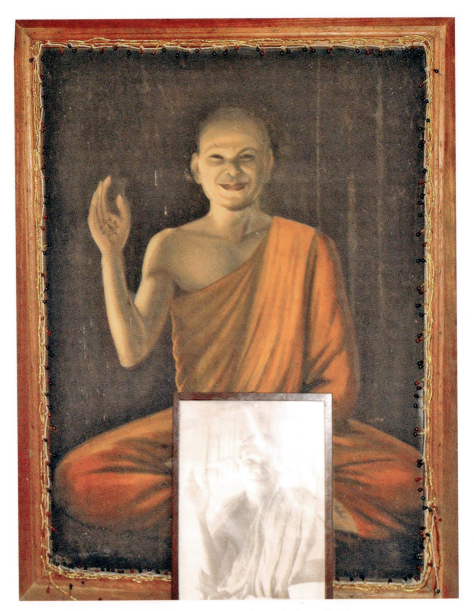

Figure 5.4. Painting of Lok Ta Nen (courtesy of Elizabeth Guthrie)

of Lok Ta Nen in the 1950s and 1960s, or to those who are doing so now, but it is important to emphasize that their numbers have always been quite small. How much momentum Lok Ta Nen's story can take on as a national myth remains to be seen.

Lok Ta Nen had several distinctive physical traits. He is said to have had holes in the fleshy area behind the ankle bone, such that you could have attached manacles. On his back was a birthmark in the shape of a crouching peacock. Almost everyone who describes him refers to his having an extremely large mouth – large enough indeed that he could put his entire fist in it. Moreover, as Samdech Daung Phâng pointed out, he had a perfect set of 32 teeth, which a Cambodian would immediately recognize as one of the characteristics of the Buddha. The most culturally resonant of his features was a chakra wheel on the palm of his hand, which, according to the current abbot of Wat Preah Thammalanka, he could make visible or invisible as he saw fit. This is depicted in iconography at the *wat*, statues and paintings and what is claimed to be a photograph in which he holds up the palm of his hand. However, the slipperiness of the iconography is indicated by the fact that one informant said that Lok Ta Nen was dark-skinned and did not look like this image at all.

Those who tell stories about Lok Ta Nen often divide their stories between the period when he was a monk and the period when he was not. Lok Pho Diep says that Lok Ta Nen ordained at Wat Tanup, the *wat* immediately to the west of Wat Preah Thammalanka, and that the monk who ordained him was Lok Kru Thlay. Others say that Lok Ta Nen assumed the robes and disrobed several times and that, in many of these cases, at least, he was self-ordained, without overly concerning himself with lines of any specific ordination. According to Samdech Daung Phâng, Lok Ta Nen ordained as a novice (as his name indicates) because the laxer disciplinary rules gave him greater freedom for magic than if he had been a *bhikkhu*. Others say that for someone like Lok Ta Nen the distinction between novice and *bhikkhu* is really beside the point.

What is clear is that Lok Ta Nen's powers of magic (*vetamon*) pre-dated his entry into the monkhood and that while his monkhood is respected, he is somehow more than just a monk. The stories of him as a non-monk emphasize his physical strength and his interest in activities such as boxing, gambling and drinking. One story tells of people trying to kill him, but his body disappeared, and it became apparent that it was not he who had been killed but a piece of wood made to seem like him. There is a vague military cast to the stories, although this was not usually explicit in people's accounts; only one village informant said that Lok Ta Nen had been a flag carrier during the post-World War II anti-colonial Issarak period, and was invincible in battle.[7] A story told by almost everyone I spoke to was that he had the capacity to take clumps of grass and turn them into troops. The link to the Issarak period may also be implied in his connection to Norodom Chantaraingsey, one of the most important Issarak leaders, who, villagers say, hid from authorities at one point in the wooded grounds at Wat Tang Thlok, another nearby temple.[8] Reports vary as to whether Lok Ta Nen had a wife and children in the period before he was a monk.

One story dating to the period before he was a monk is of a smallpox epidemic in his village. According to the story, Lok Ta Nen invited the smallpox to leave the bodies of other villagers and attack him. Soon the villagers were cured while his body became covered with smallpox. Nevertheless, after a few days his smallpox also disappeared; by taking it upon himself he had succeeded in freeing the village from the disease.

The supernatural powers attributed to Lok Ta Nen usually have to do with an ability to transform or transport his body. A male ascetic who is now a Pali teacher at the *wat* told me that Lok Ta Nen's powers had to do with his ability to 'break up elements' (*bambaek theat*). Lok Ta Nen was said to have the ability to multiply himself and be present in more than one place at once. He could also make himself small or assume the appearance of someone of a different age. This meant that he could make himself appear to be the age of a typical novice, which provides another explanation for his name. He had the ability to transport himself rapidly, and many people recount stories of him telling people headed towards a particular place that they should go on ahead of him – only to find that he was already there when they arrived. One storyteller described how he could leap as if he were flying. He was said to be able to walk through rain without getting wet. He had the ability to materialize food for guests. No one ever saw him bathe and no one ever saw him wash his clothes but there was no bad odor to him.

According to Ven. Pho Diep, Lok Ta Nen was never known for divination. He was known for having the gift of giving blessings with water (*sraoch toeuk*), which would enable people to rise to higher levels of spiritual and social status (to *laeng reaksey*). The current abbot of the *wat* says that if Lok Ta Nen blessed people with good fortune, his blessings came true, and if he cursed people, this too would come true. He taught meditation, and was also known as a healer. One former villager, still a youth when Lok Ta Nen died, when asked whether he had ever seen him do the miraculous things he was famous for, responded that he could say this much – that when Lok

Ta Nen spat, it never reached the ground, people were so eager to catch it as medicine, and the same could be said for his urine.

According to a man who lived near the *wat* in the 1960s, Lok Ta Nen was not born in Kompong Chhnang, as many believed, but in Prey Krabah district of Takeo province. Different accounts give his original name differently, one as Lok Ta Pin, whereas an inscription on a *chedei* on the *wat* grounds gives it as Touch Phong.[9] According to Samdech Daung Phâng, he was born prematurely, at seven months, as was Samdech Daung Phâng himself. His training in the vedic arts was at Phnom Tbaeng in Siem Reap and at Wat Kdey Daem in Stong district, Kompong Thom. One local lay leader (*achar*) said that Lok Ta Nen was the illegitimate son of a member of the royal family. This perhaps relates to a story, perhaps of recent origin, that Lok Ta Nen represents the reincarnation or the continued existence of a Cambodian prince from the early nineteenth century, Ang Phim. The name of Ang Phim was often invoked in millenarian movements against the French during the colonial period (Forest 1980, S'ou 1968), and to say that Lok Ta Nen was Ang Phim suggests that he could be a rallying point for political resistance. In Cambodia the figure of Ang Phim may also more abstractly represent the spirit of a teacher or *parami* whom traditional healers will sometimes call on in ritual to provide teaching through dreams or visions.

The oldest first-person recollection of Lok Ta Nen that I have encountered is one of Samdech Daung Phâng, who claims to have met Lok Ta Nen in 1939 when he himself was only nine years old. Samdech Daung Phâng, whom I have written about elsewhere (Marston 2002; see also Harris 2005: 221), is the abbot of Wat Prek Prang, near Kompong Luong in northern Kandal. He is probably the best known living critic of the reformed Buddhism dating to the early twentieth century, popularly associated with the patriarch Chuon Nath of the *Mahanikay* order, which has been the dominant form of Buddhism in Cambodia since at least World War II. He advocates his own formulation of a return to more traditional, or *boran* (lit. ancient) Buddhism. He is famed, as was Lok Ta Nen, for his ability to perform blessings with water and he has attracted a following that includes some of the most powerful Cambodian political leaders. He now has the title of *samdech*, making him one of the highest ranking monks in the country.

In 1939 Samdech Daung Phâng was not yet a monk and Lok Ta Nen was living in caves on Phnom Choeung Prey. He spent three months with him, during which time he studied literacy and nothing else. At the end of his course of study, Lok Ta Nen told him to open his mouth, and he spat into it. Samdech Daung Phâng claims, oddly, that from this time on he never had any further contact with Lok Ta Nen until after his death, when he participated in the funeral ceremonies. While Lok Ta Nen taught him directly nothing but basic literacy, Samdech Daung Phâng suggests that something else was passed on that later allowed him, through processes of meditation, to visualize other powerful letter-like symbols that are used in *yantra*.[10]

From 1939 to the late 1950s, a period of great historical change in Cambodia, I have no first-hand anecdotes of Lok Ta Nen. If he was linked to the Issarak movement, it would have been in this period. Villagers' stories of Norodom Chantaraingsey going to meditate at Wat Thammalanka are recollections from the 1960s, when he was a Brigadier-General in the Cambodian army; however, the story of him hiding out at a local *wat* would logically date to the period before 1954, when he left the Issarak movement to join the Sihanouk government (Jeldres 2003: 102),[11] perhaps suggesting contact with Lok Ta Nen from that time.

One of the most delightful stories about Lok Ta Nen, concerning events which purportedly would also have taken place in this time period, tells of him receiving Monique Izzi, who would become Norodom Monineath, the queen most closely associated with Sihanouk and the mother of King Norodom Sihamoni. I offer this story as part of the myth surrounding Lok Ta Nen and not as literal truth. The story carries weight in part because it was told to me by so eminent a public person as Samdech Daung Phâng. This at least suggests that it is a story of considerable circulation, and if it had circulation in the 1960s, it may explain something about the cult surrounding Lok Ta Nen. The story is that as a young woman, when she was just beginning to have romantic contact with Sihanouk, Monique sought out Lok Ta Nen and asked him whether she should be cautious about association with the king. Lok Ta Nen, as the story goes, encouraged her not to be shy with Sihanouk. It was soon afterwards that Sihanouk selected her to star in one of his films. The implication of this story, I suggest, is not just that Lok Ta Nen gave her good advice, but that his blessing may have given her the spiritual power (*reaksey*) necessary to rise to the occasion of being queen. The detail that gives this story its small thread of credibility is that the queen's older half-brother, Oum Mannorine, has been closely associated with Wat Preah Thammalanka.

According to one village informant, it was in 1957 that Lok Ta Nen settled at the site of Wat Preah Thammalanka. This coincides with the heady years immediately following Cambodian independence, after Sihanouk had set up his Sangkum Reastr Niyum, and after mass celebrations of the year 2500 BE – the 'half-way' point in the Buddhist era, which many saw as auspicious to the newly independent Buddhist country. Although a *preah vihear* was never built, the site was eventually made a *wat* with the sponsorship of Queen Sisowath Kossamak herself.

Lok Ta Nen was originally alone at the site, but it soon began attracting increasing numbers of visitors. There were never many other monks: three at one point and perhaps a few more later. There were, however, many more female ascetics. The site also attracted many temporary visitors from urban areas. Lok Ta Nen himself lived in a thatched hut until about 1965, when a more permanent *koti* was built. Visitors sometimes hired villagers to build meditation huts for them; there were at one site about 20 meditation huts, all made of wood. The *salom* to house the statue may have been built around 1962. Apart from the *koti*, which was only recently razed, all the structures are long gone.

URBAN ELITE INTEREST

Queen Kossamak apparently never visited the site herself, although in yearly *kathin* ceremonies she sent as her representative the governor of Kompong Cham province, Nean Theam. Although the number of monks at the *wat* was always quite small, larger numbers of monks from the different *wat*s in the area, between 60 and 100, would assemble for ceremonial activities involving dignitaries from Phnom Penh, such as the *kathin* ceremonies. Ven. Pho Diep remembers participating in these ceremonies as a young monk.

The urban visitors, most informants say, were attracted to the site as a tranquil place suitable for meditation, and they might stay two weeks at a time. A female ascetic currently resident at the *wat* says that she was living on Phnom Choeung Prey when Lok Ta Nen appeared to her in a dream, calling her to come and live at Wat Preah Thammalanka. At least one Cambodian informant, knowledgeable about Lok Ta Nen, speculated that this was a pattern which could be found in a number of those who became closely affiliated with the *wat*, an explanation which I think is consistent with what we find in other Cambodian religious movements. Such an explanation, even if we do not accept its supernatural ramifications, suggests the iconic power of figures such as Lok Ta Nen.

Although most of those who came to Wat Preah Thammalanka for periods of retreat were women, the three prominent names most remembered by people in Srok Batheay were all men: Norodom Chantaraingsey, a customs official named Chum Yoeun, and Monique's half-brother, Oum Mannorine. Oum Mannorine and his family are of particular interest because they became important contributors to the *wat* once again in the 1990s. Oum Mannorine's original connection to the *wat* was through his wife's parents, his father-in-law being a military officer who had served under the French. The couple was among those who built meditation huts at Wat Preah Thammalanka in the 1950s and 1960s and made regular short stays there for meditation. Residents of the *wat* say that it was Oum Mannorine who in the pre-war period built one of the most conspicuous landmarks of the *wat*, an unusual phallic-like cylindrical *chedei*. At this time, at the heyday of Lok Ta Nen's renown, Oum Mannorine was a colonel. He was eventually to become Secretary of State for Surface Defense, which meant that he was in charge of the paramilitary police. Born in 1924, Oum Mannonrine, like Norodom Chantaraingsey, served in a voluntary militia organized by the Japanese during World War II, when he was still in his teens (Chandler 1991: 21).

'TRADITIONAL' POWER

We do not know a great deal about the spiritual practices at the *wat* in this period. Once a year, shortly after Cambodian New Year, Lok Ta Nen would lead a ritual procession to the top of Phnom Choeung Prey. It is said that, like many of the leaders of millenarian movements in Cambodia at the present time, Lok Ta Nen was interested in building a *prasat*. He collected antiquities, mostly *yoni* and *linga*, found in the area of the *wat* – evidence, many in the vicinity believe, that the *wat* was the site of an ancient palace.

Samdech Daung Phâng emphasizes traits of Lok Ta Nen which correspond to his own agendas in promoting a certain kind of *boran* Buddhism. He says that Lok Ta Nen was well versed in traditional cosmological texts: the Traiwet, the Traida, the Traiphet, the Traiphum, and the Traiyut. According to him, the *Mahanikay* patriarch Chuon Nath, so closely identified with the reformed movement in Cambodian Buddhism (see Hansen in this volume, also Edwards 2004, Hansen 2004, Tat 1993), was suspicious of Lok Ta Nen and would have liked to have found ways of discrediting him.

This is partially confirmed by a conversation that I had in 2005 with 92-year-old Samdech Loh Lay, another titled Cambodian monk, who follows Chuon Nath's tradition closely. He said that he remembered people talking about Wat Preah Thammalanka and its royal connections, but he had never known the name of the monk. This kind of thing had never concerned him that much, he said, because his interest was in 'true Buddhism'.

Ven. Pho Diep tells an odd, resonant story that was probably one of his few personal exchanges with Lok Ta Nen. He says that there was a Boddhi tree on the grounds of the *wat* growing perfectly straight, with no branches to either side, and this was considered extremely auspicious. When Pho Diep was at the *wat* he plucked a leaf from the tree. Lok Ta Nen told him to put it in his pocket and he would *chlong phot viel bey* – he would cross safely across the three fields of war, illness, and hunger. He went on to say that if the Boddhi tree ever sprouted branches, there would be war. The Boddhi tree did subsequently sprout branches.

Another story holds that, shortly before his death, Lok Ta Nen directed that all the Buddha images in the place be painted black. He said that once he had died, people would understand what it meant. This is said to anticipate the Pol Pot period, when everyone had to wear black.

THE DEATH OF LOK TA NEN

Lok Ta Nen died in 1967. The ribald version, told by Lok Pho Diep, is that he was kicked in the testicles by a horse. One former villager said that he believed that Lok Ta Nen died at his altar. Yet another man who lived near the *wat* said that Lok Ta Nen had suddenly become ill and was being transported to Phnom Penh in a car when he died. There were massive funeral ceremonies at the *wat*, with thousands in attendance, many of them from Phnom Penh. The grounds of the *wat* were totally covered in fruit brought by mourners, intended to mask the smell of the decaying body. The body was held in state for an extended period of time, perhaps over a year. Lok Ta Nen's flesh, according to one village observer, never lost its softness to the touch, and his eyes remained open and black in color.

Instead of being cremated, the body was placed inside a *pieng*, a large earthenware jar of the sort used to store water. According to Samdech Daung Phâng, who claims to have been present, the body was placed in a sort of fetal position, with the hands raised in a prayer-like *sampheah*, a procedure associated with royalty and at least some high-ranking monks, such as Chuon Nath.[12] The *pieng* was covered with a special lid on which was the decorative image of a *kaut*, the stupa-shaped container that is used to hold the ashes of the deceased.

Legend holds that around 1973 the body in the *pieng* simply disappeared. Now, one man who lived near the *wat* at this time, whose stories about Lok Ta Nen generally took a debunking mode, challenged this story, saying that in fact, at this time, when the war was raging in the district and Lok Ta Nen's successor was in hiding, some boys tending oxen had removed the body from the *pieng* and burned it. Be that as it may, the story as generally told is that the body simply went missing. It is said, moreover, that during the Pol Pot period people sometimes caught glimpses of Lok Ta Nen walking in the forest. Legend has it that he sometimes still makes himself visible. He will take many forms, that of a child or an aged person, that of a man or of a women; the only thing that makes him recognizable is the chakra wheel on his palm.

In the 1980s, the *wat* went through a number of abbots, none of whom stayed very long or succeeded in building up the *wat* until the current abbot, Ven. Sar Long (known as Lok Chhlang), who, it is suggested, has succeed in building up the *wat* because of his own fonts of spirituality, which in some ways parallel those of Lok Ta Nen. When I first visited the *wat* in 1999, it was a rather sleepy place, although work had already begun on the construction of the *preah vihear*. Since then the *wat* has been built up very rapidly. The *preah vihear*, quite unusually, has three towers. After it was completed, a wall was built around the *wat*, a sumptuous two-storey concrete *koti* was built for Ven. Sar Long, then two enormous flagpoles were set in deep tanks of water to the east of the *preah vihear*. A new *sala chhan* (the wide-spaced 'eating hall' which is used for many public functions) is in the process of being built. Since very few *wat*s in the district would have their own cars, it is significant to mention that Wat Preah Thammalanka has had one for several years. When it was destroyed in an accident this past spring, it was replaced by a Land Cruiser, one of the vehicles most associated with wealth and power in contemporary Cambodia.

RECENT DEVELOPMENTS AT WAT PREAH THAMMALANKA

Since my first visit to the *wat* there has been, on a rising overlooking the lake, a shrine of '*brahmanical*' character, with a Vishnu-like figure (Preah Neareay) and two ascetic figures, Preahbat Beyta Tassarat and Preah Mony Eysey Akkinek. Ever since my first visit there has also been a *chedei* in which a statue of Lok Ta Nen is situated immediately in front of a Maitreya

Figure 5.5. Ven. Sar Lang, current abbot of Wat Preah Thammalanka (courtesy of Elizabeth Guthrie)

figure. To the north of the *wat* there is also now a statue of Lok Ta Nen in a reclining position, as though he were the Buddha entering nirvana. There is also, under a Boddhi tree, a recent shrine to the iconic figures of the mother and the father.

The number of monks at the *wat* has steadily increased over the years, from my first visit, when there were only 10, to 36 in 2003. The number of female ascetics (*don chi*) has remained more constant, at 10, with another three male ascetics (*ta chi*). A number of the ascetics do not come from the immediate area. Shortly before the rainy season in 2006, villagers in the district were talking about the fact that two famous young singers had recently ordained as monks in the *wat*. One only remained a monk for 11 days; the other, from a well-known family of performers, was expected to stay for the entire rainy season.

Contributions to the *wat* have come from many sources, including, early on, monks from the area who were resident at *wat*s in the US. As was the case before the war, the *wat* is heavily dependent on contributors *not* at the locality. The largest single donor has been Monique's half-brother, Oum

Mannorine. Oum Mannorine, now the Cambodian ambassador to North Korea, is best known to historians of recent Cambodia history for having led the on-the-ground defense against Lon Nol at the time of the 1970 coup, after which he was imprisoned for three years (Corfield, 1994). I have had several brief conversations with his son, Oum Wachiravuth. He has urged me not to give too much weight to his family's role at this *wat*, stressing that this is not the only *wat* to which the family is contributing[13] and that there are other major donors to the *wat*. All this is quite true, but according to Ven Sar Lang, Oum Mannorine is the only contributor with pre-war links to the *wat*. A large photograph of him and his wife is conspicuous in the abbot's *koti*, and in the district he is closely identified with the *wat*. His connection to the *wat* underlines its pre-war links to the royal family. Monks at other *wat*s in the area say that Ven. Sar Lang has visited the palace several times.

It is hard to prove that Wat Preah Thammalanka and the legend of Lok Ta Nen have any specific links to prophecy or to a particular millennial vision, and it would certainly be risky to attempt to link such ideas to the motivation of any particular donor to the *wat*. Nevertheless, elements of the story and the *wat*'s iconography suggest this link. We see evidence at the *wat* of a clear attempt to link Lok Ta Nen and the Maitreya. Ven. Sar Lang is quite comfortable in saying that some consider Lok Ta Nen a *neak mean bon*, that is, a person with a great font of merit, who throughout the Theravada Buddhist world is seen as having the capacity to effect social-spiritual transformation. Lok Sar Lang is much more cautious about saying that Lok Ta Nen might be regarded as the predicted dhammic king, Preah Batr Dhammik (see Heng Monychenda in this volume), prophesied in the *Put Tumneay* to be discovered in the humble role of a monk. When pressed, however, he will acknowledge that this is sometimes believed. In some versions of the *Put Tumneay*, a chakra wheel on the hand is a sign of Preah Batr Dhammik.[14]

Ven. Sar Lang says that today there are several persons claiming to be Lok Ta Nen. He also says that the iconic picture of Lok Ta Nen holding up his hand with the chakra wheel can be found at many places in Cambodia associated with Brahmanism. I have seen it in three places other than Wat Preah Thammalanka, but it is hard to know what it means. It can be found on the cluttered altar of the medium Ta Long, who has built a strange *prasat* near Dey Et in Kheang Svay district.[15] When asked about it, Ta Long shrugged it off as just something someone had given him. It can be found among the thousands of Buddha images in the *koti* of Samdech Lim Heng at Wat Champuk K'aek in Kheang Svay district. Lim Heng is a monk whose public role is very similar to that of Samdech Daung Phâng (see Harris 2005). The most significant case I have had contact with is a large picture of Lok Ta Nen found in one of the *prasat*s on the top of Ba Phnom mountain built with the sponsorship of a Cambodian-American medium who claims to be the reincarnation of the leader of an early nineteenth century rebellion, one of the millennial religious building projects I have been interested in.[16] The villagers who opened the door to the *prasat* for me did not seem to know the name of Lok Ta Nen, and said it was a picture of 'Ang Phim'. In this case, Ven. Sar Lang has confirmed that the medium makes some claim to being able to channel the spirit of Lok Ta Nen.

CONCLUSIONS

My intention here has not been to take the position of those who mythologize Lok Ta Nen and Wat Preah Thammalanka and depict them as central to what is going on in Cambodian religion, but merely to present them as an interesting case study in a country with many similar cases. One thing that makes this story stand out is that it has roots in the pre-revolutionary period, and the information we have about movements at that time is scarce. We know from French archives that there were other hermit-like figures who attracted followings in the colonial period, but we do not really know how common they were. Probably Lok Ta Nen was not an isolated case in the 1950s and 1960s.

Samdech Daung Phâng may be exaggerating slightly when he describes Lok Ta Nen as self-consciously *boran* in the way he himself is. It is fair to say, nevertheless, that the most clearly documented side of Cambodian Buddhism has been the progression toward reformed Buddhism (*samay*) associated with Chuon Nath, construed in the early independence period as part of the march toward modern national identity. I do not want to identify Lok Ta Nen with the timeless 'traditional' of Cambodian culture. Nevertheless, thinking of Lok Ta Nen as an alternative to Chuon Nath is instructive for what it suggests about what was supposedly being left behind by the reform movement – or more accurately, what was arising as a counterpoint and countermeasure simultaneously with modernizing Buddhism, and which developed its own networks of support, linking it in its own way to centers of power.

In the 1950s and 1960s most rural *wat*s still relied almost exclusively on the contributions of the local community for their support. Wat Preah Thammalanka, as supported by an urban following, was thus an exception to the rule. Insofar as many of the rural *wat*s in Batheay district now rely heavily on urban and expatriate donors, Wat Preah Thammalanka can be said to have anticipated the current pattern. Even so, we should keep in mind that in the time of Lok Ta Nen, Wat Preah Thammalanka was always very modest in scale. There was never a *preah vihear*, Lok Ta Nen lived in a simple *koti*, and rudimentary meditation huts were paid for by the urban followers who stayed there. The phenomenon taking place now is on a greater scale, not so much simply that of meditation retreat or individuals seeking out magical protection as that of what seems almost like competition for spiritual energy, with the flow of money from Phnom Penh much greater, and construction taking place much more rapidly.

Describing what is going on in perhaps overly simple economic terms, we can say that now that rural *wat*s are reliant on urban funds, they have to emphasize qualities that will attract the imagination of urban donors. Wat Preah Thammalanka has been fairly successful at this game by the standards of the rural district in which it is situated, although by comparison with *wat*s that really have the patronage of those in power, such as Ven Daung Phang's *wat*, Wat Champuk K'aek, or Wat Samrong Andet, the contributions to Wat Preah Thammalanka are inconsequential.

In terms of what the *wat* actually represents, one should note that to people from urban areas, it first of all represented the forest and spiritual power associated with the wilderness. This idea has its roots in Indic traditions, and is by no means a phenomenon complementing modern urbanization, although it may acquire greater intensity where urbanization is also intense.

I remain wary of drawing a sharp dichotomy between urban and rural people in Cambodia. Nevertheless, it seems to me that the original legends about Lok Ta Nen, in their quality of yarns, were very much on the order of things that could have grown up in a rural context: stories of physical and spiritual prowess exaggerated to legendary proportions. Perhaps what is most striking here is the way a type of prowess associated with the legendary military man mixed with the traits of the legendary forest monk; the iconography was further heightened by including supernatural features even associated with the Buddha himself. It is not too surprising that such a legend would achieve local circulation, or that it would be associated with a local mountain.

The local legend became slightly more than that in the 1950s. This had to do with at least two things: first, that a connection was somehow established with some members of the royal family, and, second, that public awareness of Lok Ta Nen arose at a time of great social change, when independence corresponded with much interest in the implications of the half-way point in the Buddhist era – and when many individuals were experiencing great social upheaval. The cult of Lok Ta Nen that was supported by the urban elites was more than a yarn – it became a story related to emerging narratives of nationhood.

Why, for a few urban elites, does it have so much interest now? Again, one should be very careful not to exaggerate the importance of the site. Certainly, whatever meaning the site had in the 1950s and 1960s it may, to an extent, have now. But the war and the political changes that have taken place since then have meant that even more Cambodians are groping to find ways that myth might inform political direction. I suggest that this site, like so many others in Cambodia, is one that a number of elite Cambodians have turned to for a national narrative that will provide continuity with pre-war Cambodia and a hope for future spiritual transformation. The future of the site is far from certain, but it momentarily provides a glimpse of some of the textures of contemporary Cambodian religious practice.

AUTHOR'S NOTE

Some of the research for this chapter was funded by a grant by the Center for Khmer Studies with the support of the Luce Foundation. My particular thanks go to my research assistant Chhuon Hoeur who has accompanied me on all my research trips to Batheay District, and without whom this article could not have been written.

REFERENCES

Bertrand, Didier (2004) 'A Medium Possession Practice and Its Relationship with Cambodian Buddhism: The Grū Pāramī.' In John Marston and Elizabeth Guthrie, eds *History, Buddhism, and New Religious Movements in Cambodia.* Honolulu: University of Hawai'i Press, pp. 150–169.

Brown, Robert L. (1988) 'Bodhgaya and South-East Asia.' In Janice Leoshko, ed. *Bodhgaya: The Site of Enlightenment.* Bombay: Marg Publications, pp. 61–84.

Chandler, David (1991) *The Tragedy of Cambodian History.* New Haven: Yale University Press.

—— (1996) *Facing the Cambodian Past.* Chiang Mai: Silkworm Books.

Corfield, Justin (1994) *Khmers Stand Up! A History of the Cambodian Government 1970–1975.* Clayton, Victoria, Australia: Monash Papers on Southeast Asia.

Edwards, Penny (2004) 'Making a Religion of the Nation and Its Language: The French Protectorate and the Dhammakaay.' In John Marston and Elizabeth Guthrie eds *History, Buddhism, and New Religious Movements in Cambodia.* Honolulu: University of Hawai'i Press, pp. 63–85.

Forest, Alain (1980) *Le Cambodge et la colonization Française: histoire d'une colonization sans huerts.* Paris: Harmattan.

—— (1992) *Le culte des genies protecteurs au Cambodge.* Paris: Harmattan.

Guthrie, Elizabeth (2004) 'The History and Cult of the Buddhist Earth Deity in Mainland Southeast Asia.' Doctoral dissertation, University of Canterbury, Christchurch, New Zealand.

Hansen, Anne (2004) 'Khmer Identity and Theravada Buddhism.' In John Marston and Elizabeth Guthrie eds *History, Buddhism, and New Religious Movements in Cambodia.* Honolulu: University of Hawai'i Press, pp. 40–62.

Harris, Ian (2005) *Cambodian Buddhism: History and Practice.* Honolulu: University of Hawai'i Press.

Hās' Sāvīoen (nd) *Pravaddi Draï Narottam Chantaraïsā.* (Biography of Norodom Chanrangsey) Paris: Publisher

Heder, Steve (2004) *Cambodian Communism and the Vietnamese Model, Vol. 1: Imitation and Independence, 1930–1975.* Bangkok: White Lotus.

Jeldres, Julio (2003) *The Royal House of Cambodia.* Phnom Penh: Monument Books.

Kiernan, Ben (1985) *How Pol Pot Came to Power.* London: Verso.

Kobayashi Satoru (2005) 'An Ethnographic Study on the Reconstruction of Buddhist Practice in Two Cambodian Temples: With the Special Reference to Buddhist *Samay* and *Boran.*' *Tonan Ajia Kenkyu (Southeast Asian Studies)* 42 (4) pp. 489–518.

Marston, John (2002) 'La reconstrucción del budismo 'antiguo' de Camboya.' *Estudios de Asia y África* 37 (2) pp. 271–303.

S'ou Camryn (1968) *Ācāry Svā.* Phnom Penh: Toup Lekh.

Tat, Huoth (1993) *Kalyaannamitta rabas' khñum.* (My Spiritual Friend) Phnom Penh: Buddhist Institute.

Thompson, Ashley (1999) 'Mémoires du Cambodge.' Doctoral dissertation, Université de Paris 8.

—— (2004) 'The Future of Cambodia's Past: A Messianic Middle-Period Cambodian Royal Cult.' In John Marston and Elizabeth Guthrie eds *History, Buddhism, and New Religious Movements in Cambodia.* Honolulu: University of Hawai'i Press, pp. 13–39.

Woodward, Hiram W. (1979) 'The Bayon Period Buddha in the Kimball Art Museum.' *Archives in Asian Art.* Vol. 32 pp. 72–83.

Yamada, Teri (2004) 'The Spirit Cult of Khleang Moeung in Long Beach, California.' In John Marston and Elizabeth Guthrie eds *History, Buddhism, and New Religious Movements in Cambodia*. Honolulu: University of Hawai'i Press, pp. 213–225.

NOTES

1. In the Cambodian context the word *prasat* refers to ancient Cambodian temples or to modern religious constructions with towers that in some sense evoke them. A *prasat* contrasts with the standard buildings of a Theravada *wat*, although Buddhist *wat*s may also sometimes contain what are called *prasat*s, typically religious shrines which are not specifically Buddhist in function. The *stupa* (also called *chedei*), an architectural form very much in the Buddhist tradition, is a towering structure used to hold relics or ashes (iconically a relic of the Buddha). In the Theravada tradition it is typically in the shape of a tapering inverted cone. The process whereby *prasat*s were transformed into stupas in the Middle Period is discussed in Thompson (1999).

2. The name *khleang meung* is more famously associated with a *neak ta* in Pursat province and the legend associated with him. For the Pursat story, see Yamada (2004), Forest (1992:237-247).

3. *Don chi* are female ascetics, following five to eight precepts, and typically shaving their heads and wearing white. *Don ta* are men, typically elderly, who follow similar practices without taking the next step and actually becoming monks.

4. One could speculate that an ancient pattern of migration into the area came from the floodplain of the Tonle Sap to the area of Wat Taprong and then on to other parts of the district, such as the area around Phnom Choeung Prey.

5. The Cambodian prophetic text, the *Put Tumneay*, tells of a Buddha statue being placed in the forest about 50 years before the year 2500 BE. By standard reckoning this would be 1916. However, it would seem that the statue was in fact already there at this time, perhaps as an artifact from ancient temples connected with the nearby mountain, rather than having been taken there in the early twentieth century, as the wording of the *Put Tumneay* would suggest. However, 1916 might correspond roughly to the first discovery of the statue in modern times.

6. My thanks to Elizabeth Guthrie for clarifying some of the issues involved here. Woodward (1979) has written about a similar crowned image with *naga* from Burma. Brown (1988) writes about the emergence of the iconography of the crowned Buddha in the late Angkorean period, related to the importance of Bodhgaya as a pilgrimage site and perhaps the effect of Indian Buddhists fleeing northern India and the Himalayas from Moslem invasions. See also Guthrie (2004: 152–54).

7. However, this particular informant claimed that the monk Lok Ta Nen and the non-monk who fought in the Issarak movement were two different persons.

8. Villagers say that Chantaraingsay was together with a Japanese known locally as Ta Sok.

9. One of the temple gates, constructed in 1991, has an inscription which writes about Lok Ewpuk Kmeng, called Mahahong, called Nen Piw – apparently three names for Lok Ta Nen. 'Nen Piw' literally means 'the novice who is the youngest child'. 'Ewpuk Kmeng' literally means, 'young father'. Elsewhere I have been told that Lok Ta Nen was once called 'Ta Kmeng', or 'the young grandfather'.

10   Diagram of magical power.
11   Cambodians recalling his public image in the pre-war period speak of his famous use of multiple amulets. He is generally considered as a non-Communist Issarak leader. Heder says that at one point the Communist movement considered him as an alternative, more revolutionary king, who could be installed in place of Sihanouk, but Chantaraingsey rejected this idea for fear of becoming a pawn to the Viet Minh. Sources on Chantaraingsey in the Issarak period include Heder (2004), Kiernan (1985) and (Hās' Sāvīoen).
12   Thanks to Erik Davis for this detail.
13   A sign at Wat Samrong Andet on the outskirts of Phnom Penh indicates that Oum Mannarine and his wife paid for the construction of a center for *vipassana* meditation there. The center has photographs on display dating to 1995 or 1996, from before the building was constructed, which show Oum Mannarine's wife meditating in a bamboo and thatch meditation hall together with her nephew, now King Norodom Sihamoni.
14   Personal communication, Judy Ledgerwood.
15   Ta Long is described in Bertrand (2004).
16   The historical record of the rebellion is described in Chandler 1996.

CHAPTER 6

The Recovery of the King

Alexandra Kent

Like Marston's chapter in this volume, this essay explores instances of how legend may be tapped in the shaping of political imaginings. In what follows, the mythical notion of virtuous royal power informs the narratives and practices of two middle-aged Cambodian women, one a laywoman and one a *don chi* (lay-nun). The ethnographic data for this essay was collected in February 2006 in the course of anthropological fieldwork on religious revival in Cambodia. Like the possession practices described by Bertrand (cf. Bertrand 2004), legend here becomes a living witness to culture, inscribing itself within 'social, economic, historical-political, and religious systems' (p. 150).

 While neither of the women could be considered a mainstream religious practitioner, the symbolism captured in their stories has broad resonance in Cambodia and beyond. The ideal Buddhist king was traditionally conceived of as possessing extraordinary virtue. He supported and purified the *sangha* but also deferred to the moral instructions of palace chaplains (Leclère 1899; Keyes 1994; Harris 1999). Under a truly virtuous king, who ensured that *dhamma*[1] flourished, the realm would prosper – a theme that is echoed in Heng Monychenda's discussion of ideal leadership in this volume. Further, the notion of the king as a substitute body for the welfare of the kingdom is, as Thompson (2004b) notes, limited neither to Buddhism nor to Cambodia. The two narratives here are concrete manifestations of transcendent themes, anchored in time and space; the re-ordering of Cambodia is in both cases envisaged through the recovery of the king.

RECOUNTING, PERFORMING AND RECOVERING

The two portraits sketched in this essay offer something more than narratives of recovery. Narratives are, strictly speaking, verbal recounting, which report on experience but edit out much of it along the way so as to project desires and strategies towards imagined ends (Good 1994: 139). The material below consists of narratives that are embodied and situated in a symbolically charged space. In this sense, the women discussed here are involved in the performance of healing – the 'historically contingent evocation fusing past traditions and memories with present circumstances and problems ... reflective and transformative' (Laderman and Roseman 1996: 2).

The two stories are spun around a concern with royal 'disorder' and recovery. Healing reconstitutes the person experientially, socially and culturally and in so doing may reshuffle the micro-relations of power that frame life (Kent 2005: Ch. 5). The recovery of these women's individual bodies prefigures the recovery of kingship, the physical representation of which (in the person of the king or his statuary) is a substitute not only for the body social and the body politic (Scheper-Hughes 1987), but also for the geopolitical and cultural body of the universe as imagined by the Khmer.

I approach the idea of kingship in a broad sense and intersperse the term with the word 'kingliness' in order to stress that the stories are not promoting a particular political order and its institutional forms (monarchy), but are praising a 'royal' state of being: personal virtue and dignity (see Crouzatier 2001). The stories suggest that this royal condition is attainable not only by the king but by every individual, although the king should be its exemplar (cf. Heng Monychenda's chapter in this volume). Buddhist kingliness is concerned with social and cosmological relations – relations between the human microcosmos and the supra-human macrocosmos (cf. Tambiah 1976). The desire to reinstate kingliness cannot be reduced to extolling the virtues of a specific king, although both the twelfth century king Jayavarman VII and twentieth century Sihanouk appear in stories as archetypal kings. The recovery of kingship is, rather, about the restitution of principles of conduct deemed necessary for upholding cosmos and civilization.

SPIRIT MEDIUM SOPHEA

Sophea was 51 years old when we met in early 2006. I was introduced to her by her niece, Chanta, a woman in her early twenties whom I had known for some time and who had told me, 'My aunt has special senses, like King Norodom Sihanouk',[2] she told me. 'She has *parami*'.[3]

Sophea is an educated woman. She studied French, Thai and English at school as a child in Battambang town and later also learned Vietnamese. As an adult she completed a nurse's training in Phnom Penh. When I met her she was studying for her Masters degree in Public Health in Phnom Penh. Her husband, who sadly died in 2006, was also a cultured man. At the age of thirteen he ordained as a novice in the *wat* that houses the provincial head monk of Battambang province, and he remained a monk for several years until the Khmer Rouge took control in 1975. After the Khmer Rouge regime collapsed he married Sophea and began teaching at the Pali High School in Battambang.

Some ten years ago Sophea became ill. She had difficulty breathing, was listless and weak. No form of medicine helped, so finally a friend of hers, a high-ranking official,[4] took her to see a woman he thought could help at a *wat* in Kompong Cham province. This woman was a religious renunciant, who dressed in white but did not shave her head. Instead she had a length of matted hair[5] down her back. I shall refer to her here simply as the *don chi*.[6] The *don chi* told Sophea she had a choice: to die, or to accept the *parami* that was causing her illness. She then instructed Sophea in the ritual offering of respect to the *parami*, but did not tell her its name. Sophea was disinclined to believe because of her scientific background, but she made the required offerings. That night she awoke around 4 am in a dreamlike state to see a kingly man standing before her. He pointed his finger at her and told her the name of her *parami*: 'Preah Neang Chantha Maly'.

This experience affected Sophea profoundly. She soon began organizing a ceremony to communicate her acceptance to the *parami*: 'The ceremony was like that held for the installation of a new Buddha statue, but for my ceremony we had five *achar*s instead of one, and nine monks.' When the monks had finished praying, each of the *achar*s apparently began to dance and when the fifth one began dancing Sophea too felt something enter her and take control: 'Two souls (*winnean*) were controlling me, one from the left and one from the right. They told me that from now on my health would be restored.'

From this time on Sophea began obeying her *parami*, following commands to adopt an ascetic lifestyle, living as 'brother and sister' with her husband and following the five precepts strictly. Her health problems disappeared. Nowadays, she regularly goes into trance, which she induces simply by burning incense. She explained that eight different *parami* have come to her. Each of these possesses a particular kind of power: fortune-telling, healing, protection, supernatural powers of speech and so on. When she is in trance, I have been told, Sophea's behaviour indicates which spirit is in her and the spirit then communicates with the world through her.

In 1995, one of her spirits instructed her to call a male relative[7] back from Australia. This man had moved to Australia in 1979 and had taken a degree in Law. But not long after Sophea accepted her *parami*, he began to experience spirits calling him to return to Cambodia to bring 'peace and security' to the people. These spirits, Sophea explained to me, were her spirits beckoning to him. She told him he must come back to Cambodia. He came back in 1995 and took a job in the Ministry of Justice, as a member of the royalist FUNCINPEC party. The spirits seem thus to be empowering Sophea within a politically edged network made up of various *khsae* (Khmer, lit. string, meaning social network).

Sophea told me that the spirits began contacting her because during the war many Cambodians buried their valuables in the ground at temple sites. These items, she explained, have spirits that felt they were being punished by being left underground, so they were in search of a caretaker who they could be sure would honour and respect them, and not dig them up to sell them. They decided upon Sophea as their vehicle and since then she has devoted great effort to meeting their demands, which include the restoration of two temple sites: one close to the town of Kompong Cham and one at the temple complex of Longvek, close to Udong. Sophea and Chanta decided to show me these two sites. The first is the temple at which Sophea had first learnt of her *parami* from the *don chi*. When we arrived, Sophea introduced me to the *don chi*, who shared with me something of her own story.

The wedding of the naga and the king

The temple site at which the *don chi* lives consists of an older *preah vihear* now undergoing renovation, and several new buildings under construction. Some 300 metres away is a new building that houses three ancient stone *yonis*.[8] Destructive and martial powers are believed to invest this shrine, a belief portrayed on the walls in vivid, intensely coloured battle scenes. Sophea showed me the site and told me that many *neak thom* ('big men') come to pray there to enhance their power, but she added that they would suffer bad karma if they then behaved immorally.

The *don chi* is in her late forties and has seven siblings, all of whom are married with children. She was also married earlier but her husband died

Figure 6.1. Don Chi with matted hair

during the Pol Pot regime. They had one son, who is now married. In 1984, she suffered a period of distress that caused her to become ill from that time until 1993, when she came to this temple. As soon as she arrived her illness disappeared, and she decided to become a *don chi*. She claims now to observe eight precepts and she told me that if she breaks these she will become sick again or possibly die. However, a *parami* gives her particular instructions that override the precepts. For instance, he has instructed her to follow various food taboos, including the avoidance of meat and sesame seed, and he has told her she may eat after midday because she works so hard.

In 1993 her hair was normal and she did not shave it, but after some time she began dreaming of the Hindu monkey deity Hanuman, who told her not to touch her hair. From that time on her hair became matted and thick and when I met her it reached down to her waist in a solid, flat chunk that divided into two 'feet' at the bottom. These, she explained to me, are Hanuman's feet. The long chunk is a *naga*, where the *naga* spirit resides.

One of the temple *achar*s explained to me that the *don chi*'s hair strikes fear into the *neak thom* who come to visit the temple. When they see the hair and recognize that a spirit is resident in it they are afraid to do wrong because they know that they are being observed and may be punished. The *achar* told me that I must not touch her hair because anyone apart from children and *neak mean sel* (virtuous, precept-obeying Buddhists) who does so will become sick.

At night the *don chi* sometimes dreams of a *naga* who calls her, 'Sister'. When I asked for an explanation, it was Sophea who responded:

> The *naga* once took the form of a human woman and came onto a beach to play. King Jayavarman VII caught sight of her and fell in love with this *naga* king's daughter. She told him if he wanted to marry her he would have to go under the sea with her, but he said he could not because he was a man. She told him to simply hold her tail and follow. At the time of the marriage between the *naga* daughter and King Jayavarman VII, the latter had 101 countries under his rule. While Jayavarman VII was away controlling the borders, his wife became lonely and married another *naga*. Upon his return Jayavarman VII was enraged and he sliced at his wife's *naga* brother in anger. But the blood spurted out and hit Jayavarman VII and this gave him leprosy and killed him.

This rendition of the renowned legend of the leper king[9] places the *don chi* squarely within a classic symbolic framework, replete with meanings.

As with Sophea, the *don chi*'s spiritual debut coincided with recovery from sickness. The theme of healing in relation to kingship, as Thompson (2004b: 93) has pointed out, involves the 're-membering' of that which has been dismembered, the reintegration of the past into the present in order to build health and social justice for the kingdom.[10] As the sister of the *naga* that resides in her hair and as wife of Jayavarman VII, the *don chi* personifies the link between the generative/destructive powers of the underworld and the eternal ordering power of kingship. When she re-married the universe, she regained her health.

The *don chi* and Sophea explained to me that Jayavarman VII has already been reborn and is now a 15 year old boy, the son of a high-ranking but honest man living south of the Independence Monument in Phnom Penh. This mapping of the reborn king onto the streets of Phnom Penh is rich in associations. Erik Davis (personal communication) has pointed out that positioning the invisible king south of the monument – the Mount Meru of Cambodia's modern era – places him on the legendary continent of Jambudvipa (the human realm), in the same way that the royal palace is placed immediately south of the Meru Field. Such positioning posits him as the exemplary king of modern society. The intimacy conveyed here between the *don chi* and the *dhammika* leader-to-be (see Heng Monychenda, this volume) suggests the possibility of reworking Cambodia's traumatic biography and her disordered present into a hopeful future.

The boy's true identity will not be disclosed, they explained, until Cambodia is ready to submit to his rule again, but some know, I was told, that he has x-ray vision. He is allegedly an omnipotent, omnipresent being who sees all but who himself cannot be seen. His father and grandfather, the women told me, have both been careful to keep his identity hidden because they know he would be killed if it leaked out. His ability to see but not be seen is crucial to his survival.

The story that the *don chi* shared with me is brimming with desire for the restoration of order and with subtle claims to the power to bring it about. The survival of this uncontainable source of hope and order is presented as dependent on protection from the corruption of a world gone awry – a world that, as the next story shows, is construed as devoid of justice, purity, and wholeness (health).

Figure 6.2. Statue of Preah Ko and Preah Keo

RECOVERY OF THE KING

The second site that Sophea had been instructed to restore was at Wat Tralaeng Keng at the former royal capital of Longvek, not far from Udong. As we approached this site, Sophea began to tell me the popular Cambodian legend of Preah Ko (Divine Bull) and Preah Keo (August Crystal),[11] explaining that we were going to visit the place at which the divine pair was born.

Briefly, the story of Preah Ko and Preah Keo tells of a farming couple who were to have a blessed child, provided the wife avoided eating green mangos. The wife, however, unable to resist her desire for the forbidden fruit,[12] climbed a tree to pick one and fell to her death. Upon her death a magic pair of twins was born, a calf and a human boy. The anomalous family was then banished by the villagers to the forest. But the bull soon demonstrated to local children his powers to selflessly provide prosperity, security and health from his stomach. The greedy villagers then sought to disembowel him and realized the error of their ways only after he had fled and they were left with nothing. At this time, the Siamese were trying to conquer Cambodia, and they challenged the Cambodian king to a series of contests. The Cambodian monarch had now come to understand the great value of the twins and beseeched the bull to assist. The bull obliged and, using his magical powers, won the first two contests. When they saw the bull's extraordinary powers, the Siamese wanted it for themselves. For the final confrontation, the Siamese king presented his mechanical bull, which was made of iron. Preah Ko gallantly fought but lost a horn in the battle and realized he could not win this time. The twins fled and went into hiding in the jungle. So the Siamese simply shot coins into the undergrowth and the gullible, greedy Cambodian villagers hacked away the vegetation, revealing their precious bull to the Siamese, who stole it and took it to Siam.

The themes of desire and of a lack of virtue leading to the loss of Cambodia's most valuable, integrative, healing power are woven throughout this story. This motif recurred repeatedly throughout the day that I spent with Sophea. First, we arrived at a magnificent, spreading bodhi tree with a single mango tree trunk emerging from its loins. Under the tree is a statue of a bull lying down and a boy beside it, representing the legendary figures of Preah Ko and Preah Keo.

Sophea pointed to the mango branch, explaining that this was where the mother of the twins had climbed up to reach the green mango and then fallen to her death.

We continued through a gateway leading into an area of temples and shrines. First we came to the temple of Prasat Preah Ko, raised up on an outcrop of land, with the Tonle Sap flowing behind it. Beneath the temple building was a crack in the rock at which Chanta and Sophea stopped to make an offering. Sophea explained that when Cambodia was originally raised up from the sea,[13] the *naga* holes were exposed. This one, she told me, was the entrance to a *naga* tunnel (see Figure 6.3 overleaf) that extended under the earth all the way across to Udong Mountain, several kilometers away, where the *naga* tail reached the current king's ancestral urns; the *naga* passage provided a graphic link between past and present kingship.

Sophea explained that when the Thais encroached upon this royal capital long ago the king had wanted to hide his men inside the *naga* tunnel, but she laughed: 'He could not – because there is no oxygen in there! They would all have died!' On one level, the king is thus portrayed as simply stupid, but on another as lacking the magical power and favour of the *naga*s; their realm was forbidden and dangerous for him and could not be harnessed to save the kingdom. The idea of the fallibility and foolishness of the king became increasingly pronounced as we continued our wandering.

Figure 6.3. The naga tunnel

When we entered the next large, renovated temple building of Wat Tralaeng Kaeng both Chanta and Sophea became solemn. We sat and paid respect to an empty space – an absence. In Sophea's view, we had entered the space of Cambodia's dismemberment. She explained that the centre of the hall is the site of a once-towering, four-faced stone Buddha statue. All that remains of the statue are its eight stone feet, each some one and a half metres long, and each pair facing one of the cardinal directions.

In the absence of this image, the vacuum has been filled with smaller, colourful statues but the feet, with their empty ankle sockets, still testify to the loss.

The historical events surrounding the loss of the statue in the sixteenth century have been described by several authors (Chandler 1998 [1983]; Thompson 2004a; Harris 2005). The post-Angkorean monarch King Ang Chan (1516–1566) had moved the capital from Phnom Penh to Longvek. Accounts describe the king's power at this time as absolute; the people and the monks participated fully in his order. Descriptions of Longvek by Portuguese and Spanish travelers of the time portray it as a place of fabulous wealth, with lively trading communities of Chinese, Indonesians, Malays, Japanese,

The recovery of the king

Figure 6.4. Empty sockets of missing statue's feet

Arabs, Spanish, and Portuguese. Trade products included precious stones, metals, silk and cotton, incense, ivory, lacquer, livestock and rhinoceros horn. The success of his rule was, according to the chronicles, attributed to Ang Chan's moral and religious rectitude. However, power later fell to Ang Chan's grandson Brah Sattha, during whose reign Longvek fell.

Sophea explained that the Siamese were at this time attempting to gain control of the area but the military prowess of the king was too mighty for them. However, she added, the Siamese were wily and they devised a scheme by which to dupe him:

> The Thais sent a man to Cambodia in the guise of a wise healer but in fact he made the king's daughter sick. Because the king was not a *neak mean bon*[14] he believed the monk and when his daughter fell sick he asked the monk for help. The monk told the king to get rid of the huge statue with the four-faces. In fact, the Thais wanted the statue and its power for themselves. When the king agreed to remove it, the Thais put it in one of their ships, but it was too heavy and sank in the river just by the temple. Once the statue was gone, the Thais could easily take over. Ever since then the statue has remained in the river.

Although Sophea herself did not make the association it seems that the stone manifestation of Khmer integrity is currently impotent in the realm of the *naga*s – analogous to the oxygen-depleted naga tunnel. Sophea commented on this portion of the story. 'Cambodians make their own downfall,' she said. When I asked why this had happened she almost shrieked, 'Because we Cambodians are stupid! Stupid!' She connected the legend directly to contemporary Cambodia:

> You know why Preah Ko lost a horn fighting the Thai bull? Well, it was because the Thai bull was made of metal. You see, Thailand is more developed than Cambodia. The Thais have powerful weapons and it is easy for them to beat us. But it is also easy for them to trick us. We Cambodians actually helped the Thais to steal Preah Ko and Preah Keo because we were greedy for the coins.

Taking me by the arm she then led me out of the temple building to look at a row of flowering trees that were growing at the base of the building. Pointing at these she said: 'You see those trees? Well, Cambodians are selling trees like that to Thailand so cheap. They dig them out and sell them for $50 or $100 but in Thailand they are sold for $2000 each.[15] And the powerful people (*neak thom*) are selling our forests. Cambodians are giving Cambodia away!'

When I asked her if her *parami* might be able to help stop what is going on, she told me she was afraid to get involved:

> A woman I know also has *parami*. A while ago the wife of a famous Cambodian People's Party (CPP) politician consulted her and she went into trance. Her spirit told the politician's wife that her husband was very powerful and that she could have all that she wanted, but he was going to die naked [i.e. without ceremony or the presence of monks]. Lon Nol and Pol Pot both died like that. That politician's wife then told her husband about this and he got very angry. He tried to find the medium so she had to go into hiding. So I don't dare give advice to those powerful people.

However, although Sophea believes that explicitly critiquing extant power is too risky, she nevertheless clearly identifies herself as a critic, portraying contemporary power holders as disordering, chaotic and immoral. Her spirits have instructed her to raise the statue from the river and to reinstall it. The time, she said, is not yet right, since the spirits are still angry about what has been happening, but they have entrusted her with the task. In the meantime, Sophea has been making preparations. She receives donations from people whom her spirits help and she told me she has already spent $4,000 on a piece of land not far from the site of the missing statue. In 2004, she, her relatives, the *don chi,* and the head monk of her temple consecrated this plot with a *sima*.[16] During the ceremony, she remembers, they lit many candles that burned despite the wind. She plans to pay for the construction of a building in which to install the statue that is now occupying the place of the missing image. Then there will be space to reinstall the original Buddha-king back into its correct position, at the

Figure 6.5. Prasat Sosar

heart of the cardinal points and close to the birthplace, as well as the site of the loss of Preah Ko and Preah Keo. 'That statue is very important for Khmer people because when it is installed at its original place, the country will have no more problems, but as long as it is in the river the country will continue to have problems,' Sophea remarked.

We moved on to visit Prasat Sosar, an extraordinary temple construction with seven four-faced heads atop it and inside, a forest of what were once bamboo pillars that have now been replaced by concrete imitations. The large Buddha statue protected by the bamboo forest immediately recalls the forest of the Preah Ko Preah Keo story that the Khmers had stripped away to expose their most precious being to covetous imposters.

As we sat at the entrance to the temple, Sophea began to talk about the Buddha's kingship and brahmanical spirits:

> The Buddha was a man but he was also the son of the king; he could teach people that if you do good, you receive good, if you do bad, you receive bad. Brahmanism is about strength (*mahatirit*). If you only think about *sel* [Buddhist virtue], you are easily cheated and weak and if someone fights you then, according to Buddhism, you cannot fight back.
>
> You know, the Venerable Sam Bunthoeun [a renowned Cambodian monk who established a major *vipassana* meditation centre at Udong but was assassinated in February 2003] was virtuous but still he could be killed and that was because he did not pay respect to the Brahmanical spirits, so they did not protect him.

Figure 6.6. Buddha statue with bamboo 'forest'

The Buddha statue inside Prasat Sosar, protected by the bamboo columns, graphically illustrates Sophea's ideas – that goodness and passivity cannot survive without the protection of the wild and powerful jungle.

Sophea used a recent event to explain what she meant,

I have to keep the *sel*[17] because if I break them I will get sick. I almost go crazy sometimes trying to keep my anger inside me. But the spirits help me instead. My brother has a guesthouse in Sisophon and recently someone he knew poisoned my brother's whole family so that he could break in and steal money, gold and a motorcycle. I rushed to visit my brother's family and they were very sick, drugged. Because I have a medical training I could put up intravenous lines and they got better but I also prayed to my spirits for justice. Within 24 hours the thief had crashed the motorcycle, killing his own son. The police caught him and the stolen property was returned. The spirits protect those who are pure (*borisot*).

CAMBODIA'S LEGENDARY FUTURE

As the stories of Sophea and the *don chi* interweave with popular legends, a common logic becomes apparent; the prosperity of the periphery depends upon the virtue of the centre, while conversely, the security of the centre depends upon the provision of protection by the periphery. As so tellingly represented in the legend of the leper king, the wellbeing of the kingdom and the wellbeing of the powerful yet fallible king become metaphors of and substitutions for one another (Thompson 2004b).

These two women are not simply telling moral tales about life. They are dynamically interlacing their ongoing experience with legend and symbolism. Their sickness narratives and their recoveries are structured around experience of a morally disordered world. The power to re-order life lies hidden in the past, invisible to most people. In their blind greed, the Khmers are described as offering up the treasures of their kingdom to avaricious outsiders, who then conceal it and use it to empower themselves at the expense of Cambodia. In keeping with Buddhist ideas about desire, these living legends portray blindness, selfishness and greed as the causes of Cambodia's downfall, both past and present.

Through the poetics of blindness Sophea and the *don chi* offer us a reflection upon modernity and lack of insight. The raising of the statue from the river is not simply about recovering an image *of* ordering power. It is about rediscovering insight and order from the past; if people are once again able to 'see'[18] the statue they will be transmogrified into ordered, insightful beings.

Traditional ceremonies for the consecration of new Buddha images transform these from blocks of stone or concrete into loci of sacred, life-giving power, by literally 'opening their eyes' (Swearer 1995),[19] enabling onlooker and image to participate in one another through the channel of the eyes. This kind of participatory mode of being (Tambiah 1990) may, however, be eclipsed by modern, analytical ways of knowing; Sophea's initial conflict between her medical viewpoint and the idea that her illness might be caused by a *parami* recalls, for instance, Foucault's (1973 [1963]) description of the 'clinical gaze', which brings medical truth into focus, but at the expense of other configurations of order and truth. It was only when Sophea suspended her modern, objectifying gaze that her disrupted world was made coherent and whole again; she 'saw' and communed with the king, and was healed.

These stories also speak of the necessity of the risky and inherently unstable marriage between the king, quintessence of humanity, and the natural realm, represented by the *naga*. The king is uniquely empowered; he may either virtuously uphold the natural order (*thommejeeut*) and further civilization (*arayethomm*) [20] or he may use his ego against the world, divorcing nature from culture and bringing about disfiguring disorder. These Cambodian women are, perhaps, collaborating in an effort to orchestrate a re-marriage.

The stories criticize today's leadership in Cambodia. Just as an unrighteous past king of Cambodia had once taken his sword to the honourable *naga* officials, so too, we learn, was the woman who foretold the high-ranking politician's naked death threatened by his wrath. The rampant selling off of the country's resources that is taking place in Cambodia lends fuel to Sophea's analogy between today's lack of wise leadership and the Longvek king; duped by tricksters, unvirtuous leaders give away Cambodia's riches and, with it, her integrity. As new forms of power enable consumer values to penetrate Cambodian culture and as the people rush to dig out and sell off the country's treasures, these two Cambodian critics see their world being dismembered. The vignettes here posit that it is only when the leader 're-members', marries and submits to the powers of the earth and spirits that his power will be life-sustaining and legitimate.

Partisan political interests may be worked out through myth, and we should bear in mind the party affiliations of the two women. Those who find protection in the shade of the current leaders' power[21] may appropriate similar themes to those of these stories, but in ways that contest the visions advanced here. However, I would maintain that these women are not simply the alter egos of a political party with a quasi-royalist agenda. Their mission, I submit, is not that of establishing new order cast in terms of multi-party democracy. It is, rather, to realign a world gone awry with the dictates of eternal truths – *dhamma* – to go back to the future. Kingliness, a quality which is not necessarily manifest in the person of all kings, is presented here as the preservation of cosmic balance. Stories like these depict one of the ways in which Cambodians may imagine a reconfigured order, by dredging up the country's legendary future from her drowned past.

AUTHOR'S NOTE

Warm thanks are due to the Bank of Sweden Tercentenary Foundation for generous support for this research and to Tou Seakhai for his meticulous field assistance.

REFERENCES

Ang Choulean (1997) 'Nandin and his Avatars', in H. I. Jessup and T. Zephir eds, *Sculpture of Angkor and Ancient Cambodia: Millenium of Glory.* London: Thames and Hudson, pp. 62–70.

Bertrand, D. (2004) 'A Medium Possession Practice and its Relationship with Cambodian Buddhism', in J. Marston and E. Guthrie eds *History, Buddhism and New Religious Movements in Cambodia.* Honolulu: University of Hawai'i Press, pp. 150–169.

Chandler, D. (1996) *Facing the Cambodian Past.* Chiang Mai: Silkworm Books.

—— 1998 [1983] *A History of Cambodia.* Chiang Mai: Silkworm Books.

Crouzatier, J.-M. (2001) 'Le Rôle Politique et Social du Bouddhisme au Cambodge', *Revue de Sciences Politiques.* Volume 46, pp. 19–28.

Eck, D. L. (1981) *Darsan: Seeing the Divine Image in India.* Chambersburg: Anima.

Foucault, M. (1973 [1963]) *The Birth of the Clinic.* London: Routledge.

Good, B. J. (1994) *Medicine, Rationality, and Experience: An Anthropological Perspective.* Cambridge: Cambridge University Press.

Harris, I. (2005) *Cambodian Buddhism: History and Practice.* Honolulu: University of Hawai'i Press.

—— ed. (1999) *Buddhism and Politics in Twentieth Century Asia.* London: Continuum.

Hinton, A. (2005) *Why Did They Kill? Cambodia in the Shadow of Genocide.* Berkeley: University of California Press.

Kent, A. (2005) *Divinity and Diversity: A Hindu Revitalization Movement in Malaysia.* Copenhagen: NIAS Press.

Keyes, C. F. (1994) 'Communist Revolution and the Buddhist Past in Cambodia', in C. F. Keyes, L. Kendall and H. Hardacre eds *Asian Visions of Authority: Religion and the Modern States of East and Southeast Asia*, Honolulu: University of Hawai'i Press.

Laderman, C. and Roseman, M. eds (1996) *The Performance of Healing.* London: Routledge.

Leclère, A. (1899) *Le Buddhisme au Cambodge*. Paris: Ernest Leroux.

Scheper-Hughes, N. (1987) 'The Mindful Body: a prolegomenon to future work in medical anthropology', *Medical Anthropology Quarterly*, Volume 1, pp. 6–41.

Swearer, D. (1995) 'Hypostasizing the Buddha: Buddha Image Consecration in Northern Thailand', *History of Religions*, Volume 34, pp. 271–279.

Tambiah, S. J. (1976) *World Conqueror: A Study of Buddhism and Polity in Thailand against a Historical Background*. Cambridge: Cambridge University Press.

—— (1990) *Magic, Science, Religion, and the Scope of Rationality*. Cambridge: Cambridge University Press.

Thompson, A. (2004a) 'The Future of Cambodia's Past: A Messianic Middle-Period', in J. Marston and E. Guthrie (eds) *History, Buddhism, and New Religious Movements in Cambodia*. Honolulu: University of Hawai'i Press, pp. 13-39.

—— (2004b) 'The Suffering of Kings: Substitute Bodies, Healing, and Justice in Cambodia', in J. Marston and E. Guthrie eds *History, Buddhism, and New Religious Movements in Cambodia*. Honolulu: University of Hawai'i Press, pp. 91–112.

NOTES

1   *Dhamma* (Pali, from Sanskrit, *dharma*) refers not only to the Buddha's teachings but to ultimate, eternal order.

2   Sihanouk's abdication of the throne in 2004 in favour of his son Sihamoni has done little to alter perceptions of him as the real king. A description of why this 'strategy of abdication' is so much a part of the choreographing of Cambodian kingship can be found in Thompson 2004b. 'The Suffering of Kings: Substitute Bodies, Healing, and Justice in Cambodia', in J. Marston and E. Guthrie eds, *History, Buddhism, and New Religious Movements in Cambodia*. Honolulu: University of Hawai'i Press, pp. 91–112.

3   The term *parami* is a Buddhist technical term derived from Sanskrit/Pali and means 'perfection'. It refers to the ten perfections achieved by the Buddha that enabled him to reach *nibbana*. In Cambodia the term is used popularly to refer to virtuous spirits, which make themselves apparent through a medium. A *parami* usually take the form of mythical or historical personality (see Bertrand 2004. 'A Medium Possession Practice and its Relationship with Cambodian Buddhism', in J. Marston and E. Guthrie eds, *History, Buddhism and New Religious Movements in Cambodia*. Honolulu: University of Hawai'i Press, pp. 150–169).

4   This person was an '*Oknya*' or high-ranking official. In the eighteenth century this title suggested relative proximity to central sources of power (see Chandler's 1983, p. 108 explanation).

5   Spiritually empowered people with matted hair are known in Khmer as *neak sok kandan*.

6   *Don chi*s normally shave their heads and eyebrows, and follow either eight or ten precepts.

7   This man was actually the younger brother of Chanta's mother's (Sophea's sister's) first husband, who died during the Khmer Rouge regime. Chanta's mother subsequently remarried and had three daughters, the second of whom is Chanta.

8   Lit. 'holder' or 'receptacle', representing the womb or vagina. Closely related to the *sivalinga*, it represents the potent matrix and container in which all existence is inherent and from which it emerges.

9   See Chandler 1996. *Facing the Cambodian Past*. Chiang Mai: Silkworm Books.

10 The relationship between sickness and breakdown of order is captured in the English language in the word 'disorder'.

11 Ang Choulean has discussed the continuity between Preah Ko and the Brahmanical vehicle of Siva and the function of the bull as Cambodia's palladium (Ang Choulean, 1997 'Nandin and his Avatars', in H. I. Jessup and T. Zephir eds, *Sculpture of Angkor and Ancient Cambodia: Millenium of Glory*. London: Thames and Hudson, pp. 62–70). The divine bull is associated with magical powers and mystical texts, specimens of which are hidden inside images of the bull. See also Forest's chapter in this volume.

12 The parallels with the biblical symbolism of forbidden fruit, female gender-marked original sin and the 'fall' are striking.

13 Legend has it that the founder of Cambodia was an Indian prince who fell in love with the *naga* king's daughter. When he married her, the *naga* king agreed to drain away part of the sea so that the land that was to become Cambodia would emerge (see Chandler 1983, p. 13).

14 Lit. 'a person with merit' though Sophea uses the term here to connote a 'righteous' person.

15 Sophea refers to American dollars, which are common currency in Cambodia.

16 The term *sima* refers to the monastic boundary that is ritually marked by the burial of boundary stones around the *preah vihear*. In Cambodia today eight stones are buried in pits at the cardinal and inter-cardinal points and a ninth, larger stone, is buried in front of the shrine. In this case the *sima* was to mark out a sacred-space-to-be, in anticipation of the removal of the small statue from the inner shrine and replacement of the drowned colossus.

17 *Sel* is the Khmer word for Buddhist precepts. The five precepts that lay Buddhists are supposed to keep are to refrain from lying, stealing, killing, having illicit sexual relations and taking intoxicants.

18 See, for example, Eck's discussion of the crucial importance of the eyes and 'seeing' in Indian religion (Eck 1981. *Darsan: Seeing the Divine Image in India*. Chambersburg: Anima).

19 This is the bone of contention picked up in his ethnography by Kobayashi Satoru (this volume), where older villagers argue that modern Buddhist consecration practice fails to transform the image from a mere representation into an empowered being.

20 Both of the Khmer words *thommajeeut* and *arayathomm* contain the root *thomm*, Khmer for *dhamma*. The concept of civilization is thus linguistically rendered not in contrast to nature, but as the refinement or ennoblement of the eternal laws of nature.

21 See Hinton's explication of the Khmer notion of powerful, protective 'shade' (Hinton 2005 *Why Did They Kill? Cambodia in the Shadow of Genocide.* Berkeley: University of California Press. p. 111)

CHAPTER 7

Between Forests and Families:
A remembered past life

Erik W. Davis

In an article that instituted the 'rice-field versus forest' dichotomy as an object of study among students of Cambodia, David Chandler analysed two folktales and a poetic family history, and determined that these stories provide 'contradictory, oddly satisfying answers' to the questions that pester discussions of moral order (Chandler 1996: 82). The contradictions are at least partly embodied in stories in which abandoned girls transform into birds, and crocodiles loyally but fatally attempt to serve their monastic masters. These contradictions and the satisfaction they provide do not arise from class or inter-group tensions but embody instead a single moral for all, with two interlocking parts. The first part, largely Buddhist, appeared as 'a celebration of hierarchical arrangements, operating, ideally, in the common good. The second was an attempt to survive inside the framework of what was going on' (Chandler 1996: 97).

In what follows, I review another, more contemporary, Cambodian story that also tacks its way between the two perceptions of moral order that Chandler delineates. In the process, I hope to indicate the ways in which the oppositional perception of a moral order which 'one might expect', remains embedded in narratives and lives, and how widespread identification with the values and desires of this oppositional order is managed. I believe that this process of managing the challenges to moral order provides the 'oddly satisfying' sentiment accompanying the answers.[1] I argue that these cases do not erase the oppositional from their expression, but rather re-code them to render oppositional values and desires extremely unappealing.[2] This chapter uses a few moments and memories in one person's remembered

Between forests and families: a remembered past life

lives to illuminate the representation of desire and the emotionally loaded division between the rice-fields and the forests.

My hypothesis is that we should look at morals and the concept of moral order in terms of the desiderata of the culture, that is to say, in terms of the cultural entities generally desired by social members. Further, we ought to examine those desiderata by exploring the cultural tensions that they articulate, as well as by analysing how these tensions are managed and the desiderata reproduced. Systematic, top-down analysis of these phenomena is invaluable, but neglects the intimately-felt desires such a system produces in its subjects. On the other hand, neglecting the systematic in favor of the individual risks leaving the stories we tell uprooted. Below, I shall move back and forth between these two perspectives, attempting to keep them both in view, as I examine one woman's story, and what it can tell us about the structures of 'moral order' in present-day Cambodian society.

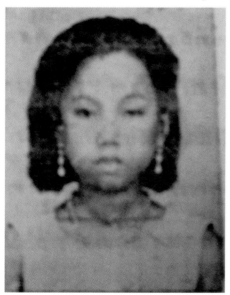

Figure 7.1. Miss Yaan as a girl (author's photo of image in 1961 'Pravatti Sangkhep Naii Nang Yaan' [A Brief History of Miss Yaan]. Ponleu Buddhicakra 3)

Miss Yaan[3] was born on Koh Suthin, Kompong Cham. A woman of standing and comfort, if not truly wealthy, she married and had two children. When her eldest was four years old, she died of what the high-ranking clerical author of her short biography called a fever, but which she herself explained was a broken heart. Shortly thereafter, she was reborn on top of a tree, a life to which I shall return shortly. After being reborn as a human being again, in Prei Veng province, she remembered her past two lives, and eventually convinced her birth family of the truth of her memories, to the extent that they took her to meet with the *Sanghareach* Chuon Nath in Phnom Penh, who determined that her memories were authentic. At the age of ten, she went with a relative to her previous lifetime's village (henceforth, references to her previous life's family and events will be denoted by the word 'original'), and led this relative to her old home, where she convinced her original family that she was indeed their mother, daughter, and sibling. Her younger siblings, now much advanced in age, and even her children, were all older than she, yet they all began calling her 'older sibling', and 'mother'. She in turn referred to them with the endearments used by those who are older towards charges in their care. Three years later, she was known to have moved 'back' to Koh Suthin, where she lived with her original father, who was then quite elderly and preparing to die.

Regarding her life on top of a tree, which took place between her two human lives, her own reminiscences tell us that she was born to a place where she had a mother to take care of her, and had a normal life. It was as if there were no day and no night, but it was always light. Any type of food she wanted to eat would immediately float to her side. When it rained she would take shelter in a hall (*sala*) or underneath the hut of a *bhikkhu*.[4] If some human came to cut down her tree, she would simply retreat to another place; she never got upset or angry with those people, but always avoided humans. When her siblings [from her previous life] performed ceremonies for her, and called her to come and find the food that they offered, she would go and eat the food and meet with her relatives. She would see a *bhikkhu* there as well, but the thought of paying homage to him never crossed her mind at all. During this period when she was born on top of a tree came a time when some groups of people had no food to eat – they were seen even picking the leaves of the shirt-button trees[5] and of the *prich* trees to eat. One day the mother who lived with her on top of the tree told her, 'Darling, go be reborn as a human being.' The young woman went out from there and saw her mother in this life harvesting rice. She entered into her mother's body and took root as a fetus in her mother's womb. (Kheum 1961)

This short but moving description contains a great deal of interest. The poetic language used to describe this life emphasizes the ease that a tree spirit enjoys. She has a mother to care for her, which roots her in the most crucial relationship of comfort in Khmer society – that of mother and child. There is no search for food, no need for labor, and the cycles of night and day have been replaced by a constant glow. The few things that might bother such a being, such as heavy rains, are easily endured by taking temporary shelter either in a *sala* (almost certainly in a temple complex) or underneath a monk's dormitory (*koti*). Timber harvest merely made her move to another tree, and did not cause her significant distress. One other aspect of this description reinforces the impression that life as a forest spirit is a life of ease in comparison with human life. Dying of a broken heart in her previous life, where she had given birth twice, she returned to take her next human birth in the body of a woman toiling in the rice fields during an apparent period of famine.

Another theme that emerges from this life as a tree spirit is the continuance of family relations throughout lives. She remembers and recognizes her original family, and is pleased to meet with them and receive their gifts. Later, when she takes rebirth in this life, she remembers her original human family and actively seeks them out, eventually rejoining that family in her original persona. As we shall see, she maintained her position in both human families, essentially welding them into one larger familial network with herself as the linchpin.

Finally, the narrative displays ambivalence towards Buddhist monks. Occupying the most holy position possible for human beings, the Buddhist monk presents himself as theoretically worthy of homage even by kings, his position spiritually and morally superseding all temporal authorities. Gifts given to the dead (such as those food offerings from her original family) are received through the intervention of the Buddhist monk. When rains fell, she sought shelter in temple settings, in *sala*s or underneath monastic dormitories. And although she noticed a monk during her time as a tree spirit, she felt no need whatsoever to pay homage to him.

I believe that we can see evidence of two distinct, oppositional perspectives on the questions of moral order in this story, as in the three examined by Chandler. The one perspective, emerging as a perspective from the forest, serves as a momentary and ultimately unsustainable critique of the other, that of the moral order of human life iconically represented by Buddhist monks. The latter effectively represents both the desires and motivations of the former, rendering the tree-spirit arcadia legitimately real but aligning it with an undesirable form of life. In the following, I shall examine the broader tensions in this disordered vision of social order before returning to the story of Miss Yaan to show how her lives and memories exist as an 'oddly satisfying' attempt to critique the order, and to make the best of her situation.

IDEOLOGICAL INVERSIONS AND THE MANAGEMENT OF DESIRE

Social structures interact with each other over years and generations, growing and developing relationships in much the same way as roots of various plants mesh and develop relationships of space and tension if left to their own devices. Yet danger surrounds them: wars can destroy them root and branch, leaving nothing but ash; or perhaps an invading structure will out-consume the older one, starving it to death. Relationships of all sorts develop over time, but like the plow, war excels precisely in the destruction of such relationships and the work of generations.

Almost to the present day in Cambodia, rice has served as the material basis of wealth and power. Land and the control of enough human power to grow rice were the basic sources of social power. The daily life of everyone in the kingdom today, including those not directly concerned with the production of rice, remains intimately concerned with its cultivation. The organization of riziculture supports the formation of specific desires and representations of 'normal' village life. The religious worldview unsurprisingly draws its characteristics most strongly from the prescriptions given to the peasants by some of those who do not themselves grow rice (kings, monks, students). The imagination expresses itself out of the materials supplied from these different sources.

The social imagination that has persisted and continues to grow into the present provides the language of desire and grows with the desires themselves. Field and forest are ideological pure types. The dualism of such division, so common in anthropology and religious thought, creates tension when exploited by the supporters of one side. We ought to understand such dualisms as influenced by a preceding decision – how to divide land and life into a symbolic dualism. This type of social imagination is more than a veneer laid over abstract and universal desires. Rather, such imaginings help create desire.

Wars have plowed through Cambodia's last two hundred years, uprooting the networks re-established in every temporary peace. The continuity of the social imagination, and the practices which perpetuate it, have assisted in producing a sense of continuity across the dark years when everything seems to burn and terror transforms its victims into other types of beings, who seek shelter where they can, including the forests that they fear. It has also produced a geography of desire, in which the forest and the field exist and symbolize desires.

I shall briefly examine a few of the desires encoded in the Khmer imagination, and the social consequences that follow from that. I shall do this through a brief examination of the process of hierarchy and power-building associated with the subsistence strategy – wet-rice agriculture – which demanded both the creation, and the creative efforts, of the Khmer people, caught between the forests and the elites, living their lives in the fields.

FAMILY

One of the dichotomies embodied in Chandler's stories as well as in Miss Yaan's is that between autonomy and dependence, which is powerfully illustrated in the workings of the Khmer family.[6] This dichotomy is perhaps the most crucial one. A person must at least belong to a group recognizable as a family, and he or she emerges into society with the help of those simultaneously most intimate and interdependent of people – the family group.[7]

Students of Cambodia have often taken the Khmer family to be a paradigm for elaboration of extra-familial hierarchies; notably, the Cambodian familial relationship seems structured according to poles of intimacy and distance (Népote 1992). The more intimate one's relationship with another, the more hierarchical that relationship, such as in the case of mother and child. The Cambodian family maps larger Cambodian society more flexibly than does the traditional Western family. Family boundaries appear loose, and various types of adoption, god-parenting, and other forms of 'fictive kinship' have been documented. One's created family, in addition to one's birth family, produces the known and civilized world that we inhabit. This network of family members defines and delimits the boundaries of the social world, the land in which one may safely travel, the people one may trust and upon whom one may rely, and the networks of intimacies that compose our emotional geographies, those spaces where we recognize the emotional landmarks, and where we can navigate with more experience and confidence than with strangers. People say that this is true of family members all the way, potentially, to the 'seventh generation', but in practice it is said precisely to assert some sort of kinship with relative strangers.

What can this mean for a discussion of a moral order, or for Miss Yaan's attempt to find her place within it? I consider three interlocking points most important. Firstly, the family is a paradigm for extra-familial relations and intimate extra-familial relations are therefore expressed in familial terms. Secondly, the extensibility of the family model to other aspects of social order appears as both product and cause of the second point – that families themselves lack clear-cut boundaries, and often include biologically unrelated people. Finally, individual power comes not only from one's incorporation into the social categories which rank prestige, such as masculinity, age, and wealth, but also from placing oneself in relationships of hierarchy and dependence upon others. Social power does not emerge from one's independence and autonomy but from one's place in what can feel simultaneously empowering and intimate, as well as crushingly oppressive. One's ability to create new networks of 'family' relations, especially if one can place oneself in a position of relative power vis-à-vis these new kin, may assist one in achieving personal success within the moral order. Miss Yaan's past-life memory has not only enabled her to join two families together into a single kin group, with her as the linchpin, but it has also allowed her to extend her own family network by placing herself in a hierarchically superior position to people older than herself, through their acceptance of her as their mother and older sibling.[8]

AGRICULTURE

An anthropological commonplace holds that a great deal can be discerned about a culture by examining the subsistence strategies it employs. Indeed, the choice of early Cambodian elites to engage in wet-rice agriculture demanded in turn the production and maintenance of a population of human laborers to work the fields and produce an agricultural surplus, which could then be extracted from them. Without a surplus, those elements we think of as composing civilization – those things we desperately desire, perhaps most especially agricultural foods like rice – are simply impossible.

On the contrary, in an increasingly venerable tradition stemming from Richard Lee and Marshall Sahlins among others, we often consider that life as a forager, without competition from expanding agriculturalists, would seem considerably easier, healthier, and more egalitarian than life as an agriculturalist, unless of course one is ruling an agricultural group.[9]

The pulsating expansion and contraction of lowland chiefdoms, kingdoms, and empires has at different times made serious and often successful attempts to integrate highlander groups, who were traditionally almost exclusively hunting and foraging groups, often also practicing low-intensity shifting cultivation. Indeed, these groups are the wellsprings from whence Khmer emerge. Zhou Da Guan reported massive numbers of slaves during the Angkorean period, kidnapped or taken by force from forest groups and mountain tribes. Chandler comments appropriately that 'It seems likely, in fact, that this is the way Cambodian society built itself up, over time, gradually absorbing and socializing "barbarians", who figure in such large numbers in the inscriptions in Angkorean times' (Chandler 2000, 72). These raids and slaving expeditions, from whom so many modern Khmer must descend, undoubtedly contributed to the well-known tensions between lowland and highland groups on the peninsula, and must have created new social representations and practices for both the slavers and the enslaved.

The problem for would-be rulers appears therefore to have lain in keeping their workers on the farm, in the *srok*, and preventing them from returning to the forests. My argument hinges on the inversion of categories common to forms of consciousness, perhaps especially the 'moral orders' that we have commonly termed ideologies. One solution to the ruler's problem is to represent the forests as places of fearful death and wild power, and the *srok* as places full of families, rice, and the artifacts of civilized life.

Judy Ledgerwood's (1990) doctoral dissertation describes the ways in which the feminine spirits of the forest are represented as malevolent, demanding spirits filled with unquenchable desire.[10] Ang Choulean, in his recent book on the *pralung* (vivifying spirits), mentions that illness attributed to the loss of the *pralung*, occurs when '[the] spirits of the forest lure some of the pralung out of the body and into the forest by conjuring up false and seductive images of their domain which is, in reality, wild and harsh.' (Ang 2004: 2)

The gendered division of territory strikes me with particular force. The forests, places of death and wildness, appear feminized as sites of unrestrained generation, while agricultural land appears as masculine space of ordered, civilized production. The spirits which vivify the Cambodian landscape are similarly mapped – feminine spirits and child spirits in the forests and in private homes, with generally masculine spirits such as *neak ta*s marking places of habitation. Monks also mark and create habitable space and unlike most other humans, can sometimes tame and conquer the wild spirits of the forests.

Chandler outlines in his article the dichotomy between forest and field, but others are also relevant to Khmer society and provide extra emphasis to the life desired by Cambodians. Cambodians have typically gendered the work of rice production, so that men create the conditions for riziculture through plowing, while women pull the seedlings and dominate the transplantation, only to return the harvested product to men for the perfecting work of threshing. Such gendering of basic work exemplifies the ways in which the main cultural desideratum of Cambodian life – rice – is classified in a way that preserves the hierarchical arrangements that make Khmer social life recognizable through generations, and keep people on the farm.[11]

Life in the forest has become, over the course of Cambodia's agricultural and political histories, a potential and situation-dependent utopia for those who find themselves working long hours in fields under unjust conditions. When such a coincidence of conditions emerges, the forest beckons, for it provides refuge from the homogenizing civilizational work of the dominant ideology, the dominant conception of a moral order, in Cambodian society. The ideological labor of articulating a moral order in Cambodia has taken previously disparate elements and welded them together, opposing them to other disparate elements. This labor creates a cultural dualism that organizes desire just as it (mis)represents space.

Cambodians have mapped these values onto the land – the forest and the rice-field, wildness and civilization, death and life, female and male. Some of these elements seem not to fit together: how can death and femaleness go together? To look at the numbers of women engaged in the labor of death-dealing, or the numbers of men engaged in reproducing life, we might well question such a combination. It certainly deserves examination.

This inverting reclassification of worlds can intervene effectively (Lincoln 1989). Both the realms of the forest and the field are realms of growth and life, but the types of life present in each realm are strikingly different. The field represents the ordered, the realm of civilized production, where rice is grown, collected, eaten, and presented in tribute, where homes, palaces and temples are built, where kings rule and society is ordered in a structured manner considered moral, and legitimated by religion. The forest is the realm of wild, superabundant generation, where all manner of life, both vegetal and animal, often terrifying, lives and thrives. It is the realm in which powerful nonhuman spirits dwell, where hunters enter at great peril to themselves, and where, in specially demarcated areas, the dead are occasionally buried (*prei khmouch*) (Ang 1986: 103–104). By means of this reclassification, the forest becomes quite literally not only the land of the dead, but also a land of exaggerated life and generation.[12]

THE CONTINUING LIVES OF MISS YAAN

The article in which I learned about Miss Yaan was published over forty years ago. I had little hope of locating her, since the combination of normal living and the traumas of the last four Cambodian decades could have wrought any combination of circumstances, making her difficult or impossible to find. Following my only lead, the site of her last residence in Kompong Cham when she was 13, I traveled there in August 2005, and after a number of inquiries, was led to a nearby temple. 'Grandmother' Yaan continues to live in the town of her original human birth in Kompong Cham province, as a *don chi*, or lay-nun. I reviewed the article from 1961 with her, since she had never seen it, and asked her to elaborate on the story and bring it up to date.

Grandmother Yaan remembers her past lives, and has, amazingly, kept her two families linked around her. She cared for her original father until his death, thereafter returning to school. Her aged mother from this life married her off at the age of 16, to a teacher who died shortly after the fall of Phnom Penh as a recent inductee into Lon Nol's armed forces. During the DK regime she moved with her three children and her mother, and although she survived the regime, she lost one child and her mother, and was nearly murdered herself.

After the Vietnamese invasion, she returned as soon as she could to her original home in Kompong Cham province and found the remaining members of her family from her previous life. She even located a half-brother from this life of whom she had not previously known, and who now serves as the abbot of the temple where she lives.

She emerged from the period of Democratic Kampuchean rule with many of the losses suffered by other Cambodians. But she also possesses a genius for reconstructing families, something she had been doing her entire life. The power that made these reconstructions possible was her memory and her desire to reconnect with those loved ones with whom she still shares, as she puts it, a destiny (*upanisaya*). What I find so interesting about her memory of past lives is the constant application of that memory to the reconstruction and expansion of the networks that link her to other human beings, placing her in a central position.

Just as the control of human labor characterized imperial modes of power during Angkor, access to human networks of power and status – relationships with those who might be able to help you, and who feel obliged to do so because of family connections – continue to permeate the power structures of modern-day Cambodia. At one point even I, a foreigner with a nose like a knife and the height of an ogre, was adopted by Grandmother Yaan: 'Now I feel that I have three surviving children to whom I gave birth', she said, including me in the count of her children from both this life and the past.

Yet Grandmother Yaan's positive genius for creating connections does not grow like a cancer, undifferentiated, consuming and incorporating all those with whom it contacts. Again, her memory plays the decisive role. Still a young girl of eleven when her original husband died, her original son, then aged fifteen, asked her to attend his father's funeral. She agreed to go to the one hundred day ceremony, but refused, despite repeated requests, to burn incense for his spirit, fearing that this would link their *kamma* in the future. This man, she recalled, had broken her heart in her previous life by having an affair with a *lkhaon*[13] actress in the troupe he managed, and she had died of this heartbreak. She wanted nothing more to do with him. She explained her refusal by claiming that performing acts of *bon* together creates networks of destiny.[14] Despite the fact that he had remarried after her death, and had eight children – a veritable treasure-trove of human wealth and connections – she refused to continue a connection with the man on whose account she had previously died. In this act of refusal are embedded the elements of the clerical monopoly on death; it is ritual action, managed and supervised by the officials of Buddhism, that creates a destiny linking two individuals together. Her refusal to allow that destiny to be maintained both acknowledges that clerical power, and expresses a desire for freedom, at least in this instance, from what it entails.

I have wanted to demonstrate the power of such practices to both create and manage desire, even at the level of a single individual. This is not to say that individuals acting in accord with the categories of the cosmos in which they live are automatons, but rather that the distinctive way in which the Buddhist imaginaire recodes the world makes it extraordinarily difficult to desire what is not permitted. Grandmother Yaan's memory and the desires created or explained by it, move her to act in ways that contest and confirm the Buddhist moral order.

The power of such productive desire results from the careful recoding of the seemingly natural symbolic associations in the cosmos: from the assimilation of female generation and reproductive power to the suffering existence held to be the lot of humanity, or else to the deathly spirits that haunt the forests. Forests themselves are gendered, made feminine and both horrifyingly abundant and full of life-in-death. They mirror the male fields and villages that have been tamed, civilized, and made safe for agriculture. Agriculture, impossible in the forests, produces that most necessary food, rice, itself embodied with a soul of its own until its death nourishes our lives. Agriculture also, not coincidentally, creates the basis of all pre-modern political power in Cambodia, the basis of an economy of extraction without which the hierarchies that populate Khmer society are rendered senseless.

The world represented to us as human is full of those things we desire, and appears to exist in direct opposition to those other things, which we dimly imagine might be possible in the other, non-human places of our world. These places – like the forests and mountains which occupy such an important place in Khmer spiritual geographies – are marked as uninhabitable by those whose demands and representations contribute to the production and management of some of our most deeply-felt desires. And yet these other things are still imagined. Grandmother Yaan's life as a tree spirit entices with its inviting vision of leisure and plenty. When asked to compare life as a human with that as a ghost, she told me that:

> Life is easier as a ghost – it's not difficult like that of human beings. Whatever I wanted to eat immediately came to me; I was never scared or anxious about working or finding enough to eat. Moreover, I never had to cook. I don't know where the food came from, but whatever I wanted appeared instantly. It wasn't like human food. I only had to see it to be satiated … If I wanted to go up into the house, I didn't climb the stairs like a human being, but floated upwards. Anywhere I wanted to go, I could go instantly … But that life isn't entirely free of pain either – if we haven't exhausted our *kamma*, we will have to return and be born again as a human being.

As for human lives, when asked which of her human lives was preferable, she replied:

> It's not easy to answer that question, because all life is so difficult. We human beings are always suffering. Even if we have wealth, we might be depressed. I was wealthy in my last life, but had lots of emotional worries. This life is very good. My husband had no other woman; why come and take

me and then immediately go off with some gold-digger? But life is always like this … I only want to escape suffering – whatever place is free of it, that's where I want to be.[15]

Grandmother Yaan's temporary but glorious life as a ghost in the forests was never a permanent possibility. Her memory of that life of ease and luxury remains, but the possibilities of offending against the seemingly stable order of the cosmos are few. Her life as a ghost represents explicitly the 'life of death'. Indeed, although the *Sanghareach* declared that she had been a type of spirit known as a Vegetal Spirit (*arukkhadevata*), she uses the word *khmouch*, signifying either a dead spirit, or a dead body. A desire for a life better than this one, with all its attendant struggles, wants, and oppressions, transforms precisely into the life impossible, the life-in-death, which marks the limits of extreme desire. These wrenching conditions can summon up a mood described by one observer as,

> between contentment and despair, in which suffering appears so associated with existence that we would willingly give up one with the other, and look forward with a sort of hope to that silent void where, if there are no smiles, there are at least no tears, and since the heart cannot beat, it will not ever be broken.[16]

We thus return to the foundational dictum of Buddhist thought. All life is stained with suffering, and the illusions of joy, plenty, and leisure merely provide the pride before the fall. For all things die and change according to the law of impermanence. The only achievement that can last is that of *nibbana* (Sanskrit: *nirvana*) – the unconditioned state of non-being, which calms not by the satisfaction of desire but by ripping desire out root and branch. Only achieving *nibbana* can calm the suffering we inherit at our birth.

> In the meantime, the world as we experience it, in multiple lives and nations, rolls on. Our lives, momentarily occupying various roles and positions, trudge forward, now experiencing a moment of gladness, followed by the sufferings of that joy's passing.

Grandmother Yaan's tales and memories help to clarify how we structure and maintain our world: where we can live, with whom we have relations, and the necessity of remaining in a society where hierarchy and hard labor are life's defining characteristics. We can only temporarily delay the world

Figure 7.2 Miss Yaan as a woman

with a flight to the forest; eventually we must return to the fields if we want to eat and live in civilization. Building families and relations appears a necessary part of surviving in that world; that in Grandmother Yaan's case this happens partly through an exceptional circumstance testifies to the power of death to manage desire. After all, her multiple remembered deaths gave her the power to reconstruct lost families. Her unusual memory provides her with the power to bridge the chasm of death, and expand the number of familial relations upon which she can rely. The extent of her social network marks her relative power and potential for social advancement. Her memory in turn forms the basis of that social network's unusually broad reach.

These days Grandmother Yaan lives as a lay-nun, dedicating herself to *vipassana* meditation and *dhamma* study. Her desires now do not include a return to life as a ghost, but to escape life altogether. The allure of death remains, and the non-being of *nibbana* offers her a way out of the choices between the forest and the field.

AUTHOR'S NOTE

I find myself grateful to many people for their help in encouraging and improving this paper, itself a substantially reduced version of a section in my forthcoming dissertation. Pong Pheakdey Boramy of the Buddhist Institute first brought the article about Miss Yann to my attention; Alexandra Kent organized a stimulating and successful workshop, and David Chandler provided much needed encouragement and suggestions. Special thanks also to Steven Collins of the University of Chicago, and Judy Ledgerwood for close readings, suggestions, and discussions of the issues involved. I dedicate this article to my own family, which expands with every new friend.

REFERENCES

Ang Choulean (1986) *Les êtres surnaturels dans la religion populaire khmer*. Paris: Cedorek.

—— (2004) *Brah Ling*. Phnom Penh, Cambodia: Reyum Publishing.

Bloch, M., and J. Parry (1982) *Death and the Regeneration of Life*. Cambridge & New York: Cambridge University Press.

Chandler, David P. (1996) 'Songs at the edge of the forest: perceptions of order in three Cambodian texts.' In D. P. Chandler ed. *Facing the Cambodian past. Selected essays 1971–1994*, pp. 76–99. Chiang Mai: Silkworm Books.

—— (2000) *A History of Cambodia*, 3rd edition. Boulder, CO.: Westview Press.

Collins, S. (1998) *Nirvana and other Buddhist Felicities. Utopias of the Pali imaginaire*. Cambridge: Cambridge University Press.

Day, T. (1996) 'Ties that (un)bind: families and states in premodern Southeast Asia.' *Journal of Asian Studies*, Vol. 55, pp. 384–409.

Kheum, T., Ven. (1961) Pravatti Sangkhep Naii Nang Yaan [A Brief History of Miss Yaan] *Ponleu Buddhicakra* 3.

Ledgerwood, J. (1990) 'Changing Khmer conceptions of gender: women, stories, and the social order.' Doctoral dissertation. Cornell University.

Lee, R. (1968) 'What hunters do for a living, or, How to make out on scarce resources.' In R. Lee and I. DeVore eds *Man the hunter*. Chicago: Aldine.

—— (1969) 'Kung Bushmen subsistence: an input-output analysis.' In A. Vayda ed. *Environment and Cultural Behavior*. Garden City (NY): Natural History Press.

Lincoln, B. (1989) *Discourse and the Construction of Society: comparative studies of myth, ritual, and classification*. New York: Oxford University Press.

Népote, J. (1992) *Parenté et Organisation Sociale dans le Cambodge Moderne et Contemporain. Quelques aspects et quelques applications du modèle les régissant*. Geneva: Olizane/Etudes Orientales & CEDORECK/Bibliothèque Khmère.

Sahlins, M. D. (1972) *Stone Age Economics*. London, New York: Routledge.

Turner, V. W. (1957) *Schism and Continuity in an African Society: a study of Ndembu village life*. Manchester: Manchester University Press.

Van Gennep, A. (1960) *The Rites of Passage*. Chicago: University of Chicago Press.

NOTES

1. This hardly seems novel; rather, I build here on the voluminous works of other anthropologists, sociologists, and historians who have examined the expression of ritual, myth, and other cultural expressions for (a) challenges to the social order, and (b) the incorporation and management of those challenges. Classic examples in the world of ritual include Van Gennep's (1960) fundamental work on the category *The rites of passage*, Turner's (1957) *Schism and continuity in an African society: a study of Ndembu village life*, and Bloch and Parry's (1982) *Death and the regeneration of life*.

2. In this way, I hope to extend rather than challenge Chandler's insights. As he points out, the dual impulses behind these stories do not allow for divergent modes of action, but rather reaffirm the sole licensed social structure.

3. The following description of Neang Yaan's life is excerpted from Venerable Kheum Tor's piece, published in 1961 (Kheum 1961. *Pravatti Sangkhep Naii Nang Yaan* [A Brief History of Miss Yaan]. *Ponleu Buddhicakra* 3).

4. The word *bhikkhu* refers to a fully-ordained monk of at least twenty years of age.

5. *Daem Lev Av, Phyllantus emblica*, a kind of tree used in traditional medicine.

6. It certainly appears at the heart of family structures far beyond the Cambodian situation as well, as a brief survey of other Southeast Asian societies will confirm. Although the structured hierarchies of the Khmer family may appear extreme, I believe that we can find the same tendencies almost universally: the link between feelings of respect and feelings of emotional intimacy may indeed inhere in the process of raising human children.

7. A family may naturally take a mind-boggling array of shapes and sizes, but we ought to consider it the unit of society just more complex than the individual. To say that humans have families is to articulate, in capsule form, ideas about family that persist in Cambodian society. It is not to say that the family is a stable form of social organization, as modern regimes throughout Southeast Asia often attempt to assert. Nevertheless, the family form has often had both state-building and state-disrupting effects in Southeast Asia. See Day (1996) 'Ties that (un)bind: families and states in pre-modern Southeast Asia.' *Journal of Asian Studies* 55: 384–409.

8. Importantly, despite the acceptance of her previous identity by her former family, Miss Yaan carefully pointed out to me that her children from this life received none of the heritable property owned by her in her past life. The two patrimonies (matrimonies would be more appropriate here) were kept strictly separated. Her statement indicates the resistance of lineages of inheritance to interventions of past-life memory and the relative strength of practices intended to preserve familial property.

9. The well-known studies of Richard Lee first brought this issue to the fore of contemporary anthropological study. See Lee (1968) 'What hunters do for a living,

or, How to make out on scarce resources' (1969); also 'Kung bushmen subsistence: an input-output analysis' Sahlins (1972) *Stone Age Economics*.

10 Ledgerwood (1990) cites Ang (1986) *Les êtres surnaturels dans la religion populaire khmer* in 'Changing Khmer conceptions of gender: women, stories, and the social order.'

11 In the increasing number of areas where much of the processing work is mechanized, the performance of this work seems to become less divided according to gender, though the different activities remain understood as men's or women's work.

12 The opposition in Indic thought between *prakrit* and *sanskrit* may also be applicable here. *Prakrit* means natural, while *sanskrit* means perfected, and the categories are evaluated accordingly. The *prakrit* world is the world of original generation, but is full of the negative, crude, aspects of that world, which in the *sanskrit* are expunged. The production of beautiful poetry, a glorious temple or palace, or a well performed ritual, are examples of Sanskritic production. Rice, the food that provides so much of the nutrition in Cambodian society, is grown entirely in the field and, by definition, cannot grow in the wild (I refer here of course only to lowland varieties, which comprise the basis of Khmer agriculture).

13 *Lkhaon* is a traditional type of lyric opera, presenting traditional stories, often drawn from the Ramayana.

14 Space does not permit exploration of the full complexity of the word *bon* (Sanskrit: *punya*) here. It can be glossed as the performance of a moral or ritual act charged with good intentions.

15 Author interview, 9 September 2005.

16 Quoted from an interview given by Eric Griffiths, reprinted in Collins (1998) *Nirvana and other Buddhist felicities. Utopias of the Pali imaginaire.*

SECTION III
Remaking Moral Worlds

CHAPTER 8

Buddhist Practice in Rural Kandal Province, 1960 and 2003
An essay in honor of May M. Ebihara

Judy Ledgerwood

If you ask rural Khmer about Buddhism today you are likely to get the reply that Buddhism is much the same as it was before war and revolution devastated their country. What is different today, they will say, is the morality of the people, their inability to live according to the tenets of Buddhism. This theme is consistent with a standard discourse of crisis and reformation in Buddhist history – time is cyclical with periods of glory, prosperity and long life that alternate with periods of death, destruction and despair. On the one hand, the current focus on such cycles is the foundation for millenarian movements and undercurrents in contemporary Khmer Buddhism. On the other hand, it raises the possibility of Buddhism as unchanging or even unchangeable – what is it about Buddhism in Cambodia that is perceived as having remained the same through the upheavals of the last thirty years?

In what follows I discuss this question by addressing the issue of religious practice in village communities.[1] If practitioners perceive their religion as the same, while dramatic changes have occurred in the structures of the religion, in the religious leaders, in the available religious texts, in certain forms of iconography and styles of religious expression, what can be the reasons for this perception? Approaching the problem from the perspective of practice, we can argue that people move, act, and perform their religious belief in ways that parallel their actions and movements of the pre-war years. Using Bourdieu's notion of 'habitus', we can think of these patterns not as consciously learned rules and principles, but as internalized results of cultural experiences, particularly those we have as young children.

What remains the same from the pre-war years in Cambodian Buddhism is the practice of merit making, the way that adult Cambodians enact the religion in their daily lives. They make choices from within a range of options that are embodied as habitus, their learned ways of thinking, feeling, speaking, moving, and so on, that come from their cultural experiences, especially their experiences as young people.

We take as a touchstone for descriptions of pre-war religious practice in rural villages the research of May Ebihara conducted in southern Kandal province in 1959–1960, in particular her doctoral dissertation (1968) and an article entitled 'Interrelations between Buddhism and Social Systems in Cambodian Peasant Culture' (1966). The research for this paper was conducted in six villages in rural Kandal province, including the village where Ebihara did her research. The ethnographic descriptions of Buddhist practice are thus not only separated across time, but also across the dramatic rupture of the desecration of religion during the Democratic Kampuchea period, and the slow process of re-establishing and reconfiguring Khmer Buddhism that is the broader topic of this volume.

CONTEXT OF THE RESEARCH

Research for this paper was conducted in the summer of 2003 as an ethnographic field school sponsored by Northern Illinois University and the Royal University of Fine Arts (RUFA). Combined research teams of American and Khmer students conducted the research in six temples in Kandal province.[2] Across the six villages, the students conducted 141 surveys with questions on Buddhist practice and ideas about Buddhism and society.[3] They performed one exercise in structured observation, kept field notes of their own observations, and conducted structured and semi-structured interviews with monks, temple committee members (*achar*s), nuns and community residents. The primary purpose of the exercise was to train students in research methodology, but the program also garnered interesting data on the daily activities in the six temples.

The temples are located in two districts, one to the east of the Mekong River and the other south of Phnom Penh. In the river district, the farmers are primarily *neak camkar*, gardening or plantation producers. Farmers in the district to the south grow wet season rice; they are *neak srai*, 'rice people' who live primarily from subsistence agriculture, though they may sometimes be able to sell some surplus. The communities are not representative of Cambodia as a whole because they are so close to Phnom Penh. Their position allows for farm income to be supplemented with wage labor in the city; some 30 per cent of households interviewed had a member working in Phnom Penh.

BUDDHIST PRACTICE

May Ebihara wrote in 1966 that in regard to Buddhist teachings,

> the intricacies of Theravada doctrine are little known to the average villager (except perhaps to those men who have been monks for extended periods of time). But certain basic precepts are known to all of them from sermons at the temple, chants or prayers committed to memory, or lessons at school … the concept of achieving merit and avoiding evil is the basic principle underlying the influence of religion on behavior. (Ebihara 1966: 177)

Cambodians say 'twer bon baan bon, twer baap, baan baap' – if you do good, you will receive good, if you do evil, you will receive evil. The results of one's accumulation of merit can be made manifest in this lifetime, with material rewards or an increase in status; or may result in a better rebirth in the next life.

The focus on merit making that Ebihara observed in 1959–1960 is also central to laypeople when they talk about Buddhism today. When asked about the role of the temple in their communities, respondents focused on the importance of being able to make merit by making offerings to the monks. Ebihara's 1966 study delineates four main practices through which merit could be earned: by ordaining as a monk, by adhering to the Buddhist precepts, by observing 'holy days' (*thngai sel*), and by gifts to the temple and the monks (pp. 177–178).[4] This paper is organized following Ebihara's categories, addressing how and by whom each of these methods of merit making is performed today.

ORDINATION

There were some 60,000 men serving as monks in pre-war Cambodia at any given time, a number that dropped to nearly zero between 1975 and 1979. The *sangha* rebuilt slowly in the 1980s, with an estimated 2,311 monks in 1982 and about 20,000 in 1991 (Keyes 1994: 62–63). With the restriction on ordination removed and new state support for Buddhism, the *sangha* grew rapidly to 50,081 by 1998–1999, 55,755 in 2003 (Ministry of Cults and Religion 1999, 2003), and to 58,828 in 2005 (Khy, this volume).

Who ordains and why? Ordination historically was the path to education, and most men were literate because they had ordained for at least a short period before they married, usually for at least one rainy season, but often for two or three years. Ordination was also a rite of passage; once a man had been a monk, his status in the community was permanently changed, he was considered mature, and a proper candidate for marriage.[5] Men who served longer periods as monks were respected in their communities and often became *achar* (lay officiants) or community leaders or both (see Yang Sam 1987: 23).

In 1959–1960, when Ebihara conducted her fieldwork, she found that some three-quarters of all the men in West Svay over 17 had been monks, remaining for an average of two to three years (Ebihara 1966: 177). But she also noted that with the rise of secular education, the number of young men choosing to ordain was declining, and among the young men under 19 none had yet sought ordination or seemed to have any immediate plans to do so (ibid.: 183). Drawing on statistics from one village in Kompong Cham, Malada Kalab found that before 1930 or so virtually all men ordained. Thereafter the numbers decline, reaching a low point of about 10 per cent in 1960 (just at the time that Ebihara noticed the decline). Kalab argues that a turning point was reached in 1963, when the government decided to recognize the certificates issued by monastic institutions as equivalent to those issued by secular institutions (Kalab 1976: 164).

In this period, even though state schools were theoretically free, education for poor boys was largely limited to primary school. To have gained further education, they would likely have had to live away from home and pay for board. Even if they lived in temples in the city, they had to pay for clothes and books. Further, Kalab found that since many schools were newly built, they charged 'fees' for construction costs and that some teachers 'demanded bribes' (Kalab 1976: 164). While girls were completely out of luck, poor smart boys had the option of ordaining and pursuing monastic education. This possibility seems to have saved the monkhood from further decline in the 1960s; after the recognition of monastic certificates, the number or ordinations rose again (ibid.: 165).

A similar situation has been recurring recently – most young men ordaining as novices in Cambodia today are poor rural boys seeking an alternative to the secular education system, which is too expensive for them. As in the 1960s, although the state education system is theoretically free, teachers charge a range of 'fees' to students.[6] For most rural families who live off subsistence agriculture, education costs are the greatest cash expense that they face annually.

The young men who ordain without the goal of studying in the monastic education system tend to ordain for shorter periods of time, perhaps for only a month or two, in part because the full three months of the rainy season (that was once the customary period for short term ordinations) overlaps with the academic school year (Chhorn Iem interview 18 March 2003).[7]

Men who were monks before the revolution and who re-ordained after 1979, and men who ordained in the 1980s when they were over 50, are now very elderly and many are dying. Nadezhda Bektimirova notes that a sharp increase in the number of temples, from about 1,500 to over 3,500 in the mid-1990s, has meant that there is a severe shortage of qualified leaders (2002: 63). Khy Sovanratana, in this volume, writes that the total number of temples in 2005 had reached 4,106; he also notes a severe shortage of qualified teachers for Buddhist schools.

Regarding the number of men ordaining in rural villages today, there are limited data available. In our research across six villages, we found that 33 out of 135 households said that someone in their house was or had been a monk (24 per cent). But if one counts only those who had ordained since 1979, the number falls to 9 of 135 or 6.6 per cent. Kobayashi found similar numbers in a village in Kompong Thom: 17.2 per cent across all age groups, but 5.9 per cent of men aged 20 to 24, 5 per cent of men aged 25 to 29 and 3.7 per cent of men aged 30 to 34 (Kobayashi 2004: 510). In the six temples that we studied there were 66 monks, 39 novices and 27 *bhikkhu*s. Three of the abbots were under 35 years old, the youngest was 28. Interestingly, in five of the six temples the majority of the monks did not come from the local communities.

When asked why they had ordained, monks gave a range of answers, including the opportunity for education, repaying the debt of gratitude that they owed to their parents, improving their karma, and for some elders, wanting to withdraw from the world. Two young novices mentioned that at their temples there was enough food to eat, implying that food supplies were not adequate in their home communities. The issue of men ordaining and moving to *wat*s in this area near Phnom Penh may be related to the broader issue of migration from poorer areas of the country to wealthier areas with more opportunities.[8] In two of the temples monks were studying in a nearby town or city. Some were studying in private English classes; one was enrolled in an MBA program.

For monks who are able to advance up the monastic educational system to upper secondary school and university (see Khy, this volume), the city offers a range of new opportunities. Perhaps rather ironically, given their vows of poverty, the lives of such educated monks are now associated with learning English, having access to computers, cell phones and other technology, and perhaps the possibility of foreign travel.

THE PRECEPTS

In order to achieve the goal of securing a better rebirth, Buddhists seek to avoid demerit (*bap*) by following the five precepts:

I undertake the precept to abstain from taking life.

I undertake the precept to abstain from taking what is not given.

I undertake the precept to abstain from improper sexual acts.

I undertake the precept to abstain from telling lies.

I undertake the precept to abstain from imbibing or ingesting substances which cause heedlessness. (Cited in Keyes 1995: 117–118)

While these imperatives are understood to be at the core of Buddhist morality, Ebihara observed that they were followed 'with varying degrees of fidelity' (1966: 177). In her research the first precept against killing was viewed as the most important. She tells the story of a villager who killed someone during the Issarak period and was subsequently ostracized and barred from the village. Now, in a country emerging from 30 years of war, it is likely that many former soldiers have violated this precept.[9]

Ebihara also noted that the injunction against taking life applied to animals. Cambodians in pre-war society would buy their meat and fish already slaughtered by members of other ethnic groups, usually Chinese or Cham. She reported that some devout elders refused to raise animals that were nurtured only to be killed (Ebihara 1966:184). When families did raise such animals, care for them usually fell to women. When it was necessary to kill a chicken or other small animal, the task was often assigned to a child, who was thought to 'know nothing', and thus could avoid the stain of sin that the act entailed (Ebihara 1968: 395). Among the families that Ebihara knew 40 years ago, some now raise animals for sale and slaughter. One woman explained to me that while she knew that her now deceased parents would not have approved, she allows her adopted daughter to raise pigs because it is profitable to do so (interview, 11 July 2003).

With regard to the injunctions against theft and lying, there is a general sense that people are not as morally responsible as they were before the years of upheaval. In response to the question on the survey 'How has Buddhism changed?', 84 responses out of 98 mentioned the relaxation of the discipline of the monks and/or the decline in morality of laypeople.

Ebihara wrote that the injunction against immoral sexual relations was 'occasionally broken', and that a double standard 'more or less sanctions adultery for males' (1966: 178). A growing literature produced by non-governmental organizations (NGOs) documents an explosion of pre-marital sex in urban Cambodia in the 1990s and 2000s.[10] It is difficult to know the degree to which this is also true in rural areas. It is extremely common for young men, married and unmarried, to visit commercial sex workers, though this has declined somewhat in the era of HIV/AIDS (East West Center 2004). Young women were ideally supposed to be closely watched and protected by male relatives until they were married; but the dramatic changes in post-war society, and in particular the explosion in the number of women working in garment factories, means that thousands of young women now live on their own in the cities (see Dirks 2005).

The prohibition against the consumption of alcohol was always the easiest precept to ignore, especially for men. Ebihara noted that there was often alcohol consumption at weddings and other ceremonies, and it was not unusual for men to relax with some rice wine or beer if they had the money. Excessive drunkenness, however, was seen as a serious moral flaw that would affect one's standing in the community and one's ability to find a wife (Ebihara 1966: 178; 1968: 390). This is much the same today, though with greater economic prosperity in the villages near Phnom Penh in the last ten years alcohol has become more affordable.

Keeping the five precepts has become a sort of rallying cry, a call by social reformers as a bottom line from which to rebuild a moral Buddhist society in the post-war era.[11] The self-proclaimed *Bodhisattva* Chan Yipon, a leader of one of several small millenarian Buddhist movements, accumulated a following traveling around the country preaching the importance of the five precepts. At each gathering he would call people forward to sign a list swearing that they would follow the precepts devoutly from that day forward. He would then display the list as a sort of talisman, using it to confirm the heralding of a new day of peace and prosperity, when ancient prophecies would be fulfilled (field notes 2003).

A focus on the precepts is also at the heart of an effort by some Khmer human rights advocates to 'localize' Western concepts of human rights by linking them to Buddhism. The Cambodian Institute for Human Rights, for example, designed training materials for teaching about human rights that explicitly connect the idea of rights to the precepts, 'not killing living things is to respect the right to life; not to steal the belongings of others is to respect the right to property' and so on (Noeu, cited in Marston 2001). The underlying idea is that motivating people to respect human rights involves teaching (or reminding) leaders of their moral obligation to follow the precepts and the other teachings of Buddhism.[12]

THNGAI SEL (HOLY DAYS)

The eighth and fifteenth days of the waxing and waning moons are Buddhist 'holy days' (literally *thngai sel*, precept days). 'Religious persons go to the *wat*', Ebihara writes, '"to ask respectfully to receive the holy precepts" (*som sul*)' (1966: 178). People might 'receive' five, eight or ten precepts; in addition to the first five, the other precepts prohibit eating after noon and before dawn; dancing, singing, listening to music or seeing shows; wearing perfumes or cosmetics; using high beds or chairs; and handling money. Holy days were described in a very similar manner by LeClere more than 100 years ago:

> On a 'holy day', as early as seven o'clock in the morning, the laity, especially the women, go to the monastery with food to be offered to the monks and with flowers and incense sticks to be presented to the Buddha, after bowing to his statue and worshiping, seated on the ground with their hands joined ... some people give alms to the poor if any turn up, alms ... On these days there are many who greet their father and mother more deferentially than usual, who refrain from arguments with their neighbours, who speak with more gentleness to their servants, who do not drink any fermented beverages, and add a dish to the usual meal of the slaves. There are a great many, however, who, while observing the holy days attend to their affairs just as on other days, with only their wives visiting the temple, while they themselves go there to pray only on the days of great religious festivals or when they have a special reason to do so (LeClere [Von Scheliha, trans.] 1899: 383).

In our research we observed elders coming to the temples on holy days; they came early in the morning, took the precepts, stayed for prayers and sermons, offered food to the monks, and stayed to eat themselves, as had been the pattern in the pre-war years.[13] Each of the temples had between 30 and 50 devotees, almost all of them elderly, with many more women than men. In our survey, 28 of 141 respondents said that they themselves took the precepts on holy days; of these, 26, or 93 per cent were over 50 years old. The majority were women.

Grandmothers who go to *som sel* will often take along small children. One elderly nun said that her children had come to know how to *soat* (chant) the request for the precepts almost as early as they could talk. She said that taking her grandchildren to *som sel* was a means of teaching them right from wrong: 'If they were afraid/respectful (*khlaic*) because of the meaning of the *dhamma*, then they would know that to kill someone was a sin, to steal something from others was a sin, and thus they would not dare to do so' (interview by Susan Spiegel, Sirak Savina and Eng Lekhena, July 2003).

DANA – THE OFFERING OF GIFTS

The other major way of earning merit for villagers is through offerings of food, money, objects and services to the temple and the monks. As Ebihara has pointed out, the monks and the laypeople are linked in a system of reciprocity (1966:178); from our research, it is clear that merit making through offerings is still at the core of Buddhist practice. 'Even respondents who were very critical of the lax discipline of young monks still praised and respected them for having chosen to be monks at all' (Spiegel n.d.: 14); because of their willingness to ordain, laypeople were provided with the opportunity to make merit.[14]

Khy Sovanratana, a contributor to this volume, has emphasized that making merit not only benefits people in their next lives, but also has immediate consequences. When people make donations they 'become dear to others'; they are given face and respect in the community, and they show people that they are trustworthy and unselfish (interview 21 March 2003). When asked in our survey if one could gain happiness in the future through merit-making activities, 87 per cent said that one could or surely could (see Spiegel n.d). There are several ways that offerings are made: as daily alms rounds offerings, as donations at festivals and ceremonies, as donations of service to the temple and as contributions to building projects.

Each morning between 9:30 and 10:30, monks walk through the villages, stopping at certain houses and waiting in silence for householders to offer food for their midday meal. The monks walk in single file in hierarchical order from the most senior to the most recently ordained. The monks walk barefoot and in silence, fixing their gaze just in front of where they are walking. Temple boys run ahead calling out to the villagers that the monks are coming. The monks have a regular routine, they know which houses give on a regular basis, and they proceed at a rapid pace. The householder (generally a woman), hearing the call, is ready in front of her house with offerings of cooked rice, cooked food, sometimes also fruit or sweets or money. The householder removes her shoes and bows in respect, holding the offering up to her forehead before spooning the rice into the monks' bowls. The temple boys carry the cooked food in multi-tiered metal containers, and stuff riel notes into bags over their shoulders.

These patterns were nearly identical in observations at 106 households across nine communities on one day (11 July 2003).[15] Twenty-five monks in ten groups, with one to four monks per group, all completed the rounds by about 10:30 am, leaving time for groups of laypeople at the temple to organize the food and present it to the monks so they could finish their meal before noon.

Ebihara noted in 1966 that really only a few houses 'with older persons' gave food to the monks on alms rounds. From our observations, this pattern seems to have continued; only certain households donate. Of those who donated, nearly all were women, 72 per cent in the southern district (where many women were off transplanting in the mornings) and 93 per cent in the eastern district. The majority, 60 per cent, were over 50 years old. Based on this very limited snapshot, it appeared that wealth was not the crucial factor in whether or not people donated; the quality of housing construction of those households that donated varied from expensive wooden houses with tile roofs to thatch houses on the ground.

When we asked specifically about the rotation system that is used to feed the monks during the annual festival of the dead (*Pchum Ben*), some 95 per cent of households reported that they participate in the system. For fifteen days the monks do not leave the temple, but households take turns cooking and bringing food to the temple. Some households participated in the system for more than one *wat*. This is another example confirming Kobayashi's observation (this volume and 2005) that the *'chomnoh'*, the social group defined by shared participation in the support of a certain temple, is 'not limited by rigid geographical or membership boundaries' (this volume).[16]

Attending annual Buddhist festivals at the temple is still extremely popular, virtually all respondents, 99 per cent, said that they attend; and, some 95 per cent, said that they make offerings when they do so. Ebihara's description of alms giving at such events is still applicable:

> Every event or festival at either temple involves the contribution of some food, money, and/or services by the villagers. For holy days or some lesser events ... some food or very small amounts of money (equivalent to three to seven cents) are given. For the important annual Buddhist festivals, the villagers typically contribute food in the form of special dishes and delicacies, some money, small offerings such as incense, and perhaps labor services (Ebihara 1966: 179).

The amount of offerings is still relatively small, ranging from less than 2,000 riels (about 50 cents) to a high of $25 US. The majority reported making offerings of between 2,000 and 10,000 riels.[17] As Kobayashi also points out, festivals draw wealthy people who are temporary participants in the temple community, including urban Khmer and overseas Khmer (who often have relatives in the village). Marston also notes that in other rural districts, including Batheay district of Kompong Cham province where he did research, rural *wats* now rely heavily on urban donors (see Marston, this volume).

While city people tend to make larger donations, local villagers cook most of the food and provide labor, which includes waiting on visitors and cleaning up. Women provide most of this labor. Men serve as temple committee members who are responsible for handling the money donated, collecting it, tallying it and announcing the names of donors and the amounts given.[18]

Smaller Buddhist ceremonies, sponsored by individuals, are celebrated throughout the year either at the temple, or in private homes. These include life cycle ceremonies, as well as blessings of various kinds. In response to our survey, 18 per cent of those interviewed said that they had sponsored a ceremony within the last year. Of these, the most popular ceremony was *Bachai Buon*, a ceremony that honors elderly parents, making merit for them as a means to repay the children's debt of gratitude. Komai likewise found that *Bachai Buon* was the favorite festival among those he interviewed in Takeo (1996: 19). As with other religious activities, sponsorship of ceremonies was related to age; 60 per cent of those who had sponsored a recent ceremony were over 50 years old. When asked in general why they had sponsored a ceremony, people most often replied, 'to dedicate merit to my ancestors', followed closely by 'to have a better life in my next incarnation'.

The fact that the majority of Buddhist practitioners across a range of activities – offering food on alms rounds, taking the precepts on holy days and participating in ceremonies – are elders is consistent with pre-war patterns. Our observations concur with Ebihara's that, 'Religiosity reaches its peak in old age when individuals come to possess more physical and psychological leisure' (1968: 395–396). Though of course in the post-war context there are additional reasons why most participants would be elders, a point we return to below in the conclusion.

RECONSTRUCTION OF TEMPLES

Five of the six temples researched for this project had been destroyed during the Khmer Rouge period. At the sixth, the walls of the *vihear*, the central worship hall, were still standing, but the roof was gone. All of the buildings of the temple complexes, including the *vihear* (central worship hall), the *sala* (teaching and dining halls), *koti* (residences for the monks), and other buildings had all been rebuilt by the time of our research. Each still had ongoing projects, including the construction of more *koti*, building of new *chedei* (reliquaries), and repair of existing buildings. These projects of rebuilding had usually begun immediately after liberation in 1979, but with initial temporary structures made of wood or even bamboo. Throughout the 1980s, little headway was made, but with the opening up of the country in the 1990s and an influx of funds from overseas Khmer, temples across the country were restored and reconstructed (see also Kobayashi, this volume).

Donating for the construction of a temple has long been considered the greatest source for earning merit.[19] In a survey of rural Thai villagers in the 1960s, Tambiah found that most thought that 'financing the entire building of a *wat* generated more merit than any other religious act' (Tambiah 1968:68). Monks who are successful at organizing and raising money for building are praised as being *pukae kosang* (powerful at building) (Marston 2008: 26).

Individual donors gain in status in this life as well as making merit for the next. Many parts of the temple and individual objects in the temple, a section of a wall for example, or a particular painting, are labeled with the name of the contributor. *Bonhchoh Sima* ceremonies, the dedication of new temples, are grand festive affairs with huge crowds. These are believed to be particularly meritorious to participate in. These large-scale building projects have become a new battleground of Cambodian politics.

Support for the *sangha* and for Buddhism has traditionally been a source of political legitimacy. Bektimirova links the reconstruction boom to the re-establishment of the monarchy and the competition for legitimacy between the royalist FUNCINPEC party and the ruling Cambodian People's Party (CPP) (Bektimirova 2002: 63–64; see also Guthrie 2002; Ledgerwood 2008).

Not everyone is enthusiastic about this surge in temple construction. Some educated urban elite bemoan the fact that funds spent on temples could be used for projects to 'develop' the country. Chhorn Iem of the Ministry of Cults and Religion said that too many temples were under construction, but that it was impossible to place restrictions on building. Monks want to preside over the building and administration of big new temples; he said that he regretted that the money was not being spent on ecclesiastical education (interview 18 March 2003).

DISCUSSION

Many aspects of village-based practice seem much the same as in 1960: the focus on merit making, the importance of the relationship between the monks and the laity, elders as the primary actors, and the role of the monks in performing ritual activity. The physical movements of the actors, the walking of alms rounds, the visit to the *wat* to ask to receive the precepts, the lighting of incense and the ritual bowing to greet a monk, serve as acts of remembrance of the way things were done before the war. These embodied patterns of practice, like hearing the sounds of familiar music, smelling the incense burning, and seeing the paintings of the Buddha's life in the *vihear* recreate a sense of place and belonging. The celebration of rituals serves to rebuild a sense of community lost in the upheavals of the 1970s and 80s (Meas Nee 1995). The act of making merit is also about gaining respect in the community by showing oneself to be trustworthy and unselfish. The reciprocal relations of giving and receiving literally bind the community together.

For today's elders, who learned Buddhist prayers and rituals at their grandparents' knees as small children chanting *som sel*, and many of whom ordained as adolescents, practising merit making is habitus. Habitus is the 'generative basis' for practices; it 'disposes' people to act in certain patterns, and 'socially competent performances are produced as a matter of routine' (Jenkins 2000: 78). Although the rituals might not be conducted in precisely the same manner as the pre-war version, because knowledge has been lost, ritual texts destroyed, or because monks have less proficiency, the elder nevertheless perceives the ritual to be the same.

At the same time, people did discuss Buddhism as having changed since pre-war times. The first theme mentioned by most interviewees was a general decline in morality among the laity and concern about the degree to which contemporary monks were lax in their discipline. Elders interviewed voiced a range of concerns, including: that it was now possible for young monks to transfer easily between temples, whereas before they had ordained and stayed in their own communities; that the amount of time that young monks spent in prayer was less than in the past; and that they seemed to be less knowledgeable about the *dhamma* and *vinaya*. Others voiced concern that monks today leave the temple to go to English classes, and that they let their eyes wander. One woman added that not only do they look around; they even call out to young women. The same woman added that some young monks today do not show proper respect for their abbot, though she said that this was because the abbot she had in mind was so young (Eng and Serei 22 July 2003).

Many young people, elders reported, are said to not be interested in religion at all, for which many blame 'modern' influences. Eng and Serei summarized their interview findings:

> … young people overwhelmingly adopt foreign cultural influences that come into society through television and the use of modern technologies. They go to watch violent action movies or they form gangs that make young people disrespectful of their elders and the monks, and make them ignore the differences between right and wrong (n.d.: 2, my translation).

This theme of moral decline coincides with Buddhist millenarian themes that are common in Cambodia in the wake of the Khmer Rouge period.[20]

A second important theme is the focus on building, and the speed with which new temples can be constructed. People commented that it used to take generations for a temple to be completed, but now they can *poh loeng* (spring up from the ground).[21] This is a result of a combination of factors mentioned above: the desire on the part of local communities to rebuild their own temples, the use of temple construction for political legitimacy on the part of government officials, the importance for monks of being seen as successful builders, and the influx of funds from (relatively) wealthy overseas Khmer.

Another possible factor in this frantic pace of building seems to lie in an increased importance of merit transfer in the aftermath of the massive mortality of the DK years. Since the early 1990s, people have been anxious to sponsor ceremonies and build *chedei* for their relatives who died in DK. When villagers were asked why it was important to make merit, they said firstly to pass merit to the ancestors, and then secondly to make a better life for themselves in the future. There is also very strong emphasis on the *Pchum Ben* festival of the dead, though it is difficult to say if this is more so than was the case in the past.

Merit transfer to one's parents is also the focus of *Bachai Buon*, the ceremony that people reported sponsoring most often recently. Children pour water over their parents' heads to ensure an auspicious rebirth. Here too it seems that the DK period magnifies the importance of the focus on this group of elders. This aging generation of DK survivors seems to deserve more than any other generation the 'physical and psychological leisure' that comes with being old. Besides owing a debt to one's parents for birth and nurturance, the adult generation today is also indebted to their parents for having kept them alive through the Pol Pot years. If the children are wealthy enough to sponsor such a ceremony, then they have truly made it back from the brink of disaster. The ritual addresses and recognizes their parents' suffering and speaks to a new stability and hopefulness.

Another more radical change is underway; some people are converting to Christianity. The Christian churches (there were three in the two districts we studied) are said to be good at 'pulling' people in by offering free English classes, money and jobs. Many people prefaced their interviews in 2003 with criticism of others in their community who had converted to Christianity. Those interviewed often assured us that they were good Buddhists, in implicit or explicit contrast to the converts. But the very need to assure someone that you are not something else alludes to the fact that a choice is now present.

Before, to be Khmer was to be Buddhist (with some rare exceptions); now it is possible to imagine otherwise. The influence of having the *vihear* of another religion nearby is one factor among an amalgamation of issues that include: the secularizing influence of 15 years of communist rule; the questioning by some of religious belief in the wake of the suffering in the DK years (Mortland 1994); the real loss of religious learning in terms of texts and knowledge known by individuals; and the influence of the 'modern' globalized world beyond Cambodia.

Clifford Geertz, writing about religious change in Indonesia and Morocco, saw that the great difference between the present situation and the 'classic religious styles' of the regions, was that these were 'no longer more or less alone in the field but besieged on all sides by dissenting persuasions' (Geertz 1968: 60). With such new possibilities comes an increase in doubt, Geertz describes this as a distinction between 'being held by religious convictions and holding them' (ibid.: 61). Although the world of the village *wat* in Cambodia in 1960 was not one of complete isolation, I would suggest that the basic beliefs and practices of Buddhism were accepted as truth by Khmer villagers enculturated with these doctrines; Buddhism provided the dispositions, the general categories that gave rise to habitus.

Arjun Appadurai writes, however, that on a global scale the 'sort of trans-generational stability of knowledge which was presupposed in most theories of enculturation ... can no longer be assumed' – here he is emphasizing the disjunctures created by global flows of people, technologies, money and ideas (Appadurai 1990: 17–18). He writes:

> [T]he invention of tradition (and ethnicity, kinship and other identity-markers) can become slippery, as the search for certainties is regularly frustrated by the fluidities ... an arena for conscious choice, justification and representation, the latter often to multiple, and spacially dislocated audiences (ibid.: 18).

The meaning of the village temple and the relationship between the monks and the laity varies across the main patrons of the temple, the wealthy overseas Khmer, the national political figures who drive out from the capital, and ordinary villagers. And while it has always been true that perspectives on religion varied across age groups, the gap has now widened dramatically. It is not only that those who are closer to death will remove themselves from the world to engage in Buddhist merit-making practices – such as giving on alms rounds and asking for the precepts – but also that the elders of today grew up steeped in these practices. With the upheavals of civil war, revolution, and tight socialist control in the 1970s and 1980s, the middle-aged generation now includes a cohort who did not sit at their grandparents' knee for the taking of the precepts; they did not grow up going through the physical motions of merit-making practice.[22]

For elders, Buddhism is a range of social habits, the re-establishment of which provides comfort and stability. For young people, Buddhism is a choice in a range of possibilities that includes not only Christianity, but also a host of secular imaginings. As the older generation of monks and *achar*s pass away, it is not clear how Buddhism will be re-imagined in the beautiful new temple complexes that have sprung up across Cambodia. Buddhism is being reconstituted in the form of its remembered past, though the perception is that it is not as pure, not as moral. This fits with Buddhist millenarian ideas of cycles of decline and restoration. Indeed it could be argued that this process of reconstitution echoes patterns in nineteenth century Khmer Buddhism (see Hansen 2004, Edwards 2004), when 'traditional' patterns were recast in reaction to colonial intrusions, and millennial prophetic texts and concerns with moral purity were central. The ideas and images of Buddhism in Cambodia today are both new and re-imagined from tradition, and ethnographic research suggests that daily merit-making practices remain at the core of village Buddhism.

AUTHOR'S NOTE

My research time in Cambodia spanned from July 2002 to August 2003, with funding from the National Endowment for the Humanities to conduct research on Buddhist prophetic texts and a combined teaching and research Fulbright Fellowship. I would like to thank both funding institutions for their support, and thank Northern Illinois University for the sabbatical that made this research possible. I would also like to thank Dr Alexandra Kent for organizing the workshop on this topic in Varberg.

REFERENCES

Arjun Appadurai (1990) 'Disjuncture and Difference in the Global Cultural Economy.' *Theory, Culture and Society*, 7 (2), pp. 295–310.

Bektimirova, Nadezhda (2002) 'The Religious Situation in Cambodia in the 1990s.' *Religion, State and Society*, 30 (1), pp. 63–72.

Bourdieu, Pierre. (1977) *Outline of a Theory of Practice*. Cambridge: Cambridge University Press.

Dirks, Annuska (2005) *Khmer Women on the Move: Migration and Urban Experiences in Cambodia*. Amsterdam: Dutch University Press.

East-West Center (2004) 'Tackling the HIV/AIDS Epidemic in Asia.' *Asia-Pacific Population and Policy*. No. 68.

Ebihara, May M. (1966) 'Interrelations Between Buddhism and Social Systems in Cambodian Peasant Culture.' In Manning Nash, ed., *Anthropological Studies in Theravada Buddhism*. New Haven: Yale University Press, pp.175–196.

—— (1968) 'Svay: A Khmer Village in Cambodia.' Doctoral dissertation, Columbia University.

Edwards, Penny (2004) 'Making a Religion of the Nation and Its Language.' In John Marston and Elizabeth Guthrie eds, *History, Buddhism, and New Religious Movements in Cambodia*. Honolulu: University of Hawai'i Press, pp. 63–89.

Geertz, Clifford (1968) *Islam Observed: Religious Development in Morocco and Indonesia*. Chicago: University of Chicago Press.

Gender and Development for Cambodia (2003) *Paupers and Princelings: Youth Attitudes towards Gangs, Violence, Rape, Drugs and Theft*. Phnom Penh: Gender and Development for Cambodia.

Guthrie, Elizabeth (2002) 'Buddhist Temples and Cambodian Politics.' In John L.Vijghen ed., *People and the 1998 National Elections in Cambodia*. Phnom Penh: Experts for Community Research, pp. 59–74.

Hansen, Anne (2004) 'Khmer Identity and Theravada Buddhism.' In John Marston and Elizabeth Guthrie eds, *History, Buddhism, and New Religious Movements in Cambodia*. Honolulu: University of Hawai'i Press, pp. 40–62.

Harris, Ian (2005) *Cambodian Buddhism: History and Practice*. Honolulu: University of Hawai'i Press.

Heng Monychenda (1995) *Five Precepts: Sole Alternative for the Reconciliation, Reconstruction and Development of Cambodia*. Anlong Vil, Battambang: Buddhism for Development.

Jenkins, Richard (2002) *Pierre Bourdieu*. New York: Routledge.

Kalab, Malada (1976) 'Monastic Education, Social Mobility and Village Structure in Cambodia.' In D. J. Banks ed., *Changing Identities in Modern Southeast Asia*. Paris: Mouton, pp. 155–169.

Keyes, Charles (1987) *Thailand: Buddhist Kingdom to Modern Nation-State*. Boulder: Westview Press.

—— (1994) 'Communist Revolution and the Buddhist Past in Cambodia.' In Charles F. Keyes, Laurel Kendall and Helen Hardacre eds, *Asian Visions of Authority: Religion and the Modern States of East and Southeast Asia*. Honolulu: University of Hawai'i Press, pp. 43–73.

—— (1995) *The Golden Peninsula*. Honolulu: University of Hawai'i Press.

Kobayashi Satoru (2005) 'An ethnographic Study on the Reconstruction of Buddhist Practice in Two Cambodian Temples: With the Special Reference to Buddhist Samay and Boran.' *Tonan Ajia Kenkyu* [Southeast Asian Studies] 42 (4), pp. 489–518.

Komai, Hiroshi (1996) 'The Role of Buddhism in the Reconstruction of the Cambodian rural Village.' Paper Presented at the National Socio-Cultural Research Congress on Cambodia, December 17–19, Royal University of Phnom Penh.

Leclère, Adhémard (1899) *Le bouddhisme au Cambodge*. Paris: E. Leroux. [Translation Renata Von Scheliha (1956) *The Buddhism of Cambodia*. Human Relations Area Files.]

Ledgerwood, Judy (2008) 'Ritual in 1990 Cambodian Political Theatre: New Songs at the Edge of the Forest.' In Judy Ledgerwood and Anne Hansen, eds *At the Edge of the Forest: Essays in Honor of David Chandler*. Ithaca, NY: Cornell Southeast AsianStudies Program (in press).

Ledgerwood, Judy and Un Kheang (2003) 'Global Concepts and Local Meaning: Human Rights and Buddhism in Cambodia.' *Journal of Human Rights* 2 (4), pp. 531–549.

Loschmann, Heike (2005) 'Buddhism and Social Development in Cambodia since the Overthrow of the Pol Pot Regime in 1979.' *Researching Buddhism and Culture in Cambodia, 1930–2005.* Phnom Penh: The Buddhist Institute Colloquium Papers.

Marston, John (2001) 'Buddhism and Human Rights NGOs in Cambodia.' Paper presented at the Religion Studies meetings, November 30.

—— (2004) 'Clay into Stone: A Modern-Day Tapas.' In John Marston and Elizabeth Guthrie (eds), *History, Buddhism, and New Religious Movements in Cambodia.* Honolulu: University of Hawai'i Press, pp. 170–192.

—— (2008) 'Constructing Narratives of Order: Religious Building and Moral Chaos.' In Judy Ledgerwood and Anne Hansen, eds *At the Edge of the Forest: Essays in Honor of David Chandler.* Ithaca, NY: Cornell Southeast AsianStudies Program (in press).

Marston, John and Elizabeth Guthrie (2004) *History, Buddhism, and New Religious Movements in Cambodia.* Honolulu: University of Hawai'i Press.

Meas Nee (1995) *Towards Restoring Life: Cambodian Villages.* Phnom Penh: Krom Akphiwat Phum.

Ministry of Cults and Religion (1999) 'Statistics (mimeo).'

—— (2003) 'Statistics (mimeo).'

Mortland, Carol (1994) 'Khmer Buddhist in the United States: Ultimate Questions.' In May Ebihara, Carol Mortland and Judy Ledgerwood eds, *Cambodian Culture Since 1975: Homeland and Exile.* Ithaca, NY: Cornell University Press, pp. 72–90.

Rajadhon, Phya Anuman (1986) *Popular Buddhism in Siam and Other Essays on Thai Studies.* Bangkok: Inter-Religious Commission for Development.

Sam Bunthoeun (2002) *A Brief Discourse on the Precepts.* Phnom Addharass, Kandal: Center for Buddhist Meditation.

Sam Yang (1987) *Khmer Buddhism and Politics 1954–1984.* Newington, CT: Khmer Studies Institute.

Spiro, Melford (1962) *Buddhism and Society: A Great Tradition and its Burmese Vicissitudes.* Berkeley: University of California Press.

Strauss, Claudia and Naomi Quinn (1997) *A Cognitive Theory of Cultural Meaning.* Cambridge: Cambridge University Press.

Swearer, Donald K. (1995) *The Buddhist World of Southeast Asia.* Albany, NY: State University of New York Press.

Tambiah, Stanley (1968) 'The Ideology of Merit and the Social Correlates of Buddhism in A Thai Village.' In E. R. Leach ed., *Dialectic in Practical Religion.* Cambridge: Cambridge University Press, pp. 41–121.

Tarr, Chou Meng (1996) *People in Cambodia Don't Talk about Sex, They Simply Do It.* Phnom Penh: Cambodian AIDS Social Research Report.

—— (1997) 'Social Contexts of Risk-Related Sexual Activity Among Young Cambodian

Males.' Paper presented at the Third International Conference on Biopsychological Aspects of HIV Infection. Melbourne, Australia, June.

UNESCO (2000) *Towards the 21st Century: National Strategy for Education for All.* Phnom Penh: UN Working Group on Poverty and Education, UNESCO.

UNFPA (2002) *Torn between Tradition and Desire: Young People in Cambodia Today.* Phnom Penh: UNFPA and the European Commission.

Wells, Kenneth E. (1960) *Thai Buddhism: Its Rites and Activities.* Bangkok: Kenneth Wells.

Unpublished documents from the 2003 field school

Eng Lekhanna and Serei Savina (n.d.) 'The Changing Role of Buddhism Before and After the War.'

Eng Lekhanna, Serei Savina and Susan Speigel (n.d.) 'A Nun's Life History.'

Rudasill, Kathryn (n.d.) 'Alms Rounds in Cambodia.'

Spiegel, Susan (n.d.) 'Buddhism in Cambodia.'

NOTES

1. Like Kobayashi Satoru (this volume), I am addressing what he refers to as 'village Buddhism', in the sense of lived practical religion, rather than the 'philosophical Buddhism' of intellectuals and learned monks. Obviously, it could also be argued that what is unchanging is the *dhamma*, the message of the Buddha's teaching.

2. The Buddhist Institute students were: Cheat Sreang, Aing Sokroeun, and Mech Samphors. The RUFA students were: To Thanarath, Sirak Sivana, Yim Many, Eng Lekhena, Iv Panchak Seila, Chen Chanratana, Mak Kun, Khun Sathal, Chey Serivath, and Seng Chantha. The American students were: Gina Curler, Margaret Karnyski, Elizabeth Markle, Katheryn Rudasill, Susan Speigel, John Stavrellis and Ellen King. The Center for Khmer Studies Assistants were: Heng Chhun Oeurn, Hak Siphirath, and Run Sambath. Special thanks are due to Dean Hor Lat of the Faculty of Archeology at the RUFA, Heng Kim Van at the Buddhist Institute and to Kim Sedara, supervisor of the Anthropology program at CKS.

3. This number of surveys is too small to be statistically relevant given the population of the villages surveyed, particularly on the riverside where population density is high. In only one of the six villages did the number of surveys completed include ten per cent of the total number of households in the village. We use the data despite this limitation as we think that it is generally indicative of trends, if not precisely statistically accurate. The findings also are consistent with those of Komai (1996). For surveys of regular villagers, households were selected randomly, choosing every third house as one walked through a village. Semi-structured interviews were conducted with religious personnel, temple committee members and self-identified temple supporters.

4. See also Kobayashi, this volume. He includes Buddhist meditation in his list of important merit-making activities, but this was not mentioned by laypeople in our study.

5   See Khy Sovanratana, this volume, on the history of the Buddhist education system for monks.

6   A study by Mark Bray (1998) documented the high costs of education placed on Cambodian parents. This survey of 77 schools in 11 provinces and Phnom Penh found that families and communities pay 74.8 per cent of the costs of primary education, with the government paying only 12.9 per cent. This is one of the lowest government contributions to primary education in the world (cited in UNESCO 2000: 23).

7   There are several parallels between this discussion and changes in patterns of ordination in Thailand. As in Cambodia, Keyes notes that religious education in Thailand is also a means of social mobility. Young village boys advance up the system to one of two religious universities in Bangkok, and then upon graduation leave the monkhood to enter mid-level jobs in secular educational institutions, business or government service (Keyes 1987: 139; see also Swearer 1995: 48).

8   Kobayashi Satoru, in his research in Kompong Thom province, found that of 24 monks and novices ordained during one rainy season, 15 were from more 'remote and forested areas' of the district (2005: 512).

9   See Heike Löschmann on Buddhism and 'political instrumentalism' for a discussion of recasting the acceptability of taking life when governments deem it necessary (2005:57). One of the central messages of Christian churches seeking converts in Cambodia today is the notion that sin can be forgiven; posters and bumper stickers declare that Jesus Christ can *leang bap*, 'wash away demerit', a concept that of course is impossible in Buddhism. This might help to explain the conversion of some former Khmer Rouge cadre, including the infamous Duch, the former director of S-21.

10 See Chou Meng Tarr 1996, 1997, UNFPA 2002, Gender and Development for Cambodia 2003.

11 See, for example, the book by Heng Monychenda entitled *Five Precepts: Sole Alternative for the Reconciliation, Reconstruction and Development of Cambodia* (1995) and the renowned meditation teacher Ven. Sam Bunthoeun's (2002) *A Brief Discourse on the Precepts*. Sam Bunthoeun was assassinated in Phnom Penh in 2003. For examples of ways that the precepts were reinterpreted for nationalist causes in Thailand, see Swearer (1995): 112–113.

12 For an extended discussion of this Buddhist recasting of Western ideas of human rights, see Ledgerwood and Un (2003).

13 Kobayashi reports some slight variation in the ways of observing holy days between two temples in Kompong Thom (see Kobayashi 2004: 513–514).

14 Susan Spiegel, John Stavrellis and Gina Curler wrote papers on the importance of merit making in village life and on the relationship between the temples that they researched and their surrounding communities.

15 There was one group of monks that did not follow this pattern. They rode a motorcycle to the nearby market and sat at a covered stand while villagers came to make offerings. When all the offerings had been made, of rice and cooked food, packaged noodles, fruit and money, the monks chanted a single blessing for all of those who had made offerings. At another temple one monk broke his silence during his walk back to the temple to take a call on his cell phone (fieldnotes 11 July 2003). For an analysis of all of the observations across the groups, see Rudasill n.d. For comparative descriptions of monk alms rounds in Thailand, see Rajadhon (1986) and Wells (1960).

16 Kobayashi's observations regarding tensions and negotiations across *chomnoh* are beyond the scope of this limited research.
17 In July 2003 the exchange rate was approximately 3,900 riels to one US dollar.
18 Other forms of labor are offered daily, temple boys serve the monks in a variety of ways, some elders (both male and female) live at the temple or come daily to help with cleaning, sorting offerings and cooking if needed. Men will sometimes offer labor for construction projects or building maintenance.
19 John Marston has written that the building of religious structures, and the narratives surrounding such construction, draws on deep roots in Southeast Asian Buddhist traditions. He documents several building projects in post-war Cambodia related to millenarian movements that he argues are linked to the theme of re-establishing order 'in the face of moral chaos and humiliation represented by the Pol Pot period and its aftermath' (2008: 9; see also Marston 2004).
20 On this theme, see Marston (2004, 2008) and this volume; Hansen and Ledgerwood (2002), Hansen (n.d).
21 This phrase is also used to discuss the appearance of structures foretold in prophecies as heralding the arrival of the new era of prosperity (see Marston on movements that link building to millenarian and nationalist ideas [2004; 2008]).
22 Kobayashi Satoru makes reference to a 'generational gap' in terms of Buddhist practices; this includes, he writes, vastly different experiences for monks depending on their age group (2005: 510). See his discussion of the influence of *'samay'* ideas, as well as the issue of control of ordinations (2005: 508–509).

CHAPTER 9

Reconstructing Buddhist Temple Buildings.
An analysis of village Buddhism after the era of turmoil

Satoru KOBAYASHI

Cambodian people suffered extraordinary social upheavals in the 1970s. Five years of internal warfare from 1970 damaged the people's way of life all over the country. Moreover, from April 1975 to January 1979 the Democratic Kampuchea regime (hereafter, DK) carried out various projects to destroy the existing society. Religion was given no place in the alternative society they planned to build. Undoubtedly, Buddhism, which had been the state religion since independence from French colonial rule and the religion of the majority of the population for centuries, was one of the aspects of culture most severely suppressed by the regime. Daily acts of faith were banned. Many Buddhist temples were destroyed. All monks were forced to renounce their yellow robes in early 1976. This brought about the complete cessation of Buddhist tradition and activities in Cambodia. The well-known fact of the huge loss of human life during the era testifies to the miserably harsh conditions endured by Cambodian society in this period.

The reality of the social destruction of the 1970s and the subsequent reconstruction after the DK era has yet to be thoroughly researched. In the early 1990s, when the country was beginning to emerge from both internal warfare and international isolation, some pioneering field studies of Cambodian social change appeared. The late May Ebihara, the only American anthropologist to have conducted full-scale rural fieldwork in pre-war Cambodia, visited her former research site and presented analyses of some aspects of social change, including villagers' narratives about life during the DK era (Ebihara 1990, 1993a, 1993b, 2002; Ebihara & Ledgerwood 2002).

As for studies of Cambodian Buddhism, Charles Keyes (1994) and Hayashi Yukio (1995a, 1995b, 2002) revealed that Buddhist monks had re-emerged in the country very early on after the fall of the DK regime. The socialist government of the People's Republic of Kampuchea organized an official ordination ceremony in the capital in September 1979, inviting Theravada monks from Kampuchea Krom, the homeland of a Khmer population in the Mekong delta region of Vietnam. Various Buddhist rituals appear to have been resumed spontaneously from that point on.

However, the Buddhist practice that reappeared in Cambodia in the 1980s was not the same as that of pre-war times. The socialist government set age restrictions for ordination, prohibiting men under 50 years of age from becoming monks. Monks were not to be differentiated according to sect. The great majority of damaged temple buildings were not yet reconstructed because of the economic difficulties in the country at the time. Buddhist activities in Cambodia did not undergo significant revitalization until 1989. In this year, the post-socialist government declared Theravada Buddhism once again the state religion. The number of monks and novices increased dramatically after the abolition of the ordination age restriction in the same year. The re-establishment of the two sects of the national *sangha*, *Mahanikay* and *Thommayut*, took place upon the return of Norodom Sihanouk to the country in 1991. The restoration of public order after the elections in 1993 clearly contributed to the revitalization of various religious activities in rural areas. Finally, in the mid-1990s, with the improvements in security and the expansion of economic activities, the floodgates of temple reconstruction in rural Cambodia were opened.

Cambodian people explain the construction of temple buildings as an act of merit making. As many scholars have pointed out, merit making plays an important role in the social, political, ritual and economic systems of Theravada Buddhist societies.[1] A Theravada Buddhist temple is, theoretically, open to everyone. Its supporting community is not determined exclusively by the geographic setting; the reconstruction of rural temple buildings attracts the interest of not only local villagers but also market dwellers, urbanites, and even Buddhists living abroad. Since it is difficult to collect funds from within local villages, the participation of distant wealthy people is highly desired. In other words, rural temple communities seek ways of networking with wealthy others through Buddhist festivals in the hope of raising funds for building reconstruction. However, in my rural fieldwork in central Cambodia, I observed tension and conflict among participants in such networking activities, although the local Buddhist leaders emphasized a sense of popular unity in Buddhism.

In this chapter, I focus on the temples and communities in and around San Kor commune, Kompong Svay district, Kompong Thom province, and analyse the ethnographic context of the reconstruction of temple buildings. The chapter aims to explore how the reconstruction activities reflect the current state of village Buddhism in post-socialist rural Cambodia. I use the term 'village Buddhism' here to draw attention to Buddhist practice as a part of people's lives. As Edmund Leach pointed out with his use of the term 'practical religion' (1968), there is a large gap between the theology of higher philosophers and the religious principles that guide ordinary people's behavior. In the following sections, I do not discuss the philosophical Buddhism maintained by intellectuals or well-educated monks, but rather the village Buddhism understandable to ordinary villagers in their everyday activities. In order to put the analysis in context, I will first briefly describe the history of the decline and reconstruction of rural lives in the research area.

DISMANTLING AND RECONSTRUCTION OF RURAL LIVES: 1970–2000

San Kor commune is located on the eastern edge of the flood area of the Tonle Sap Lake about 20 kilometers from the provincial capital of Kompong Thom, along National Highway No. 6A.[2] As is well known, the Tonle Sap Lake expands its area in the rainy season, and its floodwater reaches the south side of the highway every year in San Kor. Moreover, the area north of the highway leads to open forest. The features of the local people's livelihood variations and the history of the formation of local society are not understandable without full consideration of this environmental setting. In 2001, San Kor had a market and contained 14 villages with four Buddhist temples. During the period of my research, I lived and worked as an anthropologist in Veal village, which is located along the highway near the market and had at that time 149 households. I also conducted household surveys in Prasat village, which lies about 2.5 kilometers south of the highway with 94 households.

As is the case in most Cambodian rural areas, rice-cultivation and small-scale fishing are major traditional livelihood activities in San Kor. The paddy fields in the area may be classified into two types; the ordinary paddy fields near the hamlet and paddy fields of floating rice about 3 to 8 kilometers south of the highway. In general, the former is cultivated for consumption and the latter for sale. The household is the basic unit for these activities. In addition, there is a small population of traders. Interestingly, the existence of some active traders in the area at the beginning of the twentieth century has been confirmed. According to the historical narratives of the local people, those traders used to travel around to villages in the forest area in the North and engage in the trade of goods.[3] When they had collected a certain amount of paddy, they traveled to Phnom Penh and sometimes as far as Saigon for wholesaling. Although most of its population has long been engaged in rice growing and fishing within the area, the commune has also had communication with urban areas for a long time.

The process of destruction and recovery dominates San Kor commune's recent history. The communists took control of San Kor in 1970. The commune suffered American air raids in 1971–1972, but the people continued to organize religious activities in a nearly normal manner until 1973. Warfare then utterly transformed rural lives in 1974. In this year, the people of San Kor were forcibly relocated twice. Taking the residents of Veal village as an example, in February 1974 the local Khmer Rouge ordered the villagers to move to the forest area about 7 kilometres north of the highway. About ten days later, Lon Nol forces reached the area and ordered the people to make their second relocation, this time to the provincial capital. Six of Veal's families escaped, fleeing further north together with the Khmer Rouge, but the other sixty or so families followed the order and moved to Kompong Thom. The monks and novices of the temples in San Kor also moved to the provincial capital with their fellow villagers. The temples and villages of San Kor lost most of their residents during 1974.

In April 1975, the relocated people began to return to their original homes. However, the revolutionary organization did not allow the majority of the returnees from the provincial capital to live in their original villages. The local DK cadres considered all of them to be so-called 'new people' and divided them into two categories based on the results of DK research into their personal backgrounds. In Veal village, for instance, families whose members had participated in revolutionary movements before 1975 were allowed to live in the original village. The other families, however, were ordered to live in the newly built *sahakâr* (literally, cooperative) in the open forest about 2 kilometers north of the highway. In addition, the few families who went with the Khmer Rouge in February 1974 were considered to be so-called 'old people', and they were ordered to live in another village in the commune.

People's lives deteriorated drastically during the DK era. The effects of the DK regime's utopian social engineering project are clearly evident today. Starvation, horrific working conditions, unpredictable execution orders, and memories of the dead – all of these are frequently related in the people's life-history narratives. Moreover, the present San Kor landscape clearly reflects the physical transformation that took place during the DK era. The revolutionary organization ordered the construction of the irrigation canals and one-hundred-metre-square paddy fields. These efforts completely altered the original layout of paddy fields south of the highway.

In January 1979, the local people returned to their home villages. The reconstruction of rural livelihoods started within the context of village social order, once again largely independent of the state. Villagers reasserted their original rights to their houses and compounds. Rice cultivation began at first in the form of *krom samaki* (solidarity group), the collective agricultural production policy of the newly installed socialist government, but by 1984 these were dissolved with the consent of both residents and local authorities. In addition to village-based livelihood activities, there were people who engaged in the bicycle caravan trading to the Thai border from 1979 to 1981.[4] Security conditions in the area, however, remained relatively poor throughout the 1980s. Between 1988 and 1990 in particular, during and after the retreat of the Vietnamese troops, battles between government forces and the Khmer Rouge army occurred frequently in and around the villages of San Kor.[5] In fact, the local market that was built with government support in the early 1980s was burned down in 1990 by the Khmer Rouge. Public order in the area was finally restored after the national elections in 1993, and attention was turned to the diversification of village household economic activities in the mid-1990s. The first rice-milling machine was introduced into Veal village in 1995, and the number increased quickly. By 1998 some village households had begun wholesale trading of chickens and fish to the capital.

There has been a rapid increase since 1998 in economic migrants, in particular young women working at garment factories around Phnom Penh. Rice cultivation in the area suffered extremely bad harvests because of flooding and drought in 2000 and 2001, but some village households nevertheless had the means to rebuild their houses. In all probability, these households had daughters working at garment factories, and their remittances were more than sufficient to compensate for the bad rice harvests. This economic migration of young women has brought change to village society. Previously, it was uncommon for young unmarried women to leave for a remote place for a long period of time. This is also probably the first time that village families have received cash on a regular basis. These young women have also begun marrying men with whom they have become acquainted through their lives in the capital.

Table 9.1. Penetration of manufactured products into households of two villages

Item	Veal village (149 households)		Prasat village (94 households)	
	Households in possession	Penetration rate (%)	Households in possession	Penetration rate (%)
car	2	1.3	0	0
motorcycle	43	28.9	8	8.5
bicycle	129	86.6	72	76.6
radio	93	62.4	34	36.2
television	23	15.4	7	7.4
sewing machine	19	12.8	1	1.1
clock	85	57.0	22	23.4
gasoline engine	19	12.8	13	13.8

Source: Kobayashi 2005a

Table 9.2. Variation in building materials of house roofs

Village name	Total number of houses in village	Number of houses using different roof materials		
		Palmyra leafs	Biscite tiles	Bricks and cement
San Kor Khâ	288	226	62	0
Prasat	79	57	22	0
Chey	87	48	39	0
Sari	160	80	77	3
San Kor Kâ	79	3	74	3
Veal	118	47	69	2

Source: Author's interview with village chiefs in July, 2000.

The development of village economies is, however, rather uneven in the commune, as shown in my household socio-economic data from Veal village and Prasat village. As seen in Table 9.1, the penetration rate of manufactured products is higher among the households of Veal village than among those of Prasat village. Table 9.2 shows variations in the kinds of building materials used for house roofs in some of the villages of San Kor.

Houses with tiled roofs are more numerous in villages located near the market area than in those located far from the highway. This kind of economic distinction is evident between the villages of San Kor and the villages of the northern open forest area as well. Locals from San Kor frequently discuss the differences in lifestyles. The residents of remote villages often say that their lives are different from those of *neak phsar* (market dwellers), living near the market of San Kor. Some village householders in the market area also remarked that their lifestyles differ from those of *neak srai* (rice-cultivators).

These stories illustrate the way in which people's basic identity is based upon a contrast with 'others'. Cambodian people generally tend to express their identity in relation to socio-economic differentials. Dichotomies such as *neak srok srai* (country people) and *neak ti krong* (urbanites), for instance, are frequently encountered. In San Kor, the concepts *neak srok leu* (lit. the people in the upper country) and *neak srok krom* (lit. the people in the lower country) are used in a similar way. The former is used by the people of San Kor somewhat disparagingly to refer to the 'less developed' people from the northern forest area. This kind of self-identification may be understood as falling within the structuring of 'space'. My use of the term 'space' here refers not only to geographical and socio-economic units but also to the arena of experience and imagination within the realm of various daily interactions. Indeed, analysis of the reconstruction activities of Buddhist temple buildings in San Kor reveals the way in which people create identity and, more specifically, space. Before developing this further, however, I shall introduce the local Buddhist environment in San Kor commune.

TEMPLES, TEMPLE COMMUNITIES, AND TWO BUDDHIST TRADITIONS[6]

San Kor commune had four Theravada *wat*s in 2001 (see Table 9.3 for the basic data for the four temple-monasteries). Wat San Kor is located close to the local market. Wat Prasat Ândaet (hereafter, Wat Prasat) lies in the middle of an area of paddy fields about 3 kilometers south of the highway. It is believed that both temples were constructed at the end of the nineteenth century at the latest, and they were reconstructed in 1981. Wat Preah Krâsang was originally constructed in 1965 with assistance from Wat Prasat, and reconstructed in 1991. The last temple, Wat Krâsang Mean Rutthi, was newly constructed in 1991.

Table 9.3. Basic data of four wats in San Kor

Temple	Wat San Kor	Wat Prasat Ândaet	Wat Preah Krâsang	Wat Krâsang Mean Rutthi
Year of construction	end of 19th century	end of 19th century	1965	1991
Year of reconstruction	1981	1981	1991	-
Buildings in compound (number)	preah vihear (1), sala chhan (1), pannalay* (1), cement kot** (1), wooden kot (1), wooden hut for daun chi*** (1)	preah vihear (1), sala chhan (1), cement kot (1), wooden kot (3)	preah vihear (1), sala chhan (1), cement kot (1), wooden kot (1)	preah vihear (1), sala chhan (1), wooden kot (2)
Number of monks in 2001 Lent season	2	8	5	7
Number of novices in 2001 Lent season	22	26	7	10
Chamnoh villages	Sari, San Kor Kâ, Veal, Balang, Tang Krauch, Âmpel	Slaeng Khpos, Chey, Prasat, Kbel, San Kor Khâ, Sompavmeas, Sari, San Kor Kâ, Veal, Tang Krauch	Kbel, Krâsang Kâ	Krâsang Khâ

* *pannalay* is a building for storing scriptures
** *kot* is a building where monks live
*** *daun chi* is a female lay practitioner who holds the 10 precepts.

Source: Author's research in March 2000, July 2001.

To understand the local Buddhist environment it is crucial to review how Buddhist temples are embedded in their surrounding community. In previous studies, Buddhist temples were often referred to as the centre of the community (e.g. Ebihara 1968). However, the concrete relation between the temple and its community has been little discussed. The temple community is known in Khmer as *chomnoh* (subordinate, dependent) of the temple. Researchers typically designate the temple community as monks and novices, *achar wat* (laymen who arrange ceremonies in the Buddhist temple [Headley 1977: 1406]), and *kanakamekar wat* (temple committee, a group of persons working with secular temple affairs). However, viewing the temple as a religious institution means also considering the role of ordinary practising people. In Cambodia, it is common for people to observe the Buddhist lay precepts at one temple on one Buddhist Sabbath day and then again at another temple on the next Sabbath day. In principle, then, people may choose freely from a number of Buddhist temples to participate in Buddhist activities.

My definition of the temple community is, accordingly, *an unbounded social group, defined by shared participation in the activities of a certain temple*. The temple community may be described as having three characteristics. Firstly, openness – the community is defined by the actual practice of participation in a certain temple's activities. This implies that the community is not limited by rigid geographical or membership boundaries. Secondly, concentric rings of participants – the temple community consists of local intellectuals such as monks and *achar*s at the core, and is surrounded by ordinary villagers. Thirdly, intersection – relations between temples can be considered in terms of interactions between the core groups. Despite the impression that each temple has an independent, fixed temple community of support, in reality there is significant overlap and interaction between temple communities. This creates a fluid, flexible situation in which the villages considered as *chomnoh* of the four temples in San Kor show considerable overlap, as seen in Table 9.3. For example, Veal village is considered to be the *chomnoh* of both Wat San Kor and Wat Prasat. This means that the villagers participate in the routine activities, such as joining in rotating food preparation groups for monks, of both temples. There are many differences between the four temples in the area, but I shall focus the following discussion on two particular aspects of interest.

Figure 9.1. Preah Vihear, Wat San Kor

Figure 9.2. Preah Vihear, Wat Prasat

Figure 9.3. Preah Vihear, Wat Preah Krasang

Figure 9.4. Preah Vihear, Wat Krasang Mean Rutthi

Firstly, it is clear that history and local economic resources have a great impact upon the reconstruction process at each temple. The *preah vihear*s (ordination hall with a sacred boundary), for example, exhibit obvious differences between the two oldest temples and the two new temples (see Figures 9.1 on p. 177, and 9.2, 9.3 and 9.4 opposite). Wat San Kor has a three-storied, brick-and-mortar *preah vihear* with concrete posts. Construction was finished in 1970, and the top floor and roof were repaired between 1998 and 1999. Wat Prasat also has a brick-and-mortar *preah vihear* that was constructed in 1964 and survived through the 1970s.[7] On the other hand, the *preah vihears* of both Wat Preah Krâsang and Wat Krâsang Mean Rutthi are small and made of wood.[8] In the latter two temples, temple communities have been discussing projects for building larger and more splendid *preah vihears* for years. However, due to the shortage of funds, these plans have not progressed. If we examine the temple building reconstruction process in more detail, differences between the two oldest temples become evident. At Wat San Kor, although it was seriously damaged in the DK period, the reconstruction of buildings in the compound has progressed steadily since the early 1990s. This was made possible by the availability of ample funds from participants in the market area of San Kor and their relatives in Phnom Penh. The temple's *sala chhan* (meeting hall), with its concrete posts, was reconstructed in 1993. Other reconstruction projects have been ongoing. By contrast, Wat Prasat had only a wooden *sala chhan* built in 1985 when I first visited in March 2000. The new *sala chhan*, with concrete posts, was not completed until April 2001.

Figure 9.5. Chenh vossa, Wat San Kor

Figure 9.6. Chenh vossa, Wat Prasat

Figure 9.7. Chenh vossa, Wat Preah Krasang

Figure 9.8. Chenh vossa, Wat Krasang Mean Rutthi

The second aspect of interest are the differences in the ceremonies at each temple. At the *chenh vossa* ceremony (the celebration of the closing of the Buddhist Lent season) in 2001, for instance, all the temples organized the monks' ritual reading of *jeatok* (tales of the former births of the Buddha) to take place during the day. However, there were differences between the setting at Wat San Kor and those at the other three temples (see Figures 9.5 on p. 179, and 9.6 9.7 and 9.8 opposite). At Wat San Kor, the monks recited the sutra in the middle of the *sala chhan*, without any decorations. In the other three temples, the places where the monks recited were dressed with intricate, handmade decorations, such as the wooden fence known as *reach wat* and traditional religious objects made from banana trunks called *bay sey*. In Wat San Kor, the lay leaders explained that they had stopped preparing the decorations because there is no mention of them in the Tripitaka and they felt that this meant that they were unnecessary. The participants at the other temples, however, explained that they practised their rituals in a traditional manner based on their *propeiney cheat* (national custom). The local people in San Kor describe the former style of practice as *samay* (new/modern) and the latter as *boran* (old/ancient).

As I have discussed elsewhere (Kobayashi 2005a), two different styles of Buddhist practice represented by the Khmer words *samay* and *boran* have existed in San Kor since before the war.[9] *Samay* practice has its origin in the reformist monks' movement that developed at the core of the *Mahanikay* order of the *sangha* in the 1910s under the leadership of the two outstanding educated monks, Samdech Chuon Nath and Samdech Huot Tath. These monks insisted on the need to reconsider popular Buddhist practice according to a strict interpretation of the Buddhist scriptures. To cite a few examples, they criticized the conventional rote learning of Buddhist texts and upheld the importance of being able to explain the meaning of the Buddha's teaching. They insisted that Buddhist prayers should be chanted not only in Pali but also in Khmer at every ritual. They rejected elements of reliance upon other beings, such as spirits – elements of *promenh sasana* (Brahmanism) – in popular Buddhist rituals. They also stressed the importance of the causal circle of *kamm* (karma) in life. Wat San Kor adopted *samay* reformist practice in the 1940s and changed both monastic practice as well as the content of popular rituals in the temple. The other two temples in the commune, Wat Prasat and Wat Preah Krâsang, however, continued to uphold existing practice, which became known as *boran* in response to the introduction of reform. Many of the narratives of the local people describe the tension that exists between the adherents of the local *samay* and *boran* traditions.

However, local peoples' current references to the two traditions seem to be more complex than they presumably were in pre-war times. The difference between the two traditions, *samay* and *boran*, is still very much a part of local life today, as seen in the above-mentioned case of the preparation of the *chenh vossa* ceremony. Nevertheless, there have recently been some changes in Buddhist practice in the *boran* temples in the area. Although the local people still refer to Wat Prasat as *wat boran* (temple of old practice), and Wat San Kor as *wat samay* (temple of new practice), they are well aware that Wat Prasat adopted some of the new practices during its reconstruction process in the 1990s. Table 9.4 shows the features of recent change in practice at Wat Prasat.

Table 9.4. Recent changes at Wat Prasat

Item	Until the 1960s	In the 1990s
Place for meal of monks and novices	separated, with different lines for monks and novices	not separated
Chanting of monks and novices	separated in place and time for monks and novices	not separated
Language of chanting	Pali only	Pali with Khmer translation
Texts	palm leaf texts and printed books	printed books
Targets of offering	Buddha, *dharma*, monks and other spiritual entities	Buddha, *dharma*, monks and other spiritual entities
Offering items	flowers, candles and traditional offerings	flowers, candles and traditional offerings

Source: Kobayashi 2005a

Interestingly, the change that took place mainly in monk's practice corresponds with *samay*-style practice. I cannot explore the details of these changes here, but it is important to note that the differences between *samay* and *boran* practices are now apparent not only in comparison between temples but also within a single temple. Actually, elderly people participating in Buddhist rituals in Wat Prasat these days often describe newly ordained young monks with the Khmer phrase *samay haoey* (changed to a new/ modern one). This phrase has tones of lamentation about the current situation. This kind of expression of retrospective recognition of historical changes may exist in other cultures and societies, but the phrase seems to convey particularly profound meanings in contemporary Cambodia, which is still emerging from the social destruction of recent years.

Buddhist practice in Cambodia suffered a complete break in the DK era, and the socialist government of the 1980s did not allow the male population to become monks freely either. As seen in the case of the male population of Veal village (Table 9.5), the experiences of monks differ clearly according to age group.

Table 9.5. Statistics for men of Veal village who had been monks or novices

Age group	A. Number of males* in village	B. Number of those who had been monks or novices	Percentage of B to A
15–19	37	0	0
20–24	17	1	5.9
25–29	20	1	5.0
30–34	27	1	3.7
35–39	31	0	0
40–44	13	0	0
45–49	14	3	21.4
50–54	8	5	62.5
55–59	10	4	40.0
60–64	11	8	72.7
65–69	10	8	80.0
70–74	4	3	75.0
75–79	1	1	100.0
Total	203	35	17.2

* monks are not counted; males under 14 are omitted (ordination as a novice is not common for this group)

Source: Kobayashi 2005a

This hints at the appearance of a generation gap caused by the discontinuity of normal life. Indeed, the majority of monks in Cambodia today are young men who were born in the period between the eve of the civil war and the 1980s, and grew up without the influence of traditional cultural activities. In other words, in the post-socialist Cambodia of the 1990s, the reconstruction of tradition has been taking place through collaboration between young and old. Moreover, people use the adjectives *samay* and *boran* more generally to refer to the modern-ancient contrast in their secular lives as well. As I mentioned above, life in rural Cambodia today is currently undergoing rapid social change, which means that *samay* and *boran* elements are constantly being counterpoised. When the old people in the Buddhist temple lament '*samay haoey*', the multiplicity of meanings of the phrase begs interpretation. *Samay* and *boran* are perhaps best seen as aspects of a continuum, in which case our analytical point of departure should ideally be to aim to understand the relationship between them in everyday life.

RECONSTRUCTING BUDDHIST TEMPLE BUILDINGS

Merit-making ideology and fund raising through festival networking

If one visited Buddhist temples in Cambodia in the 1990s one was certain to see the old, damaged buildings and ongoing reconstruction. When I surveyed 39 temples in Kompong Svay and Stoeng Saen districts, Kompong Thom province in early 2000, all the temples had suffered damage to their buildings to a greater or lesser extent. The reconstruction works took up a large proportion of the monks' daily schedule in many temples. However, there were significant variations in the process of reconstruction. In some temples, the local community had planned and initiated building, but had had to stop due to a shortage of funds. I was sometimes approached by monks, *achar*s and *kenakummekar*s in these temples with requests for financial contributions. Sometimes they proposed that I help them seek contributions from Japan since, they said, the Japanese believe in Buddhism just as Cambodians do. For them, the difference between Japanese Buddhism and Cambodian Buddhism, Mahayana and Theravada, was immaterial. This personal experience highlighted for me the significance of networking among temple communities in the study of building reconstruction in Cambodia.

The popular *Bon Kathin* and *Bon Phkar* festivals both provide important opportunities for this type of networking.[10] Buddhist festivals bring people together in the name of 'we Buddhists' to make merit collectively. These festivals also provide resources for reconstruction. Unlike the community-based Buddhist annual festivals,[11] *Bon Kathin* and *Bon Phkar* have the function of pulling in Buddhists from remote area as temporary participants. In these festivals, the person who is chosen to be the main organizer invites fellow Buddhists, often a group of relatives, neighbors and friends, to make offerings to a certain temple-monastery. An atmosphere of rejoicing fills the temple from the early morning and the crowds of participants, both native and non-local, gather in the ritual at midday. These rituals inevitably include the donation of a large amount of money.

The temple community in the rural area takes special care to prepare for the *Bon Kathin* festival every year. The festival provides a chance to offer the monks' yellow robes, called *kathina* in Pali, to each monastery. As a rule, monks in a temple can accept a number of *kathina* but only on a certain day during the *kathin* season. Therefore, the rural temple community goes to great lengths to find a wealthy organizer when scheduling the date for their *kathin* so that as many people as possible can join. In my research area, Wat San Kor is active in organizing this kind of event. I observed how the representatives of the remote temples around the area repeatedly visited Wat San Kor and asked the monks, *achar*s and *kanakamekar*s to help to find a delegation organizer for their own temples' festivals. Because they are aware of the economic status of the people in the market area of San Kor, which constitutes part of Wat San Kor's temple community, they try to network with them to access financial resources.

Before the beginning of the *kathin* season of 2001, Mr. PP, a prominent *achar* of Wat San Kor, proposed organizing a special style *kathin* delegation, called *kathin samaki,* for the local people. This is a sort of cooperative delegation for offering *kathina*, which differs from the ordinary *kathin* delegation in that there is no individual organizer. Mr. PP explained that this would be a way to respond to the requests from the many temples in remote areas and he stressed that it is not so important which temples donations are made to, the crucial thing is to participate in the act of merit making. As representative of all the *achar*s and *kanakammekar*s of Wat San Kor, Mr. PP then offered the *kathin samaki*'s shares to those who wished to participate; a share cost ten thousand riel. Approximately one thousand such shares were collected from relatively wealthy families, but a considerable number of participants refused the offer and decided instead to donate individually, according to their own economic status, starting with 100 riel at every *kathin*. After gathering the 'shares', Mr. PP divided the money and gave equal portions to each of ten *kathin* delegations in the name of Wat San Kor. Sixteen *kathin* delegation groups were formed around Wat San Kor in the season of 2001; ten of which were *kathin samaki* and six of which were individually sponsored. These delegations visited temples both in the commune and outside of it, particularly in the northern forested area.

However, the *kathin samaki* that Mr. PP initiated were called into question and were stopped after only one year. According to my observations, there were two kinds of criticism of the *kathin samaki*. The first and least poignant was a theoretical argument about the legitimacy of the *kathin samaki*. This sort of critique was leveled particularly by the adherents of *boran* practice as being 'outside of our tradition'. Mr. PP replied forcefully, saying that there is nothing in the Tripitaka forbidding it. He also emphasized the importance of making merit in a pure emotional state, without paying attention to styles. Also, although all the people in the research area agreed that the ritual of *kathin* should be conducted inside the *preah vihear*, in some cases Mr. PP moved the donation of *kathina*, the central act of the ritual, from inside the *preah vihear* outside to the *sala chhan*. He said that people would be able to sit more comfortably in the *sala chhan* since the smaller area of the *preah vihear* would become very crowded. Mr. PP was concerned to adapt the ceremony to circumstances, and it is likely that his suggestions were made more acceptable by the fact that he had been ordained in Wat San Kor, had led the temple as head monk in the 1960s and was renowned for his ability to explain Buddhist doctrine. However, there was another more serious criticism. This concerned the selection of temples to be visited. Some people even openly complained about the arbitrary way in which Mr. PP and the other core members of the temple community selected the temples. Importantly, Mr. PP's knowledge of Buddhism provided no answers to these concerns.

Nevertheless, the activities of Wat San Kor facilitate a flow of resources to other temples in the area. Importantly, resources flow primarily in this manner from the market area to remote villages, from urban to rural communities. Buddhists in remote areas are keen to invite people who can mobilize resources, and the customs of Cambodian Buddhism and the ideology of merit making promote and support networking. However, this practice may, clearly, bring conflict and competition to the surface. The example of the reconstruction activities of *sala chhan* in Wat Prasat, which I observed in 2000–2001, provides useful insights on this type of contestation.

Conflict in the reconstruction process of the sala chhan in Wat Prasat

The original *sala chhan* of Wat Prasat was destroyed in a fire caused by a raid in 1974. After the DK era, the local people first rebuilt the *sala chhan* in wood, but the project to build a larger one with concrete posts was begun in 2000. The central figure in this reconstruction was Mr. CT, who was born in Veal village in 1937. He married at 21 years of age and subsequently lived with his wife's parents, cultivating paddy fields. A few years later, he started wholesale trading of chickens, and shifted to the trading of paddy in the latter half of the 1960s. In those days, he would travel to the forest area and buy paddy for cash or on credit. He survived the DK period, he said, because he was good at making wooden ox carts and building houses. In the 1980s, he sent his eldest son to Phnom Penh, where he eventually became a high-ranking official in a ministry. Mr. CT and his wife live in the village with their youngest daughter, her husband and the grandchildren.

Mr. CT took the initiative to lead the reconstruction of the *sala chhan* in Wat Prasat. He retired shortly after the marriage of his youngest daughter in 1992, and then began attending Buddhist activities enthusiastically. He ordained as a novice and spend one year in Wat Prasat, but nowadays he attends Wat San Kor more frequently than Wat Prasat. He says that this is because Wat San Kor is closer to his house. He also notes, however, that he prefers the *samay* practice of Wat San Kor, saying that it makes more sense to him, even though his parents criticized it in the past.[12] He and his family have organized several *kathin* delegations since the beginning of the 1990s, and in 1999 he managed to use his eldest son's connections to invite a group of people from Phnom Penh to come to Wat Prasat as a *kathin* delegation. This delegation from the capital was very large, and the money collected totaled some 42 million riel (approximately 10,790 US dollars).[13] After the *kathin*, he took it upon himself to purchase building materials from cities and he went to the temple frequently to take command of the reconstruction activities. In the end, the *sala chhan* was completed within one year, which is much faster than other temple reconstruction works going on in the area. However, a serious problem arose in the planning of the completion ceremony for the *sala chhan*, the last part of the reconstruction process.

The local people refer to Wat Prasat as the *boran* temple and, although monks' daily practice has become *samay* in style today, the temple continues to conduct most of the annual rituals in a manner similar to that of their ancestors. The head monk Monk TK's strong opposition to the *boran* tradition of his own temple is instructive. Monk TK was born in Chey village, San Kor, in 1973 and ordained in 1991. After staying at Wat Prasat for one year, he left to study away from the commune and moved over several *wat*s in Kompong Cham, Kandal, Pousat, Battambang, Phnom

Penh. He returned to the temple in 1996 and was promoted to head monk in 1997 at the request of the local people. However, a confrontation between Monk TK and a group of *achar*s of the temple took place just after his promotion. The *achar*s of the temple at that time were all renowned religious practitioners in the local community, who were respected for their ability to lead various rituals in *boran* style. These *achar*s had ordained at Wat Prasat in pre-war times. However, Monk TK's excellent knowledge of both Pali studies and secular social matters, acquired during his time outside of the commune, led him to oppose the temple tradition promoted by the old *achar*s.[14] This kind of contestation between young monks and old *achar*s about temple tradition had been apparent even before his promotion, but because Monk TK reacted to the old *achar*s with an inflexible attitude the conflict intensified; sometimes he forbade the monks and novices serving under him to join in *boran* rituals that had been organized by the *achar*s in response to the local people's requests. Finally, a group of original *achar*s stopped working in the temple and other *achar*s, who were less influential in the local religious scene, were brought in from the community.

At first Monk TK thought that the completion ceremony for the new *sala chhan* might provide an opportunity to ease the conflict. He had grown weary of the conflict and the social divisions it had created. He asked the officials of the department of religion of the provincial government to call a gathering of the members of the temple community of Wat Prasat in order to elect special religious officiants, called *achar bon* (festival *achar*s), to lead the completion ceremony. The outcome of this was that a group of the former *achar*s of the temple was elected. This group was going to try to organize the ceremony in cooperation with the present *achar*s of the temple. However, when they began the preparation in *boran* style, Mr. CT refused. According to him, the *sala chhan* had not been ritually dedicated to the monastery yet, so he retained the right to make decisions about the ceremony. One of the critical points of dispute was the performance of the ritual for dedicating the new Buddha statue, which had been brought from Phnom Penh by Mr. CT's family. The group of *achar*s of Wat Prasat insisted that the ritual should include a complicated procedure for transferring *parami* (perfection, goodness, virtue, power, charisma [Headley 1977: 526]) from the old statues to the new ones. However, Mr. CT adopted Mr. PP's stance on Buddhist doctrine, dismissing these ideas as unenlightened. He claimed that it was enough to consecrate the new statues by reciting Pali words and scattering flowers. In the end, the attempt at reconciliation failed, and the ceremony was held in *samay* style, in an atmosphere of great tension, with several of the older *achar*s refusing to participate even after negotiations.

CONCLUDING REMARKS

Today, the new *sala chhan* of Wat Prasat is in use, and temple activities attract many local participants. The tension between conflict and cooperation, as seen in the reconstruction processes, highlights the dilemma of reconciling the need to raise funds with preferences in practice. The various attitudes of the local people were clearly elucidated in this case. The core members of the temple community at present seem to be realists who are willing to network with the neighboring temple despite the difference in style of practice and a local history of tension caused by these differences. The ordinary villagers, who are located at the rim of the concentric temple community, did not actively debate the issue because in a practical sense both traditions provide the opportunity for them to make merit. However, some people clearly disapprove of the recent trend. The group of old *achar*s continued to criticize the role of the new *sala chhan* during my stay and expressed their feelings that the people are praying to a mere cement object, not a sacred statue ritually vested with *parami*. Moreover, they recently opted to shift their participation from Wat Prasat to the other two *boran* style temples in the commune.

The Buddhist temple in present day Cambodia is a much more complex place than the 'harmonious center of rural life' it has often been described as. While the shared ideology of merit making facilitates cooperative activity, questions of identity frequently lead to competition and conflict. The old *achar*s' ongoing attachment to *boran* practice illustrates their identification with temples and practices according to their own personal experiences and an embodied culture acquired throughout their lives. This identification is also evident in the nostalgic '*samay haoey*' that the older generation often remarks. This phrase, sometimes heard from elderly women who were not involved in the conflict, reminds us of the dynamic state of the community. Both temples and their practices are calling villagers into the space created by their imagination and memories of the past. At the same time, there is currently an increase of young people joining in temple affairs. They often express their reason for participating in a certain temple as 'because this *wat* is my/our *wat*' (*wat ni keu wat khnhom/yeung*). Importantly, all participants in the temple activities – including the group of old *achar*s, Monk TK, Mr.

CT and others – can share in this sentiment. Thus, the temple's 'tradition' is under reconstruction. The ongoing process of negotiation reflects the lively reality of the Buddhist temple as an arena at the intersection of the people's 'space', from the perspective of their varied backgrounds.

The reconstruction of the *sala chhan* of Wat Prasat also shows that reconstruction activities comprise an arena of vigorous interaction based upon economic potential and power. Under the socialist policy of the 1980s, Cambodian rural lives still faced various immediate difficulties and the dispute about Buddhist traditions had not yet surfaced. In the post-socialist era, changes began and intensified very quickly in almost all spheres of rural life. One of the results of this rapid social change since the mid-1990s is the escalation of the economic gaps within rural society. These disparities reflect larger trends throughout Cambodia in recent years. The Buddhist ideology of merit making facilitates networking between 'haves' and 'have-nots' as equals in Buddhism. However, the discrepancy between theory and practice is obvious, as seen in the case of Buddhist activities in San Kor. Mr. PP was able to effectively exploit the economic potential of the wealthy people in the market area. He also drew upon his rich and acknowledged ability to interpret practice. However, as seen in the people's criticism of the *kathin samaki* in Wat San Kor, Mr. PP's emphasis on the unity of Buddhists or equality in making merit as a principle was not sufficient for the local people. They have their own preferences for a certain temple and a certain practice, based on their perception of 'space'. Mr. CT's attitude in the reconstruction activities of the *sala chhan* in Wat Prasat represents another inconsistency. Although the Buddhist temple is open to everyone and the equality of participants as Buddhists is emphasized in the merit-making act, people also have a chance to assert power for personal benefits and disregard the interests of others in practice. However, despite the *samay*-style completion ceremony that Mr. CT initiated, the *sala chhan* of Wat Prasat is now being used for *boran*-style annual festivals. Buddhist ideology and the customary tradition of Cambodian Buddhism leave the question of conflict unanswered.[15]

The local manifestation of the *samay* or *boran* dichotomy, compromise and protest, indicates that Buddhist temples can be seen as not only arenas of interaction between individuals, but also as points of intersection between individuals' 'space'. It is not Buddhist ideology, but the recognition of the embedded nature of people's identification in geographical, socio-economic and historical ground that facilitate the interpretation of contemporary village Buddhism in any particular setting in Cambodian society.

AUTHOR'S NOTE

This is the revised version of a paper entitled 'Reconstructing Buddhist Temple Buildings in Post-socialist Cambodia: Fund raising, Merit-making ideology, Rural lives in Transition', which was presented at the workshop. Many thanks for the comments from the participants. I conducted intensive fieldwork in the research area between the years 2000 and 2002. This was made possible by research grants from the Matsushita International Foundation, Japan. I also conducted supplementary research in the area and in Phnom Penh in 2004. This was supported by the Kobayashi Setsutaro Memorial Fund of Fuji Xerox, Japan. I extend special thanks to both foundations.

REFERENCES

Bowie, Katherine (1998) 'The Alchemy of Charity of Class and Buddhism in Northern Thailand.' *American Anthropologist* 100 (2) pp. 469–481.

Ebihara, May (1968) 'Svay, a Khmer Village in Cambodia'. Doctoral dissertation. Department of Anthropology, Columbia University.

—— (1990) 'Return to a Khmer Village.' *Cultural Survival Quarterly* 14 (3) pp. 67–70.

—— (1993a) 'A Cambodian Village under the Khmer Rouge, 1975–1979.' In Ben Kiernan (ed.) *Genocide and Democracy in Cambodia: The Khmer Rouge, the United Nations and the International Community*. Monograph Series No. 41. New Haven: Yale University Southeast Asia Studies, pp. 51–63.

—— (1993b) 'Beyond Suffering: The Recent History of a Cambodian Village.' In B. Ljunggren (ed.) *The Challenge of Reform in Indochina*. Cambridge, MA, Harvard Institute for International Development, pp. 149–166.

—— (2002) 'Memories of the Pol Pot Era in a Cambodian Village.' In Judy Ledgerwood (ed.) *Cambodia Emerges from the Past: Eight Essays*. DeKalb: Northern Illinois University Southeast Asia Publications, pp. 91–108.

Ebihara, May and Judy Ledgerwood (2002) 'Aftermaths of Genocide: Cambodian Villagers.' In Alexander Laban Hinton (ed.) *Annihilating Difference: The Anthropology of Genocide*. Berkeley and Los Angeles: University of California Press, pp. 272–291.

Edwards, Penny (2007) *Cambodge: A Cultivation of a Nation*. Honolulu: University of Hawai'i Press.

Hayashi, Yukio (1995a) 'Fukkosuru Kambojia bukkyo no genzai [Present situation of Restoring Cambodian Buddhism].' *Daihorin* 62 (10), pp. 146–149.

—— (1995b) 'Kambojia bukkyo no fukko ni kansuru kisokennkyu: gentityosa houkokusiryo

[Basic study on the restoration process of Cambodian Buddhism: A report of the field research].' In *Kambojia no Syakai to Bunka: Gentityosa houkokusiryo* [Cambodian Society and Culture: a Report of the Field Research]. Tokyo: Kambojia Sogokenkyukai, pp. 290–389.

—— (2002) 'Buddhism Behind Official Organizations: Notes on Theravada Buddhist Practice in Comparative Perspective.' In Hayashi Yukio and Aroonrut Wichienkeeo eds *Inter-Ethnic Relations in the Making of Mainland Southeast Asia and Southwestern China*. Bangkok: Amarin Printing and Publishing Public Company Limited, pp. 198–230.

Headley, Robert (1977) *Cambodian–English Dictionary*. Washington D.C.: The Catholic University of America Press.

Keyes, Charles (1994) 'Communist Revolution and the Buddhist Past in Cambodia.' In Helen Hardacre, Laurel Kendall and Charles F. Keyes (eds) *Asian Visions of Authority: Religion and the Modern States of East and Southeast Asia*. Honolulu: University of Hawai'i Press, pp. 43–73.

Kobayashi, Satoru (2004) 'Kambojia Tonle Sap ko tougantiiki nouson ni okeru seigyoukatsudou to seikei no genjyou [A descriptive analysis of livelihood activities in two contemporary Cambodian villages: a case study from the eastern region of the Tonle Sap Lake].' In Amakawa Naoko ed. *Kambojia Sin-jidai* [Cambodia in a New Era]. Tokyo: Institute of Developing Economies, pp. 275–325.

— (2005a) 'An Ethnographic Study on the Reconstruction of Buddhist Practice in Two Cambodian Temples: With the Special Reference to Buddhist Samay and Boran.' *Tonan Ajia Kenkyu* [Southeast Asian Studies], 42 (4), pp. 489–518. Kyoto: Center for Southeast Asian Studies, Kyoto University.

—— (2005b) 'Kambojia, Tonle Sap ko tougantiiki nouson ni okeru syuuraku no kaitai to saihen: Ichi sonrakusyakai no 1970 nen ikou no rekisikeiken no kensyou [An examination of the demise and reconstruction of a Cambodian village since 1970: a case study from the eastern Tonle Sap Region].' *Tonan Ajia Kenkyu* [Southeast Asian Studies], 43 (3), pp. 273–302. Kyoto: Center for Southeast Asian Studies, Kyoto University.

Leach, Edmund (1968) 'Introduction.' In E. R. Leach (ed.) *Dialectic in Practical Religion*. Cambridge: Cambridge University Press, pp. 1–6.

Marston, John (2002) 'Reconstructing "ancient" Cambodian Buddhism.' Unpublished manuscript of English version of 'La reconstrucción del budismo "antiguo" de Camboya'. *Estudios de Asia y África* 37 (2), pp. 271–303.

NOTES

1 A number of anthropological studies emphasize the importance of merit-making ideology for understanding Buddhist behavior in Theravada countries. Like Theravada Buddhists in other countries Cambodians believe they can gain merit through various acts such as ordaining to be monks, keeping Buddhist precepts, performing Buddhist meditation, and offering food to monks. Contributing to temple reconstruction projects is one important way of making merit (see also Ledgerwood in this volume).

2   For the details of the people's livelihood activities and the social history in San Kor commune, see Kobayashi 2004, 2005b.

3   The community in and around San Kor commune received Chinese immigrants from the end of nineteenth century to the 1960s. Local traders in the area at the beginning of twentieth century were said to be the children of these Chinese. However, at that time, a large number of Chinese descendents engaged only in rice-cultivation and fishing. A paper dealing with this historical process of social formation is currently under preparation.

4   The men of several village households in the area would travel west to the Thai border by bicycle and purchase goods such as cigarettes and textiles in exchange for gold. They would then set out toward the East again, passing over San Kor, to the eastern region of the Mekong River and sell their goods, which, they say, were eventually distributed on the Vietnamese market. Due to the deteriorating security situation bicycle trading ceased by around 1981.

5   Vietnamese troops were stationed in the compound of Wat San Kor until 1989.

6   I have elsewhere described in detail the reconstruction of Buddhist practice in San Kor after the DK era (Kobayashi 2005a). Here, therefore, I limit my presentation to a summary.

7   It survived through the DK period because of its function as a rice storehouse.

8   These buildings in two temples in San Kor are called *salom* on some occasions. They function similarly to *preah vihear* but are different in size and construction material. When people refer to a building as *salom*, there is a connotation that the structure is transitional.

9   Some scholarly works on Cambodian Buddhism have touched upon the issue of the *samay* and *boran*. This is particularly true of the historical studies on the institutionalization and nationalization of Cambodian *sangha* (e.g. Edwards 2007), but efforts have also been made to understand macro-level religious movements in post-socialist Cambodia, where this dichotomy provides a key analytical framework (Marston 2002). The concepts of *samay* and *boran* are very relevant to village level analysis of religious activities as well, because villagers themselves describe the local Buddhist environment in these terms.

10 *Bon Kathin* is a common Buddhist annual festival in Theravada culture, which takes place at temples on a certain day of the season, which starts on the first day of old moon of the month of *Assoch* and continues until the full moon day of the month of *Kattek* in the Cambodian lunar calendar (corresponding roughly to October in the Gregorian calendar). *Bon Phkar*, the other popular festival in Cambodia, does not have a particular season.

11 These are *Bon Pisakbouchea, Bon Meakbouchea, Bon Phchum Ben* etc. In the case of these annual festivals in rural temples, participation is usually limited to the local residents of surrounding villages, so the size of donations is often smaller than at *Bon Kathin* or *Bon Phkar*.

12 He explained that he ordained at Wat Prasat because his parents preferred *boran* practice to the *samay* practice of Wat San Kor.

13 About 87 per cent of this monetary contribution was from a delegation from Phnom Penh. The largest sum of money collected at a single *kathin* that I have observed was in 2001, when some 10 million riel were donated. The average is about 3 million. This shows that the *kathin* delegation of Wat Prasat in 1999 was remarkably large.
14 Monk TK was also very interested in social matters and liked to refer to issues such as human rights and democracy in his Buddhist preaching.
15 See Bowie (1998) for further discussion of the interaction between Buddhist merit-making ideology and social inequality.

CHAPTER 10

In the Absence of Elders:
Chaos and moral order in the aftermath of the Khmer Rouge

Eve Monique Zucker

PRELUDE

In David Chandler's 'Songs at the Edge of the Forest', he describes and analyses a poem written in the nineteenth century which was a 'world of suffering, instability and war' (1998b: 85); a period analogous to the 1970s and 1980s a century later. The poem is about the rescuing of civilization from the clutches of chaos, the restoration of moral order, and the attempt to smooth over the rupture with that order's past. It dictates that a loss of merit occurred, evinced by a loss in lineage – a vacuity of ancestral past (ibid.: 85). Then it tells the story of what transpired. Following a Khmer massacre of Vietnamese, the Vietnamese attack, forcing the people to flee (ibid.: 89). The protagonist of the story then orders 'his (extended) family to leave (jat kruo), many of whom were elderly,[1] to fill their ox-carts with possessions and to leave at once' and in the haste of the departure, Chandler explains, many of the valuables end up strewn over the ground (ibid.). The poem reads: '...many possessions were lost forever, scattered along the roads and in the forest' (ibid.). These possessions, Chandler tells us, 'are the symbols of civilization, ways of expressing a frontier between the wild, undifferentiated world, and the world of hierarchies anchored in ritual and in the past' (ibid.: 89–90).

This chapter looks at the after-effects of cataclysmic violence that occurred in Cambodia over a century after the poem that Chandler describes was written, and it suggests that it was the elders themselves who might have been the most important of the valuables to be rescued in the poem.

They were the ultimate bearers of the moral and social order, for they enabled transmission of the past order and, as living ancestors, were also representatives and embodiments of that moral order. In other words, they signified and were the signifiers of Khmer civilization.

This interpretation of the meaning of elders for Khmer society takes an interesting turn in the post-Pol Pot period with which this chapter is concerned. I posit that the loss of elders during Pol Pot's revolution later became a sign of disorder that was evident in the order making process following the demise of Democratic Kampuchea. This disorder, I suggest, may be seen as a culturally specific form of chaos in that it both resists and contradicts those local notions of order that exist today but that are founded upon the pre-revolutionary past.

INTRODUCTION: CHAOS AND MORAL ORDER

Anthropologist Michael Scott (2005) has argued that chaos needs to be analysed and understood within the culturally particular visions of the phenomenon, which are often located in the mythic primordial space that precedes moral order, or are antithetical to that original moral order. Scott suggests that by attempting to understand these ideas we can see how particular historical episodes may be perceived as especially threatening in that they endanger the cosmological order and its processes. For Cambodia, the idea of a culturally specific notion of chaos has been addressed by a number of scholars of Cambodia (de Bernon, 1994; Hansen & Ledgerwood, 2005; Hinton, 2002, 2005; Mouth, 1998a; Ponchaud, 1989). However, it is above all David Chandler's work, particularly 'Songs at the Edge of the Forest' (1998b) (see above) and 'Going through the Motions' (1998a), that highlights the connection between chaos and the idea of an original ordering, which formed and substantiated Khmer ontology. In 'Songs' Chandler shows us through his analysis of nineteenth century literature how the ontological basis of humanity and civilization in Cambodia rests largely on a dichotomy between the 'wild' and the 'civil'. The 'wild' is associated with chaos whereas the 'civil' constitutes rank and hierarchy, that is, proper order. In both articles Chandler suggests that in the aftermath of chaotic historical episodes restoration of order is sought not by innovation but through a return to the traditions of the past, those of the ancestors (1998a; 1998b). Order, then, is restored by honouring the ancestors (1998a) and then maintained through the predictable transmission of stories, rituals and customs that are drawn from this ancestral past (1998b).[2]

In this chapter I suggest that like the chaos implied by the scattering of the possessions on the road in the poem that Chandler describes (1998b), the loss of elders presents a form of disorder or chaos. That is, the rupture to the moral order imposed initially by cataclysmic violence persists in its aftermath in the form of the resultant disorder. Many of the tangible and intangible forms of morality and order, including kinship structures and relations, religious institutions and other moral practices, were violated under the Khmer Rouge. In the aftermath of the violence the structuring features of the moral order that were transgressed remained unfixed and unbounded. In this disorderly state the structures of morality and order that are normally tacit may now become apparent because they have been transgressed. The necessity to engage with these structures in their disorderly and apparent state may produce a form of communal existential uncertainty that is overcome by trying to re-face and fill in the voids.[3]

I suggest here that the loss of elders is chaotic in three ways. First, the lack of elders is antithetical to and therefore chaotic relative to the moral order that was generated at the mythic moment of the birth of Khmer civilization and that forms the basis of Khmer social organization. I suggest that the loss of elders represents a structural void in a society that is organized in large part according to kinship, ranking and hierarchy. Second, the loss of elders creates an obstacle to the restoration of moral order by impeding the transmission of traditional knowledge and practice and therefore creating a disjunction with the past and the ancestors. This limits the resources that may be excavated from the past to create society anew and curtails access to the ancestors' generative power. Third, although villagers are restoring order by turning either towards tradition or towards what they consider 'modern' ideologies and practices, there is the problem of the perceived immorality of the actions of elders and ancestors in the past. I suggest that this perception contributes to the sense of disorder and obstructs the remaking of order because these immoral elders and ancestors then present a negation of the narrative of a moral past, and they undermine people's vision of the original moral order as a whole. As we shall see, it is therefore necessary that this problem be overcome by either circumnavigating it or by smoothing it over.

BACKGROUND AND SETTING

I conducted ethnographic fieldwork out of the small village of O'Thmaa nestled on the forest's edge in Kompong Speu province between 2002 and

2003 as part of a 25-month dissertation research project[4] in Cambodia that began in September 2001. My study spanned both the commune where I stayed, which I call Prei Phnom, and its neighbour, which I call Doung Srae. Prei Phnom commune at that time had a population of approximately 3,000 people whereas Doung Srae had roughly 5,500 people.[5] The two communes are strategically located in a mountainous and forested region 30 kilometres or so west of a main highway, but with Prei Phnom in the more mountainous area. The majority of the population in both of these communes occupies the lowest rungs of Cambodia's socio-economic ladder although, when I was there, some households in Doung Srae were showing signs of emerging prosperity. Both communes share similar but not identical histories as battle sites and refuges for revolutionaries and insurgents. These areas provided a base for both the Issaraks during the war of independence in the late 1940s and early 1950s and also for Khmer Rouge soldiers during the revolution from the late 1960s to 1975, and again during the civil war that lasted from 1979 to 1998. Vietnamese forces also occupied the area during the war of independence, the Lon Nol Years (1970–1975) and the People's Republic of Kampuchea (1979–1989) – albeit in the final case mostly indirectly through Khmer soldiers under their government.

Prei Phnom commune also provided a base in the Lon Nol years for another insurgent movement called the Khmae Saa (White Khmer)[6] who fought against the Vietnamese and the Khmer Rouge.[7] Another shared feature of these years was that many of the same people remained leaders throughout the upheavals, particularly in the first two periods. During the time of Democratic Kampuchea (1975–1979) most of the residents of Prei Phnom commune were moved to Doung Srae to participate in the large agricultural projects taking place there. In the years that followed, during the height of the fighting, residents of both communes were forcibly relocated to townships along the main highway. The people of Doung Srae commune were able to return to their homes a few years earlier than those in Prei Phnom (especially those in more remote villages like O'Thmaa) but generally residents of both communes returned home between the mid-1990s and 2000.

When I arrived at my fieldsite, it was immediately apparent to me that the two communes were now very different, an observation that was also shared by many of the residents of both communes.

Despite war and hardship, the commune and people of Doung Srae seemed to be thriving communally, spiritually and in some cases economically, in comparison to those in Prei Phnom. There was also a marked difference in the number of elders who had survived and returned home. Overall, more elders had survived in Doung Srae commune. The most extreme example of this is the Prei Phnom village of O'Thmaa, where only a handful of the original households remain and, when I was living there, approximately one fourth of these were headed by widows. Both Lon Nol's forces and the Khmer Rouge had considered the villagers here to be enemies and many villagers were executed, especially by the Khmer Rouge. Some villagers played a role in these killings despite or perhaps even because of the fact that those accused were often their neighbours and extended kin by blood or marriage. Doung Srae on the other hand appears to have had a smoother transition in the early Khmer Rouge years. Residents there say that although the Khmer Rouge initially did not fully trust the people of the commune they did not accuse or execute people in the early years of the revolution as they did in Prei Phnom. Instead, they even recruited members of the villages to act as leaders in other locales, indicating again that they considered this area to be more secure. Another significant difference between the two communes was that large scale agricultural projects were begun very early in Doung Srae[8] where a flatter terrain afforded more security and agricultural potential. The experience for villagers in both communes became more similar in the DK period when most of the residents from Prei Phnom were sent to Doung Srae to work on the projects there. Exceptions to this were those who were part of village exchange groups, soldiers, or members of the mobile work groups that were sent to other locations around the country.

Strong elders versus a lack of elders

Today people of both communes talk about the differences between Prei Phnom and Doung Srae in terms of the lack of elders in the former, and the presence of strong elders in the latter. They say that Doung Srae has 'strong elders' (*chi don chi ta klang*) who 'have a clear memory of the old traditions and the ways of the ancestors'. When describing Prei Phnom, on the other hand, people say that there is a 'lack of elders' (*chi don chi ta at mean*) after the war, and that traditional knowledge and practice in this commune is therefore relatively weak. This loss of elders, they say, explains why the people of Prei Phnom have lost interest in traditional practices and knowledge and instead have turned toward 'modern' (*niyum*) ideologies and ways. The commune chief of Prei Phnom explained to me:

The young people don't know much about the ancient traditions and the old people who did are dead now. These days the younger folks are into the *'niyum'* – popular ideas. However, in Doung Srae they practise the ancient customs and traditions and have a lot more elders who know how to perform these traditions.

The chief believes that Doung Srae commune has sufficient elders to direct and orchestrate traditional practices whereas in his own commune the lack of elders has prevented the transmission of this type of knowledge. The resulting ignorance of the past amongst its younger members, he argues, has led them to turn towards foreign future-oriented ideologies for their inspiration and direction.

There are other real and perceived differences between the two communes. For example, in Prei Phnom commune we see a tentative Buddhist revival with some conversion to Methodist Christianity (especially in the remote, western villages), loss of some traditional practices, and interest in contemporary (modern) fashion and thought (popular dress, music, capitalism, etc). On the other hand, in Doung Srae commune we see 'strong elders' with 'clear knowledge and memory of traditions and customs', pervasive religious participation, a strong *wat*, vibrant revival of religious practice and tradition, and 100 per cent of the population remaining Buddhist. Indicative of this concern with the past there is a current project led by the senior laymen (*achar*s) to research, record and archive traditional practices in an attempt to restore knowledge and practices associated with the past – ironically, a patently modern enterprise.[9] An excellent illustration of the disparity in traditional practices can be found in the restoration (in Doung Srae) and abandonment (in Prei Phnom) of the practice of building *phnom yong khmauch* funeral towers[10] following the termination of Democratic Kampuchea. Many families of both communes used to engage in this practice before the war and the Pol Pot regime kept them from doing so. However, while the practice has enjoyed a vibrant revival in Doung Srae, in Prei Phnom the practice has long been abandoned. Villagers in Prei Phnom say that the commune lacks elders who have the knowledge to conduct the practice. As one woman explained:

> Before, during the Sihanouk period, people used to build *phnom yong* for their parents when they died. But nowadays no one does *phnom yong* anymore when their parents die. The people who knew how to make *phnom yong* all died and we, the young generation, don't know how. In Doung Srae on the other hand they still have a lot of old people there, whereas here we don't.

In the absence of elders: chaos and moral order in the aftermath of the Khmer Rouge

This woman's explanation for the abandonment of certain traditional practices in Prei Phnom and their revitalization in Doung Srae was repeated by many of the villagers in the area. The distinction between the two communes is evident to people in both communes, but the situation is, unsurprisingly, not entirely black and white. Many residents of Prei Phnom commune express an interest in traditional practices and there are some elders there who have retained their knowledge of these matters. By the same token, the people of Doung Srae cannot be said to be uninterested in modern music, dress and ideas. Rather, the difference is a matter of degree, people's perceptions, and the level of their expressed interests.

Figure 10.1. Phnom yong khmauch

Figure 10.2. Large phnom yong khmauch

Returning to the main theme of this chapter, I suggest that the lack of elders in Prei Phnom commune represents a residual form of disorder that is left over from the chaos of war and the DK regime. In Doung Srae, the chaos and rupture of war is being mended through an appeal to tradition and the ancestral past and is evident in their current revival of traditions and rituals, and their preoccupation with excavating and reconstructing their social history. The same cannot be said of Prei Phnom, where the absence of old people has created a void not only for the present, but also in the availability of the past for the present. In Prei Phnom, the diminutive size of the elderly population, who would be able to link the past to the present, limits the resources that might be excavated from the past to fill in and enrich the present. There are simply not enough elders who remember the ways of their ancestors, and the links to those ancestors are therefore frayed or broken.

CHAOS AND THE (RE-)BIRTH OF THE MORAL ORDER

The mythical past

Khmer history begins, according to the myths, with the marriage of culture and nature. While there are several versions of this myth, in essence a princely foreigner of Indian origins marries the *naga* king's daughter, a *nagi* (Chandler, 1992; Mouth, 1998b). Out of this exogamous marriage between the prince and the *nagi*, between culture and nature, we are told, Khmer civilization was born. A number of Khmer kings then ruled the kingdom, producing a royal line of descent, and a network of kinship relations sharing common ancestry. In this manner, order was established with its attendant hierarchy and rankings. This order placed the ancestors in an elevated position not only because of their relative lineal proximity to the original kings but also for their connection to a metaphysically powerful, mythical and enchanted past. This association with the past imbues the ancestors with moral wisdom and action that is expressed as traditional knowledge and practice. Contemporary practitioners, in turn, become continuous with the mythic past and its generative power.

From this perspective, moral order is both an entity and a dynamic process. Kinship, then, constitutes both form and substance, the structure and a structuring component of moral order. In their discussion of moral order in pre-modern Southeast Asia, David Wyatt and Alexander Woodside noted: 'The language of social thought was limited ... and did not travel far beyond the use of family relationships as metaphors for broader political and social occurrences' (1982: 7). The centrality of kinship to order at that time, later during the period before Pol Pot and even today, cannot be overstated. Hence a void in vertical kinship structure caused by a lack of elders threatens the moral order as a whole; it both ruptures the order and impairs its reproduction. What are the consequences of such a gap and how do people seek to overcome it? The next section examines some of the implications and resolutions of such a cleavage.

Restoring order

Woodside and Wyatt submit that pre-modern Buddhist Southeast Asian thinkers endorsed a unitary moral order, in which everything formed part of a single existence and the binaries of being and nothingness, good and evil, etc. were no more than symbols used to 'differentiate between various elements within a given unitary whole' (1982: 6–7). The cosmic order contained everything and everything contained it. The understanding of moral order just prior to the Khmer Rouge revolution was probably not very different from this in the rural and remote areas of Cambodia, such as my fieldsite, where the ideologies presented by colonialism, nationalism and modernity had had minimal impact as compared to locales closer to the 'centre'.[11]

Despite the lack of elders, many people of Prei Phnom are attempting to restore elements of the past in an effort to surmount this uncertainty and restore a workable moral order. By re-enacting and improvising some traditional ritual practices, by recalling myths and stories that create and construct locality and a mythical ancestral past, and by gathering and transmitting fragments of local knowledge, the villagers are slowly piecing together an order that bears some semblance to that of former times. In both Prei Phnom and Doung Srae we see the reinstitution of the *Bon Dalien* harvest ritual festivities and the corresponding 'asking for rain' (*Som Toeuk Plieng*) ceremonies, the sending of sons from the villages into the monkhood, the making of offerings to the local ancestor and guardian spirits (*neak ta, me sa, arak*), and, in the case of Doung Srae, the partial reinstitution of the building of funeral towers (*phnom yong khmauch*).

For many, but not all of the people living in Prei Phnom, however, the traditional past and the order that it implies have lost some of their potency. For example, the local *neak ta* are said to be no longer as demanding or as potent as they used to be. Perhaps in response to this,[12] people have turned towards future-oriented, pragmatic ideologies that they see as 'modern' to fill the vacuum of order in a manner that answers to their everyday needs and concerns. One woman, a former Khmer Rouge cadre in her early forties, explained to me that she and her husband converted to Methodist Christianity because it is 'the only religion that can save you'. Ya, a 36-year-old former PRK soldier until 1987, and later a Khmer Rouge soldier, explained why he converted:

> I could feel God's spirit enter me. Before, when I still believed in Buddhism, I was prohibited from eating certain foods. I couldn't even eat rabbit. Even looking at one would make my eyes swell up. But when I began believing in Christianity I could suddenly eat rabbit and nothing would happen to me ... I believe in Jesus because of this. However, if I was to eat rabbit and it DID cause my eyes to swell, I also would stop believing in it.

When I asked another man from the same village, Sau, whether he had ever converted, he replied:

> No. It's like with foods that we are prohibited to eat. If we are prohibited to a certain type of food, we cannot eat it. Like rabbit,[13] I cannot eat it. It is prohibited. But the old people know about the truth of this prohibition. They say that this is a prohibition for hunters.

It is interesting in the two quotes above how this local taboo against eating rabbit is employed by people to talk about their religious orientations and their ideas about conversion. Ya sees his ability to eat rabbit as a sign of the moral potency of Christianity over Buddhism and the ways of the past. Sau on the other hand uses the traditional prohibition against eating rabbit to explain why he cannot convert – for him Christianity is indigestible. But there is more to the story – Ya does not feel welcome in the village of his ancestors whereas Sau does. Although he says that the pre-war past was a time when villagers 'loved one another' he also observed that his parents' generation committed terrible deeds against one another. As for contemporary village relations Ya sees a division between those with more and those with less. Those with more, he says, are self-interested and unwilling to offer any assistance to those neighbours with less. On the other hand he says, the situation is quite different in the village of his wife's family in Doung Srae, where villagers help one another.

To return to Ya's conversion to Christianity and the accompanying lifting of the prohibition of eating rabbit we see that this may be a means for Ya to reduce his affiliation with the village, its sordid past, and its present day difficulties by rejecting its very local culture and tradition.[14] He may in this way be attempting to cut off his relation to the village and form a stronger one to his wife's in Doung Srae. Interestingly, the metaphor of food is used to talk about these negotiations of moral order. Food is a potent moral carrier (Bloch, 2005; Trankell, 1995).[15] By eating food that his ancestors and relations would have found to be immoral he is cutting off his tie of kinship and community and also his tie to the past. Sau on the other hand uses the same metaphor to indicate that Christianity is 'other', that is, foreign and outside kin and community to assert his place in the village and his ties to the ancestors. Both men lost parents to the Khmer Rouge but Sau's mother survived and is still alive.

Ya, like all of the villagers that I interviewed who had converted to Christianity, was a former Khmer Rouge soldier and would have been a very young child[16] when the Khmer Rouge first entered the area. While most former Khmer Rouge living in the area did not convert, there nevertheless appears to be a link between the two. It is possible that the dissolution of the Khmer Rouge movement may have meant for them a double rupture to the moral order – that is, the moral order of the past previous to the Khmer Rouge as well as the bastardized substitute that was the revolutionary ideology of the Khmer Rouge. This ideology, it should be noted, also encompassed notions of modernity and a utopia of sorts.[17] In any case, these children of the revolution who grew up without much direct[18] Buddhist influences were probably easy converts for the Methodist missionaries who offered spiritual salvation as well as material in the form of food and education.

Sau and Ya were both too young during the DK to be soldiers. Later in the 1980s both joined the government army that fought the Khmer Rouge but in 1987 Ya switched sides to join the Khmer Rouge. The Khmer Rouge had executed both men's fathers in the early seventies and both men placed the blame on a local villager, who was the acting village leader, Ta Kam, whom I shall discuss below. The fact that they both lost their fathers to the Khmer Rouge at approximately the same time and in a similar manner suggests that Sau's decision not to join the Khmer Rouge or become a Christian is not simply the outcome of having lost his father. But what is interesting is that Sau is one of the people in Prei Phnom who shows an active interest in the traditions of the past. Perhaps this is because of his 89-year old mother, who not only remembers some of the traditions and stories from the past but who also enthusiastically shares this knowledge with her children and others. Her presence and influence seem to mitigate the gap whereas for

Ya (and his wife, who also lost her parents under the Khmer Rouge) the privation implied by the lack of elders seems to compound personal losses.

As the people described above show, the generation, negotiation and maintenance of moral order is a tenuous and ambiguous process fraught with uncertainties and variables.

Obstacles to restoring order: the immoral elders[19]

The morality of the generation of elders that I have been discussing so far is considered by people of both communes to be extremely questionable. People say that they 'don't understand why this particular generation did the things they did to each other', or 'why they killed one another'. Some say that 'the people of that time lacked moral knowledge or education (*at che dung*)'.

One of the few surviving elders of O'Thmaa told me that he is from the 'difficult generation'. This man, whom I call Ta Kam, has been blamed by some villagers for the deaths of several people's fathers, uncles and grandparents. He was 79 when I met him, lean and angular from a lifetime of work and poverty, with a crop of white hair that sharply contrasted the caramel colour of his gaunt face. On occasion he could be seen with his worn red-and-white-checked *kroma* (scarf) tied into a small bundle and slung over his shoulder. Giving the appearance of a wandering ascetic or a pilgrim, he would make his way along the road between O'Thmaa and Doung Srae, where he now lives with his sister's family. He was always dressed in the same way: a threadbare white shirt, mid-length trousers. Sometimes he would also be clutching a staff and bearing a wide brimmed hat to deflect the sweltering sun during his long treks.

In Doung Srae and in the village where he now lives with his sister he is welcomed as an *achar*, but in his own village, his *srok komnat*, he is shunned. On his rare visits to the village when he stays with his daughter he converses with no one apart from his daughter and no one converses with him. And yet he is related to many of the people in both communes. He explained:

> Two families here, three families there ... every village in Prei Phnom, Doung Srae ... I have a lot of relatives. I've had a long life and so I have many descendants but their parents have all died. There are only children, grandchildren, nieces and nephews left. Their parents were my siblings and cousins. There is only myself left. I am eighty years old already. The others younger than me are all gone.

In the absence of elders: chaos and moral order in the aftermath of the Khmer Rouge

Ta Kam speaks about the deaths that occurred but denies any role or responsibility. For the villagers, though, his haunting presence reminds them of the loss of family members and the executions that took place in the early 1970s, soon after the Khmer Rouge had 'liberated' the region. Villagers say that Ta Kam was the Deputy Village Chief under Lon Nol but later was chosen by the villagers to be village chief under the Khmer Rouge. The previous village chief had been executed by Lon Nol soldiers having been accused of working for the Khmer Rouge. Ta Kam himself, however, denies ever having been a village chief and says that his life under the Khmer Rouge was just like everyone else's at the time:

> Before 1975 I didn't do any work [meaning he held no special position]. I was just like other people, someone eking out a living. The war happened … After that the Khmer Rouge pushed me to drive a cart and carry cloth, rice seed, and other stuff [again not in a power position].

He says that later on during the DK regime itself, he was forced to farm when he was transferred to a southern province as part of a village exchange during the DK years. Ta Kam claims to be one of the few survivors among those who participated in the exchange but during my interviews with him he offered no explanation as to why this was so. He spent the years following the DK period moving from place to place until he eventually settled with his sister's family in Doung Srae.

As one of the oldest members of the original village of O'Thmaa he is well versed in its traditions, myths and stories. However, because of his own past, his knowledge is inaccessible to the next generation; it is tainted by his past behaviour. People will talk *about* him but they will not talk *to* him. Ironically, a man who was working in the village but came from elsewhere told me: 'If you want to hear the real, old dialect of O'Thmaa just listen to the way Ta Kam speaks.' But for the surviving villagers he has become mute, incapable of being a medium for the transmission of the past. Ta Kam represents a triple blockage to the making of moral order. First, his presence prevents people from forgetting the immoral past that ruptured order. Second, he blocks the transmission of a moral past since he cannot legitimately pass on traditional knowledge. Third, he stands as the antithesis of moral order itself by inverting the structural order that places elders and ancestors in a morally elevated position.

It may seem ironic then that Ta Kam acts as an *achar* in the neighbouring commune, where he serves the needs of the monastery. The neighbouring commune is clearly making efforts to sew up the past by turning sharply towards tradition, and their traditional treatment of Ta Kam as an elder, combined with his acceptance of this role, re-stitch him into the moral fabric of society. In this manner the tears and holes in society are mended and the surface made smooth again. However, in Prei Phnom, and especially O'Thmaa village, this is not possible for they cannot forget this man's role (and others who played similar roles) in ripping apart their world, and perhaps this is in part why alternative ideologies and orders like Christianity and even more so, 'modernity' have their appeal. As long as individuals like Ta Kam remain living, mending the gap with tradition, for these people at least, is difficult if not impossible.[20]

Ta Kam himself describes no rupture in his telling explanation of his religious activities: 'I am only looking after my next life.' For him, it seems, the process of mending the moral order is less problematic than it is for the children of his alleged victims, and one wonders whether he ever really perceived a breach in it in the first place.[21]

CONCLUSION

The loss of elders represents a local and culturally specific form of chaos that is founded upon the notion that kinship, which encompasses the ancestors, forms part of an original founding moral order and produces that order. Rupture to this order, in the form of a loss of a generation of elders, leaves a void that undermines moral order and interrupts its transmission to future generations. I have also suggested that this type of chaos is particularly acute when those elders who do remain are considered immoral. The means by which people then grapple with these ontological inconsistencies provide clues to the ways in which chaos is locally perceived.

Peter Berger observes that 'the marginal situations of human existence reveal the innate precariousness of all social worlds ... every socially defined reality remains threatened by lurking "irrealities"' (1990: 24). It is difficult for the members of a society to consciously grasp the key constituents of their overarching moral order that they share and live within, so tacit is this knowledge, so embedded in the habitus of the everyday (cf. Judy Ledgerwood, this volume). But when that moral order is damaged or threatened, its components are sometimes momentarily revealed, offering recognition of the predicament but also offering a pathway for repairing it.

It is impossible to predict what shape the future will take, but it seems reasonable to assume that the restoration of moral order may take generations. Traditions must be either passed on or forgotten, new practices rejected or adopted, and some of the immorality of the past must perhaps become vague if not altogether forgotten.

AUTHOR'S NOTE

Special thanks to David Chandler, Alexandra Kent, Michael Scott and NIAS Press' referee for comments and insights on earlier versions of this article. I am grateful for the support for this research from the Luce Foundation through the Centre for Khmer Studies and the University of London Central Research Fund. Finally, I am deeply indebted to the people of 'Prei Phnom' and 'Doung Srae' communes whom this article is about.

REFERENCES

Bataille, Georges. (1986). *Eroticism: death and sensuality* (First City Lights edition ed.). San Francisco: City Lights Books.

Berger, Peter L. (1990). *The Sacred Canopy: elements of a sociological theory of religion.* New York: Anchor Books.

Bloch, Maurice. (1986). *From Blessing to Violence : history and ideology in the circumcision ritual of the Merina of Madagascar.* Cambridge, Cambridgeshire and New York: Cambridge University Press.

—— (1992). *Prey into Hunter : the politics of religious experience.* Cambridge ; New York: Cambridge University Press.

—— (2005). 'Commonsality and Poisoning.' In *Essays on Cultural Transmisson.* Oxford, New York: Berg, pp. 45–60.

Chandler, David. (1998a). 'Going through the Motions: ritual aspects of the reign of King Duang (1848–1860).' In *Facing the Cambodian Past.* Chiang Mai: Silkworm Press, pp. 100–118.

—— (1998b). 'Songs at the Edge of the Forest: perceptions of order in three Cambodian texts.' In D. Chandler (ed.), *Facing the Cambodian Past.* Chiang Mai: Silkworm Press, pp. 76–99.

Chandler, David P. (1992). *A history of Cambodia* (2nd ed.). Boulder: Westview Press.

de Bernon, Olivier. (1994). 'Le Buddh Damnây, note sur un texte apocalyptique khmer.' *BEFEO (Bulletin de l'Ecole Francaise d'Extreme-Orient), 81,* pp. 83–96.

Duclos, Denis. (1998). *The Werewolf Complex: America's fascination with violence* (A. Pingree, Trans.). Oxford ; New York: Berg.

Hansen, Anne, & Ledgerwood, Judy. (2005). *Prophetic Histories: the Buddh Damnay and violence in Cambodia.* Unpublished manuscript, Chicago.

Hinton, Alexander Laban. (2002). 'Purity and Contamination in the Cambodian Genocide.' In J. Ledgerwood (Ed.), *Cambodia Emerges from the Past: Eight Essays.* De Kalb: Northern Illinois University Press.

—— (2005). *Why Did They Kill?: Cambodia in the shadow of genocide*. Berkeley: University of California Press.

Marston, John. (2002). 'Democratic Kampuchea and the Idea of Modernity.' In J. Ledgerwood (ed.), *Cambodia Emerges from the Past: Eight Essays*. DeKalb: Southeast Asia Publications Center for Southeast Asian Studies Northern Illinois University, pp. 38–59.

Mouth, Sophea. (1998a). *Central Conceptions of the Khmer Rouge Ideology*.Unpublished manuscript, Madison.

—— (1998b). 'The Origins of Khmer History (Working Paper).' Unpublished manuscript, Madison.

Ponchaud, François. (1989). 'Social Change in the Vortex of a Revolution.' In K. D. Jackson (ed.), *Cambodia, 1975–1978 : rendezvous with death*. Princeton: Princeton University Press, pp. 151–177.

Saigon, US Mission in. (1970). *Ten Documents Illustrating Vietnamese Communist Subversion in Cambodia – August 1969–April 1970 (Translated extracts from notebooks of North Vietnamese military personnel)* (Documents): U.S. Mission in Saigon.

Scott, Michael. (2005). 'Hybridity, Vacuity, and Blockage: visions of chaos from anthropological theory, Island Melanesia, and Central Africa.' *Comparative Studies in Society and History, 47*(1), pp. 190–216.

Taussig, Michael T. (1999). *Defacement: public secrecy and the labor of the negative*. Stanford, Calif.: Stanford University Press.

Thompson, Ashley. (2004). 'The Suffering of Kings: substitute bodies, healing, and justice in Cambodia.' In J. Marston and E. Guthrie (eds), *History, Buddhism, and New Religious Movements in Cambodia*: University of Hawai'i Press, pp. 91–112.

Trankell, Ing-Britt. (1995). *Cooking, Care, and Domestication: a culinary ethnography of the Tai Yong, Northern Thailand*. Uppsala, Stockholm: Uppsala University; Distributor, Almqvist & Wiksell International.

Wyatt, David K., & Woodside, Alexander. (1982). 'Introduction.' In D. K. Wyatt and A. Woodside (eds), *Moral order and the question of change : essays on Southeast Asian thought Monograph series*. Vol. 24. New Haven, Conn.: Yale University, pp. 1–8.

Zucker, Eve Monique. (2007). 'Memory and (Re)making Moral Order in the Aftermath of Violence in a Highland Khmer Village in Cambodia.' Unpublished PhD Dissertation, London School of Economics and Political Science, London.

NOTES

1. Emphasis mine.
2. See also Ashley Thompson (2004) on the role of the king in this process of 'healing' in the aftermath of chaos. Her essay suggests that through the king's body the past is reintegrated into the present in a manner that secures the future (cf. Alexandra Kent in this volume).

3   I am suggesting here that this unveiling or defacement of the moral order was actualised through the transgression of its constituents, leaving a state of disorder or chaos in its wake. This chaos produces existential anxiety precisely because it is a state in which discontinuity thrives. That is, it is a state in which the normal ways that society and religion may offer immortality are temporarily impotent and the limits of mortality are made clear. Peter Berger addresses this issue directly in his book *The Sacred Canopy* (1990) but the relationship between existential uncertainty and violence is also studied more broadly by Georges Bataille (1986), Maurice Bloch (1986; 1992), Daniel Duclos (1998) and Michael Taussig (1999) among others.

4   See Eve Zucker (2007).

5   Statistics from each of the commune headquarters.

6   The White Khmer (*Khmae Saa*) were at this time a guerrilla movement led by former Issarak leader Chantaraingsey. The movement was initially unaligned with the government and opposed to the Khmer Rouge, Sihanouk, and North Vietnamese. For more about the White Khmer see the US Mission in Saigon (1970).

7   According to villagers, Ta Mok was the acting leader of the Khmer Rouge base just outside the village in Prei Phnom, where I stayed during my fieldwork. They also stressed that although Ta Mok was in charge of the area for the Khmer Rouge, several other of the Khmer Rouge's highest leaders, including Khieu Samphan, also frequented the base.

8   The first dam was built between 1973 and 1975.

9   My thanks to David Chandler for reminding me of this.

10 These are very tall wooden towers under which the body is cremated following a period of burial. In Doung Srae there are two types: the more ubiquitous temporary smaller houses which are abandoned after the cremation (Figure 10.1) and the rarer, larger permanent houses where the ashes are placed following cremation (Figure 10.2). This latter type may also be used to house the ashes of other consanguineal kin.

11 It should be noted, however, that this does not mean that these movements did not affect villagers in these areas. As mentioned earlier, Doung Srae and Prei Phnom communes were bases and battlefields during the war of independence. The majority of the villagers, especially from Prei Phnom, were forced to flee the fighting and some villagers joined the resistance. Despite this and the introduction especially to nationalist ideology, it would seem that the pre-existing moral order remained resilient up until the Khmer Rouge debaucheries.

12 Conversely, this perceived decline in potency of the ancestral and guardian spirits may be as much a product of these new cultural developments.

13 I was told the taboo against eating rabbit is local to O'Thmaa along with other prohibitions, such as sitting on an upturned mortar. It is said that if one violates these taboos tigers and elephants will come and destroy the village.

14 See Eve Zucker (2007: Ch. 6).

15 Within the Khmer context certain foods are indexical to particular moral values. For example, wild game, alcohol, and forest foods are often associated with wildness whereas cooked rice, domestic meat products and domestic vegetables are associated with civility. However, these categories are not entirely fixed for people living in

16 Ya was born in 1967 which would make him 3 years old when the Khmer Rouge first arrived. Like most of the adults and former soldiers remaining in Prei Phnom commune he would have spent his formative years under the Khmer Rouge. Those who became Khmer Rouge soldiers would also have spent the major part of their adult life under Khmer Rouge ideology.

17 For a discussion of Khmer Rouge conceptions of modernity, see John Marston's thought-provoking article 'Democratic Kampuchea and the Idea of Modernity' (2002).

18 By 'direct' I mean that they did not grow up practising Buddhism by attending *wat* events, celebrating Buddhist holy days, and or other outwardly Buddhist practices because of the Khmer Rouge's negative stance towards Buddhism. This is not to say, however, that they were not implicitly exposed to Buddhist ideas through the Khmer Rouge ideology itself (see Hinton, 2005). Moreover, contact with older members, especially family members, who would have recalled the more explicit forms of Buddhist practices, would have had a significant impact when those people were available. However, this was not the case for Ya and many others like him who lost their parents to the Khmer Rouge in the early 1970s. It should, however, be added that some of those who did not convert to Christianity later made an effort to learn about the ways of their parents and ancestors.

19 See Eve Zucker (2007) especially Chapters 4, 5 and Conclusions.

20 It should, however, be noted that his living presence may provide a more immediate means of limiting the rupture since he provides the villagers with a scapegoat with which to contain the immorality of his generation. Nonetheless, he continues to be an uncomfortable reminder of that past.

21 It may be argued that Ta Kam's religious activities are his way of trying to make amends. In my discussions and interviews with him he never gave any indication that he felt particularly guilty or ashamed of anything he may have done. Instead, when he described his life he presented himself as a passive subject rather than an active agent in his choices. The only indication he gave of pro-activity or responsibility on his part was that he was looking after his interests in this life by securing his property for his children and grandchildren and his securing his own future in the next life by becoming more religious. This is why I suggest that if his religious activity is an attempt to make amends, his motive is more functional than sentimental.

CHAPTER 11

The Moral Geology of the Present:
Structuring morality, menace and merit

Penny Edwards

'All men of politics are deeply religious, but they kill. The more pious he is, the more ferocious' (Soth Polin, 1980).[1]

Whoever harms with violence
Those who are gentle and innocent,
To one of these ten states
That person quickly descends:
He would beget
Severe suffering;
Deprivation and fracturing
Of the body; or grave illness, too;
Mental imbalance;
Trouble from the government;
Cruel slander;
Loss of relatives;
Or destruction of property.[2]

'Cambodia is a society that has lost any sense of morality, riven by violence and injustice' (Kong Boncheoun, 2000).[3]

INTRODUCTION

This essay is a preliminary exploration of the visions and expectations of moral behaviour displayed by state actors and entertained by the public in contemporary Cambodia. The past decade has seen a recurrent interest in the issue of Cambodian morality, both among the general population, particularly those in their mid-twenties and above, who fear its loss, and among the male leadership, whose public rhetoric is increasingly studded with strategically timed morality tirades. A primary focus of such tirades is the female form. A secondary focus is injurious foreign influence. In this chapter, I link these notions of female propriety and sexual morality with a hierarchical social structure, and explore the gap between the moral highground invoked or projected by this recent wave of rhetoric and the reality of escalating and often unsanctioned violent crime.

In the past decade, the pace of rapid economic change, the rapacious concentration of land and other material resources in the hands of a few key families in Cambodia, an escalation of ostentation and corruption, and a rise in youth crime and recreational drug-use, has led some Cambodians to evince nostalgia for aspects of the Democratic Kampuchea regime, whose leaders are now being brought to trial for crimes against humanity. Although this nostalgia is far from widespread, its existence even among a scattering of the educated urban population is worthy of analysis.

In this article, I attempt to link legacies and patterns of violence not so much with an active process of legitimation but to the broader absence of moral sanction. While Eve Zucker's essay for this volume explores the effects of the absence of elders on contemporary mores in two Cambodian villages in Kompong Speu, I shall reflect on the apparent moral disengagement of Cambodia's leadership with issues of social violence. That disengagement has varied from a laissez-faire approach to mob killings and acid-attacks, apparent from the mid-1990s onward, to the tacit endorsement of such communal or individual actions in the late 1990s. What interests me here is the contrast between this disengagement with issues of responsibility for personal and mob violence (notably mob violence directed against ethnic Vietnamese, perceived as prime suspects for crimes of property theft, and against females engaged in extra-marital affairs), and the country's increasingly active engagement in the policing of female corporeal, sexual and conjugal morality. In comparing these policies, I examine concepts of morality, the operation of kingship, and the current feminization of notions of immorality. In so doing, I also search for congruence between the emphasis placed by the government on issues of sexual morality and some perceptions held by . I also consider the role that the state accords the *sangha* in such affairs, and examine the resonance between the government's apparent prioritization of sexual morality over broader questions of social ethics, and some recent legislation vis-à-vis the *sangha*.

Cambodia is a multi-ethnic society, with most ethnic groups subscribing to overlapping and layered sets of beliefs, incorporating, in the Khmer population, Buddhism, animism and Brahmanism. In this chapter, my focus is on ethnic Khmer, but my setting is primarily Phnom Penh, within the outlying, broader framework of the nation-state. The city, in which many ethnic groups live, is the terrain for the formulation, performance, iteration of (but not necessarily adherence to) this moral code, as applied by the ruling secular and clerical elite, in their explicit or tacit approval, condoning acts that many societies would rank as worthy of particular condemnation in that they cause excruciating harm, pain, disfigurement or death to individuals.

MORAL ECONOMY, PATERNAL RULE AND SEXUAL POLITICS

Writing of pre-industrial England, E. P. Thompson described late eighteenth century food riots as the 'last desperate effort by the people to reimpose the older moral economy as against the economy of the free market' (Thompson 1968: 73). Thompson's scholarship is perhaps best known to scholars of Southeast Asia via James Scott's seminal work *The Moral Economy of the Peasant* (1978) in which Scott applied Thompson's interpretive framework to rural actors in colonized Vietnam. Thompson's definition of the moral economy as the 'consistent traditional view of social norms and obligations' with respect to the 'proper economic function of several parties within the community' (Thompson 1971) at the 'level of royal policymaking, genteel philosophizing, and in the popular consciousness' (Hill 1971) can also be usefully applied to Cambodia at the cusp of the new millennium when many Cambodians in the older generation, while glad to be free from war, are also seeking interpretive frameworks as they adjust to the rapid dislocation of an accelerated adaptation to an unbridled free market. For the purposes of this chapter, Thompson's reading of the moral economy provides a useful point of departure for the understanding of the apparent disparity between the vestiges of material modernization in Cambodia and the veiled or explicit desire for a reversion to feudal policies of paternalism.

Paternalism was used to greatest bombast and effect by Norodom Sihanouk in his Sangkum Reastr Niyum regime (1955–1970), which promoted the nuclear family in film and popular culture, while airing debates on polygamy in parliament. Its antithesis was the faceless but omnipresent and omnipotent *angkar* (organization) of the Democratic Kampuchea Regime, which sought to destroy the family unit and make the Cambodian Communist Party the only authority to whom all must answer, but simultaneously campaigned for a puritanical sexual morality and promoted mass weddings. The notion of the state as father figure and the nation as a motherland was renewed again under the Socialist People's Republic of Kampuchea, whose attempts to continue the DK's ban on prostitution failed (Evans 2003). From 1993 to 2006, the notion of paternal rule and the emphasis on singular male authority was complicated by the fact that Cambodia was ruled as a double act with two male co-premiers. In 2004, King Sihanouk abdicated the throne in favour of his son, King Sihamoni, who is younger than First Prime Minister Hun Sen.

This same period, from 1993 to 2006, has seen a rapid reversion to pre-socialist norms, notably in the resurgence and unprecedented expansion and commercialization of the sex trade. The influx of new wealth through outside investment, speculation and corruption has also financed the resurgence of the practice of taking mistresses. During this same period, in 2004, UNESCO added Khmer classical dance to its global register of intangible cultural heritage worthy of protection. By contrast, the government has failed to adequately invest in or protect the performance of Cambodian culture on stage. In 2005 and 2006, two landmark, capital cultural institutions – the National Theatre and the Royal School of Performing Arts – were sold off to investors for profit as real-estate developments (for more on this, see Turnbull 2006). In what follows, I attempt to make sense of these apparently contradictory developments by focusing on the ways in which morality is performed and articulated in the public sphere in Cambodia today.

CULTURAL RUBRICS OF GOOD GOVERNANCE

If, in contemporary Western human rights discourse, rights come with responsibility, then, in Cambodian culture, wealth and power come with responsibility. It was perhaps this underlying expectation as much as communist propaganda that fuelled much of the outrage against the opulent excess of the wealthy urban elite in the 1970s. Today, it underlies simmering tensions in Phnom Penh between a vulnerable urban poor and the financially secure, landed minority who comprise a minute fraction of the capital's population but concentrate most of the capital's property title in a small and close-knit cluster of families.

Role models of 'good governance' exist in such Khmer literary texts as 'Dav Ek' (also known as 'Dum Dav'), where a just sovereign displays virtuosity in what is for the most part a top-down display of beneficence and protection. Listening to the plea of the minstrel Ek that the king not take his betrothed, Dav, as his royal consort, the king honours this wish and later intervenes to try and prevent the marriage of Dav to the son of the governor of Tboung Khmum. When his wish is thwarted, he wreaks a terrible and deadly vengeance on the governor, his wives, and children (Khing 2006a). Elsewhere, in the Buddhist tale 'Bogholukamar', a man of great wealth (*setthi*) who loses all of it to virtuous deeds and dies penitent is reborn in glory as King Indra, and the resplendent lineage of his orphaned son is assured through his fathering of a Bodhisattva (Khing 2006b). But wealth alone is not enough to purchase status and the wealthy and powerful can also be open to ridicule and contempt when they fail to display generosity and reciprocity. This ambiguity of wealth per se as a hold on social status is evident in the folkloric lampooning of the figure of the *setthi* in, for example, the tales of the trickster 'Thmin Chey'.

In cultural terms, the notions of responsibility and reciprocity are hinged in the concept of *kun*, which refers specifically to acts of kindness and to the onus that such acts place on the recipient to repay the donor. The concept of giving and of investment – of the intersection between material investment or practical action and spiritual returns – are also deeply ingrained in Buddhist discourse, not only in the gift-giving notion of *dana*, but also in the underlying notions of *kamma* (past actions and their accumulation, as either negative or positive moral residue that determines ones future rebirth) and *phalla* (fruits or results, usually of good deeds). Thus, when the virtuous *setthi* in 'Bhogolukumar' dies penniless, his son is happy, knowing that his beloved father has accumulated enough *phalla* to ensure him a glorious rebirth. Similarly, in the story of 'Dav Ek', the narrator blames Ek's *kamma* and his ensuing hotheadedness for the chain of events leading to the annihilation and enslavement of his rival's clan by his protector, a righteous king (Khing 2006a).

The enduring popularity of Dav Ek demonstrates some degree of cultural consensus among Cambodians that even excessive violence is justified when exercised in the fulfilment of the moral responsibility to protect and as retribution for insubordination (Hinton, forthcoming). In the 1900 manuscript version of 'Dav Ek' recently brought to light by Khing Hoc Dy, the king justifies his punishment in light of the failure of the mandarin to honour and obey a royal decree. Despite or perhaps because of this excessive punishment, 'Dav Ek' offers an oddly reassuring moral parable to the less powerful members of society in its audience. The tale underscores not the immorality of excessive violence but rather the inherent morality in the sovereign's display of the protection of politically and financially powerless members of his constituency, in this case a minstrel (Ek) who served the king not with political intrigue, but rather with the purity of his heart and the beauty of his music.

In Cambodia today, the moral climate is affected by the 'impact of genocide, poverty, fragmented institutions, the stress of post-war reconstruction, an armed society and a weak "rule of law"' (Broadhurst 2002: 1–2). This potent combination of historical legacy and contemporary inefficacy has produced, as criminologist Roderic Broadhurst has noted, 'more acts of mayhem, extra-judicial homicide and murder-robbery in Cambodia than in its neighbours' (ibid.). In his analysis of the causes and contemporary patterns of violence, Broadhurst entertains the hypothesis that 'war (and revolutionary) violence legitimated by the state carried into higher peacetime homicide', and sees a particular causal link between this process of violence legitimation and the high rate of 'suspect/offender' death, such as the communal lynchings of suspects of consumer theft (ibid.). Elsewhere, exploring the rupture between traditional cosmologies and adaptation to host country mores that have occurred among Cambodian refugees, Maurice Eisenbruch traces this 'violent stem' of cultural bereavement to the Pol Pot regime (Eisenbruch 1997).

Broadhurst notes the relative size of 'high risk groups', notably young unemployed males (Broadhurst 2002: 5). As Alex Hinton notes in his recent article on the anti-Thai riots of 2003, this group was a prime force behind the attacks (Hinton 2006). A census of the monastic population of Cambodia would also reveal a preponderance of monks in the age-range described by Broadhurst as 'high risk'. Noting the role of the *sangha* and *karma* in protecting against crime, Broadhurst also argues that the re-establishment of Buddhism in Cambodia has been 'significant in the regeneration of indigenous moral order' but that the *sangha*'s revival, and that of a moral order, 'is challenged by modernity, materialism and new forms of crime'. Refuting criticisms of Buddhism as a doctrine whose fatalism is conducive to carelessness about death, Broadhurst argues that the Buddhist 'emphasis on avoidance of suffering and the accumulation of merit' constitute powerful traditional sources of 'natural or internalized forms of social control against violence'. Thus, a recognisable basis for the establishment of clearly defined laws is embedded into the culture (Broadhurst 2002: 8–9).

SELETHOR: DEFINING 'MORALITY' IN CAMBODIA

The Khmer term most popularly used to refer to moral behaviour is *selethor*, which literally means *precepts-dhamma*.[4] In a series of interviews with laity and monks in Phnom Penh and Kratie conducted as background for this paper, Hel Rithy, a researcher at the Buddhist Institute, found that Cambodians commonly locate *selethor* in bodily deportment: in the way people meet and greet each other, in the respect that youth pay elders, and in manners of speech. In a brief history of the Cambodian term morality, Hel Rithy describes the notion of *sel* (*sila*) as 'the interaction of individuals', and emphasises the resonance between *sila* and *panna*, or wisdom: 'when conducting *sila*, one must use *panna*. Or alternatively *panna* is the medium for *sila* and vice versa'. In contemporary society, Rithy finds, the term education (*abrum*) has come to replace *panna* in definitions and evaluations of morality.[5] This finding indicates that in contemporary Cambodian society, knowledge has become superordinate to wisdom, and the secular to the religious. Interestingly, this interpretation endorses the evaluation of some of the reasons for the rise of the Khmer Rouge made by François Ponchaud in the 1970s, in which he noted how the impact of colonialism and the modernization programmes of the Sangkum had led to the devaluation of wisdom in favour of secular knowledge, with a corresponding weakening of veneration for the '*cah-tum*' (literally: old and ripe, meaning village elders) by Cambodian youth, and a dilution of the 'traditional' moral values that had held society, at least partially, together (Ponchaud 1989).

While novices and ordained monks and nuns can take eight or ten precepts, Buddhist laity in Cambodia are expected to adhere to the five main precepts (*panca sila*), and it is these, Hel Rithy explains, that form the 'pillars of social morality' in Cambodia against which behavioural standards are judged. These precepts are not to kill, not to steal, not to engage in sexual misconduct, not to lie, and not to use intoxicants. Another significant standard of moral conduct in Khmer culture is delineated not by Buddhist ethics but by past practice, through animist beliefs, most notably ancestor worship. A moral genealogy links current generations to the standard of ancestral behaviour: here, ancestors become moral arbitrators, and represent a mythical standard of morality against which contemporary generations can be judged by current elders. Animist beliefs also serve to curb excesses of human behaviour through fear of punishment by particular *neak ta* spirits Here also, punishable offences tend to involve general bodily deportment and social interaction, such as speaking ill of others under a tree spirit, or lying at court. *Neak ta*, and not the Buddha, figure as the arbiters of truth and justice in Cambodian courts, where defendants are called to swear to tell the truth not to some abstract moral standard against Buddhist scriptures, but before the very real fear of retribution by *neak ta* that they will not lie – a custom iconized most recently in the commission and erection of a statue of a prominent *neak t*a, Lokda Dambon-daek (Iron Rod) outside the Khmer Rouge Tribunal in 2006.

The Khmer term for morality, *selethor*, and the associated concepts of righteous precepts and literally, 'carrying' those precepts (*kan selethor*), are not directly congruent with the Judeao-Christian concepts embedded within the Western term morality. However, inasmuch as Buddhism, in its *thor*, imposes an individual onus on disciples of Buddha not to take human or animal life, I think it appropriate to use the notion of a moral code to describe the set and spectrum of values that determine human behaviour in Cambodian society, specifically with relation to violence and morally-loaded or encoded sanctions and justifications for such violence. This loose moral code, and its degrees of porosity, flexibility, and the manner in which it is applied, necessarily have a bearing on all those living in Cambodia, as to whether they and their actions are deemed moral or immoral according to this code.

This moral structure is calibrated by a strict socio-economic hierarchy: the crime of a petty thief caught trying to steal from a monk, or of a young teenage singer trying to 'steal' a husband from a woman of wealth and status, or of a Thai actress trying to 'steal' glory and Khmer ownership from Angkor Wat, fuel an outpouring of rage and hate which are not only accommodated within, but also apparently justified by, the hierarchical ordering of things. That hierarchy is, in turn, continually represented and rehearsed through an intricate choreography which mixes morality tales with power plays, in the form of widely-televised and highly personalized visitations by usually well-rounded and well-heeled members of government or by Oknyas[6] to rural districts, and the donations of *krama*s, *sampot*s (skirts) and money by such icons of power to their most impoverished rural constituents. The theatrics of such secular alms-giving offers a public role-reversal of an equally broadly televised scenario, that of leaders and important figures making donations to monks. In this chain of merit and menace the practice of political patronage, whereby government becomes a protection racket, is packaged as a merit-worthy, selfless and personal display of material support, and hovering above it all is the menacing possibility of its disappearance should the recipient not continue their political support. Here, the government is cast as a quasi-divine figure, a latter-day, secular mimic of the divine ruler or *devaraja* whose duty it was, in an earlier and more deeply rooted moral schema, to uphold the spiritual welfare of the realm through the sponsorship of Buddhism. This contrivance is replicated in princely titles, such as the title of Samdech (Prince) Hun Sen, a title conferred upon Hun Sen by King Sihanouk, whose own blend of statecraft and stagecraft had seen him temporarily shed his king status for the title of Prince when he abdicated the throne in March 1955 and became the President of Sangkum Reastr Niyum.

Today, the spectrum of moral values is deployed in such a way that the murder or mutilation of a subverter of the desired status quo, whether it be a petty thief or a teenage adulterer, becomes not only justified but condoned by key stakeholders, ranging from government leaders to senior members of the *sangha*. Condonement can range from silence (a lack of statements about the perpetrator of the murders or mutilation), to the displacement of responsibility (a focus on the immorality of the petty criminal or adulterer), to attempts to exonerate and explain away the violent act itself, and thereby to redeem the perpetrators. In other words, there is not simply a culture of impunity, so much as a culture of abstention from passing or voicing moral judgement.

Shades of this moral hierarchy were seen in 1970, when senior figures in the *sangha* tacitly condoned the killing of communists by monks as a justifiable defence of their religion (Yin Sambo et al. 2006/7). Often, such exhortations exonerate group action, as in a spate of mob killings of petty thieves in the late 1990s and in lynchings of Vietnamese on the streets. The lack of sanction of such acts, or the absence of outright condemnation, creates a climate in which individual responsibility can be easily handed over to the crowd, and the crime of attempting to subvert a preferred order (such as by making spurious statements about the origins of Khmer monuments, which was the trigger of the Thai riots), becomes far greater than that of attempts to restore it (by violent mass riots whose aim is, ultimately, to force a retraction of such a statement and so to revert to the status quo ante).

DEVARAJA POLITICS AND THE THEATRICALITY OF MORALITY

In Khmer culture, the notion of the *devaraja* involves upholding the spiritual welfare of the realm through the sponsorship of Buddhism. King Ang Duong, who led a resurgence of Buddhist literature, King Sisowath, under whose reign the reformist monks Chuon Nath and Huot Tath gained sway, and King Norodom Sihanouk with his active sponsorship of Buddhist higher education in the 1950s and 1960s, all performed to some extent to this ideal. However, as mentioned earlier, the bearer of the title of righteous ruler must also display justness towards his subjects. In addition, the sponsoring of material edifices, notably *wat*s has been an important function of monarchs in the past.

In his analysis of the cultural history of political power in Bali, Clifford Geertz posits the notion that statecraft was nothing more or less than stagecraft, that the expressive nature of the Balinese state was geared towards 'the public dramatization of the ruling obsessions' of the Balinese culture, notably 'social inequality and status pride', and that the audience was somehow part of the spectacle (Geertz 1980: 13, 102, 120–123). In her work on kingship in past and present Cambodia, Ashley Thompson has emphasised the deep-seated cultural attachment to kingship and the ways in which kingship, and notions of a righteous ruler (*cakkavattin*) and the saviour figure of a Buddha-to-come (Maitreya) are ingrained into popular consciousness through their symbolic encoding in Khmer visual and monumental culture (Thompson 2004).

'When it's a matter of making gifts, it's a gift from the head of State, but when it's the matter of executing some chap, that's a tribunal decision', writes Soth Polin in his semi-autobiographical novel *l'Anarchiste*, referring to the violence of the Sihanouk era and the double standards of a regime that combined elaborate public displays of beneficence with brutal repression (Soth 1980: 18). The role of gifts in cultivating images of good governance also figures in a nineteenth-century verse chronicle studied by literary scholar Khin Sok. As a sign of his virtue, the king appointed a palace minister to put an end to crime in Cambodia. Returning to Cambodia from Siam, the king called together officials of all ranks and instructed them to return to their provinces and infiltrate bandit groups, and to operate undercover until they had enough information to give him a clear picture of criminal activities (Khin 2004: 206). Once identified, the bandit chiefs were showered with gifts of jewels and titles, and offered a banquet, at which they were all greeted, arrested and put to death. The people composed a song: 'In our Kingdom, nobody is afraid of banditry anymore, thanks to our merit.' The people then worked day and night, under a royal decree, to erect *sala*s, or shelters along the roadside, while 'the King organized different theatrical spectacles and music to entertain the people'. As a result of the King's virtue, all badness disappeared from Cambodia and commerce recommenced 'Thefts, pillage, extortions ceased, people no longer were afraid. Calm and happiness reigned across the Kingdom' (ibid.: 209).

Despite popular imaging of the Sihanouk's Sangkum Reastr Niyum regime as a golden era, state violence was common. As Ponchaud recalls, Khmer Rouge captured by Sihanouk's security forces were thrown from Bokor, and left to die slowly. Elsewhere, rebels were tied to trees and left to die, bellies split open, and in 1965, 'each macabre detail of the execution of Chau Bory was projected before each cinema showing' (Ponchaud 2001: 288). Ponchaud juxtaposes these displays of violence with the impact of 'a materialist conception of merit acting in itself' independent of personal behaviour, which allowed police commissioners and notoriously corrupt high-ranking officials to 'buy back their bribes by organizing votive festivals' (ibid.: 286). Indirectly comparing Sihanouk to Machiavelli, Mao Zedong, Hitler, Stalin and Sukarno, Cambodian author Soth Polin reflects that politicians can lie, steal, cheat, break their promises, as long as their 'flesh and blood industry' (*l'industrie de chair et de sang*) keeps running (Soth 1980: 18).

Today, the political power base of new King Sihamoni and his father King Sihanouk has been seriously eroded. The latter's moral authority was particularly tainted by his coalition with the Khmer Rouge in the 1970–1975, and now economic, police and military power are firmly concentrated around Samdech Hun Sen

Since receiving the title of Samdech in the mid-1990s – a title previously almost exclusively reserved for royalty and supreme patriarchs in the Buddhist *sangha*, and therefore carrying connotations of divinity or moral authority – Hun Sen has increased his rhetoric about the need for public morality. With the exception of public remarks by King Sihanouk in the 1990s condemning mob killings as not 'humanitarian',[7] equivalent sermons from the traditional (royal) protectors of the *sangha* and state have been largely absent. A climate of impunity for serious crimes, notably contract killings and premeditated violence protecting the interests or avenging the emotions of key stakeholders in the power structure, has continued to prevail.

At the same time, the government's interaction with its subjects has taken on an increasingly Sihanoukian demeanour, down to the widely-televised and highly personalised visitations by members of government to rural districts, and the donations of *krama*s, *sampot*s and money by such icons of power to their most impoverished rural constituents

(Ledgerwood, forthcoming). In such outings, figures of government might be shown solo speaking from a podium, but such footage is enveloped with pictures of senior figures walking abroad at the centre of large coteries of followers and retainers. The moral economy of this particular crowd has cultural underpinnings in an equation of the proliferation of merit with a proliferation of retainers. Thus, in one mid-nineteenth-century text, the narrator describes an *Oknya* and his *Chumteav* (the title used for the wife of an *Oknya* or minister of higher rank) living 'happily and in a state or prosperity,' surrounded by kin, valets and servants,' while a 'virtuous king' is 'surrounded by ministers and high functionaries, Brahmins, poets, etc.' (Khin 2004: 204, 331).

In her recent analysis on the politics of state Buddhist ceremony in contemporary Myanmar, Juliane Schober describes the 'elaborate and expensive ritual theatre that the government has undertaken' and stresses the unitary, monolithic nature of the government and the multiplicity of audience (Schober 2004). In contemporary Cambodia, as in the Myanmar analysed by Juliane Schober, the projection of political power and the ceremonial life of the polity is endlessly reiterated in the public choreography of heads-of-state in state television and print media. Such spectacle can be read as simply a cynical exercise in legitimacy-building. It can also be interpreted as the performance of an expectation, of the public demonstration of the government's instantiations of good governance, however isolated and however unrepresentative of the larger picture of expropriation and dispossession. In the choreography of such secular alms-giving, the peasants are seen approaching the donors in a line-up and gratefully receiving, their body language reinforcing the economic and political hierarchy which keeps them on the receiving end (Hughes 2006).

As Caroline Hughes has shown, the figure of the material and therefore meritorious but not necessarily *moral* benefactor – the *saborosjun* – has gained saliency in Cambodia's political landscape in recent years, and is most commonly seen in media images beaming beatifically while strolling along newly-bulldozed roads, surrounded by a cortege of supporters and/or body-guards. This figure is invariably male. As Hughes shows to great effect, Premier Hun Sen plays to this figure with great skill and merges the symbolic and spiritually-enlightened figure of the *sabarasjun* with that of the *bang thom*, or strong man, who 'protects his followers and is ruthless towards his enemies'; this character-play, Hughes notes, combines both the promise of patronage and protection with the threat of menace (Hughes 2006: 479).

The spiritual genealogy of the *sabarosjun* weaves far back in Buddhist texts and readings of appropriate behaviour. The Pali word, *sappurisa*, from which *sabarosjun* is derived, means 'good, true, superior or excellent person' (Wallis 2004: 123). The following definition of the *sabarosjun*, from the Buddhist text 'Samyuttanikaya', emphasises at the outset the burden of care for elders and the importance of appropriate comportment:

> When a person supports his parents,
> And respects the family elders;
> When his speech is gentle and courteous,
> And he refrains from divisive words;
> When he strives to remove meanness,
> Is truthful, and vanquishes anger,
> The radiant one calls him
> Truly a superior [an excellent] person.[8]

In this text, we see the same equation of morality and bodily deportment that Hel Rithy found in contemporary popular definitions of morality. A *saborasjun* would appear to be an exclusively masculine role. In the televised theatre of power and patronage, high profile female figures act the role of wealthy benefactress and spiritual healer, by touching the stumps of carefully assembled mine victims, who have apparently been requested to remove their prosthetics for such occasions so that they might better represent the *kammic* rubble of war, incarnations of Cambodia's violent past and of previous negative *kamma* (French 1994).

PERCEIVED ROLE OF THE *SANGHA* VIS-A-VIS MORAL AND SOCIAL ORDER

Although the state emerged as a major sponsor of Buddhism in post-colonial Cambodia, high-ranking monks, most famously Ven. Chuon Nath, retained an independence of moral outlook, as reflected in his reported coolness towards head of state Prince Norodom Sihanouk (Meyer 1971). Nouth Narang has called this era the 'Samay Chuon Nath', when there existed a personal embodiment of both *selathor* and *panna*, when Chuon Nath matched an austere lifestyle with a steadfast commitment to learning and an investment in the propagation of Buddhist-based moral education, as in Ven. Chuon Nath's verses for youth (personal communication, HE Nouth Narang, October 2004). Although Cambodian monastic leaders have in the past encouraged Cambodians to take up arms, it is hard to imagine Ven. Chuon Nath or any of his contemporaries from the 1960s voicing the approval that senior clerical leader Ven. Bou Kry is alleged to have voiced for the killing, in the Vat Botum Vaddey monastery compound, of a suspected motorbike thief. It is possible, however, that the monastic leadership in the Sangkum was not encouraged to speak out – the political repression and media control of the 1960s would have presumably encouraged some degree of self-censorship by the *sangha*.

Today, while politicians earn merit from building pagodas and sponsoring religious ceremonies in their homes, temples and offices, monks can earn power and assurance of promotion within the state-sponsored *Mahanikay* sect by supporting selected politicians (Nissen, 2005). This support takes the form of publicized appearances and engagements, sermons and blessings, rather than electoral support in the form of votes. A particularly broadly televised scenario is that of leaders and important figures (or their personal assistants) making donations to monks, and photographed in positions embodying respect as they make their generous, detailed and widely advertised donations (x tons of rice, x crates of Fanta, x umbrellas). At the same time, the possibilities that monks enjoy for social action and political engagement are acutely circumscribed (Heng Srcang, this volume). Although monks are eligible to vote under the 1993 Cambodian constitution, their highest authority Tep Vong has ordered them to abstain from voting.

At the National Buddhist Congress in September 2005, the Supreme Patriarch of the *Mahanikay* Tep Vong ruled that monks may no longer seek alms at markets, a subject of recent debate among urban laity and the *sangha*, concerning strictures on the raising of alms at business premises. The Congress also ruled that monks could (and should) display their reverence for the state by rising to the National Anthem. The rationale for the former revision was that monks must be protected from the earthly temptations present in market settings, notably women, and that such commercial milieu were a place of moral danger. The rationale for the latter change appears to have been in keeping with a more subtle and continuous erosion of what were once distinctions between the royal, spiritual and secular realms and roles of *sdic* (king), *sangha* and *srok* (district, but which here we can read as country, as in *srok-khmae*, or Cambodia).

FEMINIZATION OF THE MORAL ORDER

The promotion of the female body as a locus for the sins of the fathers, mothers, brothers and others within national as well as religious communities, is not unique to Cambodia. Elsewhere in Asia, when foreign others 'violate' the sovereign territory of a national female subject, the full machinery of state may move to protect or defend the victim. Recent such cases involve the South Korean government's support for compensation claims against a Japan that refuses to acknowledge the existence of comfort women; the case of Sarah Balagbahan, a domestic servant from the Philippines who was sentenced to death in Singapore, and a 12-year-old girl in Japan who was gang-raped by American soldiers in 1995.[9] Balagbahan became a national hero; Korean comfort women have made a tentative step from historical oblivion to war heroine status; the Japanese schoolgirl's innocence is invoked as an incarnation of the purity of the Japanese nation under assault by Western culture. But when, as Melani Budianta writes, 'national pride is not so precariously confronted, the exploitation of women's bodies is sanctioned, regardless of the cost to women' (Budianta 2001). One way of legitimating state-sanctioned violations of the female subject is to delegitimize a particular female, or particular group of females, by depicting them as a betrayal of the national ideal. The fall from this state of hyperbolic grace to disgrace comes at a high cost. Once the female subject loses her claim to embody or represent 'national sovereignty' by failing to maintain its conceptual counterpart – namely, national morality – she is represented as deserving of dispassion, physical violence, rape and, in extreme cases, death.

Since the 1940s, when nationalist writers began to pen articles about the role of women in the nation, sexual morality has been associated with the health and strength of the Khmer nation. In her analysis of writings in the 1940s by Khmer women for Khmer news media, political scientist Kate Frieson has identified several articles that criticised 'single women and prostitutes' for 'breaking the family circle and destroying the racial lineage of Khmers', and that accused prostitutes of 'dishonour[ing] the Khmer race' (Frieson 2001: 5). More recently, in her doctoral dissertation for Australian National University, anthropologist Larissa Sandy (2006) has highlighted the complex linkages between legislation and the state's evaluation of prostitution across diverse regimes.

Since the early 1990s, increasing numbers of men in Cambodia have begun or resumed the practice of taking second wives or mistresses.

This practice had been suppressed by close to twenty years of enforced puritanical socialist morality, which reached its peak under the draconian policies of Democratic Kampuchea. Following its (re-)emergence, voices began to be heard, as early as 1993, among women, lamenting the loss of morals and imputing a superior morality to the Khmer Rouge period, when 'men could only have one wife'. By 2004, a minority of contemporary urban intellectuals ranging from their 20s to their 40s, shocked by the rapid sliding of Cambodia into what some see as a state of economic, moral and cultural anarchy, are nursing a form of nostalgia for structure, namely the structure and strictures of an authoritarian state whose rigorous moral policing of sexuality and marriage compares favourably to today's climate of impunity and promiscuity. In this moral schema, where a principal barometer of morality is a female's sexual constraint and conduct, violent acts which destroy lives and livelihoods attract less censure than such morality crimes as sleeping with a married minister or wearing short skirts to a temple.

The moral zeal of the government has surfaced and resurfaced over the past decade in a series of political sermons, rising in frequency and pitch around key religious ceremonies, and often focused on the moral duty of women to watch their skirt-lengths when visiting *wat*s. This latter topic has also been a popular talking point for members of the *sangha* and Cambodian cultural experts, in national media coverage involving issues of tradition and morality.

Since Cambodia's elections in 1993 and 1998, women have been increasingly active in political and social life. A parallel trend has seen the escalation of public acts of violence against women. The two most significant such attacks of the last decade were the contract killing of Cambodia's most popular actress, Piseth Pilika in July 1998, and the acid-attack on the seventeen year old entertainer Tat Marina in December 1999. Shot repeatedly at point-blank range, Pilika died within a week. Marina was hideously disfigured, doused in 4.7 litres of sulphuric acid. Both attacks were carried out in broad daylight. The failure of the judicial process in both cases has seen no pursuit of justice and no attempts to bring the cases to legal closure. It has been speculated that the first attack was orchestrated by Hun Sen's wife, Madame Bun Rany; Pilika's diary, as subsequently publicized in French media, strongly implied that she had been having an affair with Hun Sen. The second attack was reportedly carried out by two bodyguards together with their employer, Madame Khourn Sophal, the wife of Marina's then lover, a senior government minister named Svay Sittha. Eyewitness accounts, public wrath, and physical evidence abandoned at the scene of the crime – including a landcruiser and a mobile phone – led to the filing of charges against Khourn Sophal and the issue of an arrest warrant, but the warrant was never executed.

The widespread identification with and empathy for these victims by the Cambodian public sparked a massive public outpouring of rage and grief. More than ten thousand people traveled through and to Phnom Penh to attend Pilika's funeral in a spirit of what was described as 'nearly national mourning'.[10] No public statements of censure of condemnation of the perpetrators were issued at the time by heads of state or religious leaders. Where statements were made, they tended to focus on the behaviour of women who, by becoming the mistresses of married men, invited retribution.

Thus, one government spokesman described the acid attack on Tat Marina as a 'personal matter' for 'the first and second wife to resolve'.[11] Within months, the suspected perpetrator had reportedly resumed life as normal, and was back in the family home in Tuol Kork.[12] This paralysis of mechanisms of justice provoked the writer Kong Bunchoeun to write a fictionalized account of the attack and its aftermath, in his *The Destiny of Tat Marina* (Viesenaa Nieng Marina). The target audience of his self-described 'morality tale' included both girls who Bunchouen aims to educate 'not to become involved with married men', and 'second wives'.[13] Despite Kong's efforts, no condemnations of the act were made by any single figure of government. The subtext of this silence was that Tat Marina had brought this on herself through her own 'immoral' behaviour: her adultery had transformed her from a young, *srey sroh* (fresh girl), into a gruesome incarnation of the *srey-katleak* (unvirtuous woman), her moral failings and her sexual appetite totemized in her semi-atomized body.

The lack of legal or public moral sanction spurred copy-cat crimes, and a 'horrific surge' of acid attacks in Cambodia, most of them perpetrated by wives against their husband's lovers.[14] In 1999, the municipal court in Kompong Cham brought charges against the wife of a senior military officer for an acid attack against her husband's mistress, but refused on appeal to upgrade them to charges of attempted manslaughter, arguing that the perpetrator had intended only to 'damage' the victim's 'beauty' out of 'jealousy'.[15] In 2002, another acid attack in Kompong Cham carried out by a wife, with the help of her teenage son and daughter, blinded her husband's pregnant lover in both eyes. At the time, 'nobody dared help', and the victim was still seeking justice four years later. Sentenced to a year in prison, her assailants were released after paying a 5 million riel fine, none of which was ever seen by the victim.[16]

In 2004, Prime Minister Prince Hun Sen issued a directive to various ministries, including the Ministry of Culture, the Ministry of Religion and the Ministry of Women's and Veterans' Affairs to consider provisions for the improvement of national morality. A focal message of these morality tirades is that women should not only transmit notions of morality, as mothers, but more significantly, it seems, in policing moral boundaries through their own abstention from particular sites, professions, and dress. The conflation of dress, national culture and morality were seen recently in dress restrictions for the 'Fresh Girl Handsome Boy' (*srey sroh proh sa'at*) contest sponsored by Cambodian Television Network, a hugely popular commercial TV beauty contest, where female contestants had to wear long sampots and modest blouses completely out of sync with the figure-hugging, flesh-revealing tank-tops and tight jeans now *de rigueur* for urban women from their teens to their fifties.

From December 2005 to September 2006, three related items graced the front pages and stages of Khmer and foreign language news media in Cambodia. First was the appearance of the popular singer Chea Sovanna, in a low-back dress for a December 25th television show on the popular channel Cambodia Television Network (CTN). Sovanna was subsequently banned from CTN and was forced to issue a televised public apology to Hun Sen and Bun Rany. In her statement, which was also reported in the mainstream newspapers, *Koh Santhepheap* and *Raksmey Kampuchea*, Sovanna stated her culpability for damaging Khmer culture and the Khmer nation, by dressing and dancing inappropriately. Hun Sen accepted her apology, and Sovanna was subsequently allowed back on CTN on condition that she wore 'proper, traditional clothes'.[17] A month later, Hun Sen once again raised the spectre on national immorality, this time specifically in relation to 'elderly gangsters' and 'evil wolves' (by which he was referring to officials from the Royalist FUNCINPENC party) and their 'mistresses', whom he also referred to as 'prostitutes'. Speaking at a ground-breaking ceremony in Kompong Cham, Hun Sen proposed a law against mistresses which would have a legal basis in Article 45 of the constitution, which defines marriage as 'an arrangement of mutual consent between husband and wife'.[18]

Second, in May and June 2006, was the controversy surrounding Hun Sen's announcement, on 26 May 2006, of a ten-year ban on 3G technology.

Citing stances against debauchery on the internet in the Philippines, Vietnam and Singapore, Hun Sen stated that Cambodia needed to wait another ten years for this technology, 'until we strengthen social morality' as otherwise, even 'Buddhist monks' would 'fall down'; here he was referring to the potential of 3G technology for the rapid transfer of pornographic film media.[19] Rumours soon linked his announcement to a petition organized by *Lok Chumteav*, the first wives of Cambodian ministers.[20]

Third, in September 2006, was Hun Sen's televised announcement, during a long speech while he was filmed helping villagers plant rice in Svay Rieng, that he had ordered the Ministry of Culture to ban a planned Miss Cambodia contest. His first rationale was that Cambodians were still in poverty, and that the financial burden of such a show would ultimately fall on them. Pre-empting criticism that his decision would prevent Cambodia from displaying its culture at the Miss World forum, Hun Sen declared that if people wanted to show off Cambodian culture, they could publicize Angkor Wat or Cambodian or classical dance. Cambodia has no shortage of culture, Hun Sen continued, but no-one could claim to demonstrate 'national identity' by show-casing girls in their underpants.

Hun Sen's appeal to national and moral decorum also alluded to the potential of such activities to anger the spirit world. Referring to the conflagration of Phnom Penh's National Theatre in 1994, Hun Sen traced the genesis of this catastrophe to Cambodia's staging of the first Miss World contest. It was at the National Theatre, he continued, that people had tested the virginity (purity, *phiepborisot*) of the participants. This heinous episode had hexed the theatre, a chain of events he neatly encapsulated in the word *changrae* (inauspicious, evil) claiming that 'the (*changrae*) [that led to] the burning of the national theatre came from Miss World and that's all there is to it.' Hun Sen then stressed that the National Theatre had survived war and Pol Pot and had remained intact from 1979 onward, implying that the failure of Cambodian women to maintain due decorum was more dangerous to the Khmer nation (as embodied in the theatre) than civil war and genocide, while also underscoring the duty of the state to keep women in their proper place.[21]

Evoking doom and bad portent, the term *changrae* is used to describe animals, birds and humans in particular contexts. As one Cambodian civil servant in his forties explained the term to me, he would not give a prostitute a lift in his car because she is *changrae* and could bring him bad luck, in much the same way as owls are believed to be doomsayers in Cambodian culture. This analogy reveals much about the conflation of the 'wild' and the 'bad' in the female sexual body. Despite such associations, prostitution within Cambodian society has by and large remained socially acceptable as long as it remains invisible. In recent years, the increasing transmission of HIV/AIDS by males to the domestic environment as a result of unprotected sex with sex-workers, has accentuated the fragility of the divide between the 'immoral' world of sex outside the home and the duty-bound confines of marital sex (Sandy 2006).

One week before Samdech Hun Sen's statements about the Miss Cambodia contest and the National Theatre, the National Assembly had voted by an overwhelming majority to introduce a law against adultery. Defending the adultery law, one parliamentarian argued that it would help reduce corruption, linking the procurement of bribes to the need to meet the financial costs of keeping a mistress: in other words, the state must protect its coffers from being drained by immoral women.[22] Defending the morality campaign, Minister of Culture Prince Sisowath Panara Sereyvuth, stated that 'morality is important for our society, and even more so than corruption'. Here, morality is clearly a matter of bodily deportment rather than social action: lewd conduct can create the conditions for social moral decline, which in turn can foster corruption.[23]

When women transgress the moral codes enshrined in such cultural canons as the *chbab srey* (Cambodian code of conduct for women) the above public pronouncements tell us, they are not just violating a social code. They are themselves, as gate-keepers between the wild and the civilized, opening society up to moral rot. The notion of women as gate-keepers of the moral and biological health of the race and nation has had much currency in Asia, Europe and the Americas. Invested as icons, guardians and boundary-markers of national identity, women's bodies are routinely held up by state actors as embodiments of the ideal of national sovereignty.

The equation of notions of sexual propriety and national boundary were made explicit in cartoons about the Thai actress whose alleged controversial remarks sparked the anti-Thai riots in early 2003, where her naked, voracious and worm-infested body was depicted as evidence of Thai promiscuity. Here, a rotten female body was used as a mirror of Thai attempts to devour Cambodian culture in an ominous image which conjured both death and sex.[24]

CONCLUSION

In this chapter I have explored some patterns framing the perception of morality in Cambodian culture and contemporary society. One way of analysing the trends noted above is to consider the potential interplay between cultural understandings of morality and political expectations, on the part of both ruling and ruled, that morality is in and of itself a performance art. Like the move to protect Khmer culture at the quasi-ethereal level of United Nations resolutions, through UNESCO's inscription of Khmer dance as intangible cultural heritage, the focusing of heated debates on sexual morality in the public sphere may reflect more than mere strategizing and legitimacy-building.

The Cambodian leadership's public posturing about morality rarely tackles the deeper veins of antisocial human behaviour. Indeed, the stock responses to such crimes, rather than alienating the perpetrator, can socialise him or her by locating the victim within the lower end of the moral spectrum. In this inverse moral logic, perpetrators are not simply absolved of responsibility for their crime: they emerge as responsible citizens whose acts have helped to uphold a desired status-quo. This desired status quo is, in turn, a fiction; a microcosm in negative of the actual state of the economy and of crime at large. Government and civic relations are commonly run on a '10% rule', meaning the constant milking of individual commissions earned by one's very presence in a chain of *khsae* ('strings' of relationships) linking the supplier to the supplied through a commercialization of *kun*. National assets, from historic sites such as the Choeung Ek killing fields, to rubber plantations and rainforest, are mortgaged to the highest bidder. Large-scale crime, from police rings running motorbike thefts to cross-border human trafficking and narcotics, goes largely unpunished.

In contemporary Cambodia, notions of stability (political, economic, or familial) and attachment to, or the search for, structure, can have a distorting function. In this schema, attachment to the 'moral order' of the past can enhance the desire for the perpetuation of aspects of a moral economy associated with the duty of rulers not only to deliver some form of protection to the ruled but also to perform the part. Attachment to structure can also serve to legitimise acts of premeditated and sometimes murderous violence. On the other hand, an apparent loss of structure in daily life can encourage such phenomena as nostalgia for aspects of the Khmer Rouge era, particularly as related to the regime's draconian policing of sexual morality.

Resistance to the tumultuous effects of modernization can take many forms. In this chapter, I have focused not on popular protest, much of which is couched in such 'traditional' forms as landless citizens journeying to the capital and staging sit-ins near Samdech Hun Sen's residence and outside the palace in search of social justice. Rather, I have examined the apparent attachment of those at the lower end of society who are excluded from the more lucrative benefits of Cambodia's rapid socio-economic transition, to explanatory frameworks focused on the need to preserve sexual morality. I have also explored the apparent need among the ruling elite for legitimating narratives. Indeed, the implicit emphasis of the free market economy on the survival of those most able to meet its challenges, notably the most skilled and highly educated, also represents a threat to the socio-economic longevity of those who owe their current wealth and status principally to familial ties. In addition to free market influences, Cambodia is now also home to numerous institutions committed to developing a civil society, whose shared vision for a society based on horizontal linkages and skills-based (as opposed to contacts-based) allocation of employment and remuneration, as well as equitable sharing and taxing of national wealth and resources, represents a clear and ever-present danger to the vested interests of Cambodia's ruling elite. Faced with these challenges, one response of the Cambodian leadership has been to focus attention on the issue of female national and sexual morality. This focus on the female form and deportment can to some extent be interpreted as the search for the recuperation of a 'traditional' order whose unstated flipside is a feudal system based on rewards and patronage, similarly out of sync with the transition to a free market economy.

REFERENCES

Broadhurst, Roderic (2002) 'Lethal Violence, Crime and State Formation in Cambodia.' *Australia and New Zealand Journal of Criminology*, 35 (1), pp. 1–26.

Budianta, Melani (2000) 'Indonesian Womens responses to violence: towards an alternative concept of human security.' *Inter-Asia Cultural Studies*. 1 (2), pp. 361–363.

Eisenbruch, Maurice (1997) 'The cry for the lost placenta: Cultural bereavement and cultural survival among Cambodians who resettled, were repatriated or who stayed at home.' In M. Van Tilburg & A. Vingerhoets (eds) *Home is where the heart is: The psychological aspects of permanent and temporary geographical moves.* Tilburg, The Netherlands: Tilburg University Press, pp. 109–131.

French, Lindsay (1994) 'The Political Economy of Injury and Compassion: Refugees on the Thai-Cambodian Border.' In Thomas J. Csordas (ed.) *Embodiment and Experience: the existential ground of culture and self.* Cambridge: Cambridge University Press.

Frieson, Kate (2001) *In the Shadows: Women, Power and Politics in Cambodia*. Centre for Asia Pacific Initiatives: Occasional Papers, Occasional Paper No. 26, June.

Geertz, Clifford. (1980) *Negara: The Theatre State in 19th Century Bali*. Princeton: Princeton University Press.

Hill, Frances R. (1971) 'Millenarian Machines in South Vietnam.' *Comparative Studies in Society and History*. 13 (3) pp. 325–350.

Hinton, Alex (2006) 'Khmerness and the Thai Other: Violence, Discourse, and Symbolism in the 2003 Anti-Thai Riot in Cambodia.' *Journal of Southeast Asian Studies* 37 (3), pp. 445–468.

—— (forthcoming) 'Songs at the Edge of Democratic Kampuchea.' In Judy Ledgerwood and Anne Hansen (eds) *At the Edge of the Forest: Essays in Honour of David Chandler*. Ithaca: Cornell University SEAP.

Hughes, C. (2006) 'The Politics of Gifts: Tradition and Regimentation in Cambodia.' *Journal of Southeast Asian Studies* 37 (3), pp. 469–489.

Khin Sok (2002) *L'annexion du Cambodge par les Vietnamiens au XIXeme siècle d'apres les deux poèmes du Vénérable Batum Baramey Pich*. Paris: Éditions You-feng.

Khing Hoc Dy (2006a) *Dav Ek: Introduction, traduction annotée et textes Khmers*. Phnom Penh: Librairie Angkor.

—— (2006b) *Un auteur Cambodgien et son oeuvre: Le Bhogakulakumar du poète Nan (fin 18ème–début 19ème siècles)*. Phnom Penh: Éditions Angkor.

Kong Bunchoeun (2000) *Viesena Tat Marina*. Phnom Penh: Rainbow Publishers.

Ledgerwood, Judy (forthcoming) 'Ritual in 1990 Cambodian Political Theatre: More Songs at the Edge of the Forest.' In Judy Ledgerwood and Anne Hansen (eds) *At the Edge of the Forest: Essays in Honour of David Chandler*. Ithaca: Cornell University SEAP.

Meyer, Charles (1971) *Derrière la Sourire Khmer*. Paris: Librairie Plon.

Nissen, Christine (2005) 'Cambodia'. *Global Corruption Report*. Berlin: Transparency International. pp. 119–122.

Ponchaud, F. (1989) 'Social Change in the Vortex of Revolution.' In Karl Jackson, (ed.) *Cambodia: 1975–1978: rendez-vous with death*. Princeton, NJ, Princeton University Press.

—— (2001) *Cambodge Année Zero*. Paris and Pondicherry: Kailash.

Sandy, Larissa (2007) 'My Blood, Sweat and Tears: Female Sex Workers in Cambodia – Victims, Vectors or Agents?' Doctoral dissertation. Australian National University.

Schober, Juliane (2000) 'A Tooth Relic and the Legitimation of Power.' In Frank E. Reynolds and John A. Carbine (eds), *The Life of Buddhism*. Berkeley, Los Angeles, London: University of California Press. pp. 45–59.

Scott, James C. (1976) *The Moral Economy of the Peasant: Rebellion and Subsistence in Southeast Asia*. New Haven: Yale University Press.

Soth Polin (1980) *L'Anarchiste*. Paris: La Table Ronde.

Thompson, Ashley (2004) 'The Future of Cambodia's Past: A Messianic Middle-Period Cambodian Royal Cult.' In John Marston and Elizabeth Guthrie (eds) *History, Buddhism and New Religious Movements in Cambodia*. Honolulu: University of Hawai'i Press. pp. 13–39.

Thompson, E. P (1968) *The Making of the English Working Class*. London: Penguin.

—— (1971) 'The Moral Economy of the English Crowd in the Eighteenth century.' *Past and Present*. 50, pp. 76–131.

Turnbull, Robert (2006) A burned-out theatre: the state of Cambodia's performing arts.' In L. Ollier and T. Winter (eds) *Expressions of Cambodia: the politics of tradition, modernity and change*. London and New York: Routledge.

Wallis, Glenn (2004) *The Dhammapada: Verses on the Way*. New York: The Modern Library.

Yin Sambo, Lim Leum, Seng Hokmeng, Pong Peakdey Boramy (2006/7) 'Buddhism and Politics in Cambodia, 1954–1975.' *Siksacakr* Vol. 6, pp. 75–97.

NOTES

1   Soth Polin *L'Anarchiste* (Paris: La table ronde, 1980), p. 18.
2   Glenn Wallis *The Dhammapada: Verses on the Way* (New York: The Modern Library, 2004) p. 30 (Stanzas 137, 138 and 139).
3   Kong Boncheoun interviewed in Bou Saroeun and Phelim Kyne 'Victim's misery a modern morality tale.' *Phnom Penh Post*, June 23–July 26, 2000, p. 7.
4   The Khmer for *dhamma* is pronounced *thor*, though directly transliterated is spelled *thomm*.
5   Hel Rithy 'Morality in Cambodia: Research Report.' Unpublished paper, September 2005.
6   *Oknya* is a title of status traditionally conferred by the king but now apparently conferred by the government and widely reported to be available for purchase.
7   Sihanouk, Reported in *Rasmey Kampuchea*, 1998.
8   Sammyuttanikaya 1.11.11 [1] trans. Glenn Wallis, in Wallis, *The Dhammapada*, p. 123.
9   Michael Millett 'Rape case delay undermines US-Japan security pact.' *The Sidney Morning Herald*, July 6 2001; Michael Millett, 'Angry Okinawans tired of being good neighbours.' *Sydney Morning Herald* 3 July 2001.
10 Alain Louyot 'Qui a tué le star du Cambodge?' *L'Express*, October 7 1999. In her diary, as publicised in *L'Express*, Piseth Pilaka wrote two months prior to her assassination that she had met with Hok Lundy, who had warned her to go into hiding as Mrs Bun Rany was madly jealous and wanted her dead.
11 Seth Mydans 'Scorned wives' revenge a living death.' *The Sydney Morning Herald*, 30 July 2001, p. 9.
12 Post Staff 'Svay Sitha's acid-throwing wife at home.' *Phnom Penh Post*, June 23–July 6, 2000, p. 7.

13 Bou Saroeun and Phelim Kyne 'Victim's Misery a modern morality tale.' *Phnom Penh Post*, June 23–July 6, 2000, p. 7.
14 Seth Mydans 'Scorned wives' revenge a living death.' *The Sydney Morning Herald* 30 July 2001, p. 9.
15 Rajesh Kumar 'Women's minister pushes acid victim's cause.' *Phnom Penh Post* March 30–April 12, 2001, p. 3. FUNCINPEC Minister of Women's and Veterans' Affairs Mu Sochua, who later joined the Sam Rainsy Party, publicly took up this case.
16 'Strey rongkrueh daoy tukasit mneak som aouy tolakar rok yuthethor.' [Female victim of acid attack asks court for justice], *Rasmei Kampuchea Daily*, 19 May 2006, p. 1, 4.
17 Kuch Naren and Ethan Plaut 'Hun Sen Accepts Singer's Televised Apology.' *The Cambodia Daily*, 5 January 2006, p. 12.
18 'PM Threatens crackdown on mistresses.' *The Cambodia Daily*, Monday 27 February 2006, p. 1, 13.
19 Esther McClaren '3G Mobile ban astounds phone industry.' *Phnom Penh Post* 2–15 June, 2006, p. 1, 12.
20 UCh 'Pas de 3G, le ministre persiste et signe.' *Cambodge Soir*, 30 May 2006, p. 7.
21 'Niyuk roatmentrei prachang nine kar prolung bovar kanna' (Prime Minister opposes Miss World contests) *Rasmei Kampuchea Daily*, 6 September, pp. 1–2.
22 Sek Barisoth (2006) 'Social Morality law is sorely misguided and a sad indicator.' *Cambodia Daily* 7 September, p. 19.
23 *Cambodia Daily*. 6 September 2006, p. 1.
24 Female sexuality, voracity and the will to violence are also conjoined in beliefs about the spirits of women who die in pregnancy or childbirth, and in the clutching, greedy figure of the *mdaay-daem* – the original mother of a reincarnated child who will return to earth to claim them – the title and subject of a recent Khmer ghost story that screened in Phnom Penh.

SECTION IV

Questions of Changing Culture

CHAPTER 12

The Scope and Limitations of Political Participation by Buddhist Monks

Heng Sreang

This chapter is about the scope and limitations of political participation by contemporary Cambodian Buddhist monks. It aims to explore the relationship between the monks and politics and to examine the tension arising from conflicting views on and interpretations of the role of Khmer monks in religious and secular socio-political affairs. It also explores the impact that political participation by Buddhist monks may have on contemporary Cambodian political life.

The chapter is based on data collected from interviews carried out between March and October 2005 with 20 Buddhist monks and 30 laypeople in Phnom Penh and in Kompong Cham province. It also makes use of my own observations in recent years of debates among Cambodian intellectuals and scholars and a range of documentary data.

It is often difficult to get people to discuss political issues in present-day Cambodia. I was fortunate that in my interviews and discussions laypeople seemed keen to talk and happy to offer their opinions and reflections. However, speaking to monks about these topics was considerably harder. Monks often feel uncomfortable discussing political matters in public or with someone they do not know well. In general, they prefer to discuss these issues only among themselves. This, they explained to me, is because of warnings issued by the government after the 1998 uprising in the wake of the national elections, when monks joined in with a popular protest action. Soon after this protest, the Supreme Buddhist Patriarchs prohibited monks from participating in the local elections in 2002 and in the national elections in 2003 and in public campaigns.[1]

MONKS' 'TRADITIONAL' ROLE

The Cambodian government often encourages monks to perform a 'traditional' role as religious and moral educators of the people and to uphold the ethical foundations of society. Although the role of the *sangha* in government policies for national development and integration has been granted some official recognition, the government does not openly encourage monks to participate in secular affairs, claiming that these are the government's responsibility. Personal involvement by monks in politics – such as to campaign for law enforcement or policy implementation – is labeled 'non-traditional' (*khos-tumneam-tumlop*).

In recent years, however, Khmer Buddhism has changed in significant ways and monks have become increasingly involved in politics. This recent political activism of the Khmer *sangha* recalls the role that it played in social and political affairs in the 1940s and 1950s, when monks protested against the French colonial regime, demanding freedom, independence and the preservation of Khmer culture and language. Monks were officially granted the right to vote in elections in the constitution of 1993. However, many of them then participated in the 1998 protests against election irregularities, claiming also that the ruling party practised 'poor governance, corruption, and associated social ills'.[2] At that point, monks joined with the people to demand new leaders for the country.

The participation of Buddhist monks in the general elections and their involvement in political activities have become extremely sensitive issues for the *sangha* and the country at large. Participation resulted in subsequent imposition of restrictions upon monks, and limitation of their rights in the political arena, and this in turn has tended to fuel opposition to the government within the *sangha*. Monks who do not agree with the government's actions are labeled 'illegal' or 'false' monks[3] and this has led to the polarization of two viewpoints – 'traditionalist' and 'modernist' – regarding the role of Buddhist monks in present-day Cambodia.

The supporters of the 'traditionalist' view of monks claim that Buddhism is about teaching ways to end suffering and attain spiritual liberation and happiness by cultivating one's peace of mind. Monks, with their spiritual expertise and religious authority, should therefore educate people to live in accordance with the principles of Buddhist teachings, especially 'the Four Noble Truths and the Noble Eightfold Path'.[4] Monks, the argument goes, are not like ordinary people. Upon ordination, they detach themselves from mundane life and they should therefore adopt a neutral, compassionate stance, like the disciples of Buddha, and they should act as symbols for people to respect.[5] Any involvement in worldly matters, it is held, will cause attachment and craving, which would hazard the monks' spiritual achievements, and they would also be disturbed by politicians seeking support and popularity.

POLITICIANS ENTER THE TEMPLES

Buddhist temples depend solely on popular support. Although donations to temples from politicians as well as laypeople provide valuable materials for temple construction and for the monks' subsistence and education, many politicians today come to *wat*s in the name of their political parties.

According to Buddhist monastic principles, monks are supposed to accept anything that people offer. In Cambodia today, however, the acceptance of offerings from politicians tends to be viewed as an act of political alignment. Some monks indeed maintain close relations with certain wealthy, high-ranking leaders so as to enhance their own status, and to secure funds for luxurious, beautiful temple buildings. In this way, they are able to display the power of their own temple in relation to others. For many monks and laypeople, however, this kind of relationship is deemed improper for the *sangha* because it is seen as political and motivated by personal ambition. Critics argue that monks should be neutral and pure, while secular politics is a dirty business. Involvement in politics thus destroys neutrality and the religious prestige of monks as spiritual and moral educators and such monks will lose the respect and trust of ordinary people.[6] The Buddhist *sangha*, as Yang Sam has suggested, should therefore 'limit its scope to moral and spiritual issues and leave politics to the State'.[7]

Nevertheless, many monks, like ordinary community members, nowadays support different political parties. Yet when monks align with a party, they are seen as biased, they are less trusted by people, and they are considered 'political monks'. The political affiliations of monks thus create divisions and disharmony among people and among the monks themselves.[8] Many argue that to avoid problems such as these monks should remain neutral and independent of politicians. In this way, it is proposed, they will earn greater trust from the general public and will remain free to express their own opinions on different issues. One of the strongest proponents of this viewpoint is the *Mahanikay* Supreme Buddhist Patriarch Tep Vong.

THE VIOLENCE OF 1998

Those who advocate a traditional role for monks also contend that they do not wish to see more horrific images of the *sangha* such as those broadcast in the press in 1998, showing monks being beaten, kicked, shot at and shocked with electric batons by authorities cracking down on the peaceful demonstrations in which 34 people were killed, including at least two monks in Phnom Penh.[9] The events of 1998 have been regarded as the worst action carried out by political authorities in Cambodia since the Khmer Rouge regime. The violence shocked Cambodian people throughout the country. It created so much anger among monks, many politicians and people that the authorities were referred to as *thmil*s (cruel, non-religious people) because 'only *thmil*s would dare to beat and kill monks'.[10]

However, the opinions of the monks and those of the authorities diverge on this issue. The government maintains that monks who joined in the demonstrations were involved in partisan politics, which falls outside of their religious duties. The monks, on the other hand, argue that they had not been involved in politics; they were simply marching for peace, expressing their desire for peace and non-violence. To this day, no proper investigation of the demonstrations and the government's response to them has been conducted and no one has been held accountable for the deaths.

After the 1998 protests, the *Mahanikay* Supreme Buddhist Patriarch Tep Vong and *Thommayut* Patriarch Bour Kry signed a public announcement to prevent monks from voting and they informed the National Election Committee (NEC) that temples and Buddhist buildings should not be used for the elections. Patriarch Tep Vong subsequently declared that Cambodian Buddhism is incompatible with voting, and that monks should not use temples to do politics.[11] He proclaimed that any monks who failed to follow the orders were 'not real monks',[12] and that if any monk was to make a slight mistake, he would be punished in the *wat* or could even be expelled from the monkhood if he was involved in a demonstration.[13] To reinforce the Supreme Patriarch's warnings, the Ministry of Information issued a command on 16 June 1999 via local television and radio stations that they must submit any Buddhist monks' sermons to the Ministry of Cults and Religion for censoring or checking before broadcasting them. This regulation was reiterated by the Ministry of Information and Ministry of Cults and Religion on 24 November 2005, after monks had participated in public forums voicing concerns over human right violations; several activists had been arrested without legal charges for criticizing the government for their handling of the border conflict with Vietnam. This prohibition in fact has had little effect apart from creating more resentment among monks, politicians, and laypeople.

THE EMERGENCE OF MODERNIST MONKS

In Cambodia today, many people and monks disagree with the government's regulation and Supreme Patriarch's policy on the *sangha*. They uphold a new standpoint, seen as a new, emerging modernist viewpoint, which promotes engaged Buddhism. Supporters of this view, both monks and laypeople, want to see monks play more active roles in society – not only traditional roles – particularly in government programmes for social development. They consider the Supreme Patriarch Tep Vong's prohibition to be a form of political manipulation commanded by the ruling party. They contend that although the Cambodian constitution endows monks with the same rights as all Cambodian citizens, the ruling party nevertheless prevents monks from exercising their rights since they have seen that new movements of monks do not support the party.[14]

These people argue, moreover, that prohibitions such as those pronounced by Tep Vong are undemocratic and an obstacle to the country's development. As one monk explained, they believe that 'the prospering of the religion depends on the welfare of society … when people are poor, society is weak, and religion will deteriorate'.[15] In another interview, a student voiced the following opinion: 'Like all Cambodian people, monks are also citizens living under the laws of the state. Monks also have a duty to fulfill, just as laypeople do … They have social responsibilities for the welfare of the nation and all its members.'[16] In the words of one monk:

> We monks live solely on people's daily offerings … if people live vulnerable lives, monks will also starve … and if we are not concerned with the current vulnerability of the people, we will all die together … so we have to help people out of *dukkha*.[17]

In a series of informal interviews, several monks explained to me that they cannot live in isolation from social issues – in an individualistic fashion. They argued that they should address social ills such as corruption and poverty, gambling, illegal logging, drugs abuse and prostitution: 'We cannot stand and watch or ignore the problems around us; otherwise they will get worse and worse.'[18] Some condemned the government for allowing rampant gambling, and they claimed that they wished to hold demonstrations against the casino construction that was taking place in Phnom Penh next to the Buddhist Institute and at other sites along the Cambodian–Thai and Cambodian–Vietnamese borders, but they were afraid of crackdowns and of being accused of being false monks after the government warnings following the events of 1998.[19] They argued that the government must stop all forms of gambling since gambling, as one monk noted, is not only prohibited by the Buddhist precepts but it also increases thefts and violence, including domestic violence.

The way in which monks have become involved in politics in recent years represents a new trend for the Khmer *sangha*, and those monks who participate in these trends are considered to be modernist monks (*Preah-sang samay-tum-nueob*).

MONKS DEFY THE PATRIARCH'S PROHIBITIONS

Despite the Cambodian Buddhist Supreme Patriarchs' warnings and prohibitions of monks' participation in politics and the 2003 general elections, hundreds of Buddhist monks defied the orders and attempted to register for the election. Monks even warned that 'if monks were not allowed to register, there would be a demonstration to demand that they be allowed to vote in accordance with the rights specified in the constitution.'[20] To ensure their right to vote, they proposed that the NEC and the then King, Norodom Sihanouk, should intervene and facilitate their voting.[21]

Many monks also participated in the controversial Human Rights Day celebration on 10 December 2005 at the Olympic Stadium, Phnom Penh, which resulted in the arrests of several local human rights activists on criminal defamation charges. When one of these was later temporarily released, monks participated in a public forum held on 15 January 2006 at the Cambodian Center for Human rights (CCHR) in Phnom Penh. All of those who joined in this forum, including 19 monks, voluntarily gave thumb prints requesting that the Cambodian government unconditionally release the remaining detainees and prioritize the law over individual interests.[22] The participants also criticized the government for misunderstanding the concept of 'human rights' and for using the court of law as a tool to silence its critics.

A few months later the CCHR organized a 50-kilometre three-day march from Phnom Penh to Udong Mountain. The march was to spread the message of freedom of expression and non-violence in Cambodia. It was conducted on behalf of the 'Alliance for Freedom of Expression in

Cambodia', a coalition of 28 organizations that has protested against criminal defamation. Some 50 monks joined the walk. One of them claimed that

> we need democracy and we need freedom of expression. We don't need one party or another. We do everything for freedom of expression in Cambodia, for a nonviolent society … a monk is also a citizen, so we should be able to take part in dissent for the national destiny.[23]

In interview, monks also recalled the name of Hem Chieu, a Cambodian monk who took the lead in 1942 in opposing French efforts to romanize the Khmer script and who was considered a heroic patriot.[24]

The monks' viewpoint on this has found strong support from many Cambodians; laypeople generally regard monks as well-educated and, as a university lecturer told me, 'compared to many normal people, they are considered to be senior persons who possess knowledge of good and bad and are thus … able to make better decisions to choose who should be good leaders for the country.'[25] It is held by some that 'taking part in the elections may lead monks away from the state of neutrality, but there is nothing wrong with letting them join in social work to create prosperity for the people and the country.'[26] 'If the Supreme Patriarch does not allow the best citizens to take charge of their own country, of their own future … this is wrong.'[27] Many therefore contend that monks should have the right to participate in any activities that relate to the country's development, as long as they are not partisans or members of any political party, and do not pursue a political career or work for personal benefits since to do so would be contrary to the Buddhist *vinaya* (Buddhist monastic discipline).

CRITICISM AND CHANGE IN THE *SANGHA*'S POLICY

Many monks criticize Supreme Patriarch Tep Vong for creating difficulties for them when they tried to register to vote in the 2003 national election. Some of them call him 'a communist monk', who favours the Cambodian People's Party (CPP). They contend that although Tep Vong prohibits monks from involving themselves in politics, he himself is deeply involved.[28] Tep Vong claims that Buddhism promotes calm and peace and prevents envy, while the ambition of political parties is to seek power and money. He therefore requested that monks abstain from political activities, including voting.[29] However, on 24 June 2003, just prior to the national election, Tep Vong traveled to Svay Rieng in eastern Cambodia and told monks and nuns there that the CPP-led government had achieved a great deal: construction of roads, schools, hospitals, *wat*s and more.[30] The monks viewed this as outright propaganda that more or less amounted to an election campaign for the CPP. He did not, they noted, mention corruption or the national property sold by the government. Patriarch Tep Vong, they said, should look in the mirror to see what he is doing.[31]

Tep Vong has also been strongly criticized for his comments on political parties in Cambodia. He has said that these are today divided into two kinds: 'the older or host party and the younger or guest parties.' He names CPP 'the older or host party' and the other parties 'the younger or guest parties', and he has requested the 'younger or guest parties to limit their opposition … insult and … disputes that could lead to war, losing the peace and ownership' that the CPP has achieved since 7 January 1979.[32] Scholars, NGO workers and the people have blamed Tep Vong for having been 'too much attached to and continued [sic] to defend the ruling CPP which he belonged to and served'.[33] They also accused him of categorizing people similarly to how the Khmer Rouge leaders had divided people, when they evacuated them from towns to rural areas, displacing them from one village to another and regarding the villagers as hosts or 'old people' and the newcomers as guests or 'new people'. Critics say that 'Tep Vong goes against the Buddha's discipline, according to which Buddhist monks should not be biased'.[34]

After a lot of criticism against him, in March 2006 Tep Vong came out and publicly announced that he would rescind his 2003 voting ban and allow Cambodia's estimated 60,000 monks to vote in future elections. He said that he has consulted other *sangha* leaders and would accordingly retract the earlier ban so that monks could vote in future elections for the development of the nation.[35] The announcement (officially issued on 29 November 2006) seems to have reduced some of the tension arising from the conflicting views over monks' civil rights. Tep Vong, however, has also said that his decision just followed statements encouraging universal participation in elections by the ruling CPP's renamed and resurrected 'Solidarity Front for the Development of Cambodia Motherland'.[36] In fact, shortly before the national election in 2003, the Cambodian Prime Minister, Hun Sen, publicly declared that it is monks' right to decide whether to vote or not but that while the constitution grants monks the right to vote, he did not want to interfere with the two Patriarchs' decisions: 'I cannot oppose the prohibition by the two chief monks, and I also cannot oppose the constitution. The decision is the individual's right.'[37] His statement can be seen as an attempt to stave off a clash between monks and the government. Moreover, Hun Sen is now associating himself more closely with monks and villagers in their community, funding the construction of buildings, schools and ponds in the compounds of many *wat*s. This might seem to be an attempt to attract more support and to repair the damage done to the government's image by the attacks on monks carried out in 1998.

Tep Vong's decision to rescind the ban surprised many, but has been welcomed by the NEC, by many monks and by the opposition party, whose leaders have repeatedly claimed that 'the Supreme Patriarchs cannot ban monks from voting, because monks are like everybody else and therefore monks also have the right to vote'.[38]

What should be noted at this point is that those monks who are in favour of political activism are generally more socially engaged, though they are not properly organized; they are more concerned with the present living conditions of this life than the next life. They do not seem to reflect much on the Buddhist conception of *annata*, which means 'non-self' in Pali. Although the Buddhist teachings, as those who claim that monks should perform a traditional role argue, associate involvement in secular affairs with attachment to earthly objects and therefore the hazarding of spiritual attainment, these modernist monks counter that the next life will be determined by what they have achieved in this life time; they consider that their activities are designed to help people out of desperate life situations and that this will be meritorious for their own next life.[39] They insist, however, that monks must not side with or participate in political parties, either directly or indirectly. They have to walk a careful line between activism and politics; they must know their limitations and should avoid extreme positions. Accordingly, 'they should be independent of any political parties ... they should build their reputation and influence on their religious roles, with the help of the people on religious and humanitarian action, and not on partisan interests'.[40] Monks should not be affiliated with political parties.[41]

CAN MONKS BE NEUTRAL?

In present-day Cambodia, to a large extent, regardless of whether or not the Khmer *sangha* chooses to involve itself in politics, the *sangha* is inevitably drawn into the Cambodian political arena. Politicians frequently approach monks at *wat*s for support and they often direct their political campaigns to *wat*s, especially before general elections. Because Buddhism is so deeply respected by so many Khmer people, political leaders endeavour to associate themselves with Buddhist monks and religious movements in order to secure and maximize their legitimacy, which then enables them to build a government, carry out their political plans and consolidate their social control. They mobilize monks to help them achieve these largely political goals. Since most Cambodian people today are poor, most rural *wat*s have little choice but to be subservient to political authority in return for protection and support. Despite its prestige, the Khmer *sangha* has not recently been able the exercise its traditional influence over political authority.

1m about Buddhist *dhamma* and its relevance to their responsibilities.[42] The monks that I have interviewed say that politicians try to use the monks' hands for political power.[43] Although the politicians may seem to be carrying out honest merit making in the religious domain, most of the time it is understood rather to be a political exploitation of Buddhism; they are felt to be engaging in profit making for political power in the name of religious merit making.[44] Some monks and laypeople have told politicians not to bring politics into their *wat*s since these are places for worship and meditation: 'If politicians come to make merit in the *wat*s, they should not bring with them the name or poster of their political party, because this will weaken the religion.'[45]

CONCLUDING REMARKS

This chapter has suggested that Cambodia's development depends on both improving its governance and empowering the Buddhist *sangha* through the recognition of monks' secular roles in state programmes for national development. In Cambodia today, the *sangha* certainly plays an important role in society, but it is often under the patronage of political leaders. Cambodian leaders seem to fear that monks may become the focus of popular movements against them. They realize that people are likely to follow a monk who takes the lead in a protest action.

Preventing monks from engaging in politics is clearly not generally understood to be about a concern for their spiritual attainment but is, rather, a way of preventing them from mobilizing political dissent.

No clear distinction can be made in this regard between 'state politics' and 'party politics'. When Khmer Buddhist monks claim that they have a right to participate in state politics to ensure that the government implements its policies properly, this may be interpreted as promotion of a single party's interests. This, in turn, fuels mistrust between monks, politicians and the people. In some cases it may also be true that individual monks are in fact involved in a particular political party, for their personal interests, as noted by Christine Nissen in this volume.

It would be greatly beneficial to Cambodia if monks were allowed to enjoy civil rights and to decide on matters of general concern. Their rights and roles should not, I contend, be limited to the religious affairs of the *wats*, and isolated from the secular affairs of the state. By virtue of their religious status and leadership potential, they could be powerful instruments for seeing that government policies are correctly implemented.[46] To do this, they need to develop their participation in secular affairs rather than confining their activities to only studying and preaching, as spiritual educators. This means extending their activities to greater involvement in the community and the country as a whole, keeping people informed about the social, political and economic situation, making efforts to repair the deteriorating moral order by teaching people and leaders how to apply the Buddhist *dhamma* to their daily lives (cf. Heng Monychenda in this volume).

Khmer Buddhist monks, I believe, should play not only a legitimizing but also a critical role in relation to the state. This could then be a constructive force for the improvement and reconstruction of the social well-being and political life of the country.

However, in order to strengthen Cambodian Buddhism certain factors require reconfiguring; the civil rights of monks need to be clearly defined, the administration of the *sangha* – particularly ordination and daily work – needs to be improved and properly regulated.[47] Similarly, as Khy Sovanratana notes in this volume, monks' education, both religious and secular, needs improvement in order that monks become qualified to advise and teach the general public,[48] and so that their voices may gain an authority with which the political leaders must reckon.

AUTHOR'S NOTE

I am grateful to Mr Hak Sraon, Sok Chhay, Say Mony and V. Saron and V. Buntheourn for their help in introducing me to several monks and thus facilitating my fieldwork.

REFERENCES

Anon. 'Monks Protest Against Tep Vong's Announcement, Demand Right to Participate in Deciding Future of Country.' *Moneakseka Khmer Newspaper*, 22 January 2003 (accessed through *The Mirror*, 19 January 2003, p. 7)

Anon. 'Only Thmils Kill Monks.' *Udom Katte Khmer Newspaper*, 9 September 1998 (accessed through *The Mirror*, 6–12 September, 1998, p. 8).

Anon. 'Is Patriarch Samdech Tep Vong a Political Tool of CPP?' *Wat Phnom Newspaper*, Friday, 27 June 2003, (accessed through *The Mirror*, 22 June 2003–28 June 2003, p. 12).

Anon. 'Hun Sen: Voting or not Voting are Monks' Rights.' *Kampuchea Thmey Newspaper*, 24 January 2003, (accessed through *The Mirror*, 19–25 January, p. 9).

Bektimirova, N. (2003) 'The Sangha in Politics: Challenges and Consequences.' *Phnom Penh Post*, 21 November–4 December, p. 6.

The Center for Social Development (2001) *Good Governance-Public Forum-Elections*. Phnom Penh, January.

Chea Sotheacheath and James Eckardt (1998) 'Activist monks Dare to Defy Authority.' *Phnom Penh Post*, 12–17 September, p. 2.

Harris, I. (2005) *Cambodian Buddhism: History and Practices*. Honolulu: University of Hawai'i Press.

Lao Mong Hay (2007) 'Equanimity Would Be Supremely Great in Partisan Patriarch.' *Phnom Penh Post*, Issue 15/26 29 December–11 January, p. 15.

Locard, H. (2005) 'Haem Chiev, 1898–1943: The Umbrella Demonstration of 20th July 1942 and the Buddhist Institute Under the Vichy Regime.' In *The Buddhist Institute Colloquium: Researching Buddhism and Culture in Cambodia, 1930–2005*. Phnom Penh: The Buddhist Institute, 17 June, pp.20–38.

Lor Chandara (2006) 'Buddhist Leader to Lift Ban on Monks Voting.' *The Cambodia Daily*, Thursday, 4 May, p.16.

Melamed, S. and Pin Sisovann (2006) 'Monks Ponder Their Role in the Public Square.' *The Cambodia Daily* (Wednesday, 8 March, p. 2)

Nguyen Xuan Bach and staff. 'Old Debate on Pagoda Politics: A Rising Phoenix.' (accessed through http://www.ijf-cij.org/folder_file_for_cambodia/7.htm

Sam Rith and Charles McDermid (2006) 'Great Supreme Patriarch.' *Phnom Penh Post*, Issue 15/25 December 15–December 28, p. 2.

Yang Sam (1987) *Khmer Buddhism and Politics from 1954 to 1984*. Newington: Khmer Studies Institute, Inc.

Yun Samean (2007) 'Tep Vong Accused of Favoritism, Going Against Buddha.' *The Cambodia Daily* Tuesday, 9 January, p. 16.

Yun Samean and Kevin Doyle (2003) 'Against Decree, Monks try to Register to Vote.' *The Cambodia Daily*, Tuesday, 18 February, p. 12.

NOTES

1. All of my informants requested to remain anonymous in my research and I do not, therefore, refer to anyone by name.

2. See, Ian Harris (2005) *Cambodian Buddhism: History and Practices*. Honolulu: University of Hawai'i Press, p. 220.

3. Nadezda Bektimirova (2003) 'The Sangha in Politics: Challenges and Consequences.' *Phnom Penh Post*, November 21– December 4, p. 6.

4. Interviews, Phnom Penh, 15 April 2005. The Four Noble Truths: 1. The truth that life is suffering, 2. The truth that the cause of suffering is selfish craving for satisfaction of sensual delights, 3. The truth that the end of suffering is the end of selfish craving, 4. The truth that the path leading to the end of suffering is called the 'eightfold path'. The eightfold path consists of: 1. Right view (proper understanding of the Four Noble Truths), 2. Right intention/purpose, 3. Right speech, 4. Right action/conduct (obeying the five precepts of not killing, not stealing, not lying, not having illicit sexual relations, and not taking intoxicating drinks), 5. Right livelihood/vocation, 6. Right effort, 7. Right mindfulness, 8. Right concentration. Buddhists are supposed to know the Truth and the Path in order to acquire true knowledge which leads to Enlightenment, the end of all rebirths and suffering, to *nirvana*. See Heng Sreang (2005) *Introduction to World Philosophy*. Phnom Penh: Pannasatra University of Cambodia, pp. 81–82.

5. Interviews in Phnom Penh, 15 April 2005.

6. Interviews with students, Phnom Penh, 30 May 2005.

7. Yang Sam (1987) *Khmer Buddhism and Politics from 1954 to 1984*. Newington: Khmer Studies Institute, Inc., p. 40.

8. Interviews with students, Phnom Penh, 5 April 2005, and a monk in Kompong Cham province, 18 August 2005.

9. According to the Cambodian Office of the High Commission for Human Rights (COHCHR), however, the number of monk casualties was uncertain. The COHCHR estimate that the number of dead was greater than that given in the official report. After the uprising, the Commission found that in Phnom Penh at least 34 people were killed in August and September 1998 alone. 77 people, including 18 monks and a nun, were injured. More than 50 people, including four monks, were arrested and have not been seen since then. The report of the Special Representative of the United Nations Secretary-General for Human Rights in Cambodia (20 August–28 October 1998) stated that the bodies of some victims, including one monk, were found near Pochentong airport, on the outskirts of Phnom Penh and in the river. On 11 September, the body of a man in his early 20s, with shaven head and eyebrows, was found near the bank of the Mekong River, by the Prek Krabao pagoda in Otdom village, Peam Chhor district, Prey Veng province. The pagoda authorities believed this to be the body of a monk, although the body was dressed in what appeared to be a policeman's shirt, oversized trousers and no underwear. It was buried in the yard of the pagoda. See 'Cambodia Struggling for Justice and Peace' (Report of Missions on the 1998 Cambodian Elections), Asian Network for Free Elections (AMFREL), Asian Forum for Human Rights and Development, Thailand: Bangkok, February 1999, pp. 53–6 & 94; also, Ian Harris (2005) *Cambodian Buddhism: History and Practices*. Honolulu: University of Hawai'i Press, p. 217.

10 'Only Thmils Kill Monks.' *Udom Katte Khmer Newspaper*, 9 September 1998 (accessed through *The Mirror*, 6–12 September, 1998, p. 8).

12 Samantha Melamed and Pin Sisovann (2006) 'Monks Ponder Their Role in the Public Square.' *The Cambodia Daily* (Wednesday, 8 March, p. 2)

12 Chea Sotheacheath and James Eckardt (1998) 'Activist monks Dare to Defy Authority.' *Phnom Penh Post* 12–17 September, p. 2.

13 Nguyen Xuan Bach and staff. 'Old Debate on Pagoda Politics: A Rising Phoenix.' (accessed through http://www.ijf-cij.org/folder_file_for_cambodia/7.htm)

14 Interview with three monks in Phnom Penh, 15 May 2005, and interviews in Kompong Cham province, 30 May 2005. The Cambodian constitution (promulgated in Phnom Penh on 21 September, 1993) article 34 states that 'citizens of either sex shall have the right to vote and to stand as candidates for the election.' Many Cambodian monks regard themselves as citizens of the state, and therefore consider participation in voting to be fulfilment of their civic duty.

15 Interview with three monks in Phnom Penh, 15 May 2005.

16 Interviews with students, Phnom Penh, 30 May 2005.

17 Interview with two monks in Phnom Penh, 10 June 2005. The term *dukkha*, in *Pali*, means 'suffering', by which the monks refer to the hardships and poverty of the people or of the country.

18 Interview with three monks in Phnom Penh, 15 May 2005

19 Interview with two monks in Kompong Cham province, 18 August 2005.

20 'Monks Protest Against Tep Vong's Announcement, Demand Right to Participate in Deciding Future of Country.' *Moneakseka Khmer Newspaper*, 22 January 2003 (accessed through *The Mirror*, 19 January 2003, p. 7)

21 Yun Samean and Kevin Doyle (2003) 'Against Decree, Monks try to Register to Vote.' *The Cambodia Daily*, Tuesday, 18 February p. 12.

22 Following the arrests of its chief and deputy chief, the CCHR opened a public forum to call for public support for its request that the government stop arresting activists and release all of those already in custody. The CCHR asked people to submit signatures, names or thumb prints for petitioning to the king for his intervention. Those monks who joined the forum also submitted their thumb prints.

23 See, Samantha Melamed and Pin Sisovann (2006) 'Monks Ponder Their Role in the Public Square.' *The Cambodia Daily*, Wednesday, 8 March, p. 2.

24 Hem Chieu helped organize opposition in Phnom Penh and elsewhere in the country in the early 1940s. This led to his arrest for treason and sedition in 1942. He was then sent to Saigon and he was imprisoned (on Koh Tralach for Khmer, Con Son Island for Vietnam, Poulo Condore for Europeans). He died in 1943 at the age of 46. See Henri Locard (2005) 'Haem Chiev, 1898–19943: The Umbrella Demonstration of 20th July 1942 and the Buddhist Institute Under the Vichy Regime.' In *The Buddhist Institute Colloquium: Researching Buddhism and Culture in Cambodia, 1930–2005*. Phnom Penh: The Buddhist Institute, 17 June, pp. 20–38.

25 Interview with a university lecturer and 5 students, Phnom Penh, 10 April 2005.

26 Interview with a university lecturer, Phnom Penh, 10 April 2005.

27 Nguyen Xuan Bach and staff. 'Old Debate on Pagoda Politics: A Rising Phoenix.' (accessed through http://www.ijf-cij.org/folder_file_for_cambodia/7.htm)

28 'Is Patriarch Samdech Tep Vong a Political Tool of CPP?' *Wat Phnom Newspaper*, Friday 27 June 2003, (accessed through *The Mirror*, 22–28 June 2003, p. 12).

29 Samantha Melamed and Pin Sisovann (2006) 'Monks Ponder Their Role in the Public Square.' *The Cambodia Daily*, Wednesday, 8 March, p. 2.

30 'Is Patriarch Samdech Tep Vong a Political Tool of CPP?' *Wat Phnom Newspaper*, Friday, 27 June 2003, (accessed through *The Mirror*, 22–28 June 2003, p. 12).

31 'Is Patriarch Samdech Tep Vong a Political Tool of CPP?' *Wat Phnom Newspaper*, Friday, 27 June 2003, (accessed through *The Mirror*, 22–28 June 2003, p. 12).

32 Sam Rith and Charles McDermid (2006) 'Great Supreme Patriarch.' *Phnom Penh Post*, Issue 15/25 15–28 December, p. 2.

33 Lao Mong Hay (2007) 'Equanimity Would Be Supremely Great in Partisan Patriarch.' *Phnom Penh Post*, Issue 15/26 29 December–11 January, p. 15.

34 Yun Samean (2007) 'Tep Vong Accused of Favoritism, Going Against Buddha.' *The Cambodia Daily*, Tuesday, 9 January, p. 16.

35 Lor Chandara (2006) 'Buddhist Leader To Lift Ban on Monks Voting.' *The Cambodia Daily*, Thursday, 4 May, p.16.

36 See note 35.

37 'Hun Sen: Voting or not Voting are Monks' Rights.' *Kampuchea Thmey Newspaper*, 24 January 2003, (accessed through *The Mirror*, 19–25 January, p. 9).

38 See note 37.

39 Interview with 3 monks, Phnom Penh, 15 May 2005.

40 See note 39.

41 The Center for Social Development (2001) *Good Governance-Public Forum-Elections*. Phnom Penh, January, p. 30.

42 The Cambodian monk, Preah Maha Ghosananda, famed for having initiated annual peace walks in 1992, mentioned this several times. In 1997, after the armed conflict on 5–6 July in Phnom Penh, the head of the department of philosophy at the Royal University of Phnom Penh invited Preah Maha Ghosananda to give a lecture on Buddhist philosophy. He talked about non-violence and the step-by-step approach to peace. He said that he had met many top government officials and given his book *Step by Step* to each of them, begging them to use peaceful means to solve conflicts. But, he said, this had had little effect. In 1998 the government again used violence to crack down on peaceful demonstrations held by students, laypeople and monks.

43 Interviews with two monks in Phnom Penh, 10 July 2005, and a monk in Kompong Cham province, 5 August 2005.

44 Interviews with monks in Kompong Cham province, 5 August 2005.

45 See note 44.

46 This potential has become explicit in various recent events. Between March and April 2006, monks set out on a walk through the western provinces of Battambang and Banteay Meanchey, visiting pagodas and schools to raise awareness about the environment and HIV/AIDS, and to promote community participation to solve social

problems. See Samantha Melamed and Pin Sisovann (2006) 'Monks Ponder Their Role in the Public Square.' *The Cambodia Daily*, Wednesday, 8 March, p. 1.

47 By this I mean that ordination and daily activities should be regulated according to the monastic rules. Several monks have recently been found to have cheated people and some simply use temples as residences while they earn money for themselves by seeking alms in improper places such as in markets.

48 This educational task has begun recovery. Monks have founded 'Buddhist Centers' in Phnom Penh, Kandal and Battambang provinces and elsewhere, providing moral education and training in skills such as computer literacy and foreign languages. See Samantha Melamed and Pin Sisovann (2006) 'Monks Ponder Their Role in the Public Square.' *The Cambodia Daily*, Wednesday, 8 March, pp. 1–2.

CHAPTER 13

Buddhist Education Today:
Progress and challenges

Venerable Khy Sovanratana

Education is a central component of Buddhism. The Buddha founded the *sangha* as a community of learning, in which monks could learn from and chastise one another. When he permitted the monks to accept buildings donated by laypeople to be used as monasteries, it was with the principal aim that the monastery be used as an educational institution for monks. Wherever it spread, Buddhism paid serious attention to education. This is one of the reasons why, in ancient times, there were so many Buddhist educational institutions, both inside and outside India. Some of them attracted students, both monks and laypeople, from all over the world.

When Buddhism[1] was introduced to Cambodia, Buddhist education received due attention. But teaching and learning were carried out in the traditional way in monasteries (*wats*), mainly by and for monks. The first formal Buddhist education in modern times began with the founding in 1909 of a Pali school at Angkor Wat in Siem Reap province, northwestern Cambodia. This school was called Parama Buddhavacana Pasad.[2] Unfortunately, the school was not successful as it was located far away from the city, making administration difficult. In 1911, it was shut down. In 1914, a new Pali school named Parama Buddhavacana Monti was founded in Phnom Penh to replace the one at Angkor Wat, and it was temporarily housed at the Emerald Pagoda in the Royal Palace under the royal patronage of King Sisowath. After some time, this school was shifted to a new building adjacent to the Buddhist Institute, and its name was changed to Pali High School. Then in 1955, two years after Cambodia regained independence, it was again renamed, this time Suramrith Buddhist High School. In 1933, a Royal Decree authorized the establishment of Pali primary schools and all of these were then located in monasteries. It should be mentioned that before the official establishment of Pali primary schools in Cambodia, Pali had been studied in monasteries. This is normal practice for Theravada Buddhist monks.

To provide higher Buddhist education for monks, Preah Sihanouk Raja Buddhist University was founded in 1954. It was the third oldest Buddhist university in the world. It was headed by Ven. Huot Tath, who held the ecclesiastical title *Samdech Bodhivamsa* (Rajagana First Class), and who was also the Director General of Buddhist Education.

Unfortunately, this flourishing Buddhist education system suffered greatly in the years of conflict. After civil war broke out following the coup d'état on 17 March 1970 led by General Lon Nol, the Buddhist University, like other institutions in the country, faced hardship and difficulties. Its allocated budget was not forthcoming and in due course conditions became so dire that it had to be closed down in 1972. After the Khmer Rouge came to power on 17 April 1975 Buddhism, like other institutions, met with the darkest period of its history in Cambodia: Buddhist monasteries were either destroyed or turned into storehouses or animal shelters; Buddhist practices were prohibited and Buddhist educational institutions were abolished.

When the Khmer Rouge regime was toppled by the Kampuchean United Front for National Salvation with the assistance from Vietnamese troops on 7 January 1979, a new regime came to power called the People's Republic of Kampuchea (PRK). During the PRK period 1979–1989 Buddhism was revived to an extent and Buddhist practices were again allowed. The first ordination ceremony was held at Unalom monastery in Phnom Penh on 19 September 1979 at which time seven former monks were re-ordained.[3] For this ceremony, seven monks including a Preceptor and Assistant Preceptors were invited from South Vietnam by the state. However, up until 1988, men under 55 years of age were not permitted to receive ordination. Since then, Buddhism has gradually expanded: monasteries have been rebuilt and the number of monks has increased significantly.

From 1979 to 1991 there was only one order of monks and all monks belonged to the Kampuchean United Front for National Salvation. These were known as 'Front Monks'. However, upon his repatriation to Cambodia in December 1991 former King Norodom Sihanouk appointed Venerable Preah Mahasumedhadhipati Tep Vong as the Supreme Patriarch of the *Mahanikay* Buddhist Order, and Venerable Bour Kry as the Supreme Patriarch of the *Thommayut* Buddhist Order.[4] This effectively re-established the two sects of Cambodian Buddhism that had existed before the Khmer Rouge regime. By 2005, there were 4,106 monasteries and 58,828 monks and novices of both Orders in the whole country.[5] Of these, 3,980 monasteries and 57,509 monks and novices belonged to the *Mahanikay* Order, while the *Thommayut* Order had 126 monasteries and 1,319 monks and novices. Both orders fall within the Theravada tradition.

THE RE-ESTABLISHMENT OF BUDDHIST EDUCATION

Today's Buddhist education in Cambodia began with the official re-opening of a Buddhist primary school on 2 December 1989 by Chea Sim, then a member of the Central Bureau of the Kampuchean Peoples' Revolutionary Party, President of the National Assembly and Chairman of the Kampuchean United Front for National Salvation, at Wat Tuol Tum Poung in Phnom Penh.[6] In his speech at the opening ceremony he said:

> The renaissance of the monastic school will be the ground in which to plant Buddhist knowledge, to ensure the revival of our national culture and soul. It will contribute to the strengthening of pure morality, the spirit of solidarity, national unity, and international solidarity for our nation. (Free translation)

As mentioned, from the fall of the Khmer Rouge regime on 7 January 1979 up until 1988, young men were not allowed to become ordained, although some young men were secretly ordained and led clandestine monastic lives in certain monasteries. Towards the end of 1988, the state issued a circular permitting young candidates to become monks. After this, ordination ceremonies were held in many monasteries in all of the provinces. Within a short time the number of monks, young monks in particular, increased so rapidly that by 1989 it became necessary to open monastic schools for them.[7] Prior to the official opening of the Buddhist schools, there had been some Pali and Buddhist studies operating unofficially in a few monasteries in the provinces.

Since the official opening of the first Buddhist primary school, many such schools have followed suit, both in the capital and in the provinces. In 1992, Buddhist secondary education began with the re-establishment of Suramrith Buddhist High School on the premises of the former Preah Sihanouk Raja Buddhist University. In 2004, the High School was relocated to its original, pre-1975 location. In 1999, when the first batch of monk students had completed their Buddhist upper-secondary education, the

Preah Sihanouk Raja Buddhist University was re-opened at its former location in Phnom Penh to provide higher Buddhist education to monks.

The present system of Buddhist education largely follows the structure that was in place prior to 1975. The curriculum, which consists of both religious and secular subjects, has been reproduced, with some adaptations to modern conditions.

Buddhist monastic education is divided into three levels of studies:

1. Buddhist primary education
2. Buddhist secondary education
3. Buddhist higher education

1. Buddhist primary education (Buddhika pathama siksa)

Buddhist primary schools are attached to and mainly looked after by monasteries. In 2001, Buddhist primary schools were discontinued in Phnom Penh, though some have been upgraded to Buddhist Secondary Schools.[8] At present, Buddhist primary schools officially exist only in the provinces, though some monasteries in outlying districts of Phnom Penh still provide Buddhist primary education to newly ordained monks. The main reason given for discontinuing Buddhist primary schools in the capital is that there is insufficient accommodation, and the number of monks is too great, which means it would be difficult for them to find food by going on alms rounds.

Buddhist primary education consists of three years of study, at the end of which candidates who pass the state examination receive the title of *Maha*. This qualification entitles the monk to sit the entrance examination for Buddhist secondary school.

The study programme includes Pali, Buddhist discipline, biography of the Buddha, Buddhism and the secular subjects that are taught in grades 4, 5, and 6 at the public schools. As a requirement for their study of Pali, the first year students are required to memorize a grammar book by heart. In the second and third years they are taught to translate the commentary of the Dhammapada word by word into Khmer. Although a few Pali teachers have endeavoured to change certain aspects of the course and teach Pali by composing sentences and structures, the old method continues to be followed.

In 2005, there were 555 Buddhist primary schools spread throughout the country, attended by 14,492 monk students.[9] Since the re-opening of Buddhist schools, 17,887 (2005 figures) monk students have completed and obtained Certificates of Buddhist Primary Education.

2. Buddhist secondary education (Buddhika madhyama siksa)

Buddhist secondary education started with the re-opening of Suramrith Buddhist High School in 1993 in Phnom Penh. It consists of two levels, lower secondary and upper secondary, each comprising three years of study. The duration of lower secondary education is now one year less than it was in the 1960s. The reason for the reduction by one year was, firstly, to match the duration of secondary education in secular schools and, secondly, to produce graduate monks as quickly as possible since Cambodian society is in a great need of qualified monks.

The programme of the Buddhist lower secondary studies includes Pali, Sanskrit, Buddhist discipline, Buddhism, English and the secular subjects taught in grades 7, 8, and 9 at the public schools. Besides grammar, Pali is studied by translating commentarial texts, such as 'Mangaladipani' (Commentary of Mangalasutta), 'Visuddhimagga, Kankhavitarani' (Commentary of Patimokkha).

In 2006, there were 23 Buddhist high schools in Cambodia that provided Buddhist secondary education to 3,826 monk students. As of 2005, 2,880 monks had completed their studies and received Certificates of Buddhist Lower Secondary Education.[10] Of the 22 high schools, seven are situated in Phnom Penh. The locations of the 22 schools are as follows:

1. Preah Suramrith, Phnom Penh
2. Samdech Bour Kry, Phnom Penh
3. Roath Saroeun, Phnom Penh
4. Samdech Nun Nget Lanka, Phnom Penh
5. Samdech Uom Suom Mahamontrey, Phnom Penh
6. Samdech Loah Lay Sansam Kosal, Phnom Penh
7. Samdech Tep Vong (Nirot Raingsey), Phnom Penh
8. Chumpouvoan, Phnom Penh
9. Oeung Thuong, Battambang
10. Samdech Chuon Nath, Kompong Cham province
11. Samdech Chea Sim, Takeo province
12. Prey Veng, Prey Veng province
13. Reach Bo, Siem Reap province
14. Svay Rieng, Svay Rieng province
15. Khemarak Raingsey, Kompong Chhnang province
16. Chum Kriel Kampot, Kampot province
17. Preah Sovannatther Uom Iem, Posat province
18. Takhmao, Kandal province

19. Banteay Meanchey, Banteay Meanchey province
20. Sa San-Chea Choam, Kratie province
21. Udam Muniratana Eng Huoy, Kompong Thom province
22. Intagnean Suisse, Sihanoukville
23. Choeung Chhnok, Kompong Cham.[11]

Most Buddhist high schools, especially those in the provinces, will likely proceed to provide upper secondary education to the students when they have completed the lower secondary studies. Consequently, the number of Buddhist high schools offering upper secondary education will increase year by year. As of 2006, there were 1,863 monks doing Buddhist upper secondary studies in ten Buddhist high schools, while 314 monks had passed the final examination and obtained Certificates of Buddhist Upper Secondary Education.

So far, ten Buddhist high schools provide upper secondary education:

1. Preah Suramrith, Phnom Penh
2. Samdech Bour Kry, Phnom Penh
3. Toath Saroeun, Phnom Penh
4. Oeung Thuong, Battambang province
5. Samdech Chuon Nath, Kompong Cham province
6. Prey Veng, Prey Veng province
7. Chum Kriel Kampot, Kampot province
8. Khemarak Raingsey, Kompong Chhnang province
9. Posat, Posat province
10. Reach Bo, Siem Reap province.[12]

The programme of Buddhist upper secondary studies includes Pali, Sanskrit, Buddhist discipline, Buddhism, comparative religion, English, and the secular subjects taught in grades 10, 11, and 12 in the public schools. Pali language and grammar are more advanced at this level, including composition of Pali verse and translation of Khmer texts into Pali, and vice versa.

3. Buddhist higher education (Buddhika Udam Siksa)

The Preah Sihanouk Raja Buddhist University (SBU) was re-opened in 1999 in order to provide higher education in Buddhism and relevant fields of study to those monks who had completed their Buddhist upper secondary studies. The University conducts an entrance examination for the selection of 50 students each year. In the first three academic years, it was able to maintain only one department, the Department of Buddhist Studies.

In response to the increasing number of applicants, the University established the Department of Education Science in 2003. This department annually admits 50 students who have passed a competitive entrance examination. This means that from 2003 until 2006, one hundred students were selected for each academic year.

On 23 January 2006, the Preah Sihanouk Raja Buddhist University was upgraded by a sub-decree of the Royal Government of Cambodia to a fully-fledged university with the addition of two more departments and a centre: the Department of Pali, Sanskrit and Foreign Languages, the Department of Khmer Literature, and the Centre of Teachers' Training.[13] Therefore, currently the university comprises four departments and a centre. From the academic year of 2006 onwards the university will be admitting 200 students each year.

In 2006 there were 403 students studying at the University.[14] The first three batches of 65 students had already graduated from the University with Bachelor of Arts degrees in Buddhist Philosophy, and the first group of 24 students had graduated with Bachelor of Education degrees. Some of the graduates have now become teachers at Buddhist secondary schools. Some of the others are pursuing their Masters degrees at various universities in Cambodia and abroad.

According to the prospectus, the main objectives of re-establishing the University are as follows.[15]

1. To give Cambodian Buddhist monks a deep knowledge of religious and secular fields in order that they may become a firm knowledge base from which Cambodian people may benefit, and so that they may teach as well as propagate true Buddhist teachings far and wide, both inside and outside the country.

2. To train Cambodian Buddhist monks to become an integral part of our national intellectual resources, to contribute to national development in social morality, to upgrade the quality of life of Buddhists through education, teaching, etc.

3. To train Cambodian Buddhist monks to have the competence, depth of knowledge and skills to preach the *dhamma*, explain and interpret the Buddha's teachings, and provide guidance to people concerning their way of life.

4. To train Cambodian Buddhist monks to become well-qualified scholars, who have wisdom and good conduct, and are able to perpetuate and promote Buddhism well.
5. To train Cambodian Buddhist monks to become scholars with erudition and expertise in Buddhism, to do research, write books and propagate Buddhism both at home and abroad.

The re-establishment of the Buddhist University thus aimed to cultivate monks' solid knowledge in both religious and secular fields in the hope that graduate monks will then serve both Buddhism and society.

In 2005, Preah Sihamoni Raja Buddhist College was founded by Samdech Bour Kry, the Supreme Patriarch of *Thommayut* Buddhist Order,[16] to provide higher Buddhist Studies to the monks. Situated in Wat Svay Popé, this Buddhist College consists of two departments: the Department of Buddhism and the Department of Administration. It admits 100 monk students annually.

This college would seem to have been established with the intention of providing greater opportunities to the monks of the *Thommayut* Order, whose number is still small. At present only a few of them have studied up to tertiary level. However, current enrolments show that the vast majority of monk students of the college are from the *Mahanikay* Order.

Since the number of monks completing Buddhist upper secondary education is increasing significantly each year, the Ministry of Cults and Religions is now planning to open two colleges as branches of Preah Sihanouk Raja Buddhist University in the near future, one in Kompong Cham province and another in Battambang province.[17] This will provide opportunities for monks to continue higher education in their provinces without coming to Phnom Penh. This will help to limit the number of monks in the capital and will also help to ensure that there are qualified and educated monks to teach Buddhism to the people in the provinces.

STUDY OF DOCTRINE AND DISCIPLINE

In addition to the three levels of Buddhist monastic education, there is another form of Buddhist education called '*Dhamma-Vinaya*'. This consists of three years and is divided into three levels known as *Thnak Trey, Thnak Toa,* and *Thnak Ek*. This is a traditional way of studying Buddhism and it does not have a systematic administration. As was the case in the 1960s, all the schools today remain on monastery premises and are directly managed by monasteries. While some are one-classroom schools, others do not have classrooms per se. Some monks learn under volunteer teachers, while others learn by reading books themselves. Then, depending upon their level of knowledge, they may take the annual examination that is held by the Office of Dhamma-Vinaya of the Directorate of Buddhist Education and by provincial Departments of Cults and Religious Affairs countrywide. The examination is also open to the general public. The papers include the biography of the Buddha, Buddhist discipline, selected kindred sayings, and the Buddha's verses.

According to statistics obtained from the Ministry of Cults and Religious Affairs, in 2005, there were 768 *Dhamma-Vinaya* schools attended by 15,836 students throughout the country.[18] It is very difficult to assess how accurate this figure is since *Dhamma-Vinaya* studies do not have a formalized system of administration. Moreover, *Dhamma-Vinaya* examination appears to have lost its appeal to monk students. Some monks do not find the examination important any more, while others take the examination only for the sake of the certificate. One of the reasons for this indifference is the lack of encouragement from the authority concerned. Monks interviewed by the author say that the certificates of *Dhamma-Vinaya* are not useful for their purposes even within the *sangha* community.

THE PROGRESS OF BUDDHIST EDUCATION

Since its re-establishment in 1989, Buddhist education has taken great strides, particularly after the UN-sponsored general elections of 1993. Buddhist primary schools have jumped in number from 23 in 1990 to 584 in 2005. Buddhist secondary schools have increased from one in 1993 to 30 in 2005, and these are found in most of the major provinces of the country. The number of monk students in the three levels of education has also shot up rapidly.[19] There are now Buddhist primary schools even in such remote provinces as Uddor Meanchey, Preah Vihear, Ratanakiri and Mondolkiri.

Before 1975, Buddhist monastic schools were concentrated to Phnom Penh. Although primary schools existed in some provinces, Buddhist secondary schools were only to be found in the capital and in Battambang province. The establishment of a great number of provincial Buddhist secondary schools means that monks in rural areas have the opportunity to receive Buddhist higher education without coming to Phnom Penh. Previously, some monks had to abandon their studies because they could not find accommodation in the capital, the only place at which they could obtain Buddhist higher education. The new availability of Buddhist education in the provinces not only saves Buddhist schools in the capital from becoming too densely populated but also provides a valuable contribution to the development of human resources in rural areas.

As mentioned above, Phnom Penh has eight Buddhist secondary schools offering Buddhist lower secondary education, and three high schools offering Buddhist upper secondary education. This is an unprecedented number. Before the Khmer Rouge took power, there was only one Buddhist high school namely, Suramrith Buddhist High School.

The communiqué of the 14th Annual Conference of High Dignitary Buddhist Monks in 2005 adopted the principle that each district should have at least one Buddhist primary school, and in each province there should be a Buddhist secondary school.[20] This will enable Buddhist monastic education to spread more widely throughout the country, especially in the remote provinces.

CHALLENGES OF BUDDHIST EDUCATION

Despite its rapid progress, Buddhist education in Cambodia today is faced with many challenges. The rapidly increasing number of monks and novices means that more learning facilities have to be provided. However, since the national economy is struggling, education in general has received insufficient attention and resources. Since Buddhist monastic education falls under the management of the Ministry of Cults and Religious Affairs, which is not a prioritized ministry in government policy, it has received less attention than other areas of education. The government prioritizes particular fields in its policy, and secular education (which falls under the Ministry of Education) is one of these.

The number of Buddhist schools at all three levels is inadequate to provide education for the growing number of monks and novices. If we compare the total number of monks in the whole country and the number of monk students in the three levels of education, we see that two thirds of monks are not attending Buddhist schools.[21] The number of monks who have graduated from Buddhist high school or from the Buddhist University is still very small. The shortage of Buddhist schools is felt country-wide, and it is most acute in the remoter districts of the border provinces.

Acquiring teaching materials has been a major problem. Chea Krasna, a Pali teacher of Samdech Oum Suom Mahamontrey Buddhist Secondary School, has stated that he has been a Pali teacher there since 1990 and the major problem for him and other teachers at the school is the shortage of textbooks and documents for use in teaching.[22] The Buddhist educational institutions do not yet possess textbooks of their own for secular subjects. Instead, they make use of the textbooks from the Ministry of Education for teaching non-religious subjects such as mathematics, physics, chemistry, history, geography. Even textbooks on Buddhist subjects are often unavailable or are in inadequate supply. Those available have generally been written and published prior to 1975 and there are no plans to bring textbooks up to date or to compose new ones. Almost all Buddhist schools also lack teaching materials and laboratories. Some Buddhist schools do not even possess a library, while the libraries of some Buddhist schools are poorly managed and do not contain enough books.

The lack of teachers is another serious problem. Venerable So Sarith, Director of Samdech Nun Nget Lanka Buddhist Secondary School, explained, 'We do not have enough teachers, and most of the teachers are hired from outside … Some hired teachers do not come regularly, which makes students lose interest in their studies.'[23] Pali teacher Chea Krasna concurs. The shortage of teachers, especially teachers of religious subjects, is felt everywhere, at the three levels of Buddhist education. For instance, all of the country's Buddhist primary schools together – which have 776 classrooms and 14,492 monk students – have only 888 teachers, of which 89 are formal teachers, 232 are teachers on contract and 567 are volunteer teachers.[24] This shows that many schools lack permanent or properly trained staff.

The same problem exists within higher Buddhist education. The Preah Sihanouk Raj Buddhist University currently has only ten academic and administrative staff. It therefore hires three times as many teachers from outside to fill the vacancies. These outside teachers often fail to come to class and consequently the teaching programme cannot follow the schedule correctly. The Ministry of Cults and Religious Affairs has tended to recruit only a limited number of teachers to the Buddhist primary and secondary schools and the government has no plan to provide enough teachers to Buddhist schools.

As with other civil servants in Cambodia, the teachers of Buddhist monastic education are so badly paid that they have to resort to other forms of employment to earn a sufficient income. The hourly remuneration for visiting teachers is also very low and payments are often appallingly delayed.[25] In addition to these problems, Buddhist education does not have its own funds or resources to run the schools, and management is not always reliable. For example, the Buddhist university, where the author is a lecturer, does not even possess enough funding to run examinations.

All these problems have resulted in poor standardization and a relatively low quality of Buddhist education. Before the civil war broke out, Buddhist education was considered to be of a good standard and its certificates were highly regarded. Nowadays, by contrast, there are constant complaints about its low standard.

CONCLUSION

Modern Buddhist education in Cambodia began in 1909. The present system, however, began with the re-opening of a Buddhist primary school at Tuol Tum Poung, Phnom Penh, in 1989. Since then, the number of Buddhist primary schools attached to monasteries has increased rapidly and Buddhist secondary schools too have reached a hitherto unprecedented number. They can be found in most of the 24 provinces and in the major cities of the country, with the bulk in Phnom Penh. For higher Buddhist education, there is the Preah Sihanouk Raj Buddhist University in Phnom Penh, which was re-opened in 1999 and is the only higher Buddhist educational institution in the country.

Besides the formal, three-level Buddhist education, there are also three grades of *Dhamma-Vinaya* study. This education has no proper, systematic administration or schools, but state examinations are held annually for the three grades and certificates are issued to successful candidates by the Ministry of Cults and Religious Affairs, with approval from the Supreme Patriarchs of both Buddhist Orders.

In spite of rapid growth, Buddhist education is faced with many problems. The shortage of administrative and academic staff at all three levels has impeded progress. The low levels of reimbursement to teachers have also resulted in the frequent absence of teachers. Due to lack of funding, all Buddhist monastic schools suffer from insufficient teaching materials and poor school maintenance.

Given all of this, it is difficult to know what direction Buddhist education is taking. It is very much in a period of trial and error at present. Most aspects of it are being restructured and are searching for ways to move forward. Thus far, it continues to lack proper curricula. The textbooks at primary and secondary levels are inadequate or non-existent, particularly textbooks for secular subjects. As the youngest institution in the field, the Buddhist University faces a Herculean task. It lacks all the resources necessary to run decent courses. The most significant lack is human resources in the form of competent and qualified administrative and academic staff.

These problems are all the more significant given that the country as a whole is swamped by a myriad of problems and Buddhist education remains the only hope for most Cambodians. We Cambodians hope that it will become strengthened in the not too distant future and once again become the backbone of Cambodian society that it used to be, and guide the country towards real peace, happiness and prosperity.

AUTHOR'S NOTE

The author would like to thank Dr Alexandra Kent for her warm invitation to the conference 'Reconfiguring Religion, Power and Moral Order in Cambodia', for which this paper was originally written.

SELECTED BIBLIOGRAPHY

Buddhist Institute (2006) *A History of Buddhist Education.* (In Khmer). Phnom Penh: The Buddhist Institute.

Chay Yi Heang (2004) 'Buddhism and Problems of Education.' (In Khmer) *Kampuja Suriya Journal*, Year 58, No.1–2. Phnom Penh: The Buddhist Institute.

Chhorn Iem (2000a) 'The Curriculum of the Preah Sihanouk Raj Buddhist University' (Unpublished). Phnom Penh.

—— (2000b) 'Fundamentals of Buddhist Education.' (In Khmer) Paper presented at the 3rd National Socio-Cultural Research Congress on Cambodia. Phnom Penh: The Royal University of Phnom Penh.

Harris, Ian (2005) *Cambodian Buddhism: History and Practice.* Honolulu: University of Hawai'i Press.

Hean Sokhom (2001) 'Rehabilitation of Monk Education in Cambodia.' (In Khmer). Paper presented at the Fourth Socio-Cultural Research Congress on Cambodia. Phnom Penh: The Royal University of Phnom Penh.

Huot Tath (1968) *L'Enseignement du Buddhisme: Des Origines à Nos Jours.* Phnom Penh: The Buddhist Institute.

—— (1959) 'History of Preah Sihanouk Raj Buddhist University.' (In Khmer). *Buddhika Seksa* [Journal of Buddhist Studies]. Phnom Penh: The Preah Sihanouk Raj Buddhist University.

—— (1970) *Buddhism in Cambodia: A Short History.* (In Khmer). Phnom Penh: The Buddhist Institute.

Khy Sovanratana (1999) 'Buddhism in Cambodia: The Past and Present.' (Unpublished). Essay submitted to the Department of Pali and Buddhist Studies, University of Kelaniya, Sri Lanka.

Klot Thyda (2002) *The Understanding of Buddhism in Khmer Society*. (In Khmer). Phnom Penh: The Preah Sihanouk Raj Buddhist University.

Ly Sovy (2004) *Pravat Preah Sangh Khmer* [History of Cambodian Monks In 8th, 9th and 10th Decades of 20th Century] (In Khmer). Phnom Penh: Ecole Française D'Extreme-Orient.

Pang Khat (1970) Buddhism in Cambodia. *Série de Culture et Civilization Khmères*. Tome 8. Phnom Penh: The Buddhist Institute

—— (2001) 'History of Buddhism in Cambodia.' In *Buddhasasana 2500*. Third Reprint. Phnom Penh: The Buddhist Institute.

Ray Pok (1957) *Cambodian Buddhism*. (In Khmer) Phnom Penh: The Buddhist Institute.

Saddhatissa, Hammalawa (1990) *Pali Literature of South-East Asia*. Singapore: Singapore Buddhist Meditation Centre.

Sao Chanthol, Long Kim Leang, Chhun Chor, and San Saing (2005) 'Training of Buddhist Monks in Cambodia.' (In Khmer). B.A. Dissertation submitted to Preah Sihanouk Raj Buddhist University, Phnom Penh.

Zepp, Ray (2004) 'Experiencing Cambodia.' (Unpublished collection of articles).

NOTES

1   Buddhism practised in present-day Cambodia is Theravada. However, from about the second to early thirteenth centuries, other schools of Buddhism, i.e. Sarvastivada, Mulasarvastivada, Sammitiya and Mahayana also existed in Cambodia. In certain periods, there existed two Buddhist sects alongside Brahmanism.

2   Buddhist Institute, 2006. *Pravat Buddhika Siksa* [A history of Buddhist education]. Phnom Penh

3   Ly Sovy (2004) *Pravat Preah Sangh Khmer* [History of Cambodian Monks: In 8th, 9th and 10th Decades of 20th Century], Phnom Penh, p. 1.

4   Ibid. In his speech at the 14th Annual Conference of High Ranking Buddhist Monks (12 September 2005), Ministry of Cults and Religions, Phnom Penh, the Supreme Patriarch Tep Vong also said this.

5   Statistics (2005) obtained from the Directorate-General of Buddhist Education, Ministry of Cults and Religious Affairs, Phnom Penh.

6   From a report of the Official Opening Ceremony of The Buddhist Primary School obtained from Tuol Tum Poung monastery, Phnom Penh.

7   In 1989 there were 8,000 monks and novices living in 2,800 monasteries (Hean Sokhom [2001] 'Rehabilitation of Monk Education in Cambodia.' [In Khmer], paper presented at the 4th Socio-Cultural Research Congress on Cambodia, Phnom Penh).

8   Interview with the President of Tuol Tum Poung Monastery's Lay Committee, 6 August 2005.

9   Khun Haing, Speech to the Annual Buddhist Conference of High Ranking Monks, Phnom Penh, 12 September 2005.

10. Report obtained from the Directorate of Buddhist Education, Ministry of Cults and Religions, Phnom Penh, 2006
11. Ibid.
12. Ibid.
13. Sub-decree dated 23 January 2006, signed by Hun Sen, Prime Minister of Cambodia, obtained from the Preah Sihanouk Raja Buddhist University.
14. Speech to the Annual Buddhist Conference of High Ranking Monks, Phnom Penh, 12 September 2005.
15. Taken from Chhorn Iem (2000a) 'The Curriculum of the Preah Sihanouk Raj Buddhist University.'
16. Cambodian Theravada Buddhism is divided into two Orders, namely, *Mahanikay* and *Thommayut*. *Mahanikay* is by far the larger of the two.
17. Speech by H.E. Min Khin, Secretary of State, Ministry of Cults and Religions, in charge of Buddhist Education, during the opening ceremony of the thesis defences for the final year students of the Buddhist University, 30 January 2007.
18. Khun Haing, Speech to the Annual Buddhist Conference of High Ranking Monks, Phnom Penh, 12 September 2005.
19. Hean Sokhom (2001) 'Rehabilitation of Monk Education in Cambodia.' [In Khmer], paper presented at the 4th Socio-Cultural Research Congress on Cambodia, Phnom Penh), p.75.
20. *Sangha Prakas* of the 14th Annual Conference of High Ranking Buddhist Monks, 13 September 2005, Phnom Penh.
21. Of the 58,828 monks in the country, only 19,075 monks are enrolled in formal education.
22. Author's interview with Chea Krasna, Mahamontrey monastery, Phnom Penh, 6 August 2005.
23. Author's interview with Venerable So Sarith at Lanka monastery, Phnom Penh, 19 August 2005.
24. A report obtained from the Directorate of Buddhist Education, Ministry of Cults and Religious Affairs, Phnom Penh, 2005.
25. Interview with Venerable So Sarith, Director of Samdech Nun Nget Lanka Buddhist High School, Phnom Penh, 2005.

CHAPTER 14

Buddhism and Corruption

Christine J. Nissen

> The role of the police station is to act as a fair place for the people to solve conflicts. Nevertheless, they take money from people when they solve conflicts. They take money for the purpose of going to bars, drinking, having beautiful girls, gambling, and giving jewellery to their wives. For example, they have a car, and they cannot save to buy a car if they are not corrupt ... It affects society because people are poor. People are victims. Poor people get hurt because of the unfair police station.

The above is a quote from Mrs Vanny, a housewife in her mid-50s who lives in an accessible rural area in Cambodia. The citation illustrates a general perception, shared by the majority of the Cambodian population, that corruption is not socially accepted. In fact, recent research even suggests a decline in acceptance of corruption from 1998 to 2004 in Cambodia. This might seem to contradict descriptions of Khmer society as undergoing moral decline (see Penny Edwards, Heng Monychenda in this volume). However, research on corruption also contains comprehensive data showing how Cambodians strategically, consciously or unconsciously, use their vocabulary and explanations of corruption to legitimize their own involvement in corrupt practices. This has been theorized as a moral economy of corruption (Olivier de Sardan 1999). Thus, corruption is as frequently denounced in words as it is practised in fact.

The apparent paradox in the Cambodian discourse of corruption is interesting in the light of how people create a folklore of corruption (Myrdal 1968). Many Cambodians are also concerned about politicization of the monkhood, which they deem to be the intrusion of 'moral' corruption into the moral order of the society – a symbolic pollution (or corruption) of the sacred. The objective of this paper is to explore what role Buddhism plays in the everyday discourse of corruption and how logic taken from religion is drawn upon to address corruption. I shall analyse this by outlining how the paradox in the discourse of corruption is not only apparent in relation to bureaucracy, where corruption is widely known to flourish, but it is also visible, albeit in a different form, in people's view of Buddhist institutions. I shall also examine how a fatalistic bureaucratic outlook (Herzfeld 1992) – a way for people to find meaningful explanations for their unsuccessful dealings with bureaucracy – is similar to the way in which Buddhist logic is used in the moral economy of corruption. This provides us with the framework of 'languages of corruption' in a local Khmer context.

Universal definitions are sometimes proposed for setting the limits of acceptable behaviour in public administration. However, they may help little in understanding the significance of corruption to locals. During my fieldwork in Cambodia it became clear that people who might be perceived by outsiders as engaging in corrupt exchanges do not necessarily interpret their own practices according to such unequivocal standards. Practices that some would label corrupt may be considered by others to be, for instance, the symbolic establishment of obligatory ties and thus as morally rational and praiseworthy (Scott 1972: 10; Blundo and Olivier de Sardan 2006: 113). The concepts of 'corruption' and 'Buddhist logic' used in this paper are therefore taken from the narratives of the participants of the study. I thereby shift the vantage point from that of the researcher-interviewer to that of the interviewee whose perspective is sought. I make use of an interactional approach and apply critical practice theory. 'Corrupt practices' thus refers to a broad spectrum of practices and should not be mistaken for a legal definition.[1] This leaves room for the discrepancy between local practices and legal definitions, which often derive from European law. As we shall see, people in Cambodia are 'culturally intimate' with corruption (Herzfeld 2005), because of the logics of patronage and Buddhism. This intimacy enables people to deal with corruption in everyday life.

I shall begin by contrasting Cambodians' trust in state institutions with their trust in local pagodas, where trust is expressed as generalized trust based on integrity ratings. The contrast illustrates the moral status of the pagodas and the role Buddhism plays in constituting social and moral order. Further, the low integrity rating scores for state institutions in general show that bureaucratic fatalism is at play. The discussion of trust is then further explored through my informants' remarks on how the religious and the social orders are interwoven. I find that the dynamic of the paradox in the discourse of corruption is also manifest in how people deal with Buddhism;

Figure 14.1. Poster showing how 'Corruption Breeds Poverty' (courtesy of the Centre for Social Development).

the fatalism of Buddhism resembles that found in relation to bureaucracy. This brings us to a discussion of morality and how people create a moral economy of corruption. I conclude that in order to understand the paradox we must abandon the assumption that the values entailed in the constructed moral economy of corruption are necessarily at odds with the way people deploy their Buddhist logic. Furthermore, for the Khmer, the religious and the social belong to different but closely related orders of truth. I argue that a violation of the boundary between them, such as the politicization of the monkhood, is a form of symbolic corruption that is perceived to have more extensive consequences for moral order than state corruption has.

SOCIO-CULTURAL ORDER – BUDDHISM AND PATRONAGE

As other papers in this volume make clear Buddhism and patron–client relationships are significant features of life in rural Cambodia. They operate in producing meaning, in justifying practices and in deciding what constitutes right or wrong behaviour. I therefore propose that Cambodian society should be viewed as a 'socio-cultural totality' (Tambiah 1990: 136) in which instrumental and performative symbols and actions are intertwined and fused. However, Buddhism and the hierarchical order that is structured upon patron–client relationships not only shape rationales in daily life, but may also be subject to contestation and political interpretation (Hughes 2006; Kent 2005).

The influence of Buddhism and patronage structures is especially visible in lowland Cambodia where Theravada Buddhism has long played an important role as the dominant religion and Buddhist monks are still called upon to perform a number of functions in rural life. Monks participate in all formal village festivals, ceremonies, marriages, and funerals and they occupy a unique position in the transmission of Khmer culture and values. By his way of life, a monk provides a living model of the most meritorious behaviour a Buddhist can follow, and Buddhists achieve good karma by earning merit and avoiding misdeeds (see for example Alain Forest's, Anne Hansen's and Judy Ledgerwood's contributions to this volume for fuller descriptions).

The notion of karma means that an individual's experiences are consequences of previous acts, including those in former incarnations. Karma acts as an incentive to perform acts that will reduce suffering in this or future lives. A wealthy man is assumed to be benefiting from meritorious acts performed in a previous life, and his wealth in turn enhances his ability to accumulate good karma for his next life. This suggests that a certain resignation and fatalism is embedded in Buddhism for the less fortunate, who cannot afford to gather merit through generosity. By contrast, the Buddhist belief that a position of power is the reward for having performed meritorious deeds in previous lives to an extent legitimizes the relationship between public position and private gain, which from a Western neo-political perspective would be seen as corrupt. However, to maintain stores of merit, prosperous people should redistribute their wealth back down the social hierarchy to produce, in Scott's terms, 'legitimacy of dependence' (Scott 1977). Within the bureaucracy this enables leaders to favour their subordinates.

A statement by Mrs Tani, a poor women whom I interviewed in rural Cambodia, describes this delicate system of social division in Cambodian society. She was describing how police officers came to her house to take money from her:

> It is like when a hen catches frogs for her chickens. The frog asks why the hen catches frogs but then he is eaten. You know, there is no reason for the frog to ask the hen but he should just try to be invisible.

According to Buddhist logic a frog might hope to become a hen in his next life. Mrs Tani's metaphor captures not only the power differential between herself and the police but it also posits them as belonging to distinct groups, each with its own possibilities and means; the police live off lower ranking people, which the latter quietly accept, thus reproducing hierarchical order. The literature on corruption repeatedly finds that those who benefit from corruption accept it while those who are excluded tend to condemn it (Blundo and Oliver de Sardan 2006: 113; Lambsdorff et al. 2005). However, the quote above adds a further nuance. While the 'frogs' may collectively condemn the behaviour of the police, they nevertheless see 'hens' eating 'frogs' as part of a natural order, one that may be traced back through traditional gift-giving practices in Cambodia. This reveals common cultural principles that are viewed as both embarrassing and inevitable. However, these principles may be contested when the social basis of reciprocity shifts and when the power of money and the vulnerability of poverty instead govern access to jobs and services such as health, education, the judiciary and water.

TRUST IN STATE INSTITUTIONS COMPARED TO BUDDHIST INSTITUTIONS

Much recent research suggests that trust and perceptions of corrupt practices have a strong reciprocal relationship (Čábelková 2001; Tonoyan 2005; Uslaner 2005) and that the discourse of corruption is a key arena through which the state, citizens, and other organizations and aggregations, such as religious institutions, come to be imagined (Gupta 1995). Exploring the level of trust and the discourse of corruption thereby provides us with insight into how people experience different spheres of society.

Table 14.1. Integrity rating showing that state institutions rank very negatively compared to private and Buddhist institutions

Number of respondents =2000	Aware (%)	Net Opinion (%)
NGOs	75%	+59%
Private schools	40%	+42%
Your local pagoda	95%	+29%
The military	71%	+21%
Private hospitals	94%	+20%
Public schools	98%	+12%
Water service provider	28%	+7%
National Election Commission	83%	+2%
Village chief	99%	-10%
Electricity provider	32%	-10%
Media (radio, TV, newspapers)	81%	-13%
Senate	37%	-13%
National Assembly	62%	-24%
Public hospitals	96%	-28%
Commune administration	98%	-32%
Political parties	86%	-35%
Office of Council of ministers	52%	-38%
District administration	87%	-41%
Central government and administration	87%	-42%
Provincial administration	80%	-44%
Police excluding traffic police	92%	-55%
Traffic police	82%	-61%
Tax authority	69%	-68%
Judge/ court	85%	-77%
Customs authority	64%	-83%
Average level of integrity across **negatively** rated institutions		-40%

Table 14.1 shows that fully 95 per cent of the respondents report that they are aware of the existence of their local pagoda. Table 14.1 also illustrates the integrity rating of institutions in Cambodia and shows that state

institutions, with the interesting exception of the military, are perceived very negatively and that the average level of integrity across the negatively rated institutions amounts to a net opinion of minus 40 per cent. At the opposite end of the spectrum are the private and Buddhist institutions. NGOs, private schools, and the local pagodas receive a considerably higher integrity rating of 59 per cent, 42 per cent, and 29 per cent respectively.

Societies with a low level of trust in anonymous others and institutions, are thought to promote a higher perception of corruption than high-trust societies (Tonoyan 2005 & Uslaner 2005). This is consistent with the empirical data in this study, which show a clear correlation between corruption severity and integrity rating; low generalized trust towards the state institutions influences people's negative experiences of corrupt practices in local bureaucracy.

Mrs Vanny's account above of police behaviour (rating among the lowest in Table 14.1 with a net opinion at -55 per cent) clearly illustrates the stigmatization of corruption. Mrs Vanny has a stereotypical perception of all policemen as corrupt, while Mrs Tani describes them as living off the lower ranking people simply because they are able to do so. These two women's views were shared by many of my informants. This speaks of a folklore of corruption and a fatalistic attitude toward bureaucracy, according to which people expect to encounter corrupt behaviour when facing the police and other state institutions. This has given rise to an irony in the discourse of corruption, whereby people's rejection of corruption has led them strategically to choose to pay bribes up-front to officials in order

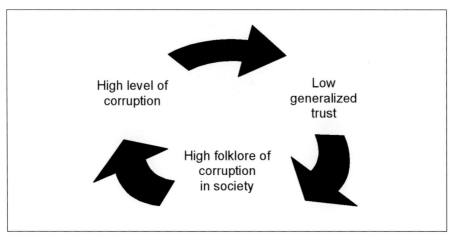

Figure 14.2. Cycle of trust and corruption

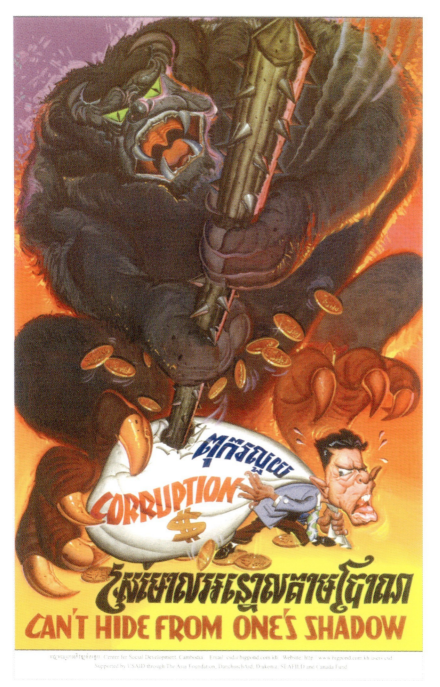

Figure 14.3. Poster showing the moral burden of corruption (image courtesy of the Centre for Social Development).

to keep some control of the payment. This creates a habitual vicious cycle of low trust and corruption as illustrated in Figure 14.3 opposite.

Low generalized trust thereby increases the negatively loaded folklore of corruption in society, which further generates an actual high level of corruption, which results in further low generalized trust, and so on. The more corruption develops, the more it becomes engrained in social habits and the more deeply it becomes inscribed in the moral economy and the less possible it is to reduce it (Olivier de Sardan 1999: 32). However, the circle can also be inverted by swapping 'low' for 'high' and 'high' for 'low'. In this way, generalized trust generates a low perception of corruption, which results in a low level of actual corruption. This second circle fits to some extent to people's perception of Buddhist institutions represented by the local pagoda.

The local pagodas are viewed as institutions that secure social and moral order. This is evident in the statement below by Mrs Sopheary, a woman in her mid-40s who comes from a rural area and who contributed generously to the pagoda for the Khmer New Year Festival:

> I respect and celebrate Buddha and give to the poor and old people because I respect Buddha. When I see poor people on the road I'll give, I also give to monks and they will divide to the poor and the old people and I'll get a good next life ... Rich people who have a lot of money from doing bad and give much to the pagoda, they will not get a good life, they will not get it back ... When people do corruption then they will have a bad next life, because doing corruption and oppressing people is to do something bad. But corruption is not only one person. It is many people so they will all get something bad in the next life, even if they do it because of their low salary.

Mrs Sopheary believes that the Buddhist institutions uphold social and moral order in society by redistributing money from the rich to the poor and punishing people who act badly with bad karma. She further explains the principles of Buddhism as rejecting corruption, since the religion rejects material greed, but at the same time she believes that your position and possibilities in life are determined by your moral habitus.

Statements like hers indicate that the state and the Buddhist institutions in Cambodia are viewed separately, according to separate imaginations. But there are also many similarities; both institutional forms are represented in local communities, both see women primarily as clients and men primarily as patrons, both require money from people in order to sustain themselves, and both have a role in maintaining social and moral order; one in a formal way through laws and the other in a more informal way through beliefs and practices.

The state, however, is in a crisis of legitimacy and faces profound distrust from its citizens, as shown in Table 14.1. This might mean that people are turning towards Buddhism to find moral order, a notion supported by the increased numbers of pagodas built after the fall of Democratic Kampuchea in 1979 (Kobayashi 2005). Nevertheless, the integrity rating of the pagodas is not particularly positive, with a net opinion of only 29 per cent. One explanation for this could be the folklore of increased politicization of monks and Buddhist institutions. As we shall see, this explanation cropped up in interviews with some local men.

POLITICIZED BUDDHISM

Mr Sen is an elderly layman whom I met in a pagoda in a remote village. He explained his critical view of the monkhood and how Buddhism has become corrupted:

Figure 14.4. Khmer New Year ceremony, monks receive donations from the laity and offer blessing in return (author's photo)

> Some monks collect the money in the pagoda and after one or two years they take that money and get married and build a house. The money collected is to be used in the pagoda but if the monk can collect the money he might take it and use it himself ... Sometimes the governor forces the monks to do something and if they refuse to do it they will go to prison or something. Therefore the monks decide to follow the governor.

Mr Veasna from another pagoda echoes Mr Sen's contempt for the mix of corruption, politics and religion:

> Some of the people in the government belong to a party and go to the pagoda and become monks because monks are very popular, but really they are not monks because they don't respect Buddha ... I work for a good monk, not for a bad monk. A bad monk is a monk who does not follow Buddhism and behave well. Monks are only monks if they do good things. People in monk's robes who do bad things are not really monks.

The two statements show how the religious and the social orders are interwoven. They further demonstrate how the dynamic of the paradox in the discourse of corruption is also present in the ways that people deal with Buddhism, especially in the way Mr Veasna distinguishes between good monks (the ones he works with) and bad monks ('the Others').

Another elderly patron, Mr Kinal, who comes from another small village, explained how Buddhism used to create social order. From his statement it is evident that social and moral order can be sustained by both religious institutions and the state but that they use different means. He regrets that Buddhism's role in securing order in society has declined and he argues that the state therefore needs to make laws for people to follow instead:

> Before, people believed in Buddhism and could not do anything bad because they would be punished in the next life. When people believe in Buddhism they must have an honest spirit and work honestly with other people. Nowadays, people believe less in Buddhism, and less in other religions also, because they only believe in what they see and they cannot see the next life. Officials in the government are involved in a lot of corruption because they do not believe ... If people trust less in Buddhism then the government must create laws for people to be afraid of and follow because when people do not believe in Buddhism they do something bad and make corruption.

Both the state and Buddhist institutions have fallen victim to low trust and corruption and lack integrity as institutions in which Cambodians can find moral guidance – the state considerably more than the Buddhist institutions. However, while the state in general is viewed as corrupt, people explain the politicization of the monkhood with great regret and as a symbolic pollution of the whole society; pollution of the sacred leads to a general moral breakdown. Yet, the connection between politics and Buddhist institutions is certainly not new in Cambodia. Buddhism has been the state religion since 1991, and while it provides the state with an ideological basis it also provides political leaders with legitimacy and monks with influence (see Heng Sreang's and Heng Monychenda's chapters in this volume).

One interpretation of my results is that some of the negative perceptions of the state are projected onto Buddhist institutions because of the 'antagonistic symbiosis' between the religious and state spheres. Another interpretation could be that this symbiosis is, to the detriment of both institutional forms, being torn apart, which leads to a separation between sacred and profane or between ideology and practice.

Nostalgia for the past should not be overlooked in the above citations. Neither should the dynamics of the restoration of public order through the building of pagodas after the fall of Democratic Kampuchea. As Kobayashi has pointed out, when people speak about their faith they do so in personal rather than in theological terms (Kobayashi 2005), which should alert us to individual distinctions similar to those noted in people's vocabulary on corrupt practices. The men quoted above all maintain that they believe strongly in Buddhism. Meanwhile, they keep a critical eye on state institutional development and fear that its moral corruption may penetrate even the religious realm and thereby bring about the dissolution of the entire moral order.

THE MORAL ECONOMY OF CORRUPTION AND BUDDHISM

Cambodians distinguish between corruption in which they are the ones paying for a service and corruption in politics, which they do not usually experience directly but believe to be widespread. In the first form they conceptualise the action on the basis of their relation to the taker and the act is accordingly sometimes labelled as a kind of gift. This operates as a moral economy of corruption based on Buddhist logic, which we will examine below. They may alternatively view the practices as improper and spread denigrating rumours about the person who took their money but mostly leave it at that. In the case of politics, the behaviour is labelled corruption and since it is assumed that politics inevitably involves corruption, it is generally thought that even good people will become corrupt after entering politics.

The expression 'a moral economy of corruption', a reshaping of Thompson's (1971) and Scott's (1976) concept of 'moral economy', refers to corruption as a socially embedded logic that depends on cultural and socio-economic matters (Olivier de Sardan 1999: 25–26). I utilize this term and find that the moral economy of corruption in Cambodia is used as an excuse by people seeking to justify their own corrupt practices while publicly denouncing the practice in others. The same person may in one context denounce and in another justify similar corrupt practice. We see an example of this in a quotation from a female member of a commune council in an accessible rural area. Locals complain about her taking money. She told me:

> Corruption is oppression ... Corruption means that powerful people with money can hurt us. I think the unofficial payment that people are willing to pay [to commune council members] is not the problem because we do not ask for that when we do something like write papers. People give to us willingly; we do not ask them for payment ... It is up to the people themselves whether or not they give.

The explanation that this commune council member employs legitimizes her acceptance of money. However, when referring to those who take from her she calls on the same fatalism about bureaucracy as others do, describing those more powerful than her as corrupt and herself as victim. By transferring responsibility for corruption onto others, be it superiors or 'the system', civil servants are able to engage in the general discourse and folklore, in which corruption is deplored and the powerful are stereotyped as those who are corrupt. This rationale is embedded in the way many people perceive themselves as being poor, regardless of age, gender and whether they are from poor or well-off households. This general self-identification is related to the construction of identity in terms of 'we the poor' versus 'them the rich'. The rich are corrupt and 'Other'. This resembles the way in which 'bad monks' are perceived to belong to 'the Other', as seen earlier in this chapter. This interpretation of corruption represents the division between a 'culture of corruption' model for them, the bureaucrats, the rich, 'the Other', versus a 'victim of circumstances' model for us (Miller et al. 2001).

A further example of the 'other-ing' of corruption is the following statement by a policeman who asked me for US$500–1,000 to pay the general police officer and ministry people to arrange a promotion for him:

> I work here and I have no idea about being involved in corruption but in other provinces they are involved in corruption … It is up to the family of the police if they get involved in corruption. Some families of police are poor and need the money. Some families are rich and need to be happy. Many policemen are involved in corruption. Among 100 policemen, I think 80 or 90 are corrupt … I do not practise corruption because some people speak badly about you if you practise corruption. I do not like that.

By labelling one's own bribes as 'gift-giving' (*luy sakun* or *luy banthaem* when referring to the low salary of civil servants) as opposed to 'corruption' (*luy puk roaluy*) the individual promises him/herself good karma and the transaction is rendered a moral deed. This vocabulary is seldom questioned because it functions to protect against personal failure and becomes an excuse when dealing with bureaucracy, a kind of 'secular theodicy' (Herzfeld 1992: 5–7). The level of society hierarchically immediately above ego, categorized as belonging to 'the Other', is described as consisting of people who exploit their position. While the social hierarchy in Cambodian society can be viewed as 'feeding' the distinction between 'rich' and 'poor', the folklore of corruption reproduces not only the practice of corruption but also the notion of victimization.

Buddhist beliefs rest upon the idea of a hierarchical order that is dependent on moral habitus. The better karma one has, the higher rank on the ladder and the better life one will get. Since it is held that all rich are corrupt but that corruption will be punished by loss of merit, it makes sense for people to label their own practices as not corrupt. Hence the paradox that corruption is as frequently denounced in words as it is practised in fact. I would argue that the Buddhist logic of karma and punishment is the basis of the moral economy of corruption, through which people legitimize their own corrupt practices by labelling them gift-giving or something similarly moral. An argument from Mrs Sotha, a woman in her late-30s, supports this:

> We know the monks are not always honest but when I give, I give to Buddha through the monk and then it is up to the monk to be honest. I will still get merit even though the monk keeps the gift for himself.

Mrs Sotha does not see herself as responsible for the monk's behaviour. She insists that her merit is secured even if the monk does not spend the money as prescribed. Of course there is a difference between paying bribes and giving to the monks but people use the same dichotomy: 'it is a good

Figure 14.5. A monk chanting at Khmer New Year ceremony with donations in front of him (author's photo).

deed to give and this will benefit me later on', either in terms of merit or in the form of service provision. This way of thinking echoes the way in which people distinguish between their own actions (always characterized as honest) and other people's corrupt actions in the bureaucracy. The social order represents, in this case, a refraction of the divine through the divisive complexity of everyday experience and practices. The personal justification that takes place in the moral economy of corruption should therefore not be viewed as being at odds with people's understanding of Buddhist morality. It is merely a reproduction of the basic Buddhist logic by which people rationalize their own behaviour through reference to their lack of power and, therefore their lack of responsibility. Hence, 'culture and power exist in a complex and mutually determining relationship' (Hughes and Öjendal 2006: 419). In this sense we see that people employ Buddhist logic in the creation of a moral economy of corruption as a means of dealing with what is an undeniable social fact.

CONCLUSIONS

The moral economy of corruption is a type of narrative and a symbolic system that has roots in local norms, such as Khmer Buddhist values, according to which it is the individual act, at times rewritten to fit individual needs, that determines merit and karma. Thus, corruption functions, as does Buddhism, as an idiom through which people try to create coherence in the world they inhabit. In the Cambodian folklore of corruption people condemn corruption and describe themselves as victims at the same time as they legitimize their own actions according to the moral economy of corruption. A cultural intimacy of corruption is thus established. Corruption in Cambodia needs to be understood in terms of how these strategies of personal legitimization and simultaneous collective condemnation are linked to the moral ordering of society, to Buddhism and to systems of patronage.

Unlike ordinary people, monks cannot easily legitimize their corrupt behaviour because they have vowed to forgo attachment to material possessions. Laypeople, however, may use the excuse that what is available to them is the result of merit gathered from former lives. This illustrates the fact that the theological and the social belong to different, interwoven orders of truth. Violation of the boundaries between the two realms, represented by the politicised monkhood, is seen as a symbolic pollution of the sacred. This is deemed to disrupt moral order to a greater degree than the commonplace corruption of the bureaucracy, where the folklore portrays corrupt practices as expected. Furthermore, Buddhist institutions seem to be idealized in the aftermath of the Khmer Rouge era with a nostalgia for the past that is not matched in attitudes towards present-day state institutions.

Because of the low levels of trust in state institutions in Cambodia, Buddhism may play a role in upholding social norms and social hierarchy. This role seems limited and the folklore of corruption towards Buddhist institutions, even expressed by loyal supporters, must be understood as a further threat to Buddhism's significance in everyday life. However, it may be inappropriate to speak of a moral breakdown. Rather, Cambodia may be witnessing a change in social structure, with the state and religious institutions losing their monopoly on the flow of information to people (cf. the high integrity rating for NGO's with a net opinion at +59 per cent). Local experiences and vocabularies are now increasingly mixed with global experiences and vocabularies of corruption.

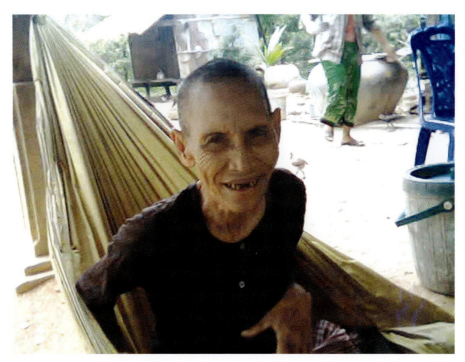

Figure 14.6. An old man and patron from a rural village watching over his household from his hammock (author's photo).

An interesting next step in this discussion would be to examine which strategies people use to manoeuvre in this language of corruption towards Buddhist institutions. When dealing with the bureaucracy people use informal structures, such as networks of relationships, which operate in parallel with the formal structures. For religion, however, different strategies are required. Exploring these strategies further may assist in the establishment of anti-corruption policies that would be to the benefit of both the state and the Buddhist institutions.

AUTHOR'S NOTE

This study would not have been possible without the valuable support, enlightening discussions and input from my colleagues at the Center for Social Development and the Center for Advanced Study, both in Phnom Penh, or without funding from DanChurch Aid, Diakonia, the Royal Danish Embassy in Bangkok and the World Bank. Furthermore, I would like to thank my supervisors Mikael Gravers and Nils O. Bubandt, University of

Århus, for their valuable help and encouragement. Similarly, I thank my good friend Robin Biddulph. Most importantly, I thank Modern, Sen, Soptheary, and Narin. I am deeply grateful to them for their insight and will to teach me from their experiences and views of the world.

REFERENCES

Andvig, Jens C., O-H Fjeldstad, I. Amundsen, T. Sissener and T. Søreide (2000). *Research on Corruption – A Policy Oriented Survey*. Chr. Michelsen Institute and Norwegian Institute of International Affairs, Norway.

Blundo, G. and Jean-Pierre Olivier de Sardan (2006) *Everyday Corruption and the State – Citizens & Public Officials in Africa*, London & New York: Zed Books.

Čábelková, Inna (2001) 'Perceptions of Corruption in Ukraine Are They Correct?' CERGE-EI Working Paper, No. 176. The Center for Economic Research and Graduate Education of Charles University (CERGE), Prague (http://www.cerge-ei.cz/pdf/wp/Wp176.pdf)

Center for Social Development (2005) *Corruption and Cambodian Households – Household Survey on Perceptions, Attitudes and Impact of Everyday Forms of Corrupt Practices in Cambodia*. Center for Social Development: Phnom Penh.

Gupta, Akhil (1995) 'Blurred Boundaries: The Discourse of Corruption, the Culture of Politics, and the Imagined State.' *American Ethnologist*, 22 (2), pp. 375–402.

Herzfeld, Michael (1992) *The Social Production of Indifference – Exploring the Symbolic Roots of Western Bureaucracy*. Chicago and London: The University of Chicago Press.

—— (2005) *Cultural Intimacy – Social Poetics in the Nations-State*, Second Edition, New York and London: Routledge.

Hughes, Caroline (2006) 'The Politics of Gifts: Tradition and Regimentation in Contemporary Cambodia.' *Journal of Southeast Asian Studies*, 37 (3) pp. 469–489.

Hughes, Caroline and Joakim Öjendal (2006) 'Reassessing Tradition in Times of Political Change: Post-War Cambodia Reconsidered.' *Journal of Southeast Asian Studies*, 37 (3), pp. 415–420.

Johnston, M. (1996). 'The search for definitions: the vitality of politics and the issue of corruption.' *International Social Science Journal*.Vol. 149, pp. 321–335.

Kent, A. (2005) 'Compassion and Conflict: remaking the pagoda in rural Cambodia.' *Svensk religionshistorisk årsskrift*. Stockholm University, pp. 131–153.

Lambsdorff, J. G., M. Taube and Mattias Schramm (2005) 'Corrupt contracting – Exploring the analytical capacity and new institutional economics and new economic sociology.' In Lambsdorff, J. G., M. Taube and Mattias Schram (eds) *The New Institutional Economics of Corruption*. London and New York: Routledge Taylor & Francis Group, pp. 1–5.

Miller, William L., Å.B. Grødeland and T.Y. Koshechkina (2001) *A Culture of Corruption? Coping with Government in Post-communist Europe*. Budapest: Central European University Press.

Myrdal, Gunnar (1968) *Asian drama: An Inquiry into the Poverty of Nations, Vol 2*. New York: Pantheon.

Nissen, Christine J. (2005) *Living Under the Rule of Corruption – An Analysis of Everyday Forms of Corrupt Practices in Cambodia*. Phnom Penh: Center for Social Development.

—— (2006) 'Like the frog and the hen – An Anthropological study of the folklore of corruption in rural Cambodia.' Masters dissertation, Institute of Ethnography and Social Anthropology, University of Aarhus, Denmark.

Olivier de Sardan, Jean-Pierre (1999) 'A Moral Economy of Corruption?' *The Journal of Modern African Studies*, 37 (1), pp. 25–52.

Kobayashi, Satoru (2005) 'An Ethnographic Study on the Reconstruction of Buddhist Practice in Two Cambodian Temples: With the Special Reference to Buddhist *Samay* and *Boran*.' *Tonan Ajia Kenkyu [Southeast Asian Studies]* 42 (4), pp. 489–518.

Rose-Ackerman, Susan (2004) 'The Challenge of Poor Governance and Corruption.' A Copenhagen Consensus Challenge Paper, Copenhagen Consensus, mimeo, April 2004 (www.copenhagenconsensus.com).

Ruud, Arild Engelsen (2000) 'Corruption an Everyday Practice. The Public-Private Divide in Local Indian Society.' *Forum for Development Studies*, NUPI, No. 2, November, pp. 271–294.

Scott, James C. (1976) *Moral Economy of the Peasant – Rebellion and Subsistence in Southeast Asia*. New Haven: Yale University Press.

Thompson, E. P. (1971) 'The Moral Economy of the English crowd in the Eighteenth Century.' *Past and Present*, No. 50, pp. 76–136.

Tonoyan, Vartuhi (2005) 'The Bright and Dark Sides of Trust: Corruption and Entrepreneurship – A Cross-Cultural Comparison of Emerging vs. Mature Market Economies.' Höhmann, H. H. and F. Welter (eds) *Trust and Entrepreneurship: A West-East Perspective*. Cheltenham, UK Northampton, Mass.: Edward Elgar.

Uslaner, Eric M. (2005) 'Trust and Corruption.' Lambsdorff, J. G., Taube, M. and Schramm, Matthias (eds) *The New Institutional Economics of Corruption*. London and New York: Routledge Taylor & Francis Group (chapter 5).

Visvanathan, Shiv and H. Sethi (1998) *Foul Play – Chronicles of Corruption*. New Delhi: Banyan Boods.

NOTE

1   The problem of defining 'corruption' has been the subject of much debate. See, for example, Visvanathan & Sethi (1998), Johnston (1996), Andvig et al. (2000), Rose-Ackerman (2004) and Anders & Nuijten (2006). It has been argued that since corruption is a typically 'Western' concept it may not be applicable or it may mean something different in other settings. In Cambodia, however, while corruption is not socially accepted, Table 14.2 illustrates the complexity of corruption practices as reflected in the Khmer language. See also Nissen (2006).

Table 14.2: Vocabulary, from extortion to gifts of kindness

Payment type	Khmer terms*	English meaning
Extortion	**Luy keng pravanh**	Exploitation money
	Luy keapsangkat	Money paid under pressure
	Luy hot cheam reastr	Money from sucking people's blood
	Luy lob lun	Money from ambition/greed
	Luy Bokpras	Money cheated out of someone
Corruption	**Luy puk roaluy**	Corrupted/spoiled money
	Luy rok krao	Money outside one's salary
	Luy ngonget	Dark money
	Luy kraom tok	Money under the table
	Luy luocleak	Money paid secretly
	Luy min sucaret/ tuccaret	Dishonest money
	Luy kraocbab/ min srabcbab	Money outside the law
	Luy khubkhitnea	Money agreed upon for illegal action
	Luy kec pun	Money to evade taxation
	Luy pak puok	Money shared among a clique
	Luy col hopao aekacun	Money going into a private pocket
Bribery	**Luy (sisamnok) Sok pan**	Money to persuade an official to do something
	Luy tinh toek cet	Money to buy someone
	Luy sokcet	Money to buy a favour
Payments to arrange service provision	**Luy roatkaa**	'Government money'
	Luy tinh kaangea	Money to process the paper
	Luy camnay phlov kat	Short-cut money/money to speed up procedures
	Luy thvieu ouy sevakarngea toancet	Money to speed up procedures
	Luy camnay knong kaa tumneak tum noang	Money to establish a relationship

continued overleaf

Payment type	Khmer terms*	English meaning
Payment to encourage service provision	**Luy loek toek cet**/ luong(lom) cet	Money to encourage an official to do his job
	Luy yok cet ke	Money to please someone
	Luy cun cea rungvoan	Prize money
Tips after service	**Luy toek tae**	Tea money
	Luy toek beer	Beer money
	Luy tlay tuk bic	Ink money, (lit. Bic liquid money)
Gifts after service	**Luy sakun**	Money out of gratefulness for service received
	Luy kun bamnac	Money out of gratefulness for service received
	Luy deng kun	Money out of gratefulness for service received
	Luy arkun	Money out of gratefulness for service received
	Luy tobkun	Money out of gratefulness for service received
Financial contributions	Luy vipeak'tean	Contribution (e.g. to local project)
	Luy banthaem	Additional payment to please the poorly salaried
	Luy bampenh kar khvakhaat	Financial support (e.g to school for underpaid teaching staff)
	Luy bampan	Money to feed someone/assistance
	Luy cumnuoy	Money to help someone/assistance
	Luy chamnay upaktham	Financial support
	Luy amnoy	Donation
	Luy cuy sangkruoh	Donation
Unsolicited gifts expressing kindness	Luy sandan'cet	Unsolicited payment from the heart
	Luy sobboros	Charity money
	Luy metathoa	Compassion money
	Luy monusthoa	Humanity money

* The 'bold' Khmer words are the most commonly used words for that category.

CHAPTER 15

Development Workers as Agents of Cultural Change

Vandra Harris

The history of social change tracks the engagement between the forces competing for moral power and legitimacy in any given society. This volume is primarily concerned with religion as a moral force; however, this chapter shifts the focus to consider international development as one of many forces contributing to the shape of religion, power and moral order in contemporary Cambodia. By considering the role and attitudes of development workers, it is possible to gain a broader understanding of the way development may influence Cambodian culture. Interviews with practitioners in Cambodia reveal a critical openness to cultural change and a deliberate approach to shaping culture by means of development. Their attitudes to cultural change are consistent with Bhabha's (1994) notion of hybridity, whereby cultures are constantly negotiated and recreated in the face of different influences. Development workers also label culture and cultural change in ways that support their selective approach to cultural change through development.

Appadurai (1996, pp. 43–44) proposes that the pace of cultural change experienced in the world today poses a challenge to enculturation, or the reproduction of culture. In this context, he suggests, culture becomes 'an arena for conscious choice, justification, and representation' in which cultural reproduction is politicised. Development workers in Cambodia report that they are making choices about the kind of culture that they want to see and they are using development as a vehicle to meet those goals. Religious groups may also be seen to be working to mould culture in constructive ways, which may lead us to conclude that active engagement between clergy and development workers in Cambodia could enhance cultural outcomes for ordinary Khmer. I conclude, however, that the best outcomes can be achieved through these groups continuing to work side by side rather than in active collaboration.

DEVELOPMENT IN CONTEMPORARY CAMBODIA

Development is one of many contexts in which cultures meet and are transformed. It exercises a powerful influence, not only because of its scope but also because of the multitude of forms it takes, the money involved and the vast numbers of individuals and organisations it engages. From the time of the 1991 Paris Peace Accords Cambodia has received steadily increasing amounts of foreign assistance. In 2003, Cambodia received US$508 million in Overseas Development Assistance (OECD n.d.), which represented 12% of the nation's GDP (UNDP 2005) and about one third of the government's budget (Langran 2001, p. 159).

Foreign donors control recipients of funding by demanding that they comply with a range of conditions (Dudley 1993, p. 19; Hoksbergen 2005, p. 161). Furthermore, donor governments openly represent development as a means of pursuing their own national interest, as can be seen in the statement by the Australian Agency for International Development (AusAID) that aid is given for three reasons, namely that it 'reflects our desire to help those less fortunate than ourselves ... improves our regional security ... [and] creates jobs and opportunities for Australians' (AusAID, n.d.). Development is an avenue by which foreigners try to influence Cambodian politics and society. Exploring the development encounter therefore enables us to recognise one of the key cultural forces at work in Cambodia today.

Different cultures overlap in this encounter, creating a space in which culture is negotiated (see Bhabha 1994, p. 2), and my focus is the role of development workers in these negotiations. In examining this, I take a 'contact' perspective, which Pratt describes as 'emphasiz[ing] how subjects are constituted in and by their relations to each other ... not in terms of separateness ... but in terms of copresence, interaction, interlocking understandings and practices, often within radically asymmetrical relations of power' (1992, p. 7).

Development workers are integral agents within development processes and may constitute 'the starting point and life force' of their organisation (Rugendyke 1992, p. 294). They function in regions of liminality between NGOs and communities, between bureaucracy and local cultures, and often between speakers of different languages. Moving between the communities and the funding organisations, development workers are boundary-crossers who may have special insight into the complexities of implementing development, and privileged access to the communities in which they work. People who are continually crossing between cultural groups in this way are always somehow 'Other,' whichever space they are in (see Anzaldua 1987), and this gives them a unique outsider–insider perspective. Hooks (1990, p. 153) believes that this marginal perspective creates a 'radical possibility' for creativity. The creativity that I believe is generated in the margins of development is seen in development workers' mediation of development as a cultural force.

These practitioners are often overlooked or assumed to be neutral actors, but the development workers' own understanding of poverty, development, and of themselves as agents within it, fundamentally shape the way they approach these processes (O'Leary and Meas 2001). Recognition of this agency has led to references to development workers as brokers of development processes, who shape development in small ways (Jackson 1997) and as 'mediat[ors] between different knowledge systems' (Hilhorst 2003, p. 190). Practitioners may, however, be unaware of the power that they hold in the communities in which they work, and may therefore not be aware of the extent to which they affect the development process (O'Leary and Meas 2001). As Jacobsen (2005) points out, Cambodians perceive power as residing in particular symbols and behaviours. The fact that development workers do not characteristically bear the more conventional markers of power may be part of the reason that they do not perceive themselves to be powerful.

My research consisted of a comparative study of the perspectives of development workers in Cambodia and the Philippines regarding the interaction between development and culture. In this chapter I draw on the Cambodian data, collected in late 2003 by means of informal interviews with 21 development workers in urban and rural areas of Cambodia.[1] A snowballing technique was used to establish contact with potential interviewees, and all of the initial contacts had a religious connection, being drawn primarily from an ecumenical development network of which I was a Board member, and also a Cambodian colleague working with Buddhist and Quaker organisations in Cambodia. As a result, many of those whom I interviewed worked with organisations with some religious connection, primarily Christian or Buddhist. Pseudonyms are used when referring to the research participants.

NGOs AND DEVELOPMENT WORKERS IN THIS STUDY

The practitioners who took part in this research and the organisations they worked for were very diverse. Many practitioners had been involved in development in Cambodia for at least a decade, and very few organisations had strong and collaborative relationships with overseas partners or funders. The stories of two Cambodian practitioners from this study illustrate some of the experiences of funding relationships, and the sorts of cultural issues that practitioners are choosing to address through development.

Lida[2] is the director of a women's NGO that was created and funded by an Australian women's organisation, and which works in northeastern areas of Cambodia. The organisation became a Cambodian NGO in 2000, when the funding organisation decided to close the NGO, but the local staff chose to continue the work independently, now seeking funding from a variety of organisations for each project they plan. An important aim of their work is to 'hand back' development work to villages when the local community is confident and able to take control, and they have done this in 11 villages.

Speaking about the difficulty of matching community needs with funder priorities, Lida stated that she found it easier to secure funding for HIV/AIDS projects than for community development, which the organisation had identified as most important. She recounted a situation in which she was able to get funding for a home-based care project for people with HIV/AIDS, but that her organisation wanted to do prevention because they had not identified many HIV patients in the areas they were working in. The particular irony of this situation was that the organisation was able to secure this funding, but none for food security, 'so people can't eat'. Lida believes that this is in part the result of pressures on funding bodies, who are often accountable to other financial sources, as well as a lack of knowledge about (and interest in) Cambodian culture.

Lida described the frustrations of beginning to work with women in villages, many of whom are shy and 'not confident to speak', reflecting that 'most haven't been to school, [so they] think they know nothing [and wonder] "how can I do this if I'm illiterate?"' Participating in a review process revealed to staff that pushing people to participate can actually bring about negative effects, while being patient allows the women to become 'proud' and 'really excited' about their membership of the group. Reflecting on the organisation's key focus on domestic violence, Lida stated that there has been an important change, for there is 'still domestic violence, but now women complain'. While the men may have initially found this challenging, they soon became quite positive about their wives' newfound confidence.

Commitment to promoting such cultural change means that Lida's organisation accepts whatever funding it can obtain, and adjusts the projects to include components to address issues such as gender, violence and nutrition. Lida does not report this change to the funding bodies, since her experience shows that the funders are not interested in non-financial project outcomes, only caring that 'the money is spent on time'. This dynamic, mentioned by several other practitioners, allows Cambodian development workers a great deal of flexibility, because the relationship with the funding body is not sufficiently close for there to be effective communication about the actual practices and goals of the local workers, including where this relates to culture.

Dara[3] is another practitioner who spoke clearly about the ways that his organisation works for cultural change. He is a male development worker in his 30s, working with a rural organisation with a focus on community development in the northeastern region of Cambodia. He has been working with this organisation since it was founded in 1992, when many NGOs entered Cambodia with the UNTAC mission. Like many of the practitioners that I spoke to, Dara had been a refugee during the Khmer Rouge era and had gained his development knowledge by working in the field. In spite of having a medical background, when Dara returned to Cambodia, he encountered discrimination that made it difficult to find work, as rifts emerged between 'returnees and residents'. The international NGOs that entered Cambodia at the commencement of the UNTAC mission did not discriminate on this basis, and welcomed the English-language skills that many refugees had acquired in the border camps.

The organisation was founded by three Australians who had secured funding from AusAID to help achieve their aim of creating a Cambodian NGO. At the completion of the first three-year phase, the three Australian founders withdrew over a nine-month period, and one of them continues to function as an adviser to the organisation as necessary. At the end of the second-year phase and with 'not much warning', the funding was not renewed, and since that time the organisation has received funding from a variety of sources, currently reporting to four different funders.

With the withdrawal of the founders in 1995, the organisation was established as a Cambodian NGO, and it has continued to operate in three-year phases that conclude with an evaluation that informs the design of the next phase. The initial phase was called 'rebuilding community', and aimed to address the discrimination that accompanied the return of refugees from the Thai border. Evaluation revealed that the 'the poor were not being helped by the project', so the second phase was 'combating poverty' by means of a variety of strategies including community organising and training of village workers and Village Development Council representatives. The evaluation at the end of this phase revealed that the phase had been unsuccessful because the poor had been constructed as victims, and concluded that many people were poor because they were unable to access services, and this led to a phase focused on 'promoting structural change at the village level'. When I spoke to Dara, the organisation was in its fourth phase – 'advancing civil society' – which focused on communities working together, both within and between villages.

Like the other practitioners in this research, both Dara and Lida are committed to social and cultural change in Cambodia and are guided by a clear vision. In general, practitioners found it hard to articulate their cultural goals but they were keen to describe the work they do and the ways in which they use development to reinvent Cambodian culture.

CONTINUITY AND CHANGE

Many forces have contributed to the history of cultural change in Cambodia. Hansen (2004) discusses the central place of religion in Cambodian identity, engaging with and affected by other cultural forces. Development practitioners addressed religion and other contemporary cultural influences, and in general they approached cultural flows critically, rejecting some forms of cultural change, particularly those that they were unable to mediate or influence. It will come as no surprise that development workers identified the Khmer Rouge as the most damaging cultural influence in Cambodia's recent history. Sophal,[4] for example, stated that the danger of being killed directly or indirectly by the Khmer Rouge meant that 'everyone had to develop a new way of life: anything to survive'. Development workers reported that this period still has a significant impact on people's behaviour and on contemporary expressions of Cambodian culture.

In spite of its dominance in these discussions, the Khmer Rouge regime was not the only negative cultural influence mentioned, but nor was all cultural change identified as negative. Rather, practitioners expressed a belief that while culture may change in ways that are positive or negative, change itself is normal. Bunna[5] explained this most clearly, saying that, culturally there's always change, from one to another set of traditions. However the effect or the results of that change have a lot to do with what the inputs are. [For example] there was the war input, and traditions changed as a result of that. But now in the time of peace, they have community development, they have new economic development ... and [the result] is a lot of change, [which happens] in different ways according to the context and the way people think and respond to those inputs.

This brings to mind Hinton's (2005, p. 145) identification of acceptance of cultural change as key to both Buddhism and the Khmer Rouge ideology.

Practitioners consistently listed several cultural influences in addition to the Khmer Rouge. Samnang[6] outlined a brief history of cultural influences on Cambodia, which spanned 'the French then the Japanese then the Americans', followed by the Khmer Rouge 'with the backing of Chinese government', then a 'Vietnamese regime backed by the US government',[7] concluding that 'we still have some influence of whatever, I don't know: Western, Eastern, middle ...'. A similar opinion was expressed by Sok,[8] who stated that while 'neighbouring cultures are influencing Cambodian culture, they cannot [destroy] Cambodian culture'. He referred to the cultural 'threat' of neighbouring countries, but felt that they posed no continuing danger, saying, 'I don't think that Cambodian culture will become like American culture – or other countries' [culture]'.

There was also lamentation about the impact of the media, particularly in relation to young people. Ratana,[9] for example, said that television and movies 'always promote other countries' culture; they forget to put [movies and television programs] together for the young generation about our culture' with the result that 'our young people forget the culture'. According to practitioners, this meant that young people were learning behaviour that was less respectful, more individualistic and more consumption-driven.

Although Cambodian development workers named a variety of cultural influences, they nevertheless expressed a sense of Cambodian culture maintaining its integrity and uniqueness even as it was changing. This is particularly striking when compared with the perspective of Filipino development workers I interviewed (see Harris 2005), who consistently claimed that cultural change was destructive, referring to an 'authentic' Filipino culture that was destroyed by the arrival of the Spanish colonisers. Benhabib (1995) proposes that perceptions of cultural continuity rely on the retention of a central core when other aspects of culture are changed, and this is consistent with the responses of Cambodian practitioners in this study.

When Cambodian practitioners spoke of development, they described it as a means of attaining cultural change and reconstruction. An example of the tone of the responses can be seen in the comments made by Max, an expatriate development worker in Cambodia.[10] When asked, 'Do you think that development changes culture?' He answered 'I hope so!' He gave examples of targeted cultural changes, which included 'focusing on the poorest – for people [in Cambodia] to do this is a cultural change ... [and also] women's status is changing as a result of participating in development'.

The cultural project of Cambodian development workers focused on the ways people interact with each other. Building community-mindedness and collaboration were frequently named as key goals, demonstrating that these practitioners share concerns about weak social cohesion. Vinet[11] stated that voluntarily helping each other is a quintessentially Cambodian trait that was all but destroyed under the Khmer Rouge regime, and which now constitutes the target of many development projects. Similarly, Ratana said that 'before, they didn't know how to work together as a team [but] now community participation means they work together'. Development was therefore named as a way to strengthen communities by rebuilding their sense of connection to one another.

Practitioners also displayed a belief that they can change culture selectively, as seen in the statement by Ek[12] that development 'is good for Cambodian people because most of the things we encourage them to change are the bad things. We don't change all of the culture, we change the bad culture'. This deliberate, selective approach to cultural change also reflects the notion of transculturation, whereby in the process of indigenising cultural influences, local people 'determine to varying extents what gets absorbed into their own cultures and what it gets used for' (Pratt 1994, p. 31). Cambodian development workers' acceptance of the notion that culture is constantly changing as it interacts with the environment allows them to feel confident to act as part of the process, and to direct some of these changes. The cultural forms that result from these processes are still seen to constitute 'Cambodian culture', distinct from the cultures of their neighbours or the West, but incorporating influences from those cultures. This process of transculturation is a particular product of the contact zone, since it is a space of cultural contact and negotiation (see Pratt 1994). This is no less the case when the contact zone concept is applied to development.

LABELLING CULTURE

Hansen points to the centrality of Buddhism in the 'development of different and competing discourses of authentic "Khmerness"' in the latter part of the twentieth century (2004, p. 60). Development practitioners contributed to their own discourse of authenticity, although this was not centrally focused on religion. As they spoke about transforming culture, development workers labelled cultural forms in different ways depending on the extent to which they approved of them. The ability to label culture in this way demonstrates power, and yet the 'power' of development workers is complex. They occupy a lowly position in the hierarchy, being the field workers who are relegated to the 'dirty' jobs, yet they may find themselves in positions of significant power in the context of the village, where they acquire authority through their association with development knowledge and funds (Jackson 1997, p. 244). In this way, development workers are 'often on the lowest rung of the organisation in terms of status and authority but [are] capable of making, or breaking, a project' (Jackson 1997, p. 237). Further to this, there is pressure on these practitioners to function both according to community expectations and according to development theory or project demands, and these may well be in conflict with one another (O'Leary and Meas 2001). This can be seen, for example, in the loss of authority experienced by field workers who attempt to operate in an egalitarian fashion (Jackson 1997, p. 246).

One practitioner who discussed this loss of authority was Ruth,[13] an expatriate practitioner who explained that Cambodian villagers go out of their way (and beyond their means) to treat practitioners as 'a higher person', for example giving them the best water and food even when they cannot afford it. According to Ruth,

> the irony is that to not play the bigger person role means that you lose respect in the eyes of those who are 'under' you. It's a catch-22, in that if you actually become too much like the people, they can think, 'Well what are you about anyway?'

Offering a particularly vivid example of this, Ruth described an international organisation working from a model based on reincarnation theology, whereby staff moved into the slums to live beside the people they were working with. While this ideology aims to improve relationships and outcomes by having staff live with the poor, the response in this instance was one of shock and bemusement, with people saying to the workers: 'This is not going to encourage us to get out of poverty, because if we see that people like you can end up in poverty again, then we don't want to [copy you].' While this organisation may have believed that it could act as a model for breaking down structures that constrain people, in fact their choice to renounce their place in the hierarchy resulted in a loss of credibility, which made them less able to meet their goals. Ruth recognised that these strategies can be very effective in other countries, but believes that they do not fit well with the particular social and cultural context of Cambodia.

When development workers spoke positively about specific cultural forms, they often gave them the positive association of being pre-revolutionary culture. Dara[14] explained that in his organisation 'our activities focus on restoring the culture of traditional society, because we have learned that some of the traditional culture has been lost since the war time'. Other practitioners were more specific, as can be seen in Vinet's statement that prior to the Khmer Rouge, 'if we did something at the community level, we did not pay, we just worked together … but after the Pol Pot regime, much of that solidarity, helping each other, disappeared'. While their assessment of causality may be challenged, what is of interest in this paper is what practitioners imply through the labels they use. While the practitioners may be referring to actual historical cultural practices, invoking tradition in this way is a means of valorising their cultural goals. Labelling positive traits as indigenous gives them a level of credibility that makes it easier for the development workers to (re)introduce these concepts, consistent with Narayan's (1997, p. 21) discussion of venerability, in which ideas or practices acquire status by virtue of their age rather than necessarily carrying intrinsic value.

It is interesting, however, that the label of 'authentic culture' was not always coterminous with 'good culture'. This was perhaps because the actions of the Khmer Rouge made a romantic perception of Cambodian culture less feasible. Seanglim Bit points out the dissonance experienced by Cambodians in attempting to reconcile the glorious picture of Cambodia's past with the results of the Khmer Rouge regime, noting that the 'contrast between the two extremes, from the very proud and powerful to the very weak and defeated, has to be incorporated into a collective sense of national identity' (1991, p. 84). Practitioners did not invoke the glorious Angkor period, but rather referred to the period immediately prior to the Khmer Rouge and a culture that was experienced by people who are still alive. The implication was that they were able to draw on personal experience to identify authentic and constructive Cambodian traits. One practitioner (Ratana), however, challenged this, asserting that most development workers relied on cultural rhetoric rather than their own experience when talking of this time, since the majority of them would have been less than ten years old when Pol Pot came to power.

In spite of this question, development workers' negative assessment of certain cultural changes reflects their perception that many changes have been detrimental to the people at the grassroots and the most excluded in Cambodian society, who are primarily targeted by much development work. Likewise, practitioners' positive appraisal of their own work stems from their expectation that they are effectively managing change to benefit these same people. These comments may be better understood by recollecting James Scott's assessment of village power relations, which suggests that the nostalgic and apparently selective memory of the community's poorest members is a result of the fact 'that so many of the innovations of the past decade have worked decisively against their material interests' (1990, p. 179). Rather than comprehensively labelling cultural change as negative, development workers appeared to appraise the changes in terms of how the communities with which they work were affected by them.

DEVELOPMENT AND RELIGION

Marston (2004) discusses the use of religion to capture ideas of nationalism and identity, describing the ways religion can become a tool of those with cultural or political aspirations. Similarly, Hansen (2004, p. 60) points to the many movements in Cambodian history which have been based on the 'assumption that Theravada Buddhism was an "essential" component of Khmerness'. The other chapters in this volume demonstrate that many religious institutions in Cambodia are working in ways that benefit Cambodian society, from education (see Khy Sovanratana, this volume) to providing trustworthy institutions (see Nissen, this volume). Development practitioners' work was clearly grounded in ideas of Cambodian identity and nation, and religion was perceived as an important component of these, yet development and religion appeared to be understood as distinct realms of activity. The practitioners whom I interviewed had a positive attitude towards Buddhism and its role within contemporary Cambodian society, and they pointed to ways in which Buddhism and development interact. Rith[15] was one of those who explained the benefits of development by pointing to its role in rebuilding Buddhism, as a central part of the broader cultural reconstruction. He reflected that 'when development came, [it] changed culture ... [for example] Buddhism was destroyed during the Khmer Rouge regime, now development starts it again'.

Many of the development workers I interviewed were working for organisations with Christian or Buddhist affiliations. Although evangelising activities disqualify projects from financial support from some foreign donors, such as AusAID,[16] non-evangelical activities by or with religious organisations can be eligible for funds. The practitioners were therefore in the interesting position of being able to cooperate with religious institutions such as *wat*s and churches on specific activities (for example outreach to the poor) but not to promote membership of the institutions. This may be one reason that development workers in this study did not report collaborating directly with religious groups. Another reason may be that they see the tasks of development and religion as different, if at times complementary.

A significant question that remains, then, is whether development workers should collaborate with religious leaders and organisations in their work. To my mind, the answer to this pivots on perceptions of cultural authority. With Cambodian culture in flux, and with an absence of elders (see Zucker, this volume), development workers have sometimes claimed the authority to define culture. They do not state their claim as exclusive, for example invoking Buddhism as an important cultural force parallel to development. They do, however, valorise Cambodian influences over foreign development influences on culture, explaining that development funders rarely take enough time to gain an understanding of Cambodian culture. Having located themselves in a realm of cultural authority, development workers are able to use development projects as a conduit for this newly acquired power.

This leads to the question of who ascribes cultural authority. According to Scott, the practice of culture entails a 'more or less constant ideological struggle' between the rich and poor members of any given community (1990, p. 199; see also Hall 1997, p. 24). Occurring on a subtle level, these struggles are fought 'over facts and their meaning, over what has happened and who is to blame, [and] over how the present situation is to be defined and interpreted' (Scott 1990, p. 178). In this way, the issue of who has the power to influence culture has tangible implications for the poor or excluded members of a community, as they are often the ones on the losing end of this struggle. Development workers may therefore be viewed as subversive, since one of their articulated goals is changing culture to benefit the weak. Development workers, of course, are not always completely altruistic, but I do believe that it is important to have faith that the majority of people working in development are genuinely committed to the poor, even if they may at times be blind to the effects of their own power.

On this basis, I would suggest that close collaboration between development workers and religious organisations in Cambodia is not to be desired. If there is no reliable basis for ascribing cultural authority, then perhaps affirming a variety of authorities is the best option, in that it allows for the possibility of competition. This in turn opens spaces for active cultural dialogue, since conflicts or differing priorities can demonstrate that culture is an arena of active choice, and this choice is central to cultural liberty, which the United Nations names as 'vital' to human development (UNDP 2004, p. 1). There is a sense in which this embodies a democratic approach to culture, in which people are able to make their own cultural choices. While development workers acknowledge the possibility of making conscious decisions about culture, this may not be widely accepted (or even considered) in the broader Cambodian community. Inviting Cambodian people more generally to participate in the active and ongoing construction of their culture diffuses the power of development or religion to define culture, and mitigates the question of cultural authority.

CONCLUSION

These practitioners express a positive attitude towards certain forms of cultural change and a belief that they are able to influence culture selectively in order to create a contemporary, hybridised Cambodian culture. While they reject the wholesale imposition of Western values, they can see the potential for positive input from both 'traditional Cambodian culture' and Western sources. In particular, they desire to recast culture in ways that increase social integration and foster cultural continuity.

I propose that a key reason that development workers believe that development brings positive cultural outcomes is the power that they have in development processes. Since they are able to influence the projects as they apply them, they know that they can mediate development. While development workers have relatively low power in relation to the development structures within which they function, practitioners are powerful in relation to the communities they work with, and it is in this context that they are able to name cultural change in ways that authorise or discredit it.

Encouraging development workers and religious organisations to continue to work in a parallel manner rather than in active collaboration diffuses cultural authority, which facilitates broader participation in the definition of culture. If cultural democracy is understood in the sense of a greater proportion and cross-section of society feeling able to influence culture, then continuing to support a low level of collaboration between religion and development would appear to be a positive move in this direction.

REFERENCES

Anzaldua, G. (1987). *Borderlands/La Frontera: The new Mestiza.* San Francisco: Aunt Lute.

Appadurai, A. (1996) *Modernity at Large: Cultural dimensions of globalization.* Minneapolis: University of Minnesota Press.

AusAID (n.d.) 'About Australia's Aid Program', available at http://www.ausaid.gov.au/makediff/whatis.cfm, viewed December 2005.

Benhabib, S. (1995) 'Cultural Complexity, Moral Interdependence, and the Global Dialogical Community.' In M. C. Nussbaum and J. Glover (eds) *Women, Culture and Development: A study of human capabilities.* Oxford: Clarendon Press: pp. 235–255.

Bhabha, H. K. (1994) *The Location of Culture.* London and New York: Routledge.

Dudley, E. (1993). *The Critical Villager: Beyond community participation.* London and New York: Routledge.

Hall, S. (1997). 'The Local and the Global: Globalization and Ethnicity.' In A. McClintock, A. Mufti and E. Shohat (eds) *Dangerous Liaisons: Gender, Nation and Postcolonial Perspectives.* Minneapolis and London: University of Minnesota Press: pp. 173–187.

Hansen, Anne (2004) 'Khmer Identity and Theravada Buddhism.' In J. Marston and E. Guthrie (eds) *History, Buddhism, and New Religious Movements in Cambodia.* Honolulu: University of Hawai'i Press: pp. 40–62

Harris, V. (2005) 'The Development Contact Zone: Practitioner perspectives on culture, power and participation in Cambodia and the Philippines.' Doctoral dissertation, Centre for Development Studies. Adelaide, Flinders University.

Hart, G. (2001). 'Development Critiques in the 1990s: Culs de sac and promising paths.' *Progress in Human Geography* 25 (4): pp. 649–658.

Hilhorst, D. (2003) *The Real World of NGOs: Discourses, diversity and development.* London & New York: Zed.

Hinton, A. L. (2005) *Why did they kill? Cambodia in the shadow of genocide.* Berkeley: University of California Press.

Hoksbergen, R. (2005). 'Building Civil Society Through Partnership: Lessons from a case study of the Christian Reformed World Relief Committee.' *Development in Practice* 15 (1): pp. 16–27.

Hooks, B. (1990) *Yearning: Race, gender and cultural politics*. Boston, MA: South End Press.

Jacobsen, T. (2005) 'Power in Cambodian Texts and Contexts: A ptdaim–mukh taxonomy.' Paper presented at the conference Reconfiguring Religion, Power, and Moral Order in Cambodia, Varberg, Sweden, 27–29 October 2005.

Jackson, C. (1997) 'Sustainable Development at the Sharp End: Field worker agency in a participatory project.' *Development in Practice* 7 (3): pp. 237–246.

Langran, I. V. (2001) 'Cambodia in 2000: New hopes are challenged.' *Asian Survey* 41 (1): 156–163.

Marston, J. (2004) 'Clay into Stone: A Modern-Day Tapas.' In J. Marston and E. Guthrie (eds) *History, Buddhism, and New Religious Movements in Cambodia*. Honolulu: University of Hawai'i Press: pp. 170–192.

Narayan, U. (1997) *Dislocating Cultures: Identities, traditions and third-world feminism*. London and New York: Routledge.

O'Leary, M. and N. Meas (2001) *Learning For Transformation: A study of the relationship between culture, values, experience and development practice in Cambodia*. Phnom Penh: Krom Akphiwat Phum.

OECD (n.d.) Aid at a Glance: Cambodia 2001–2003, available at http://www.oecd.org/dataoecd/1/15/1879774.gif, accessed December 2005.

Pratt, M. L. (1992) *Imperial Eyes: Travel writing and transculturation*. London: Routledge.

—— (1994) 'Transculturation and Autoethnography: Peru, 1615/1980.' In F. Barker, P. Hulme and M. Iverson (eds) *Colonial Discourse/Postcolonial Theory*. Manchester: Manchester University Press.

Rugendyke, B. A. (1992) 'Compassion and Compromise: The policy and practice of Australian non-government development aid agencies.' Doctoral dissertation Thesis, Armidale, NSW, University of New England.

Scott, J. C. (1990) *Weapons of the Weak: Everyday forms of peasant resistance*. Delhi and Oxford: Yale University Press.

Seanglim, B. (1991) *The Warrior Heritage: A psychological perspective of Cambodian trauma*. California: Seanglim Bit.

UNDP (2004) *Human Development Report 2004: Cultural liberty in today's diverse world*. New York: UNDP.

—— (2005) Country sheet: Cambodia. Available at http://hdr.undp.org/hdr2006/statistics/countries/country_fact_sheets/cty_fs_KHM.html, accessed December 2005.

NOTES

1. Of this number, 17 were Cambodian and four were expatriate workers.
2. Interview number 12, Phnom Penh 14 October 2003.
3. Interview number 2, Battambang 20 September 2003.
4. Sophal is a male development worker in his 30s who is a development consultant for several organisations. He has studied overseas and given particular attention to the cultural aspects of development in Cambodia. Interview 7, Battambang 24 September 2003.
5. Bunna is a male development worker in his 30s and is the Director of a very small, regionally based NGO that secures funding on a project-by-project basis. He was a refugee during the Khmer Rouge period and later studied overseas. Interview 1, Phnom Penh, 16 September 2003.
6. Samnang is a male Development worker in his 30s, who has worked with community development NGOs and an international organisation and now works with an NGO in an associated area. He began his NGO work when he was a refugee during the Khmer Rouge era. Interview 6, Battambang, 23 September 2003.
7. While this is not an accurate reflection of political alliances at the time, it is a useful insight into this person's perception of the range and complexity of international influence on Cambodia.
8. Sok is a male former development worker in his 30s, who is now employed by the government to carry out community development work in the same area as when he was in the NGO sector, working with a variety of funders. Interview 5, Battambang, 23 September 2003.
9. Ratana is a female NGO Assistant Director in her 40s who works with an NGO network organisation. She has studied overseas and is based in the capital city. Interview 19, Phom Penh 22 October 2003.
10. Max is an expatriate NGO Assistant Director in his 40s who works with the Cambodian partner of an international NGO. He has worked in the region for over ten years, and is based in the capital city. His organisation has a secure funding base. Interview 20, Phnom Penh, 22 October 2003.
11. Vinet is a female development worker in her 40s who recently joined the Cambodian arm of an international NGO. She is based in the capital city and her organisation has a secure funding base. Interview 13, Phnom Penh, 15 October 2003.
12. Ek is a male development worker in his 40s, who works with the Cambodian partner of an international NGO. He works in a regional area and his organisation has a secure funding base. Interview 11, Takeo, 1 October 2003.
13. Ruth is an expatriate development worker in her 30s who works as a consultant with a variety of organisations. She has lived in Cambodia for a number of years and is married to a Cambodian. Interview number 22, Phnom Penh, 25 October 2003.
14. Dara is a male development worker in his 30s, working with a rural organisation that was started by expatriates and which receives ongoing practical support from them. For a decade the organisation received ongoing bilateral funding, but in recent years has had to seek funding from a variety of sources. Interview 2, Battambang 20 September 2003.

15 Rith is a male development worker in his 30s, who works with the Cambodian arm of an international NGO. He works in a small community and his organisation has a secure funding base. Interview 8, Battambang, 29 September 2003.

16 Many Cambodian NGOs receive their funding from NGOs in other countries rather than directly from foreign governments. These funding NGOs, however, often receive a significant proportion of their finances from their government's development agencies. This therefore ties them and their partner organisations to the conditions of the funding government.

CHAPTER 16

In Search of the Dhammika Ruler

Heng Monychenda

IDEAL POLITICAL CONFIGURATION IN CAMBODIA

The ideal of political configuration in Cambodia is based upon the trinity of Jati (Nation), Sasana (Religion) and Mohaksatra (King), in which religion refers to Buddhism, the predominant religion in Cambodia. This can be seen in Cambodia's National Anthem, which consists of three sections, starting with a prayer for the protection of the king, followed by a statement of pride in the nation and of being the Khmer who built Angkor Wat, and ending with recognition of the importance of Buddhism in maintaining peace and development.

The Jati (Nation) and the Sasana (Religion) pillars may be compared to the two wheels of the chariot that maintain balance in society while propelling it forwards: one wheel is called *anachak* (the 'wheel' of state affairs) and the other is *Buddhachak* (the 'wheel' of Buddhism). In Cambodia today there is tremendous interest among the people to embrace *Buddhachak*[1] (the way of life according to Buddhism) and to harmonize it with *anachak* (modern state governance) in an effort to rebuild the country.

The third pillar (king) is traditionally understood to be the charioteer who may steer the chariot of society towards victory or failure in warfare. The ideal king or leader in the Khmer imagination is known as *Preah Batr Dhammik* (the Dharmic King) or Just Ruler. The search for a Just Ruler has been going on for centuries and Khmer still foster hopes that one day the *Preah Batr Dhammik* will come to govern their country.

THE WHEELS OF POWER

In general, Khmer people believe that peace and development can only come about when the government knows how to unite modern state

In search of the Dhammika ruler

governance, *anachak*, with traditional state governance, *Buddhachak*, both conceptually and in practice. While *anachak* is more concerned with the system and structure of worldly power, *Buddhachak* focuses upon the personal capacity and qualities of the individuals who want to bring peace and development to their country.

Two institutions in particular are relevant to the Khmer understanding of the powers that influence socioeconomic life. The first of these is the *wat* (Buddhist monastery), a grassroots institution that was traditionally under the common ownership of ordinary people. *Wats* provided literacy, economic assistance (loans), offered refuge in times of poverty and were the point of departure for dreams of approaching the second important institution, the *veang* (Royal Palace). To many Khmer, the *veang* represents a place in which everything is possible. It is the symbol par excellence of power and wealth, a kind of heaven on earth and the focus of the longings of ordinary people. The *veang* is also the place of residence of the king and the royal family, who are understood to be the reincarnations of Devadas (gods/angels) or of people who acquired great merit in previous lives, and it is therefore envisaged as the source of the power to rule and to save the people from suffering. Typically, when a villager comments on the magnificence of

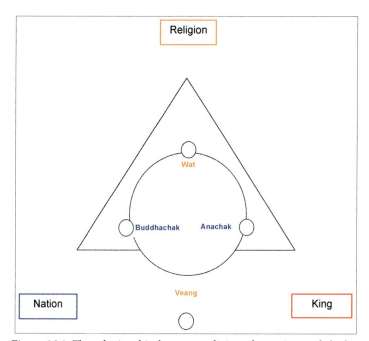

Figure 16.1. The relationship between religion, the nation and the king

a large house, he might say: 'Wow! This house is as big as the temple!' while an urbanite would be more inclined to use the palace simile and say: 'Wow! It is as big as the Royal Palace'. In essence then, the *wat* is a symbol of village prosperity and development while the *veang* symbolizes wealth and power in the city.

The *wat* may be understood as a source of fuel that inspires the lives of common people. It is a nuclear point around which people can unite in troubled times, and it is a wellspring of social and ethical values concerning leadership. Traditionally, a man who had never been a monk would not be considered 'complete' by his fellow villagers. Most of the post-Angkorean kings spent a period of time in the monkhood in order to fulfil the ten perfections (*parami*). Cambodian Buddhists consider this period essential to achieving the status of a good king, a good royal family member, or a good leader; the present king ordained twice in Paris, Prince Ranaridh ordained for one week in India, and Sam Rainsy ordained for one week in Cambodia. The present Prime Minister of Cambodia, Hun Sen, has never been a monk but he often publicizes the fact that he was once a temple boy. The basic principles that anyone – ruler or commoner, monk or layperson – would acquire from the *wat* were: *dana* (generosity)[2], *sila* (precepts)[3] and *bhavana* (development)[4].

The relationship between the *veang* and the *wat* is dynamic and yet ideally it is finely balanced. The *veang* requires the support of the *wat* and its parishioners and it reciprocates by providing support and prosperity to the *wat*. However, the *veang* is also sensitive to the moral influence of the *wat*, and it is difficult for the *veang* to maintain its status if its power and wealth are not seen to be based upon *dhamma*,[5] if they are not obtained through adherence to *dhamma*,[6] and are not born of *dhamma*.[7] Indeed, a ruler must publicly declare before the monks that his leadership is based upon these three tenets before making an offering to the monks, be it for making merit, paying gratitude, or even for political purposes.[8]

ANALOGIES FOR JUST LEADERSHIP

The two wheels of the chariot (*anachak* and *Buddhachak*) need a charioteer or a driver to lead people towards a goal. The two cannot be separated and need to be in balance. However, nowadays when Cambodians talk about the importance of the leader they often use the analogy of the naval captain rather than that of the charioteer. For instance at the end of official speeches speakers often praise the leader by saying: 'May the Lord Buddha blessyou so that you can navigate the Cambodian ship (*doeknomm neavear Kampuchea*) safely to land.' I ask myself why the traditional analogy of the chariot has suddenly been replaced in the popular imagination by that of the ship and why the importance of the two wheels for peace and development has been lost while all focus is now upon the captain. I cannot help but ask whether this changing pattern of thought reflects a change in Cambodian leadership towards Caesarism: a captain with a ship, but no chariot that requires religious cooperation.

Ever since the time of Jayavarman VII (r. 1181–c. 1220), Cambodia has suffered foreign occupations or civil wars. Jayavarman VII has become the ideal ruler in popular Cambodian consciousness and Cambodians still nurture dreams of recovering the glorious days of Jayavarman VII. This king has come to represent the ideal ruler who truly controlled the two wheels of the chariot for leading the country successfully: he extended territories, he brought about development, and he was devoted to Buddhism. The search for someone similar to Jayavarman VII or *Preah Batr Dhammik* (the Messiah of Cambodians), and the hope that *Preah Batr Dhammik* will come to save the country, has been passed down from generation to generation, with support in the Buddha's predictions. The book entitled the *Put Tumneay* (Buddha's Prediction) describes what this ideal ruler will look like, and when and where he will appear. It is interesting to note that the Buddha's Prediction mentions a Chinese man (from the incarnation of an angel called Visnukara), who will be carrying a *kompi* (Prediction book, Sutra, Canon) that will help in recognition of the *dhammika* king. Recently, I indeed received two letters from an elderly man living in the United States telling me that he has found a person who has the qualities of *Preah Batr Dhammik* and he is convinced that this man will save Cambodia from misery.

These hopes and this searching are motivated by the frustration that Cambodians feel about that fact that their recent leaders have not been able to reduce the suffering of the people. The more suffering they face, the stronger their hopes of finding *Preah Batr Dhammik*.

WHO WILL BE THE *PREAH BATR DHAMMIK*?

According to Cambodian thought, *Preah batr Dhammik* is a person who upholds the Tenfold Virtues of the Ruler[9] and who has supernatural powers such that enemies cannot harm him. People scrutinize the practice of the ruler closely to see whether he follows the Tenfold Virtues as prescribed by the Buddha. The Buddha also advised that rulers should practice the 12 Duties of the Great Ruler,[10] the Fivefold Policy of Socioeconomic Development,[11] and accountability towards society and nature.[12] However, it is clear that Cambodians have failed to consider various other qualities of the rulers as taught by the Buddha, or perhaps our monks have failed to preach sufficiently about these. Or maybe it is greed, anger and ignorance that have made Cambodians ignore or fail to implement Buddhist teachings. Cambodians have therefore focused upon the Tenfold Virtues of the Ruler, which deal with the individual behaviour of the leader, but have tended to overlook the Buddha's teachings about system of government (*Dhammadhippateyya*),[13] the role of the government (*Dhammikarakkha*),[14] the rule of law (*Ma Adhammakara*),[15] wealth distribution (*Dhananuppadana*),[16] moral order (*Samanabrahmana-paripuccha*)[17] and political platform/public policy (*Rajasanggaha 5*).[18]

THE JUST RULER AND THE JUST POPULACE

The failure of Cambodians to identify and the interminable wait for the *Preah Batr Dhammik* to appear, the incomplete preaching of monks on the *dhamma* for the rulers, and the failures of Cambodia's rulers have caused Cambodians much suffering. I therefore propose that Cambodians begin to actively cultivate a new *Preah Batr Dhammik* instead of passively waiting for a *Preah Batr Dhammik* to appear. It is time that we start to save ourselves before any *Preah Batr Dhammik* arrives to perform his task.

I would argue that *Preah Batr Dhammik* is simply a title for those who believe in dhammocracy[19] (*dhammadhippateyya*), respect for *dhamma*, love of *dhamma*, taking *dhamma* as the principle of life, and honouring *dhamma* as the 'flagship'. Therefore, it seems to me, it is not only rulers who must comply with *dhammic* rules, but all citizens of the country should cultivate these qualities in themselves. A Just Ruler may well be able to lead the country towards peace and development but the Just Populace is essential in choosing the Just Ruler and for checking up on his performance. This may seem like an unrealistic pipe-dream, but I would argue that it is a more practical solution than waiting for the voluntary appearance of *Preah Batr Dhammik* or waiting for a Chinese fortune-teller to reveal the true *Preah Batr Dhammik*.

In one of my books, *Preah Batr Dhammik* (1991), I contend that everyone can and should be *Preah Batr Dhammik* in contemporary Cambodia. The issue that seems worthy of discussion is: How are we to change common understandings of the concept of *Preah Batr Dhammik*? How might we begin to integrate dhammocracy and dhammikaship into the Prime Minister's cabinet and his public servants? How might the populace absorb dhammikaship, and what will be the role of the *wat* in this? Further, when power is no longer in the hands of the king, what kind of support might the king offer in order to realize the recurring dreams of his subjects? How may we make the subjects believe that by complying with dhammocracy and dhammikaship the government will be praised and re-elected, and peace and development will prevail?

RECONFIGURING POWER AND MORAL ORDER

Cambodians today face major questions concerning who holds worldly power and who is responsible for moral disorder. The *veang* is no longer the source of power and wealth. The *wat* has lost many of its former roles in society, the charisma of the *wat* and of monks has been damaged by war and the destruction wrought by the Khmer Rouge, and it has been weakened further by modern state government and by modern education. This decline can be seen in the replacement of the pronoun *acchkdei*, which monks used to use to represent 'I', by *atma*. *Atma* means I, while *acchkdei* actually means the ability to understand and explain the correct way of life, ability to manage conflict, ability to manage the *wat* as a place to which villagers may send their children for education.[20] Cultivation of the kind of relationship between the *wat*/monks and the villagers, as articulated through the word *acchkdei*, may help recover trust among villagers that their monks can help them reconfigure power and shape a political culture based on dhammocracy.

The challenge for the *wat* would then be, on the one hand, to play a greater role in educating, explaining, and disseminating information to villagers so that they know what qualities good leaders and representatives should possess and what kind of government system would best protect the interests of Cambodians, provide peace and development, maintain the rule of law, manage fair wealth distribution, improve the moral order, make sound public policy, and take care of the environment.[21] This would help villagers and city people alike to make better decisions in recruiting or electing their representatives and their leaders. On the other hand, the trustworthiness of the monks, in the eyes of the people, would be judged according to the extent to which the monks were able to influence power-holders and provide 'therapeutic' *dhamma*, or even detoxify maleficent power-holders. The task is not easy but it is not impossible.

Moral order in Cambodia is said to be declining. One example of this is the way in which primary and secondary school teachers, dissatisfied with their low salaries, oblige children to take extra, private classes with them. This damages the morality of the children and becomes a blueprint for their own behaviour when they grow up. People assume that if the teachers were to receive a higher, more appropriate salary from the government they would stop this behaviour. Corruption is another aspect of moral decadence, as is the increasing use of drugs by youths, which in turn gives rise to social disorder, and the high rate of HIV/AIDS infection. One may point out these problems to the monks and expect them to solve them, but this is not easy when the number of qualified monks does not match the magnitude of the problems. However, the socially-engaged Buddhism launched ten years ago by Buddhism for Development has proven effective in engaging monks actively in social work and in trying to help solve the problems that Cambodia faces. See the story of the organization at and its founder at http://www.bfdkhmer.org/founder_2_1.html.

Socialization into a moral order must also be carried out by the government, parents and schools. Unfortunately, post-war trauma and the nightmare of the Khmer Rouge delay the recovery of moral order and they also provide good excuses that may be trotted out when power is mismanaged or the moral order is corrupted. Buddhism for Development is now launching a program called Mother Karuna that aims to cultivate the role of mothers in healing these problems and in 'detoxifying the poisons' of men, who are the dominant leaders in Cambodia today. We hope that our work will encourage women to become female *dhammika* Rulers – another wheel that may match the traditional wheel of male *dhammika* Rulers.

CONCLUSION

There is nothing intrinsically wrong with living in hope of good things to come, though doing so may take time. Good leaders will come. Some of them may already have arrived. The real problem is whether these leaders are able to enact their just leadership. When the system of government is dhammocratized and the rule of law prevails, good people will be able to show their faces as *dhammika* leaders.

The role of Buddhism in Cambodia is still vital for the future of political figures, for Cambodians as well as in the world at large. The role of monks and *wat*s in helping to shape the behaviour of the leaders and in making the government system more dhammocratic is important. This includes active engagement with the daily lives of the Buddhist laity, not only in terms of the four *bhavana*[22] or development issues but also regarding decision making about the system of government, policies, and leadership.

Monks need to be aware that they are monks, and that they must live within the framework of the *vinaya* (law) taught by the Buddha, particularly regarding involvement in political manoeuvering in relation to the government and political parties. Proper and adequate education for monks in this new world order needs to be considered in capturing and managing the changing opportunities and threats caused by globalization.

REFERENCES

Indapañño Heng Monychenda (2003) *Preahbat Dhammik*, a publication of Buddhism for Development, third revised edition. Phnom Pen.

Venerable Khiev Chum, (1972) *Pracheathippateyya Chastum* [Ancient Democracy]. Phnom Penh: Treyrath Library.

NOTES

1. This refers to the Noble Eightfold Paths of the Buddha: Right View, Right Thought, Right Speech, Right Action, Right Effort, Right Livelihood, Right Awareness, and Right Concentration.
2. *Dana*: Two kinds; material gifts and the gift of truth.
3. *Sila*: Five precepts: abstain from killing, stealing, sexual misconduct, false speech, and intoxicants.
4. *Bhavana* means development. There are four kinds of development: physical development, moral development, emotional development and development of wisdom.
5. *Adhammiko* (the opposite of *dhammiko*).
6. *Adhammaladdho* (the opposite of *dhammaladdho*).
7. *Adhammeneva* (the opposite of *dhammeneva*).
8. Offering Announcement: *Ayaŋ no bhante pindapato dhammiko dhammaladdho dhammeneva uppādito màt`pituadike gunavante uddissa imaŋ saparikkhàraŋ saŋghassa dema te gunavantadayo imaŋ attano santakaŋ viya maññamànà anumodantu anumoditvàna yathichitasampattihi samijjhantu sabbadukkhà pamuñcantu.* [Dear Venerable monks! All of our foods are based upon *dhamma*, obtained through adherence to *dhamma*, and are born of *dhamma*. We dedicate these foods to our ancestors, such as mothers and fathers. May they acknowledge these foods (merits) as theirs and then may they be released from all kinds of suffering. May they achieve the state of human being, the state of deities, and the state of nirvana as they desire.]
9. The Tenfold Virtues of the Ruler (*Dasabiddharajadhamma*): *dana* (charity), *sila* (morality), *pariccaga* (self-sacrifice), *ajjava* (honesty), *maddava* (kindness), *tapa*

(self-control), *akodha* (non-anger), *avihinsa* (non-violence), *khanti* (tolerance), and *avirodhana* (conformity to the law).

10 12 Duties of the Great Ruler: *cakkavatti-vatta*:

(1) *Dhammadhippateyya ca Dhammikarakkha*: supremacy of the law and righteousness and provision of the right watch, ward, and protection for one's own folk, (2) for the army, (3) for administrative officers, (4) for civil servants, (5) for professionals, traders and farmers, (6) for town and country dwellers, (7) for the religious, (8) for beasts and (9) birds. NB this duty refers to the ideals presented in note 9.

(10) *Ma Adhammakara* (to let no wrong-doing prevail in the kingdom).

(11) *Dhananuppadana* (to let wealth be given or distributed to the poor).

(12) *Samanabrahmana-paripuccha* (see and ask for advice from the men of the religious life – monks who maintain moral standards. See Indapañño Heng Monychenda (2003) *Preahbat Dhammik*, a publication of Buddhism for Development, third revised edition, p. 203.

11 Ràjasaṇggaha Five: (1) *Sassamedha* (policy for agricultural development), (2) *Purisamedh*a (policy for promoting human resources), (3) *Sammapasa* (policy for promoting employment), (4) *Vacapeyya* (policy for public relations), and (5) *Niraggala* (policy for national security). (S.I.76; A.11.42, Pali Text Society). See Indapañño Heng Monychenda (2003) *Preahbat Dhammik*, p. 205.

12 The concept is taken from the Three Refuges of Buddhism: Buddha, *dhamma*, and *sangha*.

13 When referring to Dharma or law this is called *Dhammadhipateyya*; when referring to a person who established it is called *Pracheathipateyya* (Democracy). Venerable Khiev Chum, a Buddhist scholar of the early 1970s, defined this as the system of democracy in his book *Pracheathippateyya Chastum* [Ancient Democracy], pp. 62–64.

14 See note 9.

15 See note 9.

16 See note 9.

17 See note 9.

18 See note 10.

19 Dhammocracy = (Dhammo, Pali, *dhamma*) + -cracy = this author's own combination.

20 Khmer Dictionary, The Buddhist Institute Edition, 1967.

21 See notes 9, 10, 11 and 12.

22 See note 4.

Index

Achar 23–24, 27, 95, 111, 114, 148, 150, 163, 176–7, 184–185, 188–189, 200, 206–207
Ananda 45–46, 51, 53
Anderson, Benedict 30
Ang Chan, King 22, 118–119
Ang Choulean 125, 127, 135, 142
Ang Duong, King 26, 40, 221
Ang Phim, Prince 95, 103
Angkar 7, 63, 74, 81, 215
Angkor 3–4, 18–19, 22, 27, 32, 125, 127, 138, 302
Angkor Wat 4, 22, 220, 231, 257, 310
Anti-Thai riots 218, 232
Apppadurai, A. 162, 293
Australia 112
Australian Agency for International Development 294, 297, 304
AUSAID. See Australian Agency for International Development
Ava 22
Ayutthaya 18, 20, 22–23

Bali 222
Bangkok 20, 23, 26–28, 40–41, 45, 288
Banyan 67
Baphuon 22
Batheay 85–88, 98, 104–105, 157
Battambang 111, 187, 261–262, 264–265
Baudelaire, Charles 35, 42
Bayon 18
Bocola, Sandro 42
Bektimirova, Nadezhda 151, 159
Benhabib, Seyla 299
Berger, Peter 208
Bit Seanglim 302
Bodhisattva 45, 153, 217
Bokor 223
Bon Kathin 184–185
Bon Phkar 184
Bonhchoh Sima 158
Bourdieu, Pierre 147
Bour Kry 9, 244, 258, 261–262, 264
Brahmanism 18, 30, 85, 102, 122, 181, 214
Broadhurst, Roderic 218
Buddhachak 310–312
Buddhavacana 45, 257
Buddhism for Development 316
Buddhist Institute 6, 27–28, 219, 246, 257
Buddhist Socialism 6, 29
Bachai buon 157, 161
Bun Rany 228, 230

Cambodian Institute for Human Rights 154
Cambodian Peoples' Party 9–10, 120, 159, 247–248
Cambodian Television Network 230
Cham 152
Chan Yipon 153
Ceylon. See Sri Langka
Chandler, David 40, 128, 131, 133, 135–136, 142, 195–197
Changrae 231

Chap Bin Suvannajoto 52
Chau Bory 223
Chea Krasna 266–267
Chea Sim 259, 261
Chea Sovanna 230
Chedei 19, 95, 98, 100, 158, 161
Chenh vossa 181–182
Chhorn Iem 151, 159
Chiang Mai 18–20
China 3, 9, 75
Choeung Ek 71, 73, 75–76
Choeung Prey 88
Chuon Nath, Venerable 29, 43, 47–52, 95, 98–99, 103, 130, 181, 221, 225–226, 261–262
Christianity 29–30, 161–162, 200, 204–205, 208
Chul Kiri 88
Chulalongkorn, King. See Rama V
Chum Yoeun 98
Coedes, George 49
Cold War 9, 68, 75
Communist Party of Kampuchea 63, 215
CPK. See Communist Party of Kampuchea
CPP See Cambodian Peoples Party

Daung Phang, Venerable 93, 95–96, 98–99, 103–104
Dav Ek 216–217
Davis, Erik 12, 115
Democratic Kampuchea 7–8, 62, 64–69, 71, 73–76, 78, 137, 148, 161, 169, 170, 172–173, 179, 183, 186–187, 196, 198–200, 202, 205, 207, 214–215, 228, 281, 283
Devaraja 16, 221
Dhammacariyeavangs Et, Venerable 35–36
Dhammalikit SanghanayokLvi Em 46
Dhammalikhit Sanghanayok Uk, Venerable 46, 48
Dhamma-vinaya 35, 38, 41, 45–47, 49–52, 264–265, 268
Dhammika 13, 115, 311, 313, 316
Dhammocracy 13, 314–315
DK. See Democratic Kampuchea
Don chi 12, 88, 101, 109, 111–112, 114–115, 121, 123, 137
Doung Srae 198–207, 209

Ebihara, May 148–150, 152–158, 169
Ecole Française d'Extrême Orient 49
Eisenbruch, Maurice 218
Edwards, Penny 13, 272
Emerald Pagoda 257

Forest, Alain 5, 12, 39, 275
Foucault, Michel 124
Four Noble Truths 242
FUNCINPEC 112, 159

Ganesa 21
Gautama Buddha 21, 23, 38, 55
Geertz, Cliford 162, 222
Grandmother Yaan 137–141
Guthrie, Elizabeth 1

Habitus 147–148, 159, 162, 208, 280, 285
Hallisey, Charles 53
Hansen, Anne 5, 12, 25, 98, 275, 298, 301, 303
Hanuman 114
Harris, Ian 1
Harris, Vandra 13
Hel Rithy 219, 225
Hem Chieu 247
Heng Monychenda 13, 17, 102, 109–110, 115, 251, 272, 283
Heng Samrin 67–69
Heng Sreang 9, 13, 30, 226, 283
Hinton, Alexander 7, 12, 218, 299
HIV/AIDS 153, 232, 296, 316
Hooks, B. 295
Hughes, Caroline 224
Huot Tath, Venerable 29, 44, 48, 52, 181, 221
Hun Sen 9, 67, 75, 216, 221, 223–224, 228, 230–232, 234, 248, 249, 312

Ieng Sary 68–70, 73–74
Indra 21, 217
Isan 20
Izzi, Monique. See Norodom Monineath, Queen
Issarak. See Khmer Issarak

Jacobsen, Trudy 295
Japan 55, 98, 184, 191, 227, 249, 299

Jayavarman V, King 2
Jayavarman VII, King 2, 4, 18–19, 91, 110, 114–115, 313

Kalab. Malada 150
Kambujasuriya 35, 43, 46–47
Kampuchea Krom 28, 170
Kampuchean People's Revolutionary Party 9
Kanakamekar 176, 185
Kandal 12, 95, 148, 187, 261
Keng Vannsak 29
Kent, Alexandra 1, 2, 12, 22
Keyes, Charles 170
Khing Hoc Dy 217
Khmer Issarak 93–94, 96, 152, 198
Khmer Republic 7, 64
Khmer Rouge 7–8, 12, 30, 62–69, 72, 74–77, 111, 158, 160, 172–173, 197–199, 203–207, 219, 223, 228, 233, 244, 248, 258–259, 266, 287, 297–300, 302–304, 315–316
Khmer Rouge Tribunal 220
Khmer United Front for the Salvation of Cambodia 8, 258
Killing Fields. See Choeung Ek
Kim Hak 46–47
Kobayashi, Satoru 12, 13, 151, 156–158, 283
Koh Santhepheap 230
Kompong Cham 67, 85, 97, 111–112, 129, 137, 150, 157, 187, 229–230, 241, 253, 261–262, 264
Kompong Chhnang 88, 95, 261–262
Kompong Luong 95
Kompong Speu 12, 197, 214
Kompong Svay 171, 184
Kompong Thom 12, 60, 95, 151, 167, 171–172, 184, 262
Khourn Sophal 228–229
KPRP See Kampuchean People's Revolutionary Party
Kratie 219, 262
Krom samaki 173
Kusinara 46, 54

Lanna 18
Lan Xang 18, 32
Leclère Adhémard 154
Ledgerwood, Judy 12–13, 135, 208, 275
Lee, Richard 134
Leper king 114, 123
Lévi-Strauss, Claude 86
Longvek 19, 22–23, 112, 116, 118–119, 124
Lon Nol 6–7, 102, 120, 137, 172, 198–199, 207, 258
Luat Dam 63
Loh Lay, Venerable 99
Lvi Em 46, 52, 54

Mahanikay 9, 26–29, 95, 98, 170, 181, 226, 243–244, 258–259, 264
Mahavimaladhamm Thong, Venerable 38–39, 43, 48–49, 51
Mae chi 9
Maitreya Buddha 23, 91, 100, 102, 222
Mao Zedong 223
Mara 21
Marston, John 1, 12, 109, 157, 303
Marxism–Leninism 7
Mecca 40
Menam 17
Mekong 17, 148, 170
Methodism 200, 204, 205
Ministry of Cults and Religious Affairs 159, 244, 264–268
Ministry of Education 70, 71, 266, 267
Ministry of Information 244
Miss Yaan 129, 131, 133–134, 137
Mondolkiri 265
Mongkut, King. See Rama IV
Mount Meru 115

Naga 21, 91, 112, 114–115, 117, 120, 124
Naga king 114, 127, 202
Nandin 21
Nang Yaan. See Miss Yaan
Narayan, U. 302
Naresuan, King 22
Neak camkar 148
Neak mean bon 5, 23, 102, 119
Neak mean sel 114
Neak phsar 175
Neak srai 148, 175
Neak ta 4, 21, 88, 135, 203, 219, 220
Neak thom 112, 114, 120
Nissen, Christine 13, 251, 303

Noble Eightfold Path 242
Norodom, King 5, 15, 26–27
Norodom Chantaraingsey, Prince 94, 96, 98
Norodom Monineath, Queen 96
Norodom Sihamoni, King 96
Norodom Sihanouk, Prince and King 6, 110, 170, 215, 222, 225, 246, 258
Norodom Yukanthor, Prince 27
Northern Illinois University 148
North Korea 9, 102
Nouth Narang 225

O'Thmaa 197–199, 206–208
Oum Mannorine 96, 98, 101–102
Oum Wachiravudh 102

Pagoda at the Hill of Men (Wat Phnom Pros) 65–67, 73, 80
Parakkambhu, King 18
Panara Sereyvudh 232
Parami 95, 110–112, 114, 120, 124, 188–189, 312
Paris Peace Accords 1, 9, 34, 75–76, 294
P'aw 87–88
Patimokkha 16, 20, 261
Pchum Ben 156, 161
People's Republic of Kampuchea 8, 66–67, 170, 198, 216, 258
Philippines 227, 231, 295
Phnom Penh 3, 5, 7–8, 13, 19, 27, 38, 48, 63–64, 67, 85–86, 91, 97, 99, 104, 111, 115, 118, 130, 137, 148–149, 151, 153, 172, 173, 179, 187–188, 215–216, 219, 229, 231, 241, 244, 246, 257–262, 264–266, 268
Phnom Taprong 88
Phnom yong khmauch 200, 203
Pin Yathay 78
Pol Pot 12, 63–64, 68–70, 72–74, 85, 99–100, 114, 120, 196, 200, 203, 218, 231, 302–303
Pol Pot period. See Democratic Kampuchea
Ponchaud, François 219, 223
Prasat 88, 98, 102, 103
Prasat (village) 171, 174
Prasat Preah Ko 117
Prasat Sosar 121–122

Preahbat Beyta Tassarat 100
Preah Mony Eysey Akkinek 100
'Preah Neang Chantha Maly' 111
Preah keo 23, 116, 117, 120–122
Preah ko 21, 23, 116–117, 120–122
Preah Neareay 100
Preah Sihanouk Raja Buddhist University 258–260, 262–264, 267–268
Preah vihear 91, 97, 100, 104, 112, 179, 186, 265
PRK. See People's Republic of Kampuchea
Prei Phnom 199
Protestanism. See Christianity
Put Tumneay 78, 102, 313

Rama 21
Rama II, King 25
Rama IV, King 25–26, 39–41, 45, 54
Rama V, King 26, 39, 41
Ramayana 21
Ratanakiri 265
Reamker. See Ramayana
Reamthipodey, King 23
Royal Library 36, 39, 47
Royal University of Fine Arts 148

Sahlins, Marshall 134
Saigon 172
Samaneravinaya 48
Sam Bunthoeun 10, 122
Sandy, Larissa 227
Sanghareach 17, 130, 140
Sangkum Reastr Niyum 29, 97, 215, 219, 221, 223, 226
Sattha, King 119
Schober, Julianne 224
Scott, James 215, 303
Scott, Michael 196
Siam 4, 18, 22, 23, 25–26, 39–40, 42, 45, 55, 117, 222. *See also* Thailand
Siem Reap 35, 95, 257, 261–262
Sihanouk. *See* Norodom Sihanouk
Sima 4, 121
Singapore 227, 231
Sisowath, King 26, 221, 257
Sisowath Kossamak, Queen 97
Sithor 19
Siva 16, 21
Sukhotai 18

Son Ngoc Thanh 28
Soth Polin 222–223
Sri Lanka 16, 18, 20, 54
S–21. See Tuol Sleng
Superior Pali School 27
Suramrith Buddhist Hugh School 257, 259, 261–262, 266
Suryavarman I, King 2
Suryavarman II, King 2
Suttantabreyjea Ind 43

Tambiah, Stanley 41, 158
Ta Kam 205–208
Takeo 95, 157, 261
Ta Nen 85–88, 91–105
Tat Marina 228–229
Tboung Khmum 217
Tenfold Virtues of the Ruler 313–314
Tep Vong, Venerable 8–10, 226, 243–245, 247–249, 258, 261
Thailand 9, 17, 20, 75, 120
Thmin Chey 217
Thommayut 9, 25–29, 170, 244, 258–259, 264
Thompson, Ashley 91, 109, 115, 222
Thompson, E.P. 215, 284
Tilok, King 19
Thngai sel 149, 154
Tonle Sap 88, 117, 171
Touch Phong 95
Tripitaka 181, 186
Tuol Kork 229
Tuol Sleng 67, 71–73, 75–76
Tuol Tum Poung 259, 268

Uddor Meanchey 265
Udong 22–23, 112, 116, 122
Udong Mountain 117, 246
Umbrella War of 1942 5
United Nations Transitional Authority in Cambodia. See UNTAC
UNTAC 76, 297
U Nu 55
Uttamamuni Um–Sur, Venerable 35, 39, 48, 53–54

Vajiranana, Venerable Prince 39, 46, 54
Veal 171–174, 177, 183, 187
Vickery, Michael 10
Vietnam 3–4, 8–9. 26, 67, 70, 74–76, 170, 215, 231, 245, 258
Vishnu 16, 21, 100
Visnukara 313
Vossa 20

Wat Bathom 85–87
Wat Champuk K'aek 103–104
Wat Choeung Prey 88
Wat Damnak 35
Wat Kdey Daem 95
Wat Krasang Mean Rutthi 175, 179
Wat Prasat 175, 177, 179, 181–182, 186–190
Wat Preah Krasang 175, 179, 181
Wat Preah Thammalanka 85–88, 91, 93, 96–100, 102–104
Wat Prek Prang 95
Wat Samrong Andet 104
Wat San Kor 175, 177, 179, 181–182, 185–187, 190
Wat Svay Popé 264
Wat Tan Thlok 94
Wat Tanup 93
Wat Taprong 88
Wat Tralaeng Kaeng 116, 118
Wat Tuol Tum Poung 259
Wat Unnalom 38, 44
Weber, Max 16
West Svay 150
"Wheel of History" 8, 63
Woodside, Alexander 202–203
World War II 93, 95, 98
Wyatt, David K. 202–203

Ya 204–206
Yang Sam 243

Zhou Da Guan 135
Zucker, Eve 11–13, 214, 304

NIAS Press is the autonomous publishing arm of
NIAS – Nordic Institute of Asian Studies, a research institute
located at the University of Copenhagen. NIAS is partially funded by the
governments of Denmark, Finland, Iceland, Norway and Sweden
via the Nordic Council of Ministers, and works to encourage and
support Asian studies in the Nordic countries. In so doing, NIAS
has been publishing books since 1969, with more than two
hundred titles produced in the past few years.

COPENHAGEN UNIVERSITY

Nordic Council of Ministers